The Smell of Slavery

Offering an original contribution to the growing subfield of sensory history, Andrew Kettler uses smell as a frame of analysis for constructions and perceptions of race and the environment in the age of Atlantic slavery. Kettler recounts how proponents of slavery defined African bodies as noxious and pungent and therefore inferior and deserving of enslavement. African slaves were deemed "excremental" by their owners, and, as such, vastly inferior to their masters and trapped in a pre-modern state of being in which modern hygiene and other trappings of enlightenment remained beyond their reach. By branding African bodies as odoriferous, slave owners equated them with animals or beasts of burden: well-equipped for hard labor. Kettler vividly and effectively shows how the sense of smell was used to aesthetically define specific populations as lacking the necessary humanity to become full subjects, and in so doing demonstrates that the roots of racism transgressed intellectual and political arenas and included the realm of the senses.

Andrew Kettler is an Ahmanson-Getty Fellow at the UCLA Center for 17th- & 18th-Century Studies at the William Andrews Clark Memorial Library.

T0351991

The Smell of Slavery

Olfactory Racism and the Atlantic World

ANDREW KETTLER

University of California, Los Angeles

CAMBRIDGE
UNIVERSITY PRESS

CAMBRIDGE
UNIVERSITY PRESS

Shaftesbury Road, Cambridge CB2 8EA, United Kingdom

One Liberty Plaza, 20th Floor, New York, NY 10006, USA

477 Williamstown Road, Port Melbourne, VIC 3207, Australia

314–321, 3rd Floor, Plot 3, Splendor Forum, Jasola District Centre, New Delhi – 110025, India

103 Penang Road, #05–06/07, Visioncrest Commercial, Singapore 238467

Cambridge University Press is part of Cambridge University Press & Assessment, a department of the University of Cambridge.

We share the University's mission to contribute to society through the pursuit of education, learning and research at the highest international levels of excellence.

www.cambridge.org
Information on this title: www.cambridge.org/9781108796385

DOI: 10.1017/9781108854740

First published 2020
First paperback edition 2022

A catalogue record for this publication is available from the British Library

Library of Congress Cataloging-in-Publication data
NAMES: Kettler, Andrew, author.
TITLE: The smell of slavery : olfactory racism and the Atlantic world / Andrew Kettler, University of California, Los Angeles.
OTHER TITLES: Olfactory racism and the Atlantic world
DESCRIPTION: New York, NY : Cambridge University Press, [2020] | Includes index.
IDENTIFIERS: LCCN 2019057477 (print) | LCCN 2019057478 (ebook) | ISBN 9781108490733 (hardback) | ISBN 9781108854740 (ebook)
SUBJECTS: LCSH: Slavery – Social aspects – Atlantic Ocean Region. | Smell – Social aspects – History. | Odor – Social aspects – History. | Blacks – Atlantic Ocean Region – Social conditions. | Atlantic Ocean Region – Race relations – History. | Slave trade – Atlantic Ocean Region – History. | Racism – History.
CLASSIFICATION: LCC HT871 .K47 2020 (print) | LCC HT871 (ebook) | DDC 306.3/620974–dc23
LC record available at https://lccn.loc.gov/2019057477
LC ebook record available at https://lccn.loc.gov/2019057478

ISBN   978-1-108-49073-3   Hardback
ISBN   978-1-108-79638-5   Paperback

For A. I. S.
Love. Trust. Marriage.

Contents

List of Figures   *page* viii

Preface: Making Scents of the Middle Passage   ix

Acknowledgments   xxi

   Introduction: *Pecunia non Olet*   1

1 The Primal Scene: Ethnographic Wonder and Aromatic
   Discourse   40

2 Triangle Trading on the Pungency of Race   77

3 Ephemeral Africa: Essentialized Odors and the Slave Ship   123

4 "The Sweet Scent of Vengeance": Olfactory Resistance
   in the Atlantic World   155

   Conclusion: Race, Nose, Truth   195

Index   220

Figures

1.1 Print of "Pears Soap Advertisement based on Aesop's fable, 1884." This advertisement appeared in *The Graphic* on December 18, 1884. Courtesy of the British Library *page 71*

2.1 Print of portrait of Benjamin Rush, by Charles Willson Peale, 1818. Courtesy of the National Independence Historical Park 108

2.2 Print of "Free Labour: Or The Sunny Side of the Wall." Included within London. Thos. McLean 26 Haymarket. 1833. June 19th. John Carter Brown Library. Political Cartoons. Accession Number: 72–149. Courtesy of the John Carter Brown Library 116

3.1 Print of "A Spiritual Healer, Paramaribo, Suriname, ca. 1831." Source: Pierre Jacques Benoit, *Voyage a Surinam ... cent dessins pris sur nature par l'auteur* (Bruxelles, 1839), plate xvii, fig. 36. Courtesy of the John Carter Brown Library 140

4.1 Print of "Training Bloodhounds, Saint Domingue." Included within Marcus Rainsford, *An Historical Account of the Black Empire of Hayti* (London, 1805), facing, p. 423. Courtesy of the Library Company of Philadelphia 175

Preface

Making Scents of the Middle Passage

William Shakespeare was a wedded man, but occasionally the traveling playwright found respite in unwedded arms. His travels took him across his merry isle as a new form of English character, a popular celebrity who gained notoriety increasingly throughout his lifetime. Sonnet 130 portrays one of the many loves of this wayward playwright; an adoration for a historically nebulous woman who provided the narcissistic genius a reprieve, most likely in a brothel, possibly in his wandering heart.[1] The section, which Shakespeare composed at the end of the sixteenth century and personally devoted to the "Dark Lady," a central character in many of his celebrated Sonnets numbered 127 to 152, describes this affection while offering substantial indications to a central argument of this book: that Anglo-Atlantic racism began in the body, emerged from the popular mind and the popular stage, and was experienced well before Enlightenment codes of racial knowing were defined within the increasingly scientific literatures of the late eighteenth century.[2]

Shakespeare's "Dark Lady" had: "eyes ... nothing like the sun;/ Coral is far more red than her lips' red;/ If snow be white, why then her breasts are dun;/ If hairs be wires, black wires grow on her head./ I have seen roses damask'd, red and white,/ But no such roses see I in her cheeks;/ And in

---

[1] Stephen Greenblatt, *Will in the World: How Shakespeare Became Shakespeare* (New York: Norton, 2004), 233–249.

[2] For recent works on Atlantic racism, medicine, and the Enlightenment, see Andrew Curran, *The Anatomy of Blackness: Science & Slavery in an Age of Enlightenment* (Baltimore, MD: Johns Hopkins University Press, 2011); Rana Hogarth, *Medicalizing Blackness: Making Racial Differences in the Atlantic World, 1780–1840* (Chapel Hill: University of North Carolina Press, 2017).

some perfumes is there more delight/ Than in the breath that from my mistress reeks."[3] That aromatic line, that reeking breath emerging from heaving lungs beneath breasts that were "dun," or brown, was part of an Elizabethan conceit that African bodies and cultures smelled.[4]

For this study of racial consciousness in the Atlantic World, it is prudent to contrast Shakespeare's wanton tone for fragrant otherness with the aromas of whiteness portrayed as part of John Stafford's collected commonplace book, *The Academy of Pleasure* (1665). In the poem "The Contemplative Lover," a similar lyrical infatuation involved the sense of smell emanating from a lover's breath. Contrastingly for the metropolitans reading Stafford's collection, this "baulmy incense" came from a paramour whose skin was "more pure, more white, more soft" than the allegorically portrayed furs of the ermine. The "fragrant breath" emanating from this porcelain woman as "odoriferous art" could "drive away grim death" and "transform" the infatuated poet "to a Flower Fashioned like a heart."[5] Whiteness, or the breath that sprung from English female beauty, could metaphorically stop death. Darkness, or the lungful that bounded from an African woman in Shakespearean London, reeked of something much more malevolent for freshly expectant English noses.[6]

[3] William Shakespeare, *Shakespeare's Sonnets*, eds. Barbara Mowat and Paul Werstine (New York: Simon & Schuster, 2009), quotes on 268–269. For this specific series of sonnets, see Dympna Callaghan, *Shakespeare's Sonnets* (Malden, MA: Blackwell, 2007), 54–55; Kim Hall, "'These bastard signs of fair': Literary Whiteness in Shakespeare's Sonnets," in *Shakespeare and Race*, eds. Catherine Alexander and Stanley Wells (New York: Cambridge University Press, 2001), 64–83.

[4] For debates on the "Dark Lady" as African, see Kim Hall, *Things of Darkness: Economies of Race and Gender in Early Modern England* (Ithaca: Cornell University Press, 1995), 66–73; Gwyn Williams, *Person and Persona: Studies in Shakespeare* (Cardiff: University of Wales Press, 1981), 115–130; Robert Fleissner, *Shakespeare and Africa: The Dark Lady of His Sonnets Revamped and Other Africa-Related Associations* (Philadelphia: XLibris, 2005), 27–37; Leighton Brewer, *Shakespeare and the Dark Lady* (Boston: Christopher Publishing House, 1966), 21–29.

[5] *The Academy of Pleasure: Furnished with all Kinds of Complementall Letters, Discourses, and Dialogues; with Variety of New Songs, Sonets, and Witty Inventions* (London: John Stafford, 1665), quotes on 30–32.

[6] For standard introductions to olfactory racism, see Constance Classen, "The Odor of the Other: Olfactory Symbolism and Cultural Categories," *Ethos* 20, 2 (1992): 133–166; Mark Smith, *How Race Is Made: Slavery, Segregation, and the Senses* (Chapel Hill: University of North Carolina Press, 2006); William Tullett, "Grease and Sweat: Race and Smell in Eighteenth-Century English Culture," *Cultural and Social History* 13, 3 (2016): 307–322.

The idea that Africa and her peoples were pungent mounted through the later seventeenth century to lead later European populations to believe in the desirability of increased purification, which partially arrived through rhetorically defining the African other through diverse spiritual, biological, and scientific languages about odor, miasma, contagion, and pollution.[7] These racialized aromatic roots of English sensory culture later informed Anglo-Atlantic slaveholders throughout the Americas, who often discussed African odors as a mark of biological inferiority. For many writers of the eighteenth century, racial definitions moved from material concerns with African cultures and a perceived lack of cleanliness among sub-Saharan Africans to biological definitions of inherent racial differences.[8] Among these later scholars was the lexical founder of American liberty, Thomas Jefferson, who infamously argued within his ardently racist Query XIV of *Notes on the State of Virginia* (1785) that Africans "secrete less by the kidnies, and more by the glands of the skin, which gives them a very strong and disagreeable odor."[9] These sensory ideals originally modified within earlier forms of English literature and, throughout the Early Modern Era, agitated within a global intelligence network that rested on ideas of progress, scientific reason, and Enlightenment.[10]

During the Early Modern Era, blackness and whiteness were increasingly defined upon a cultural binary, whereby whiteness often symbolized virginity, purity, and floral essences, and blackness was marked by an inherent dirtiness, sinfulness, and odor. Controlling the rhetorically

---

[7] For colonization, disease, race, and othering, see Warwick Anderson, "Excremental Colonialism: Public Health and the Poetics of Pollution," *Critical Inquiry* 21, 3 (1995): 640–669; Alison Bashford, *Imperial Hygiene: A Critical History of Colonialism, Nationalism and Public Health* (Basingstoke: Palgrave Macmillan, 2004); Nélia Dias, *La Mesure des Sens: Les Anthropologues et le Corps Humain au XIXe Siècle* (Paris: Aubier, 2004).

[8] For the transition from monogenetic racism to polygenesis, see Richard Popkin, *The Third Force in Seventeenth-Century Thought* (Leiden: Brill, 1991); Robert Sussman, *The Myth of Race: The Troubling Persistence of an Unscientific Idea* (Cambridge, MA: Harvard University Press, 2014), 11–63.

[9] Thomas Jefferson, "Notes on the State of Virginia," in *The Literatures of Colonial America: An Anthology*, eds. Susan Castillo and Ivy Schweitzer (Malden, MA: Blackwell, 2001 [1785]), 530–536, quote on 533.

[10] For racism and the links between core and periphery, see Ann Laura Stoler and Frederick Cooper, "Between Metropole and Colony: Rethinking a Research Agenda," in *Tensions of Empire: Colonial Cultures in a Bourgeois World*, eds. Frederick Cooper and Ann Laura Stoler (Berkeley: University of California Press, 1997), 1–58; G. V. Scammell, "Essay and Reflection: On the Discovery of the Americas and the Spread of Intolerance, Absolutism, and Racism in Early Modern Europe," *The International History Review* 13, 3 (1991): 502–521.

created filth of blackness through the slave trade initiated the first stage in the construction of capitalism through forms of linguistic and sensory discourse that preconditioned primitive accumulation.[11] As the continental philosopher Alain Badiou recently described: "After demonizing black cats, the Devil's dark powers, crows, witches in black rags, the darkness of death, and the blackness of the soul, we so-called Whites of Western Europe had to invent the fact that the majority of Africa's inhabitants clearly constituted an inferior 'race,' condemned to slavery and then to the forced labor of colonial occupation simply because this enormous population was 'black.'" This constructed form of negative blackness positioned a commodification process that subjected African bodies into diverse states of what Frantz Fanon termed "non-being." Through the discursive and material aspects of this exclusionary procedure, Africans became objects to be traded, rather than considered fully human. Such nefarious discourses formulated African bodies into objects within vast sensory engagements defined through an exaggerated and most absurd form of racial knowing.[12]

Tortured within the holds of ships upon the Middle Passage where odor situated bodies within the grinding economies of the Atlantic World, slaves felt the oppression of olfactory discourse and pungent materiality on their very bodies.[13] In Alexander Falconbridge's *Account of the Slave Trade on the Coast of Africa* (1788), the reformed slave trader and surgeon described the embodied and existential threat of odor and disease beneath the decks where Africans lay "in the blood and mucus, that had

---

[11] For economic forms of primitive accumulation within the Atlantic Slave Trade, see Robin Blackburn, *The Making of New World Slavery: From the Baroque to the Modern, 1492–1800* (London: Verso, 1997), 509–517; Barbara Solow, *The Economic Consequences of the Atlantic Slave Trade* (Lanham, MD: Lexington Books, 2014), 98–109.

[12] Alain Badiou, *Black: The Brilliance of a Noncolor*, trans. Susan Spitzer (Cambridge: Polity, 2017), quote on 91. See also Joseph Washington, *Anti-Blackness in English Religion, 1500–1800* (New York: Edwin Mellen Press, 1985), 90–97; Robert Young, *White Mythologies: Writing History and the West* (London: Routledge, 2004), 32–52; Calvin Warren, *Ontological Terror: Blackness, Nihilism, and Emancipation* (Durham, NC: Duke University Press, 2018), 26–61; Frantz Fanon, *Black Skin, White Masks* (London: Pluto, 2017 [1952]), 139–140, 159–160; Bénédicte Boisseron, *Afro-Dog: Blackness and the Animal Question* (New York: Columbia University Press, 2018), 160–166.

[13] For experiences of the Middle Passage and commodification, see Sowande' Mustakeem, *Slavery at Sea: Terror, Sex, and Sickness in the Middle Passage* (Urbana: University of Illinois Press, 2016), 55–75; Stephanie Smallwood, *Saltwater Slavery: A Middle Passage from Africa to American Diaspora* (Cambridge, MA: Harvard University Press, 2008), 122–137.

flowed from those afflicted with the flux, which ... is generally so violent as to prevent their being kept clean." These souls persisted in the "excruciating" mental and physical pain of being chained below shipboards within fluid spaces filled often with the contaminated excrement of their continental brethren.[14]

During the abolitionist debates against the slave trade of the late eighteenth century, British politicians, Atlantic planters, and English citizens read often of these stenchful conditions from diverse sources.[15] The former slave trader turned preacher and abolitionist composer John Newton's *Thoughts upon the African Slave Trade* (1788) described the "heat and smell of these rooms" below the decks of ships as "insupportable, to a person not accustomed to them." The odors, following the miasma theories of effluvium, night air, and bad air within the medical profession at the time, were believed to cause great "fevers and fluxes" among the ill and dying slave populations, who often perished as "poor creatures" devoid of the Christian assistance Newton deemed essential to human instruction. While later penning the effusive notes for "Amazing Grace," the Anglican cleric Newton must have thought considerably of the "noisome and noxious effluvia" that metaphorically infected the entirety of the slave trade that he once participated in and came to prominently oppose.[16]

It was not only in cramped cabins below deck where slaves found odor to be a detriment to their terrible familiarities and laboring lives. Throughout the Atlantic World, there were numerous cases of master's punishments that either used odor as a part of the violent ceremonies for reprimanding slaves or created putridity as evidence of their malevolent rituality. The infamous and vile Jamaican planter Thomas Thistlewood's illustrious "derby dose" involved the culminating act of punishment whereby a fellow slave defecated in the mouth of a captured runaway who had braved the mountainous West Indian countryside. Thistlewood applied this climaxing act many times throughout the eighteenth century on his Jamaica plantations that were known foremost for hundreds of

---

[14] Alexander Falconbridge, *An Account of the Slave Trade on the Coast of Africa by Alexander Falconbridge* (London: Phillips, 1788), quotes on 27–29.

[15] For British abolitionism and the slave ship, see Marcus Rediker, *The Slave Ship: A Human History* (New York: Penguin, 2008), 308–342; Seymour Drescher, *Econocide: British Slavery in the Era of Abolition* (Chapel Hill: University of North Carolina Press, 2010 [1977]), 162–187.

[16] John Newton, *Thoughts upon the African Slave Trade ... The Second Edition* (London: Buckland and Johnson, 1788), quotes on 33–36.

instances of rape and repeated brutishness against slave bodies.[17] As described within the oft-published abolitionist collection *Mirror of Misery* (1814), the punishment of ingested excrement was not uncommon throughout the later Atlantic World, and the ritual could often involve amusement for planters and their wives rather than function solely as a vile form of punishment from all-too-commonly abhorrent masters.[18]

The smell of slavery also consistently emanated from sick bays on plantations due to the putrefying wounds commonly emblazoned upon the backs of slaves by the master's whip.[19] Akin to these countless lashings upon the productive fields of the Caribbean, on vindictive planter Arthur Hodge's estate in the British Virgin Islands of 1811 slaves would frequently be dipped in copper kettles until their skin seared off from their muscles. The disturbed Hodge also purposefully drowned and revived his slaves through a sadistic game of power, torture, and castigation. As well, the British planter often disciplined slaves through making them drink boiling water, which destroyed throats and stomach lining and led to slow, waiting, and miserable deaths. Hodge was executed for his crimes against property, but his use of torture upon slaves should never be considered a psychopathic anomaly within an Atlantic World where nearly unlimited power over black bodies led to sick bays, like Hodge's saddened dens, that were full of such pungency that those visiting the plantation avoided the slave dwellings due "to the offensive smell proceeding from the wounds occasioned by cartwhippings on Negroes therein confined."[20]

---

[17] Trevor Burnard, *Mastery, Tyranny, and Desire: Thomas Thistlewood and His Slaves in the Anglo-Jamaican World* (Chapel Hill: University of North Carolina Press, 2009), 104, 183. For more on rape in Jamaican slavery, see Sasha Turner, *Contested Bodies: Pregnancy, Childrearing, and Slavery in Jamaica* (Philadelphia: University of Pennsylvania Press, 2017), 215–218.

[18] *The Mirror of Misery; or, Tyranny Exposed* (New York: Samuel Wood, 1814), 32–33.

[19] For more on planter violence in the Atlantic World, see Randy Browne, *Surviving Slavery in the British Caribbean* (Philadelphia: University of Pennsylvania Press, 2017), 44–71; Marisa Fuentes, *Dispossessed Lives: Enslaved Women, Violence, and the Archive* (Philadelphia: University of Pennsylvania Press, 2016), 100–123; Rachel Feinstein, *When Rape Was Legal: The Untold History of Sexual Violence During Slavery* (New York: Routledge, 2018); Thavolia Glymph, *Out of the House of Bondage: The Transformation of the Plantation Household* (Cambridge: Cambridge University Press, 2012), 63–96; Lamonte Aidoo, *Slavery Unseen: Sex, Power, and Violence in Brazilian History* (Durham, NC: Duke University Press, 2018); Lisa Ze Winters, *Mulatta Concubine: Terror, Intimacy, Freedom, and Desire in the Black Transatlantic* (Athens: University of Georgia Press, 2018), 67–106; Thomas Foster, *Rethinking Rufus: Sexual Violations of Enslaved Men* (Athens: University of Georgia Press, 2019).

[20] *Papers relating to the West Indies; viz. Correspondence between the Earl of Liverpool and Governor Elliot: In Reference to the Trial and Execution of Arthur Hodge, for the*

Punishments became common throughout the colonial spaces of the Atlantic World, but slavery was centrally about commodified labor and keeping a profitable stock of healthy working slaves.[21] At the owner's whim and under the overseer's knout, slaves worked to create profit in fields and factories that were often deteriorating and pungent. Each form of labor presented odors through which slaves persevered. Specifically, slaves were often employed in the process of "heaping up dung" to fertilize the fields of West Indian islands devoted to sugar production.[22] Slaves also habitually hauled cane trash, which could often become quite ill-smelling when rotting in the oppressive humidity of the Caribbean Basin. Upon burning, the fumes of cane trash may also have become a sweet-scented and redolent reminder of the "damp vapours" that frequently hung above the "scalding liquid" where "skimmers" constantly worked in boiling houses – aromas that must have often reminded reticent slaves of the countless and repetitive days of labor devoted to sweetness forever lost to the master's command.[23]

Tortured in holds, beaten on plantations, and made to work for master's profit in the stinking cotton dens, rum distilleries, and tobacco factories of the Atlantic World, slaves never stopped resisting.[24]

Murder of a Negro Slave: Ordered, by the House of Commons, to be printed, 26 June 1811 (London: House of Commons, 1811), quote on 6–7. Courtesy of the John Carter Brown Library.

[21] For centrality of labor in slavery, see Justin Roberts, *Slavery and the Enlightenment in the British Atlantic, 1750–1807* (Cambridge: Cambridge University Press, 2018); Dale Tomich, *Through the Prism of Slavery: Labor, Capital, and World Economy* (Lanham, MD: Rowman and Littlefield, 2004), 32–55; Abigail Swingen, *Competing Visions of Empire: Labor, Slavery, and the Origins of the British Atlantic Empire* (New Haven, CT: Yale University Press, 2015), 140–171; Daina Ramey Berry, *The Price for Their Pound of Flesh: The Value of the Enslaved, from Womb to Grave, in the Building of a Nation* (Boston: Beacon, 2017), 58–90.

[22] *An Account of Duckenfield Hall Estates Negroes, Jamaica, 1806* (Manuscript: Codex Eng.183 2-Size). Courtesy of the John Carter Brown Library.

[23] John Dovaston, *Agricultura Americana or Improvements in West-India Husbandry Considered Wherein the Present System of Husbandry Used in England is Applied to the Cultivation or Growing of Sugar Canes to Advantage*, 1774 (Manuscript: Codex Eng. 60, Volume I), 18–19, 46–48, 109–110, quotes on 158–159. Courtesy of the John Carter Brown Library.

[24] For persistent slave resistance, see D. A. Dunkley, *Agency of the Enslaved: Jamaica and the Culture of Freedom in the Atlantic World* (Lanham, MD: Lexington Books, 2013), 15–32; Eric Robert Taylor, *If We Must Die: Shipboard Insurrections in the Era of the Atlantic Slave Trade* (Baton Rouge: Louisiana State University Press, 2006), 85–103. See also transgression and anticolonialism within Srinivas Aravamudan, *Tropicopolitans: Colonialism and Agency, 1688–1804* (Durham, NC: Duke University Press, 1999), 29–70.

Abolitionists noticed these forms of resistance, many of which came from an aromatic sense of smell buried deep within different aspects of African ethnic memory. In the poem "The Worn-Out Negro Slave," read much during the 1820s within abolitionist circles, the image of a slave in need of protection emerged again as a character suffering "midst filth and stench, in gloom and midnight shade,/ Beneath the deck, in iron fetters bound,/ In dreadful rows, close packed, we there were laid,/ Where comfort, ease, or rest, were never found."[25] Later abolitionists found in these portrayals of odor and disease a way to relay suffering for a newly moralizing Anglo-Atlantic public, first through work to abolish the pestilential trade at the turn of the eighteenth century and then through applying odor within discussions of freedom and the rights of the subject stolen by the broader institution of slavery in discussions of emancipation, apprenticeship, and American forms of war-torn freedom that would only arrive decades later.[26]

Upon earning their emancipation from slavery, with backbreaking labor and resistance tracked over many centuries, many Africans and African Americans throughout the Atlantic World spoke from a place of profound sensory longing to return to an essentialized Africa often remembered through libidinal celebration and goals of romantic communalism. Regularly, abolitionists heard these corporeal desires and transmitted much of African sensory yearning to the pages of the growing Anglo-Atlantic public sphere.[27] In "The Negro's Vigil," written in the direct wake of the first formal stage of British abolition in 1833 by the Scottish poet James Montgomery, who had spent much of his life in Barbados living near numerous slave populations, the longing for

---

[25] "The Worn-Out Negro Slave," in *Third Report of the Female Society, for Birmingham, West-Bromwich, Wednesbury, Walsall, and Their Respective Neighbourhoods, for the Relief of British Negro Slaves* (Birmingham: Richard Peart, 1827–1828). Courtesy of the John Carter Brown Library.

[26] For commodification in the slave trade and debates on subject, object, and agency, see Simon Gikandi, *Slavery and the Culture of Taste* (Princeton: Princeton University Press, 2011), 50–96; Walter Johnson, *Soul by Soul: Life Inside the Antebellum Slave Market* (Cambridge, MA: Harvard University Press, 1999), 117–188; Frank Wilderson, "The Prison Slave as Hegemony's Silent Scandal," *Social Justice* 30, 2 (2003): 18–27.

[27] For British abolitionism and the public sphere, see Brycchan Carey, *British Abolitionism and the Rhetoric of Sensibility: Writing, Sentiment and Slavery: 1760–1807* (New York: Palgrave Macmillan, 2005); J. R. Oldfield, *Popular Politics and British Anti-Slavery: The Mobilisation of Public Opinion against the Slave Trade, 1787–1807* (Manchester: Manchester University Press, 1995), 155–184; Christopher Leslie Brown, *Moral Capital: Foundations of British Abolitionism* (Chapel Hill: University of North Carolina Press, 2006), 209–258.

African airs focused an emotionality that linked smell and these forms of embodied continental memory. The verse, told from the constructed perspective of the slave newly freed, portrayed a universalized and singular African trumpeting: "Climb we the mountain, and stand/ High in the mid-air to inhale,/ Fresh from our Father-land,/ Balm in the ocean-borne gale."[28] For many abolitionists, Africans, and African Americans throughout the Atlantic littoral, aromatic scents infused a sensory discourse counter to the racialized economic ideology that dark bodies inherently reeked.

In Sarah Tucker's *Abbeokuta, or Sunrise within the Tropics* (1853), the English missionary to the Yoruba and celebrated author similarly imagined what the trail from the coast to interior freedom must have been like for recolonized Africans returning from their places within the slave societies of the Atlantic World. Part of this journey involved the former slaves breathing in the air of fragrant flowers that might transport "to them instinct with life of other days, and would bring back, with increasing force, the associations of their childhood."[29] Such abolitionist and missionary rhetoric expresses that the dialogues of odor within the Atlantic World took on more than simply racist connotations of the smell of African bodies. For different African ethnic groups, creolized African Americans, and many abolitionists who supported the causes of freedom, there was beauty and honor in longing for the smells of remembered African pasts.[30]

Despite these romantic goals, slaveholders of the American South during the Antebellum Era justified the perpetuation of their peculiar institution through an increasing intellectual exchange with freshly engaged scientific communities in Europe that continued to discuss the supposed inferiority of African peoples through the sense of smell. During this

[28] James Montgomery, "The Negro's Vigil," Publisher's Broadside (London: Z. T. Purdy and J. Montgomery, 1834). Manuscript ZBA2572 in the Michael Graham-Stewart Collection, Royal Museums Greenwich, UK.

[29] Sarah Tucker, *Abbeokuta: Or, Sunrise within the Tropics: an Outline of the Origin and Progress of the Yoruba Mission* (London: J. Nisbet, 1858 [1853]), quote on 48–49. For more on the African idea of nostalgia and a desire for ethnic homelands among slaves on the Middle Passage, see Ramesh Mallipeddi, "'A Fixed Melancholy': Migration, Memory, and the Middle Passage," *The Eighteenth Century* 55, 2–3 (2014): 235–253.

[30] For African and slave resistance within both American and British narratives of abolitionism, see Claudius Fergus, *Revolutionary Emancipation: Slavery and Abolitionism in the British West Indies* (Baton Rouge: Louisiana State University Press, 2013), 176–198; Ousmane Power-Greene, *Against Wind and Tide: The African American Struggle against the Colonization Movement* (New York: New York University Press, 2014), 17–45.

tumultuous and defining era for concepts of American liberty, the nose increasingly became a renewed disciplinary apparatus, freshly motivated through religious, sexual, and scientific narratives to mark black bodies through specific and aromatically informed institutions of control.[31] Akin to the pseudoscience of phrenology, these newly involved scientific, religious, and civilizing connotations for the nose became essential for slaveholders and scientific racists to continue justifying their beliefs regarding the inherent inferiority of African minds and bodies.[32]

Representing such growing ideals among the educated and aristocratic classes of the Atlantic, selected Southern publications of the early nineteenth century work of French biologist Julien-Joseph Virey were printed within *Natural History of the Negro Race* (1837). These selections categorized different African nations through their odors, increasingly tied to an objective language of science and medicine on the eve of Social Darwinism. Virey specifically noted that when all "negroes sweat, their skin is covered with an oily and blackish perspiration, which stains cloths, and generally exhales a very unpleasant porraceous smell."[33] The medical nuances applied within Virey's text regarding skin scents and stinking pores exposes the very intensity of the desire to codify African smells during the late Enlightenment as the encyclopedias and scientific methods of the elite instigated the era of Scientific Racism and provided new justifications for white dominance that warranted grander forms of conquest and colonialism in Africa and the Global South. With these global and racial motives influencing public spheres, medical fictions became scientific facts, resonating with positivist vigor, esoteric language, and

---

[31] For American proslavery rhetoric, see the religious supports of evangelicalism within John Patrick Daly, *When Slavery Was Called Freedom: Evangelicalism, Proslavery, and the Causes of the Civil War* (Lexington: University Press of Kentucky, 2002), 57–72; and the transnational links within Larry Tise, *Proslavery: A History of the Defense of Slavery in America, 1701–1840* (Athens: University of Georgia Press, 1987), 75–96.

[32] For introduction to phrenology, see Stephen Tomlinson, *Head Masters: Phrenology, Secular Education, and Nineteenth-Century Social Thought* (Tuscaloosa: University of Alabama Press, 2013), 286–345; Britt Rusert, *Fugitive Science: Empiricism and Freedom in Early African American Culture* (New York: New York University Press, 2017), 121–125; James Poskett, *Materials of the Mind: Phrenology, Race, and the Global History of Science, 1815–1920* (Chicago: University of Chicago Press, 2019). See also Kenneth Greenberg, *Honor & Slavery: Lies, Duels, Noses, Masks, Dressing As a Woman, Gifts, Strangers, Humanitarianism, Death, Slave Rebellions, the Proslavery Argument, Baseball, Hunting, and Gambling in the Old South* (Princeton, NJ: Princeton University Press, 1998), 3–23.

[33] Julien Virey, *Natural History of the Negro Race*, trans. J. H. Geunebault (Charleston, SC: D. J. Dowling, 1837), 44–54, quote on 44.

economic incentive to mark the African laborer as biologically different than those opposingly racialized economic classes grasping for control of the means of production.[34]

As part of these increasingly professional, racist, and scientific languages of pro-slavery and colonialist discourse, Southern academic Josiah Priest's *Slavery, As It Relates to the Negro, or African Race* (1843) used the inherent "strong odor of the negro's body" to similarly justify numerous uninhabited beliefs regarding how African slaves digested complex or raw foods easier than Europeans. With few limitations to the dreadful social constructions of racial thought during the Antebellum Era, Priest argued that slave bodies included both a pungent odor and smoother alimentary processes because African groups had frequently ingested human flesh while living as cannibals during their extraordinary biological past.[35] This type of distorted linking of Africans to a fabricated historical world of cannibalism and odor justified continued religious support for the nefarious economic system of the Old South.[36]

Priest's stretched narrative and the multinational adoption of Virey's pseudoscience portray that the popularity and success of olfactory racism rested on the viral ability of smelling to support nearly all racial discourses about the African and African American, which provided justifications for

[34] For the British moral mission in Africa, see Catherine Hall, *Civilising Subjects: Metropole and Colony in the English Imagination, 1830–1867* (Oxford: Polity, 2002), 332–338; Tim Fulford, Peter Kitson, and Debbie Lee, *Literature, Science and Exploration in the Romantic Era: Bodies of Knowledge* (Cambridge: Cambridge University Press, 2008), 228–270; Alison Twells, *The Civilising Mission and the English Middle Class, 1792–1850: The "heathen" at Home and Overseas* (Basingstoke: Palgrave Macmillan, 2009), 125–142. See also the general understanding of what manners were to be cultivated among the others of the world in Paul Langford, *Englishness Identified: Manners and Character 1650–1850* (Oxford: Oxford University Press, 2001), 137–147, 219–225; Peter Kivy, *The Seventh Sense: Francis Hutcheson and Eighteenth-Century British Aesthetics* (Oxford: Clarendon Press, 2003), 46–54, 266–282.

[35] Josiah Priest, *Slavery, As It Relates to the Negro, or African Race* (Louisville, KY: Brown, 1849 [1843]), quote on 228–229. See also Kyla Wazana Tompkins, *Racial Indigestion: Eating Bodies in the 19th Century* (New York: New York University, 2012).

[36] For more on religious support for American proslavery, see Charles Irons, *The Origins of Proslavery Christianity: White and Black Evangelicals in Colonial and Antebellum Virginia* (Chapel Hill: University of North Carolina Press, 2008), 55–96; Mitchell Snay, *Gospel of Disunion: Religion and Separatism in the Antebellum South* (Chapel Hill: University of North Carolina Press, 1997), 53–77; Elizabeth Fox-Genovese and Eugene Genovese, *The Mind of the Master Class: History and Faith in the Southern Slaveholders' Worldview* (Cambridge: Cambridge University Press, 2005).

the continued dominance of white bodies in the Caribbean, the perpetuation of slavery throughout the American South, and the rise of capitalism within increasingly colonized spaces of Africa during the nineteenth century.[37] Following these numerous olfactory discourses, *The Smell of Slavery* specifically demonstrates that the shifting of odor upon the racialized other is a timeworn tradition that was expanded within the Atlantic World to provide narratives of disease, pollution, miasma, and labor to justify numerous reprehensible colonial and capitalist trajectories that situated and disciplined African bodies into a governable discursive and biopolitical space for commodification and political dominance during the Early Modern Era and well into the Scramble for Africa.[38]

---

[37] For capitalism and slavery, see Sven Beckert and Seth Rockman, "Introduction: Slavery's Capitalism," in *Slavery's Capitalism: a New History of American Economic Development*, eds. Sven Beckert and Seth Rockman (Philadelphia: University of Pennsylvania Press, 2016), 1–28; Daniel Rood, *The Reinvention of Atlantic Slavery: Technology, Labor, Race, and Capitalism in the Greater Caribbean* (New York: Oxford University Press, 2017), 197–202; Gerald Horne, *Apocalypse of Settler Colonialism: The Roots of Slavery, White Supremacy, and Capitalism in Seventeenth Century North America and the Caribbean* (New York: Monthly Review Press, 2018); Sven Beckert, *Empire of Cotton: A Global History* (New York: Knopf, 2015).

[38] For commodification and slavery, see Trevor Burnard, "Collecting and Accounting: Representing Slaves as Commodities in Jamaica, 1674–1784," in *Collecting Across Cultures: Material Exchanges in the Early Modern Atlantic World*, eds. Daniela Bleichmar and Peter Mancall (Philadelphia: University of Pennsylvania Press, 2013), 177–191; Elizabeth Fox-Genovese and Eugene Genovese, *Fruits of Merchant Capital: Slavery and Bourgeois Property in the Rise and Expansion of Capitalism* (New York: Oxford University Press, 1983).

Acknowledgments

Many dedicated and accommodating scholars have been of assistance to this project, both from great distances and through closer personal contact. Primarily, the academic community at the University of South Carolina was essential in the production of this monograph, reading and critiquing the arrangements of this work at each phase. As this book partially emerged out of a lengthy dissertation that covered many topics other than race and smell, my doctoral committee deserves chief consideration. That committee, composed of Mark Smith, Matt Childs, Woody Holton, Daniel Littlefield, and David Shields, have consistently stayed with this project beyond final submission of the dissertation and as I have moved on to different early career stations.

My dissertation advisor, Mark Smith, has been specifically essential through providing constant critique and support to the theses included within this project, even with the revisions I provide to his own essential studies on the social constructions of race in the Americas. His work on the history of the senses and approach to mentorship have been a driving force for my intellectual and academic maturation. The nuanced materialism applied within his analyses on both sensory history and the Old South harkens back to the days of Eugene Genovese, when history mattered as subversive praxis.

Matt Childs has also provided a continually optimistic energy for this project and has consistently offered essential historiographical critiques and the finest of academic psychotherapy regarding this moment of the academic job market. Woody Holton arrived later to my project but has provided constant review during even the most burdensome recent times within the American political spectrum. During my time serving at the

Institute for African American Research at South Carolina, Daniel Littlefield always kept an open door for questions on the goals of an academic life and the histories of slavery, race, and nation central to this project. David Shields provided the primary critiques behind my first publication on the history of the senses and has continued to contribute important assistance for my continuing scholarship on topics of discourse, taste, and sensory consciousness. Many others also deserve thanks regarding this project during our shared time at South Carolina, including Don Doyle, Kathryn Edwards, Kent Germany, Nicole Maskiell, Carol Harrison, Valinda Littlefield, Kevin Dawson, Michael Woods, and S. P. MacKenzie.

While at South Carolina, I also participated within and served as Chair of the Atlantic History Reading Group. The scholars who have been through that weekly roundtable provided this work with a current historiographical focus that burgeoned footnote upon footnote of density to this generally philosophical project for historical study. I would specifically like to thank Chaz Yingling and Neal Polhemus for their consistent reading of my manuscript and tangential readings of my other sensory scholarship. Finding lifelong colleagues and friends may be the most important part of graduate school, and Neal and Chaz, Gary Sellick, Tim Minella, Brian Dolphin, Cane West, Randy Owens, Evan Kutzler, Lewis Eliot, and Patrick O'Brien have provided the foremost intellectual assistance to this project and the essential friendships that continue to make academic life worth pursuing. As well, portions of this project were thankfully critiqued within this reading group and at South Carolina by Tyler Parry, Erin Holmes, Antony Keane-Dawes, Robert Greene, Stephen O'Hara, Katherine Crosby, Caleb Wittum, Carter Bruns, Mitch Oxford, Maurice Robinson, and Jill Found.

After leaving South Carolina to serve as Early American History Fellow at the University of Toronto, my work faced fresh critique that forced changes to an already ballooning academic mission. Concision and focus were found often from revisions furnished by the scholars in the Senior Common Room at University College. Specific researchers at Toronto who provided guidance on this monograph include David Clandfield, Mairi Cowan, Adrienne Hood, and John Yeomans. I would also like to thank the academic direction and support during my time at Toronto provided by Donald Ainslie, Christina Kramer, and John Marshall. While in Toronto, as this project took final shape, my initial editor at Cambridge, Deborah Gershenowitz, maintained an important sponsorship that allowed this project to mature with the correct level of deadline management and laissez-faire nourishment. As I begin a current posting as Ahmanson-Getty Fellow at the William Andrews Clark Memorial Library, I would also like to thank the scholars at UCLA and the Center for 17th- & 18th-Century Studies for continuing support for my early academic career. Specifically, I would like to acknowledge Brenda Stevenson and Sharla Fett for the opportunity to contribute to the 1619 Anniversary Series on American Slavery.

Numerous other scholars have assisted with this project from its inception nearly ten years ago. At the University of Nebraska-Omaha, where I formulated the outlines of this venture, I would specifically like to acknowledge John Grigg. As well, I give thanks to Tracy Leavelle, David Peterson, and Mark Scherer for serving on my committee. In more recent years, this project has also received support from a wide range of academics. Hsuan Hsu has provided multiple intellectual spaces to debate this work at conferences through his organizational efforts and tireless critical eye. I met Chris Blakley while researching in Barbados and have been happy to talk often of this project with a scholar facing similar academic decisions and scholarly goals. Paul Musselwhite, Bevan Sewell, Marlene Eberhart, Jacob Baum, Linda Roland Danil, Michael Bull, and Daniela Hacke have provided critical impetus through publication support of some of my tangential sensory work. As well, throughout the many years of this project, I have often discussed this monograph and presented at numerous conferences with leading scholars in the fields of Critical Race Theory, American slavery, and the history of the senses. Due to the many encounters at these venues, I also would like to acknowledge Craig Koslofsky, Walter Johnson, David Howes, Melanie Kiechle, Alix Hui, Tracy McDonald, Chris Woolgar, James Walvin, and Constance Classen for their important notes, inspiration, and academic interest.

Aspects of this monograph have been presented at: The University of South Carolina History Center, the Northeastern Conference on British Studies, the Midwest Popular Culture Association, Under Western Skies IV, the Southern Association for the History of Science and Medicine, the College English Association, the British Association for American Studies, the American Comparative Literature Association, the Popular Culture Association/American Culture Association, the Southern Historical Association, the Consortium on the Revolutionary Era, the Missouri Valley History Conference, the Knowing Nature Conference at the Folger Shakespeare Library, the Organization of American Historians, the Association for the Study of Literature and the Environment, the Early Modern Interdisciplinary Graduate Forum at the University of Toronto, the Canadian Historical Association, the Sensing the South Workshop at Mississippi State University, the African Studies Association, and the Senses and the Sacred Conference at the University of York. I offer a heartfelt thanks to those numerous settings for the space to present and hear criticism on the many interdisciplinary contours of this monograph.

This project was also supported by numerous grants and fellowships. My final year of dissertation writing was funded by the Bilinski Educational Foundation. I researched at the National Archives in Kew using funds provided by the University of South Carolina, which arrived from the Institute for African American Research and a Wilfred and Rebecca Calcott Award from the History Department. My research at the Barbados Department of Archives and the Barbados Museum and Historical Society was financed by the Ceny Walker Institute at South Carolina. Exploration at the Jamaican Archives Unit was funded by an Atkinson/Wyatt Dissertation Fellowship from South Carolina. As well, investigation at libraries within South Carolina was partly supported through a Walter Edgar History Scholarship from the Columbia Committee of the National Society of the Colonial Dames of America in the State of South Carolina.

While in Toronto, I earned a Harcourt Brown Travel Fellowship for Research at the Newberry Library in Chicago. Other recent investigations for this project have been performed at the Huntington Library, the John Carter Brown Library, and the Massachusetts Historical Society. While at the Huntington under the auspices of a Mayers Fellowship, I discussed this project often with David Torres-Rouff, who granted a critical eye and important academic lunch conversation to fill the lengthy California midafternoons. While in Pasadena, I was also glad to have had the opportunity to discuss this project and academic expectations often with both Daniel Richter and Lindsay O'Neill. At the John Carter Brown Library, I researched under the support of a New World Comparative Studies Fellowship. I thank Neil Safier and Bertie Mandelblatt for their academic backing and Anthony di Lorenzo, Jeremy Mumford, and Céline Carayon for the conversation. At the Massachusetts Historical Society, where I served under a short-term Mellon Fellowship, I would like to thank Kid Wongsrichanalai and Katy Morris for their research guidance as well as Angela and Jeremy Lowther for the lodging and entertainment.

As well, I write today with great thanks to the Canadian healthcare system. During my time in Toronto, my life was shocked into a fresh and troublesome place by an unforeseen health crisis. There is no doubt, even in this focused mind of a reasoning academic, that if this personal calamity had occurred in the United States my life would have been further shattered due to the horrible contingencies and profiteering of the American healthcare industry. Beyond the importance of an academic position at the University of Toronto, the stipulation of being in Canada, in a place that must clearly be a socialist hellscape, saved many aspects of what could have been a shattered career and a wasted life.

When you enter upon the winding paths of life, you never expect the health challenges that come. Leveling up into the test and making your way forward through the darkest of physical pains always becomes the only choice forward. Often, however, understanding that singular selection of striving onward takes time and assistance. Initially, in my case, that support came from a healthcare industry that prizes the human over the dollar, that asserts healthcare as a human right that should never destroy a family with choices between disparaging debt or debilitating disease. Leveling up, finding that next plane of living, discovering a lifeway through the discomfort, then comes from the people around you. Family and friends, colleagues and advisors, the respected and the loved, all helped me through the hurt to find spaces of peace that, when in the darkest moments of illness, we never expect to again encounter.

I therefore also write today with thanks to my siblings, close personal friends, and extended family that every note of support or opposing forms of tough love helped me through the worst moments. Likewise, I send always a message of love and gratefulness to the memories of my grandparents, who, even within the thoughts of this agnostic mind, somehow still touch me with a love of knowledge and ephemeral support from the place beyond. To my parents, whose loving care can never truly be correctly thanked, I offer that I will forever strive to be the son that you deserve. And, as always, I bestow a heartfelt thank you and love to my Amanda, who has shown me the beauty of life even in the darkest moments of catastrophe. I promise to reward you each day with my own renewed positive outlook, to provide the same wondrous support you have imparted upon me, as we look forward to our own marriage, family, and future. Two kids forever in love.

We live in a selfish time, an era of Randian ethics where healthcare profits dispense a Malthusian genocide and disaster capitalism upon ill bodies. This is structural and seemingly impenetrable, which consequently creates burdened feelings upon the sick who frequently must balance their own survival against their ability to support or exist within their families. Terms like "pre-existing condition" are thrown around to protect a reprehensible structure that allows pharmaceutical representatives, insurance companies, finance capitalists, and doctors foregoing their Hippocratic Oath to house millions in bank accounts while children living in their same cities die without the healthcare that could be provided through a greater balance of wealth and compassion.

Because the structure of the market protects stockholders over the ill, society perpetuates with implicitly genocidal discourses against the unhealthy, creating excessive spaces of selfishness that remove natural empathy for diseased persons within the human community. A false consciousness perpetuates the idea that nothing can be done to help the ill, that there are barriers preventing the rich from providing monies to help the sick, that somehow the cash would be stolen or funnelled or wasted. Those succumbing to banality within the structure assert protocols, rules, and roadblocks between the ill and the compassion they deserve. But those bureaucratic and corporate barriers do not need to exist, and they only seem to function as a way to protect callous and greedy structures of the medical industry and government administration. These false barricades between rich and poor are dishonest discursive constructs within a self-perpetuating superstructure that justifies greed over healthcare for all.

My own life would have continued regardless of the care that was provided in either Canada or the United States. My crisis was temporary and overcome. But, for many, this is not the case. Impoverished and sick children face a life where their parents must balance supplying their overpriced medicines against eating enough food. Elderly patients similarly suffer through a healthcare industry that uses their bodies as vectors for pills to profit within a bureaucratic mess of matching funds and uncaring capitalist insatiability. Mansions rise in the countryside as evidence of an American pharmaceutical and medical industry that traps bodies into biopolitical spaces for the extraction of greater monies. Chronic disease builds wealth instead of creating greater empathy, preventing the sick citizen from ever dreaming of their full potential because they face a wall of costs.

We trumpet "research and innovation" as the reason for exorbitant prices and sing an elegy to all the drugs that never cure because they keep the chronically ill alive and pumping, while never fully understanding the costs of those pills upon the empathic structures that keep society caring. Deep into the tissue of civilization, hatred for the sick grows because they are believed to overburden the economy. The ill are believed to take money from the finite economic structure, and consequently they become another degraded class, a lesser assemblage, a threat to the pocketbooks of the avaricious. But the amount of wealth in the economic structure is not predetermined. That old mercantilist tale is simply a hegemonic invention made to trick the subaltern. We do not need to fight for a fixed amount of pennies, as wealth can be created, innovations can generate more currency, and believing otherwise is simply false consciousness educated upon the masses by those who have the majority of the existing funds and find, in disputes among the impoverished, the continuing ability to divide, conquer, and accumulate.

The failing American healthcare system that burdens the function of the economy is not the fault of the ill, just as poverty is not the fault of the poor. The more desperate a medical condition, the greedier capitalist mouths froth with the ability to profit. Greed attacks the structures of our economies much more than illness. Such a system must be destroyed. Children should not die because they lack currency, when healthcare executives, wayward physicians, and pharmaceutical representatives spend millions on little stones and shiny things. This is disaster capitalism upon the body, and it must be changed.

Let us strive for a world after 2020 in which the reasonable and compassionate can return hearts and minds to a progressive space and remove the generational stains of historically abhorrent narcissism that currently protects unfeeling and sickening discourses of healthcare, immigration, structural racism, and tainted historical memory. Overcoming the shockingly subordinate sins of 2016 that made some believe they needed performative and evil forms of criminality in the halls of power to face an uncaring world will allow society to find again persons revitalized from social occlusion, who can then rise from their illnesses with the human right of care, despite the sickening economics of sordid scions, corporations made persons, and both of their falsely conscious certainties of a cruelly unchanging world.

Introduction

Pecunia non Olet

Although understood during previous centuries through popular and folk traditions that allocated the plagues of the Early Modern Era to possible pestilence from vapors, the foremost English academic treatment of what came to be called miasma theory appeared within Robert Boyle's *Suspicions about the Hidden Realities of the Air* (1674).[1] Although centrally about overturning the idea that air was benign within chemical reactions, Boyle's Royal Society text described how objects that decayed into "effluvium" caused diseases that penetrated the defenses of the human body through the nasal passages. For Boyle and his cohort of early modern scientists, miasma often meant odor, and the detection of pungency signified the existence of disease within the environment. Deriving from humoral traditions of medical diagnosis that linked the nose directly to vulnerable parts of the brain, miasma theory articulated that objects created pungent smells that denoted the menace of infection.[2]

---

[1] Robert Boyle, *Tracts Containing I. Suspicions about Some Hidden Qualities of the Air: with an Appendix Touching Celestial Magnets and Some Other Particulars: II. Animadversions upon Mr. Hobbes's Problemata de vacuo: III. A Discourse of the Cause of Attraction by Suction* (London: W. G. for M. Pitt, 1674), 38–48. For an earlier summary, see Thomas Thayre, *Treatise of the Pestilence: Wherein Is Shewed All the Causes Thereof, with Most Assured Preseruatiues against All Infection; and Lastly Is Taught the True and Perfect Cure of the Pestilence, by Most Excellent and Approved Medicines* (London: Short, 1603), 8–13. See also Jayne Elizabeth Lewis, *Air's Appearance: Literary Atmosphere in British Fiction, 1660–1794* (Chicago: University of Chicago Press, 2012), 43–79; Robert Boyle, *Essays of the Strange Subtilty of Effluviums* (London: W. G. for M. Pitt, 1673).

[2] For the general application of miasma theory to early modern religious conceptions that "all things that smell evil, are evil," see Piero Camporesi, *The Incorruptible Flesh: Bodily Mutation and Mortification in Religion and Folklore* (Cambridge: Cambridge University

To control overpowering scented objects that caused sickness within early modern bodies, Boyle and the Royal Society consequently engaged the sense of sight to analyze substances of decay at more minute spaces for bodily governance.[3]

Following fresh understandings of cleanliness, miasma theory, and godliness related to concerns over the invasions of poor airs, the English polymath Thomas Tryon presented extended discourses on the philosophy of the five senses for early modern readers that portrayed the senses as similarly engaged within philosophical combat.[4] In his *Letters upon Several Occasions* (1700), Tryon submitted various dialogues about the traits of individual senses and their particular roles for protecting English bodies from the increasing threats of the outside world, implicitly affording standards of worth and proper comportment for each individual sense.[5] To become a proper Englishperson, sensory routinization and

Press, 1988), 80–84. Miasma theory was generally displaced by germ theory within scientific fields during the middle of the nineteenth century through the work of John Snow, Jakob Henle, Louis Pasteur, and Robert Koch. However, miasma remained a popular way to understand the link between disease, breathing, and smell well into the twentieth century. John Farley, "Parasites and the Germ Theory of Disease," in *Framing Disease: Studies in Cultural History*, eds. Janet Lynne Golden and Charles Rosenberg (New Brunswick, NJ: Rutgers University Press, 1997), 33–49; John Pickstone, "Death, Dirt, and Fever Epidemics: Rewriting the History of British Public Health, 1780–1850," in *Epidemics and Ideas: Essays on the Historical Perception of Pestilence*, eds. Terence Ranger and Paul Slack (Cambridge: Cambridge University Press, 2011), 125–148.

[3] For critical theory, literary dissemination, and ideas of intellectual contagion, see Peta Mitchell, *Contagious Metaphor* (London: Bloomsbury Academic, 2012), 1–36; Margaret Pelling, "The Meaning of Contagion: Reproduction, Medicine, and Metaphor," in *Contagion*, eds. Alison Bashford and Claire Hooker (London: Routledge, 2014), 15–38.

[4] Thomas Tryon, *A Treatise of Cleanness in Meats, and Drinks, of the Preparation of Food … and the Benefits of Clean Sweet Beds … Also of the Generation of Bugs, and Their Cure. To Which Is Added, A Short Discourse of the Pain in the Teeth, Etc.* (London: S. P., 1682), 8–13. For more on discourses of smell and science during later decades, see the initial decline of miasma theory within academic circles in William Tullett, *Smell in Eighteenth-Century England: A Social Sense* (Oxford: Oxford University Press, 2019), 67–87.

[5] For Royal Society, sensory skills, and the rise of the eye, see Jessica Riskin, "The Divine Optician," *American Historical Review* 116, 2 (2011): 352–370; Alan Salter, "Early Modern Empiricism and the Discourse of the Senses," in *The Body as Object and Instrument of Knowledge: Embodied Empiricism in Early Modern Science*, eds. Charles Wolfe and Ofer Gal (Dordrecht: Springer, 2010), 59–74; Todd Borlick, "The Whale Under the Microscope: Technology and Objectivity in Two Renaissance Utopias," in *Philosophies of Technology: Francis Bacon and His Contemporaries*, ed. Claus Zittel (Leiden: Brill, 2008), 231–249; Lorraine Daston and Peter Galison, *Objectivity* (New York: Zone Books, 2007), 48–59.

the education of particular sensory skills became necessary as protections from both the invasion of bad airs and the increasingly probing nature of fresh worldly encounters arriving to English ports. For smelling, as within the works of botanist and physician John Floyer during coterminous decades, Tryon taught Englishpersons to cultivate "greater talents" of the sense to avoid the "penetrating" and "stinking Foggs, Scents, and Vapours" that are "extreamly hurtful to the Mind and Body." Tryon spent more space on smelling than upon the other senses throughout his celebrated letters because, like many early moderns, he understood that the nasal passages remained consistently open to the threats of contaminated, malignant, and lingering airs that affected both the comportment of the body and the functions of the susceptible mind.[6]

Because of these intense fears of invasion from psychological melancholy and physiological disease caused by zymotic miasmas, night airs, and bad vapors, Europeans consistently understood water as corruptive throughout much of the Early Modern Era. This consistent fear provided even greater impetus for a burgeoning perfume industry due to the unswerving fears of bathing that commonly informed various European discourses.[7] Similarly applying the idea of perfumed cleanliness and miasma theory, Richard Mead, Royal Society member and physician to King George II during the early eighteenth century, believed that the use of positive smells would cure the diseased effects of negative odors, through a battle between supposed contagions, perfumes, and curatives.[8] The longstanding and persistent eighteenth-

---

[6] Thomas Tryon, *Tryon's Letters upon Several Occasions* (London: Conyers and Harris, 1700), 1–7, 85–87, quotes on 117–125. See also the varied use of sensory skills to discover scents to battle disease throughout John Floyer, *Pharmako-Basanos. Or, The Touch-Stone of Medicines. Discovering the Vertues of Vegetables, Minerals, & Animals, by Their Tastes & Smells. In Two Volumes* (London: Michael Johnson, 1687); Mark Jenner, "Tasting Lichfield, Touching China: Sir John Floyers' Senses," *The Historical Journal* 53, 3 (2010): 647–670.

[7] Georges Vigarello, *Concepts of Cleanliness: Changing Attitudes in France since the Middle Ages* (Cambridge: Cambridge University Press, 2008), 14–45; Kathleen Brown, *Foul Bodies: Cleanliness in Early America* (New Haven, CT: Yale University Press, 2009), 37–38; Mark Jenner, "Quackery and Enthusiasm, or Why Drinking Water Cured the Plague," in *Religio Medici: Medicine and Religion in Seventeenth-Century England*, eds. Ole Peter Grell and Andrew Cunningham (Aldershot: Scolar Publishing, 1996), 313–340.

[8] Richard Mead, *A Short Discourse Concerning Pestilential Contagion: And the Methods to Be Used to Prevent It* (London: William Bowyer for Buckley and Smith, 1720), 2–4, 50–54; Richard Mead, *The Medical Works of Richard Mead M.D. Physician to His Late Majesty King George II. Fellow of the Royal Colleges of Physicians at London and Edinburgh, and of the Royal Society* (Edinburgh: Donaldson and Elliot, 1775), 257, 539–540, 597.

century understanding of disease and pestilential invasion often focused on these concepts of pungent contamination and deodorization through counteractive and antiseptic smells. Within these considerations, odors essentially indicated disease, usually emanating from rotting animal carcasses and vegetal materials that were deemed to create invasive vapors from decaying objects. These beliefs continued for much of the general population within Europe and North America well into the nineteenth century.[9]

During the Early Modern Era, the senses went to war.[10] Within various discourses, as with the sensory contests fundamental to Thomas Tomkis's *Lingua, or the Combat of the Tongue and the Five Senses for Superiority* (1607), each of the senses was granted a narrative strength for battling to earn a greater part of the future English and broader Western sensory consciousness.[11] Numerous other plays and prose chronicles allocated support for individual senses regarding the importance of each sense for goals of Christian morality, childhood education, and for gaining social prominence in

[9] For more on miasma theory, see Steven Connor, *The Book of Skin* (Ithaca: Cornell University Press, 2004), 210–214; P. C. Baldwin, "How Night Air Became Good Air, 1776–1930," *Environmental History* 8, 3 (2003): 412–429; Melanie Kiechle, *Smell Detectives: An Olfactory History of Nineteenth-Century Urban America* (Seattle: University of Washington Press, 2017), 35–37, 174–175; Katherine Arner, "Making Yellow Fever American: The Early American Republic, the British Empire, and the Geopolitics of Disease in the Atlantic World," *Atlantic Studies* 7, 4 (2010): 447–471.

[10] For texts with senses at battle, see John Davies, *Nosce Tiepsum* (London: Richard Field, 1599); Richard Brathwayt, *Essays Upon the Five Senses* (London: Anne Griffin, 1635 [1620]), 70–74. See also the summaries of sensory battles within Elizabeth Robertson, "Afterword: From Gateways to Channels. Reaching towards an Understanding of the Transformative Plasticity of the Senses in the Medieval and Early Modern Periods," in *The Five Senses in Medieval and Early Modern England*, eds. Annette Kern-Stähler, Beatrix Busse, and Wietse de Boer (Leiden: Brill, 2016), 286–296; C. M. Peterson, "The Five Senses in Willem II Van Haecht's Cabinet of Cornelis Van Der Geest," *Intellectual History Review* 20, 1 (2010): 103–121; Jo Wheeler, "Stench in Sixteenth-Century Venice," in *The City and the Senses: Urban Culture Since 1500*, eds. Alexander Cowan and Jill Steward (Aldershot: Ashgate, 2007), 25–38.

[11] Thomas Tomkis, *Lingua: or, The Combat of the Tongue, and the Fiue Sences for Superiority* (London: Okes for Waterson, 1622 [1607]). For embodied sensory experience and historical methodology, see Joy Monice Malnar and Frank Vodvarka, *Sensory Design* (Minneapolis: University of Minnesota Press, 2004), 37–39; Pamela Smith, *The Body of the Artisan: Art and Experience in the Scientific Revolution* (Chicago: University of Chicago Press, 2004); Bruce Smith, *The Acoustic World of Early Modern England: Attending to the O-Factor* (Chicago: University of Chicago Press, 1999), 12–13; Kate Lacey, *Listening Publics: The Politics and Experience of Listening in the Media Age* (Cambridge: Polity, 2013), 6–8; Bruce Smith, *The Key of Green: Passion and Perception in Renaissance Culture* (Chicago: University of Chicago Press, 2009), 6–10.

the sycophantic salons and courts of high society.[12] The affective power of these narratives led to later bodily alterations in the function of the five-sense hierarchy, which moved smell to a much lower space of importance within Western culture, in part because miasma theory defined that nearly all odors were inherently a threatening signifier of malady, emanating smell signified a lack of morality, and overpowering scents presented a deficiency of social graces.[13]

Numerous scholars have traced this important decline of smell as a marker of a modernity that applied smelling to partly justify ideas of the progressive centralized state, concepts of shame, and social ordering.[14] Within this debate about the need of Western states to remove nearly all smells as a marker of disease to the singular body and the wider body politic, *The Smell of Slavery* argues that ideas of race became important to define both a lack of civilization within black populations and for more aggressively coding African bodies as the very cause of infection, as

---

[12] For more on senses debated during the Early Modern Era, see Hristomir Stanev, *Sensory Experience and the Metropolis on the Jacobean Stage (1603–1625)* (Farnham: Ashgate, 2014), 18–20; Laura Giannetti, "Of Eels and Pears: A Sixteenth-Century Debate on Taste, Temperance, and the Pleasures of the Senses," in *Religion and the Senses in Early Modern Europe*, eds. Wietse de Boer and Christine Göttler (Leiden: Brill, 2013), 289–305; Elizabeth Harvey, *Sensible Flesh: On Touch in Early Modern Culture* (Philadelphia: University of Pennsylvania Press, 2003); Carla Mazzio, "Introduction: Individual Parts," in *The Body in Parts: Fantasies of Corporeality in Early Modern Europe*, eds. David Hillman and Carla Mazzio (New York: Routledge, 1997), xi–xxix; Jonathan Sawday, *The Body Emblazoned: Dissection and the Human Body in Renaissance Culture* (London: Routledge, 1995), 1–11; Viktoria von Hoffmann, *From Gluttony to Enlightenment: The World of Taste in Early Modern Europe* (Urbana: University of Illinois Press, 2016).

[13] Immanuel Kant summarized the Enlightenment understanding of the sense of smell, stating that it "does not pay us to cultivate it or to refine it in order to gain enjoyment; this sense can pick up more objects of aversion than of pleasure (especially in crowded places) and, besides, the pleasure coming from the sense of smell cannot be other than fleeting and transitory." Constance Classen, "Other Ways to Wisdom: Learning through the Senses across Cultures," *International Review of Education* 45, 3–4 (1999): 269–280, quote on 272. For more on the anti-olfactory ideals of Kant, see Hannah Arendt and Ronald Beiner, *Lectures on Kant's Political Philosophy* (Chicago: University of Chicago Press, 1990), 65–66, and Immanuel Kant, *Analytic of the Beautiful, from the Critique of Judgment* (Indianapolis, IN: Bobbs-Merrill, 1963 [1790]), 28–36. See also Ann-Sophie Barwich, "Up the Nose of the Beholder? Aesthetic Perception in Olfaction as a Decision-Making Process," *New Ideas in Psychology* 47 (2017): 157–165.

[14] For inspirational work for the field of sensory studies, see Norbert Elias, *The Civilizing Process* (Oxford: Blackwell, 2000 [1939]); Sigmund Freud and Joan Riviere, *Civilization and Its Discontents* (London: Hogarth, 1929 [1903]). See also social construction of sensation within Kelvin Low, "The Social Life of the Senses: Charting Directions," *Sociology Compass* 6, 3 (2012): 271–282.

specifically commodified objects that produced the very miasmas that
brought contagion upon creation.[15]

DISENCHANTING AROMA

For the Western racist, historically and structurally, the mental understanding regarding the material reality of the racially marginalized matters
little when the body can be educated to feel and sense racial disgust
through forms of false sensory consciousness inscribed upon the organs
of perception.[16] *The Smell of Slavery* explores articulations of the African

---

[15] For an introduction to medicine and the black body during the Early Modern Era, see
Suman Seth, *Difference and Disease: Medicine, Race, and the Eighteenth-Century British
Empire* (Cambridge: Cambridge University Press, 2018); Emily Senior, *The Caribbean
and the Medical Imagination, 1764–1834: Slavery, Disease and Colonial Modernity*
(Cambridge: Cambridge University Press, 2018); Andrew Curran, *The Anatomy of
Blackness: Science & Slavery in an Age of Enlightenment* (Baltimore, MD: Johns
Hopkins University Press, 2011); Rana Hogarth, *Medicalizing Blackness: Making
Racial Differences in the Atlantic World, 1780–1840* (Chapel Hill: University of North
Carolina Press, 2017); Ikuko Asaka, *Tropical Freedom: Climate, Settler Colonialism, and
Black Exclusion in the Age of Emancipation* (Durham, NC: Duke University Press,
2017), 139–166; Sharon Block, *Colonial Complexions: Race and Bodies in Eighteenth-
Century America* (Philadelphia: University of Pennsylvania Press, 2018), 10–34.

[16] For debates on Cartesianism and phenomenology in sensory studies, see
Antonio Damasio, *Descartes' Error: Emotion, Reason and the Human Brain* (London:
Random House, 2008), 223–244; E. A. Grosz, *The Incorporeal: Ontology, Ethics, and
the Limits of Materialism* (New York: Columbia University Press, 2017), 1–14;
Maurice Merleau-Ponty, *Phenomenology of Perception* (London: Routledge, 2014
[1945]); Maurice Merleau-Ponty, *Sense and Non-Sense* (Evanston, IL: Northwestern
University Press, 1991 [1948]); Jean-François Lyotard, *Phenomenology* (Albany, NY:
State University of New York Press, 1991), 48–55; Hans Jonas, *The Phenomenon of Life:
Toward a Philosophical Biology* (Evanston, IL: Northwestern University Press, 2001
[1966]). During the 1980s, the anthropology of the senses emerged from the work of
Constance Classen and David Howes to question the Cartesian focus on standard sensory
hierarchies and the universalizing body of phenomenological analysis. Paul Rodaway,
Sensuous Geographies: Body, Sense, and Place (London: Routledge, 2011), 3–40;
David Howes, *Sensual Relations: Engaging the Senses in Culture and Social Theory*
(Ann Arbor: University of Michigan Press, 2010), 29–60; Paul Stoller, *Sensuous
Scholarship* (Philadelphia: University of Pennsylvania Press, 1997), 4–23; Sarah Pink,
"The Future of Sensory Anthropology/the Anthropology of the Senses," *Social
Anthropology* 18, 3 (2010): 331–333. In recent decades, a new field of carnal hermeneu-
tics has emerged to reassert phenomenology of the body through non-universalizing
languages that frequently were believed to displace non-Western sensory traditions.
Christopher Watkin, *Phenomenology or Deconstruction?: The Question of Ontology
in Maurice Merleau-Ponty, Paul Ricoeur, and Jean-Luc Nancy* (Cambridge: Cambridge
University Press, 2012); Evan Thompson, *Mind in Life: Biology, Phenomenology and the
Sciences of Mind* (Cambridge, MA: Belknap, 2010), 253–260. In the most recent change
to the field of sensory studies, scholars following the work of Brian Massumi highlight the

body through the changing functions of the European nose, as part of a nasal social construction that was both informally contoured and an important part of formal community developments during the Atlantic Slave Trade. The civilizing process that led to a significant decline of olfactory sensations with the rise of Western modernity emerged through changes within fields of racial embodiment. The foundational reason that the eye became the arbiter of truth within scientific study was because subjective odors threatened many burgeoning English and Western concepts of race, identity, and cultural superiority.[17]

At its broadest, *The Smell of Slavery* therefore adds to a growing field of study that focuses on the importance of discourse for the construction of embodied historical experience.[18] Scholars of historical bodies frequently argue that the perceptions of the five senses are culturally constructed.[19] The other, through this understanding of embodiment, enculturation, and

importance of the event and affect upon sensory perception. Brian Massumi, *Semblance and Event: Activist Philosophy and the Occurrent Arts* (Cambridge, MA: MIT Press, 2013), 39–86; Ruth Leys, *The Ascent of Affect: Genealogy and Critique* (Chicago: University of Chicago Press, 2018); John Protevi, *Political Affect: Connecting the Social and the Somatic* (Minneapolis: University of Minnesota Press, 2009), 3–32.

[17] For broader histories of odor, see James Knox Millen, *Your Nose Knows: A Study of the Sense of Smell* (San Jose, CA: Authors Choice, 2001); Roy Bedichek, *The Sense of Smell* (Garden City, NY: Doubleday, 1960), 147–174; Avery Gilbert, *What the Nose Knows: The Science of Scent in Everyday Life* (New York: Crown, 2008); Kelvin Low, *Scents and Scent-Sibilities: Smell and Everyday Life Experiences* (Newcastle: Cambridge Scholars, 2009); Gabrielle Dorland, *Scents Appeal: The Silent Persuasion of Aromatic Encounters* (Mendham, NJ: Wayne Dorland, 1993), 45–62; Ruth Winter, *The Smell Book: Scents, Sex, and Society* (Philadelphia: Lippincott, 1976), 87–104; Nathalie Wourm, "The Smell of God: Scent Trails from Ficino to Baudelaire," in *Sense and Scent: An Exploration of Olfactory Meaning*, eds. Bronwen Martin and Felizitas Ringham (Dublin: Philomel, 2003), 79–100; Annick Le Guérer, *Scent, the Mysterious and Essential Powers of Smell* (New York: Turtle Bay, 1992); Gabrielle Glaser, *The Nose: A Profile of Sex, Beauty, and Survival* (New York: Atria, 2002); Mandy Aftel, *Essence and Alchemy: A Book of Perfume* (New York: North Point, 2001), 11–47.

[18] C. Y. Chiang, "The Nose Knows: The Sense of Smell in American History," *Journal of American History* 95, 2 (2008): 405–416; Mark Smith, "The Senses in American History: A Round Table Still Coming to 'Our' Senses: An Introduction," *Journal of American History* 95, 2 (2008): 378–381; Mark Smith, "Making Sense of Social History," *Journal of Social History* 37, 1 (2003): 165–186; David Howes, "Charting the Sensorial Revolution," *Senses and Society* 1, 1 (2006): 113–128; George Roeder, "Coming to Our Senses," *Journal of American History* 81 (December, 1994): 1113–1122.

[19] David Abram, *The Spell of the Sensuous: Perception and Language in a More-Than-Human World* (New York: Pantheon, 1996); Mark Johnson, *The Meaning of the Body: Aesthetics of Human Understanding* (Chicago: University of Chicago Press, 2007), 89–91, 279–280; Mark Smith, *Sensing the Past: Seeing, Hearing, Smelling, Tasting, and Touching in History* (Berkeley: University of California Press, 2007), 133–138.

education, is commonly assembled within an ontological space rather than experienced as an objective material reality. Within discourse, these sensory experiences of the body are frequently constructed through language that alters the biological function of the five senses. As well, as a part of certain forms of social conditioning, the odors, tastes, and sounds of the other are perceived not only through the linguistic episteme through which they take meaning but also in traces imprinted upon the body before language articulated those perceptions into words.[20]

Out of these historiographical fields of body knowledge and discursive analysis emerged the history of the senses, which asserts as a primary marker of the field's historiography that the ontological breaches caused by the discovery of the New World, the invention of the printing press, changes in religious practice during the Reformation, and the taxonomic desires of the Enlightenment produced an increased separation, streamlining, and reordering of the senses during the Early Modern Era.[21] This monograph accesses these discourses on the making of modernity to

[20] For embodied racial knowledge, see Helen Ngo, *The Habits of Racism: A Phenomenology of Racism and Racialized Embodiment* (Lanham, MD: Lexington Books, 2017), 135–174; Alexis Shotwell, *Knowing Otherwise: Race, Gender, and Implicit Understanding* (University Park: Pennsylvania State University Press, 2011), 14–15, 34–36; Constance Classen, "The Odor of the Other: Olfactory Symbolism and Cultural Categories," *Ethos* 20, 2 (1992): 133–166; Mark Smith, *How Race Is Made: Slavery, Segregation, and the Senses* (Chapel Hill: University of North Carolina Press, 2006), 1–10; Will Jackson and Emily Manktelow, "Introduction: Thinking With Deviance," in *Subverting Empire: Deviance and Disorder in the British Colonial World*, eds. Will Jackson and Emily Manktelow (Basingstoke: Palgrave Macmillan, 2015), 1–21; Jonathan Reinarz, *Past Scents: Historical Perspectives on Smell* (Urbana: University of Illinois Press, 2014), 85–112; Yadira Perez Hazel, "Sensing Difference: Whiteness, National Identity, and Belonging in the Dominican Republic," *Transforming Anthropology* 22, 2 (2014): 78–91; Mark Smith, "Transcending, Othering, Detecting: Smell, Premodernity, Modernity," *Postmedieval* 3, 4 (2012): 380–390.

[21] For classic works on sensory changes and modernity, see Marshall McLuhan, *The Gutenberg Galaxy; The Making of Typographic Man* (Toronto: University of Toronto Press, 1962); Dominique Laporte, *History of Shit* (Cambridge, MA: MIT Press, 2000 [1978]); Walter Ong, *Ramus, Method, and the Decay of Dialogue: From the Art of Discourse to the Art of Reason* (Cambridge, MA: Harvard University Press, 1958). Important in the introduction of the olfactory into these academic and popular deliberations was historian Alain Corbin's work on French discourses of deodorization in eighteenth-century *Paris, The Foul and the Fragrant* (1983), and Patrick Süskind's widely read novel, *Perfume: the Story of a Murderer* (1986). Alain Corbin, *The Foul and the Fragrant: Odor and the French Social Imagination* (Cambridge, MA: Harvard University Press, 1986 [1983]), 65–70; Patrick Süskind, *Perfume: the Story of a Murderer* (New York: Pocket Books, 1986). See also Rodolphe El-Khoury, "Polish and Deodorize; Paving the City in Late Eighteenth Century France," in *The Smell Culture Reader*, ed. Jim Drobnick (Oxford: Berg, 2006), 18–28; Peter Burke, "Urban Sensations: Attractive and Repulsive,"

discover significant differences between premodern and modern sensory consciousness through proclaiming that odor was decreasingly perceived within European metropoles from the era of Johannes Gutenberg until the twentieth century.[22] As Western Europe deodorized conceptually and materially, the Atlantic World afforded a space for European consciousness to emplace odors upon new bodies in an ostentatious game of sensory imperialism that combined ecological scents with new forms of literary, medical, and scientific race-making.[23]

Premodern European sensory worlds are best exemplified through the Catholic mass, which combined sensations to elicit reverence for the material representations of the trinity. In these sensory engagements, the tones of choirs mixed with the aroma of incense to create an immersive sensory experience whereby sounds, smells, tastes, sights, and tactile experiences frequently combined to create a common sensory wonderment that inherently trusted olfaction for greater social application.[24]

---

in Volume III of *A Cultural History of the Senses*, ed. Constance Classen (London: Bloomsbury, 2014), 43–60.

[22] For more debates on general olfactory decline, see Constance Classen, David Howes, and Anthony Synnott, *Aroma: The Cultural History of Smell* (London: Routledge, 1994); Constance Classen, *Worlds of Sense: Exploring the Senses in History and Across Cultures* (London: Routledge, 1993); Chris Sladen, "Past Scents: The Importance of a Sense of Smell to the Historian," in *Sense and Scent: An Exploration of Olfactory Meaning*, eds. Bronwen Martin and Felizitas Ringham (Dublin: Philomel, 2003), 149–168; Mark Jenner, "Follow Your Nose? Smell, Smelling, and their Histories," *American Historical Review* 116, 2 (2011): 335–351.

[23] Holly Dugan exposed that those in power during the Early Modern Era often used aroma to display olfactory spectacles to amuse the subdued masses. Dugan's work also emboldens a significant aspect of Atlantic history that focuses on material culture and the experience of encountering and expanding new mercantile commodities through the senses. Holly Dugan, *The Ephemeral History of Perfume: Scent and Sense in Early Modern England* (Baltimore, MD: Johns Hopkins University Press, 2011). See also Sally Barnes, "Olfactory Performances," *TDR* 45, 1 (Spring 2001): 68–76.

[24] Katelynn Robinson, *The Sense of Smell in the Middle Ages: A Source of Certainty* (London: Routledge, 2019); Michel Jeanneret, *A Feast of Words: Banquets and Table Talk in the Renaissance* (Chicago: University of Chicago Press, 1991), 263–265; Suzanne Evans, "The Scent of a Martyr," *Numen* 49, 2 (2002): 193–211; Susan Ashbrook Harvey, *Scenting Salvation: Ancient Christianity and the Olfactory Imagination* (Berkeley: University of California Press, 2006); Bissera Pentcheva, *The Sensual Icon: Space, Ritual, and the Senses in Byzantium* (University Park: Pennsylvania State University Press, 2010); Eric Palazzo, "Art and the Senses: Art and Liturgy in the Middle Ages," in Volume II of *A Cultural History of the Senses*, eds. Constance Classen and Richard Newhauser (London: Bloomsbury, 2014), 175–194; Catherine Saucier, "The Sweet Sound of Sanctity: Sensing St. Lambert," *Senses and Society* 5, 1 (2010): 10–27; David Chidester, "Symbolism and the Senses in Saint Augustine," *Religion* 14, 1 (1984): 31–51; Constance Classen, *The Color of Angels:*

Because of the propensity of incense and sulfuric hell to understandings of both religion and medicine within premodern worlds, the sense of smell was often seen above the ground as clouds of aroma that portended fragrant spiritual experience and possible malevolent contamination. Consequently, premodern European sensory worlds prized the sense of smell for various medical, environmental, and spiritual procedures, ranging from the use of scented herbs in medicine to the ideal of the odor of sanctity that arose from specifically religious persons.[25]

Indulgent olfactory life was common prior to the Early Modern Era, and the mixing of spiritual worlds with the material environment often came through the beauty of collaborating ecological fragrances with otherworldly admiration.[26] For example, the poetry of botanist Nicholas Breton's *Smale Handfull of Fragrant Flowers* (1575) proclaimed: "Whom we may see in hande to haue/ this litle branche of Flowres greene./ Which sents and sauours passing well,/ the redyest way to heauen to smell."[27] European doctors prior to the Enlightenment, who generally followed the olfactory traditions of Galen that the nose was directly connected to the brain through a hollow tube and thus more

Cosmology, Gender, and the Aesthetic Imagination (London: Routledge, 1998); Piero Camporesi, *The Anatomy of the Senses: Natural Symbols in Medieval and Early Modern Italy* (Cambridge: Polity, 1994); Mary Thurlkill, *Sacred Scents in Early Christianity and Islam* (Lanham, MD: Lexington, 2016); Katherine Rinne, "Urban Ablutions: Cleansing Counter-Reformation Rome," in *Rome, Pollution, and Propriety: Dirt, Disease, and Hygiene in the Eternal City from Antiquity to Modernity*, eds. Mark Bradley and Kenneth Stow (Cambridge: Cambridge University Press, 2012), 182–201.

[25] Le Guérer, *Scent*, 39–50, 70–77; Dugan, *Ephemeral History*, 23–25; Classen, *Color of Angels*, 16–56; Ian Maclean, *Logic, Signs and Nature in the Renaissance: The Case of Learned Medicine* (Cambridge: Cambridge University Press, 2002), 77–80, 153–161, 198–199; Gerhard Jaritz and Verene Winiwarter, "On the Perception of Nature in Renaissance Society," in *Nature and Society in Historical Context*, eds. Mikuláš Teich, Roy Porter, and Bo Gustafsson (Cambridge: Cambridge University Press, 1997), 91–111; François Quiviger, *The Sensory World of Italian Renaissance Art* (London: Reaktion, 2010), 125–136.

[26] Laszló Bartosiewicz, "'There's Something Rotten in the State ... ': Bad Smells in Antiquity," *European Journal of Archaeology* 6, 2 (2013): 175–195; Victor Rodriguez-Pereira, "Sabrasa olor: The Role of Olfaction and Smells in Berceo's Milagros de Nuestra Senora," in *Beyond Sight: Engaging the Sense in Iberian Literatures and Cultures, 1200–1750*, eds. Ryan Giles and Steven Wagschal (Toronto: University of Toronto Press, 2018), 31–46.

[27] Nicholas Breton, *A Smale Handfull of Fragrant Fowers Selected and Gathered out of the Louely Garden of Sacred Scriptures, Fit for any Honorable or Woorshipfull Gentlewoman to Smell Unto* (London: Richard Jones, 1575), quotes on 7–8.

susceptible to outside influences upon body and mind, also employed a greater appreciation for smells when searching for proper pharmaceutical treatments from plants, often collected in vernacular compendiums like Rembert Dodoens's oft-translated and seminal botanical tracts, the additions to that work within the many editions of John Gerard's *Herball, or General History of Plants* (1597), the frequent editions of Thomas Cogan's *The Haven of Health* (1584), and William Coles's later *Adam in Eden* (1657).[28] With aromatic plants and their shepherding signatures within simples, many early modern doctors also used their noses to discover variations in the aroma of countless human sicknesses.[29]

During the Early Modern Era, new sensory regimes emerged.[30] The central aspect of most of these modern sensory understandings relayed

---

[28] Rembert Dodoens, *A New Herbal*, trans. Henry Lyte (London: Gerard Dewes, 1578 [1554]); John Gerard, *The Herbal or General History of Plants* (New York: Dover, 1975 [1633 Edition, Original Edition, 1597]); Thomas Cogan, *The Haven of Health* (London: Anne Griffin, 1636 [1584]), 42–56; William Coles, *Adam in Eden, or, Natures Paradise the History of Plants, Fruits, Herbs and Flowers with their Several Names ... the Places Where they Grow, Their Descriptions and Kinds, Their Times of Flourishing and Decreasing as also Their Several Signatures, Anatomical Appropriations and Particular Physical Vertues* (London: J. Streater for Nathaniel Brooke, 1657).

[29] Vivian Nutton, "Galen at the Bedside," in *Medicine and the Five Senses*, eds. W. F. Bynum and Roy Porter (Cambridge: Cambridge University Press, 1993), 7–16; Bruce Stansfield Eastwood, "Galen on the Elements of Olfactory Sensation," *Rheinisches Museum Für Philologie. N. F.* 124, 3–4 (1981): 268–290; Michael McVaugh, "Smell and the Medieval Surgeon," *Micrologus* 10 (2002): 113–132; Carole Rawcliffe, "'Delectable Sights and Fragrant Smelles': Gardens and Health in Late Medieval and Early Modern England," *Garden History* 36, 1 (2008): 3–21; Laurence Totelin, "Smell as Sign and Cure in Ancient Medicine," in *Smell and the Ancient Senses*, ed. Mark Bradley (New York: Routledge, 2015), 17–29; Richard Palmer, "In Bad Odour: Smell and Its Significance in Medicine from Antiquity to the Seventeenth Century," in *Medicine and the Five Senses*, eds. W. F. Bynum and Roy Porter (Cambridge: Cambridge University Press, 1993), 61–68; Letta Jones, "Plants and Smell – For Whose Benefit?," in *Sense and Scent: An Exploration of Olfactory Meaning*, eds. Bronwen Martin and Felizitas Ringham (Dublin: Philomel, 2003), 115–128; Alessandro Arcangeli, "The Trouble with Odours in Petrarch's *De Remedis*," in *Sense and the Senses in Early Modern Art and Cultural Practice*, eds. Alice Sanger and Siv Tove Kulbrandstad Walker (Farnham: Ashgate, 2012), 19–30.

[30] For more on debates regarding sensory change during the Early Modern Era, see Jacob Baum, *Reformation of the Senses: The Paradox of Religious Belief and Practice in Germany* (Urbana: University of Illinois Press, 2019), 1–12, Walter Ong, "The Shifting Sensorium," in *The Varieties of Sensory Experience: A Sourcebook in the Anthropology of the Senses*, ed. David Howes (Toronto: University of Toronto Press, 1991), 25–30; Julie Stone Peters, "Orality, Literacy, and Print Revisited," in *Time, Memory, and the Verbal Arts: Essays on the Thought of Walter Ong*, eds. Dennis Weeks and Jane Susan Hoogestraat (Selinsgrove, PA: Susquehanna University Press, 1998), 27–61; Carolyn Purnell, *The Sensational Past: How the Enlightenment Changed the Way We Use Our Senses* (New York: Norton, 2017), 44–45, 102–122.

a greater importance to the eye, which became the sense of truth and validation within the New Science and for the rise of tastefully civilized aesthetic observations during the eighteenth century.[31] Within religious traditions, the eye also became more important due to a Reformation focus on the written word and literacy among the masses.[32] As the eye rose as a particular sense of distance and reason, the lower contact senses of smell and taste were marginalized as inferior and overly subjective.[33] With the denigration of smell, cleansing through freshening perfume meant to minimize and remove the odor of the body became an even greater mark of modernity that began to set Western groups apart from the others of the world who frequently defined imaginatively perfumed bodies as positive markers of subjective identity.[34] This monograph adds to this multivalent

---

[31] Barbara Maria Stafford, "Presuming Images and Consuming Words: The Visualization of Knowledge From the Enlightenment to Post-Modernism," in *Consumption and the World of Goods*, eds. John Brewer and Roy Porter (London: Routledge, 1993), 462–477; David Summers, *The Judgement of Sense: Renaissance Naturalism and the Rise of Aesthetics* (Cambridge: Cambridge University Press, 1994), 179–181; Georgia Warnke, "Ocularcentrism and Social Criticism," in *Modernity and the Hegemony of Vision*, ed. David Michael Kleinberg-Levin (Berkeley: University of California Press), 287–308.

[32] For more on the importance of material culture and the senses to debates on religious change, see Baum, *Reformation of the Senses*, 133–168; Sally Promey, "Religion, Sensation, and Materiality: An Introduction," in *Sensational Religion*, ed. Sally Promey (New Haven, CT: Yale University Press, 2014), 1–22; Beatrice Caseau, "The Senses in Religion: Liturgy, Devotion, and Deprivation," in Volume II of *A Cultural History of the Senses*, eds. Constance Classen and Richard Newhauser (London: Bloomsbury, 2014), 89–110; Volker Schier, "Probing the Mystery of the Use of Saffron in Medieval Nunneries," *Senses and Society* 5, 1 (2010): 57–72; Matthew Milner, "The Physics of Holy Oats: Vernacular Knowledge, Qualities, and Remedy in Fifteenth-Century England," *Journal of Medieval and Early Modern Studies* 43, 2 (2013): 219–245; Rachel King, "'The Beads With Which We Pray Are Made From It': Devotional Ambers in Early Modern Italy," in *Religion and the Senses in Early Modern Europe*, eds. Wietse de Boer and Christine Göttler (Leiden: Brill, 2013), 153–175.

[33] For more on olfactory decline and the rise of the eye, see Louise Vinge, *The Five Senses* (Lund: Gleerup, 1975), 71–103; Joseph Moshenska, *Feeling Pleasures: The Sense of Touch in Renaissance England* (Oxford: Oxford University Press, 2014), 1–14; Robert Romanyshyn, *Technology as Symptom and Dream* (London: Routledge, 1989), 30–60, 125–127.

[34] For cleansing and deodorizing of England, see Keith Thomas, "Cleanliness and Godliness in Early Modern England," in *Religion, Culture, and Society in Early Modern Britain: Essays in Honour of Patrick Collinson*, eds. Patrick Collinson, Anthony Fletcher, and Peter Roberts (Cambridge: Cambridge University Press, 1994), 56–83; Mark Jenner, "Civilization and Deodorization? Smell in Early Modern English Culture," in *Civil Histories: Essays Presented to Sir Keith Thomas*, eds. Peter Burke, Brian Howard Harrison, Paul Slack, and Keith Thomas (Oxford: Oxford University Press, 2000), 127–144; Zygmunt Bauman, "The Sweet Scent of Decomposition," in *Forget Baudrillard?*, eds. Chris Rojek and Bryan Turner (London: Routledge, 1993), 22–46; Jean-Pierre Goubert, *The Conquest of Water: The Advent of Health in the Industrial Age*

paradigm of secularization, disenchantment, and the bordering of racial odors through displaying that the senses were further divided and classified during the Early Modern Era. This narrative of racial streamlining through the senses demonstrates how Europeans used the power of the printed word to shift odor from their own bodies to that of the African other in order to support ideas of transnational European whiteness and Christian purity.[35]

European cultures experienced a shift from an aromatic past to the deodorizing tendencies of the Early Modern Era. The decline of odor began with the plague, which instituted ideas of healthful deodorizing; with the printing press, which created an optic world above the magical sensorium of the past; and through the civilizing process, which altered the function the sensory hierarchy for both the court elite and the lower classes who emulated emerging bourgeois sensory aesthetics. In his analysis of a later sensory modernity, Donald Lowe focused on the rise of bourgeoisie sensory regimes within Victorian England as a "displacement" or "superimposition of one culture of communications media over another." For Lowe, the rise of this seminal bourgeoisie culture of limiting sexuality within the public sphere contributed to the decline of odor through lessening the power of perceived genital and perfumed aromas related to threatening female sexuality.[36]

(Princeton, NJ: Princeton University Press, 1989); Valerie Allen, *On Farting: Language and Laughter in the Middle Ages* (New York: Palgrave Macmillan, 2007), 42–51.

[35] For social and political power altering the senses, see Davide Panagia, *Political Life of Sensation* (Durham, NC: Duke University Press, 2010); Karin Bijsterveld, *Soundscapes of the Urban Past: Staged Sound As Mediated Cultural Heritage* (Bielefeld: Transcript, 2013); Carolyn Birdsall, *Nazi Soundscapes: Sound, Technology and Urban Space During Nazi Germany* (Amsterdam: Amsterdam University Press, 2012), 12–19; Hans Rindisbacher, "The Stench of Power," in *The Smell Culture Reader*, ed. Jim Drobnick (New York: Berg, 2006), 137–147.

[36] Donald Lowe, *History of Bourgeois Perception* (Chicago: University of Chicago Press, 1982), 5–9, 101–103, quotes on 7. See also Peter Gay, *Education of the Senses* (New York: Norton, 1999); David Howes, "Freud's Nose: The Repression of Nasality and the Origin of Psychoanalytical Theory," in *Nose Book: Representations of the Nose in Literature and the Arts*, eds. Victoria De Rijke, Lene Oestermark-Johansen, and Helen Thomas (London: Middlesex, 2000), 265–282. For more on sexuality and odor, see Janet Hopson, *Scent Signals: The Silent Language of Sex* (New York: William Morrow, 1979); Rachel Herz, *The Scent of Desire: Discovering Our Enigmatic Sense of Smell* (New York: William Morrow, 2007); P. A. Vroon, Anton van Amerongen, and Hans de Vries, *Smell: The Secret Seducer* (New York: Farrar, Straus & Giroux, 1997); James Vaughn Kohl and Robert Francoeur, *The Scent of Eros: Mysteries of Odor in Human Sexuality* (New York: Continuum, 1995); Catherine Maxwell, *Scents & Sensibility: Perfume in Victorian Literary Culture* (Oxford: Oxford University Press, 2017); Érika Wicky, "Perfumed Performances: The Reception of Olfactory Theatrical

The Smell of Slavery describes an earlier foundational displacement
that occurred in the deep recesses of the Western European body during
the Early Modern Era.[37] That groundwork of modern sensory consciousness created categories of race, class, and gender within embodied perceptions as a means to support the rise of the nation-state and her capitalist
motifs.[38] Rather than starting from an analysis of race construction as
part of scientific or political dialogues, the methods of this monograph
explore varying natures of perception through understanding that the

Devices from the Fin de-siècle to the Present Day," in *Media Archaeology and Intermedial
Performance: Deep Time of the Theatre*, ed. Nele Wynants (Basingstoke: Palgrave
MacMillan, 2019), 129–144.

[37] For more on sensory shifts of modernity within historical study, see early work within
Robert Mandrou, *Introduction to Modern France, 1500–1640: An Essay in Historical
Psychology* (New York: Holmes & Meier, 1976), 50–57; Lucien Febvre, *The Problem of
Unbelief in the Sixteenth Century, the Religion of Rabelais* (Cambridge, MA: Harvard
University Press, 1982 [1942]). See also Hans Rindisbacher, *The Smell of Books:
A Cultural-Historical Study of Olfactory Perception in Literature* (Ann Arbor: University
of Michigan Press, 1992), 13–16. For more on smell and literary criticism, see J. Douglas
Porteous, *Landscapes of the Mind: Worlds of Sense and Metaphor* (Toronto: University of
Toronto Press, 1990), 4–7, 24–45; Jonah Lehrer, *Proust Was a Neuroscientist* (Edinburgh:
Canongate, 2011), 79–81. Other aspects of olfactory decline explored in recent studies
include analyses of the natural environment, technology, and religious practice. Classen,
Worlds of Sense, 22–36; Constance Classen, "Sweet Colors, Fragrant Songs: Sensory
Models of the Andes and the Amazon," *American Ethnologist* 17, 4 (1990): 722–735;
Constance Classen, "The Sensory Orders of 'Wild Children,'" in *The Varieties of Sensory
Experience: A Sourcebook in the Anthropology of the Senses*, ed. David Howes (Toronto:
University of Toronto Press, 1991), 47–60. See also Anthony Synnott, "Puzzling over the
Senses: From Plato to Marx," in *The Varieties of Sensory Experience: A Sourcebook in the
Anthropology of the Senses*, ed. David Howes (Toronto: Toronto Press, 1991), 61–69;
Guido Giglioni, "Sense," in *Renaissance Keywords*, ed. Ita Mac Carthy (New York:
Routledge, 2017), 13–30.

[38] Olfactory categories were also important in the construction of different meanings for
male and female bodies. Faith Wallis, "Signs and Senses: Diagnosis and Prognosis in Early
Medieval Pulse and Urine Texts," *Social History of Medicine* 13, 2 (2000): 265–278;
Faith Wallis, "Medicine and the Senses: Feeling the Pulse, Smelling the Plague, and
Listening for the Cure," in Volume II of *A Cultural History of the Senses*, eds.
Constance Classen and Richard Newhauser (London: Bloomsbury, 2014), 133–152;
Jennifer Evans, "Female Barrenness, Bodily Access and Aromatic Treatments in
Seventeenth-Century England," *Historical Research* 87, 237 (2014): 423–443; Gail
Kern Paster, *The Body Embarrassed: Drama and the Disciplines of Shame in Early
Modern England* (Ithaca: Cornell University Press, 1993), 40–41; Amy Eisen Cislo,
*Paracelsus's Theory of Embodiment: Conception and Gestation in Early Modern
Europe* (London: Pickering and Chatto, 2010), 36–42; Marjorie Boyle, *Senses of
Touch: Human Dignity and Deformity from Michelangelo to Calvin* (Leiden: Brill,
1998), 18–19; Cora Fox, "Isabella Whitney's Nosegay and the Smell of Women's
Writing," *Senses and Society* 5, 1 (2010): 131–143.

body retains tacit knowledge about how to experience the world often before categories are formalized in the languages of learning. Such tacit knowledge exists within the body and can be transferred between persons through forms of social consciousness that are not always explicitly linguistic.[39] Bodies are educated to sense the world in specific ways through texts, or forms of media, and through more informal forms of diffusion, whereby social characters are modeled on the experiences of interpersonal behavior. Smell is a specifically important facet of embodied racialization as the sense confuses these discussions of the discursive and material, the conscious and subconscious, the self and the other, and the sensed and imagined.[40]

[39] Michael Polanyi, *The Tacit Dimension* (Chicago: University of Chicago Press, 1966); Joy Parr, "Notes for a More Sensuous History of Twentieth-Century Canada: The Timely, the Tacit, and the Material Body," *Canadian Historical Review* 82, 4 (2001): 720–745; Karen Cerulo, "Scents and Sensibility: Olfaction, Sense-Making, and Meaning Attribution," *American Sociological Review* 83, 2 (2018): 361–389; Geert Thyssen and Ian Grosvenor, "Learning to Make Sense: Interdisciplinary Perspectives on Sensory Education and Embodied Enculturation," *Senses and Society* 14, 2 (2019): 119–130. See also Robert Sullivan, *The Geography of the Everyday: Toward an Understanding of the Given* (Athens: University of Georgia Press, 2017), 133–154; Caroline Jones, David Mather, and Rebecca Uchill, *Experience: Culture, Cognition, and the Common Sense* (Cambridge, MA: MIT Press, 2016). For more on the history of emotions, embodiment, and sensibilities, see Lucien Febvre, "Sensibility and History: How to Reconstitute the Emotional Life of the Past," in *A New Kind of History*, ed. Peter Burke (London: Harper Row, 1973), 12–26; Gail Kern Paster, *Humoring the Body: Emotions and the Shakespearean Stage* (Chicago: University of Chicago Press, 2004), 22–27; Monique Scheer, "Are Emotions a Kind of Practice (And Is That What Makes Them Have a History)? A Bourdieuian Approach to Understanding Emotion," *History and Theory* 51 (May, 2012): 193–220; Daniel Wickberg, "What Is the History of Sensibilities? On Cultural Histories, Old and New," *American Historical Review* 112, 3 (2007): 661–684; Martha Craven Nussbaum, *Hiding from Humanity: Disgust, Shame, and the Law* (Princeton, NJ: Princeton University Press, 2004), 70–88.

[40] For modern understandings of the biology of sensing odors, see the analysis of levels of odor recognition that combines biological triggers with learning and memory within Donald Wilson and Richard Stevenson, *Learning to Smell: Olfactory Perception from Neurobiology to Behavior* (Baltimore, MD: Johns Hopkins University Press, 2006), 243–264; the Nobel Prize–winning work on olfactory receptors within Linda Buck and Richard Axel, "A Novel Multigene Family May Encode Odorant Receptors: a Molecular Basis for Odor Recognition," *Cell* 65, 1 (1991): 175–187; the biology of the sense of smell and education of odor presences into adulthood within J. A. Mennella and G. K. Beauchamp, "Olfactory Preferences in Children and Adults," in *The Human Sense of Smell*, eds. David Laing, Richard Doty, and Winrich Breipohl (Berlin: Springer-Verlag, 1991), 167–180; the discovery of the place of odor within deeper parts of the brain during the early nineteenth century within Lyall Watson, *Jacobson's Organ and the Remarkable Nature of Smell* (New York: Norton, 2000); and background on animal scenting and human retention within D. Michael Stoddart, *The Scented Ape* (Cambridge: Cambridge University Press, 1990); D. Michael Stoddart, *Adam's Nose,*

To some extent, because odor was deemed a cause of disease and evidence of illness in the body, smell has been consistently denigrated within Western cultures since the rise of modern sensibilities after the Renaissance.[41] By the late eighteenth century, the fragrant garden signatures of the sixteenth century had become inherently suspicious to many European noses.[42] The first volume of Irish novelist Oliver Goldsmith's *A History of the Earth and Animated Nature* (1774) presented a significant discourse on the place of smell as such a troublesome and subjective sense. Goldsmith found in this prejudice of odor a reason to remove smell from his botanical and zoological analyses. He argued that because "the sense of smelling gives us very often false intelligence," humans should not follow the nasal passages to find either agricultural sustenance or create aesthetic judgments.[43] English doctor Erasmus Darwin's *Botanic Garden*

and the Making of Humankind (Hoboken, NJ: Imperial College Press, 2015), 41–118; Luca Turin, *The Secret of Scent: Adventures in Perfume and the Science of Smell* (New York: Ecco, 2006), 4–9.

[41] Robert Jütte, *A History of the Senses: From Antiquity to Cyberspace* (Cambridge: Polity, 2005), 8–12; Jim Drobnick, "Introduction: Olfactocentrism," in *The Smell Culture Reader*, ed. Jim Drobnick (Oxford: Berg, 2006), 1–9; Constance Classen, "Foundation for an Anthropology of the Senses," *International Social Science Journal* 153 (September, 1997): 401–441. See also Emily Friedman, *Reading Smell in Eighteenth-Century Fiction* (Lewisburg, PA: Bucknell University Press, 2016); David Le Breton, *Sensing the World: An Anthropology of the Senses*, trans. Carmen Ruschiensky (London: Bloomsbury Academic, 2017), 166–171.

[42] For academic resistance to significant olfactory decline in modernity, see Diane Ackerman, *Natural History of the Senses* (New York: Random House, 1990), 15–25; Smith, "Transcending, Othering," 380–390; Emily Cockayne, *Hubbub: Filth, Noise & Stench in England 1600–1770* (New Haven, CT: Yale University Press, 2007). Much of the current debate on whether olfactory sensations declined within Western Europe also focuses on concerns regarding incense, anti-Catholicism, and the Reformation. Matthew Milner, *The Senses and the English Reformation* (Farnham: Ashgate, 2011), 4–6, 108–110, 185–186, 348–350; Dugan, *Ephemeral History*, 31–41; Jacob Baum, "From Incense to Idolatry: The Reformation of Olfaction in Late Medieval German Ritual," *The Sixteenth Century Journal* 44, 2 (2013): 323–344; Holly Crawford Pickett, "The Idolatrous Nose: Incense on the Early Modern Stage," in *Religion and Drama in Early Modern England: The Performance of Religion on the Renaissance Stage*, eds. Jane Hwang Degenhardt and Elizabeth Williamson (Farnham: Ashgate, 2011), 19–38; David Robertson, "Incensed over Incense: Incense and Community in Seventeenth-Century Literature," in *Writing and Religion in England, 1558–1689: Studies in Community-Making and Cultural Memory*, eds. Roger Sell and A. W. Johnson (Burlington: Ashgate, 2009), 389–409.

[43] Oliver Goldsmith, *A History of the Earth and Animated Nature: In Eight Volumes* (Dublin: J. Christie, 1813 [First Edition, 1774]), 130–133, quote on 131. See also Cynthia Wall, *The Prose of Things: Transformations of Description in the Eighteenth Century* (Chicago: University of Chicago Press, 2006), 70–95.

(1791) similarly represented that modern Western culture mislaid smelling as a subjective and wandering sense.[44] These increasingly suspicious relations of smelling had much to do with materially deodorizing conditions of newly modern English life and the nascent sewage systems, industrial pumps, and sulfuric fumigations of growing British urban spaces.[45]

[44] Erasmus Darwin, *The Botanic Garden: A Poem in Two Parts* (New York: Swords, 1798 [1791]), 106–108. Numerous scholars have noted that the analysis of smelling is often made difficult because most terms for smell are reliant on metaphors to individual and subjective experiences and through the use of essentially symbolic language. Daniel Press and Steven Minta, "The Smell of Nature: Olfaction, Knowledge and the Environment," *Ethics, Place & Environment* 3, 2 (2000): 173–186; Felizitas Ringham, "The Language of Smell," in *Sense and Scent: An Exploration of Olfactory Meaning*, eds. Bronwen Martin and Felizitas Ringham (Dublin: Philomel, 2003), 23–36; William McCartney, *Olfaction and Odours; An Osphrésiological Essay* (Berlin: Springer-Verlag, 1968), 1–15; David Trotter, *Cooking with Mud: The Idea of Mess in Nineteenth-Century Art and Fiction* (New York: Oxford, 2000), 98–142; Clare Batty, "A Representational Account of Olfactory Experience," *Canadian Journal of Philosophy* 40, 4 (2010): 511–538; Fiona Borthwick, "Olfaction and Taste: Invasive Odours and Disappearing Objects," *The Australian Journal of Anthropology* 11, 2 (2000): 127–140; Clare Batty, "Olfactory Experience I: The Content of Olfactory Experience," *Philosophy Compass* 5, 12 (2010): 1137–1146; Clare Batty, "Olfactory Experience II: Objects and Properties," *Philosophy Compass* 5, 12 (2010): 1147–1156; Roland Harper, E. C. Bate-Smith, and D. G. Land, *Odour Description and Odour Classification; A Multidisciplinary Examination* (New York: American Elsevier, 1968), 16–35; Hannah Higgins, *Fluxus Experience* (Berkeley: University of California Press, 2002), 44–46; Dan Sperber, *Rethinking Symbolism* (Cambridge: Cambridge University Press, 1975), 111–123.

[45] More recent case studies on the rise of bacteriology and industrial sewage have also portrayed aspects of the scientific, institutional, and medical aspects of olfactory decline. Matthew Newsom Kerr, *Contagion, Isolation, and Biopolitics in Victorian London* (Cham: Springer, 2018); David Barnes, *The Great Stink of Paris and the Nineteenth-Century Struggle against Filth and Germs* (Baltimore, MD: Johns Hopkins University Press, 2006); Sergio López Ramos, *History of the Air and Other Smells in Mexico City, 1840–1900* (Bloomington, IN: Palibrio, 2016); David Inglis "Sewers and Sensibilities: the Bourgeois Faecal Experience in the Nineteenth-Century City," in *The City and the Senses Urban Culture Since 1500*, eds. Alexander Cowan and Jill Steward (Aldershot: Ashgate, 2007), 105–130; David Pike, "Sewage Treatments: Vertical Space and Waste in Nineteenth-Century Paris and London," in *Filth: Dirt, Disgust, and Modern Life*, eds. William Cohen and Ryan Johnson (Minneapolis: University of Minnesota Press, 2005), 51–77; Michael Brown, "From Foetid Air to Filth: the Cultural Transformation of British Epidemiological Thought, Ca. 1780–1848," *Bulletin of the History of Medicine* 82, 3 (2008): 515–544; Stephen Halliday, *The Great Stink of London: Sir Joseph Bazalgette and the Cleansing of the Victorian Metropolis* (Stroud: Sutton, 2001), 108–163; Christine Rosen, "Noisome, Noxious, and Offensive Vapors, Fumes and Stenches in American Towns and Cities, 1840–1865," *Historical Geography* 25 (1997): 49–82; Andrew Hurley, "Busby's Stink Boat and the Regulation of Nuisance Trades, 1865–1918," in *Common Fields: An Environmental History of*

However, the most significant and lasting aspects of olfactory decline did not emerge within modernizing English culverts. Rather, the marked consciousness of olfactory decline for Western cultures occurred foremost within the Atlantic World, wherein identity construction marked specific bodies as scented and whiteness as contrastingly deodorized through an education of the senses that coded race as a means of economic control through hegemonic discourse. In accordance with Andrew Rotter's recent analysis of British and American imperial schemes that called for multisensory analyses to better uncover the goals, successes, and failures of imperial projects, *The Smell of Slavery* consequently explores the sense of smell within a discourse of racism and resistance that affected the tacit knowledge of Atlantic, British, and European noses.[46]

The field of Atlantic history inherently focuses the importance of global interactions upon the structures of economies and the alterations of cultures within Europe, Africa, and the Americas during an era defined by the rise of the Atlantic Slave Trade, the centralization of mercantilist Western state apparatuses, and the commodification of scientific and

---

St. Louis, ed. Andrew Hurley (St. Louis: Missouri Historical Society, 1997), 145–162; Elizabeth Shove, *Comfort, Cleanliness and Convenience: The Social Organization of Normality* (Oxford: Berg, 2003), 4–9, 21–41; Virginia Smith, *Clean: A History of Personal Hygiene and Purity* (Oxford: Oxford University Press, 2008), 224–263; Suellen Hoy, *Chasing Dirt: The American Pursuit of Cleanliness* (Bridgewater, NJ: Replica, 2000), 147–170; C. Dallett Hemphill, *Bowing to Necessities: A History of Manners in America, 1620–1860* (Oxford: Oxford University Press, 2002), 129–159; Richard Bushman, *The Refinement of America: Persons, Houses, Cities* (New York: Knopf, 1992), 238–262; Richard Bushman and Claudia Bushman, "The Early History of Cleanliness in America," *Journal of American History* 74, 4 (1988): 1213–1238.

[46] Andrew Rotter, *Empires of the Senses: Bodily Encounters in Imperial India and the Philippines* (Oxford: Oxford University Press, 2019); Andrew Rotter, "Empires of the Senses: How Seeing, Hearing, Smelling, Tasting, and Touching Shaped Imperial Encounters," *Diplomatic History* 35, 1 (2011): 3–19. For more on the senses, sensory skills, and nation building, see the recent analysis of Latin American nationalism within Francine Masiello, *The Senses of Democracy: Perception, Politics, and Culture in Latin America* (Austin: University of Texas Press, 2018), 19–70. See also sensory colonialism within Jean Comaroff, "The Empire's Old Clothes: Fashioning the Colonial Subject," in *Cross-Cultural Consumption: Global Markets, Local Realities*, ed. David Howes (Abingdon: Taylor & Francis, 1996), 19–38; Constance Classen, "Touching the Deep Past: The Lure of Ancient Bodies in Nineteenth-Century Museums and Culture," *Senses and Society* 9, 3 (2014): 268–283; Haunani-Kay Trask, *From a Native Daughter: Colonialism and Sovereignty in Hawai'i* (Honolulu: University of Hawai'i Press, 1999); Brandy Nalani McDougall, *Finding Meaning: Kaona and Contemporary Hawaiian Literature* (Tucson: University of Arizona Press, 2016), 146–154.

political theories within the discourses of the later Enlightenment.[47] These various economic and social forces of the Atlantic World birthed Western modernity through invasive forms of knowledge, rather than simply from imperial forms of understanding. As literary critic Charles Taylor has aptly summarized: "The belief that modernity comes from one single universally applicable operation imposes a falsely uniform pattern on the multiple encounters of non-Western cultures with the exigencies of science, technology, and industrialization."[48] Atlantic history exposes these flaws within the universalizing narratives of imperial history and earlier forms of the history of science and medicine through presenting a contested modernity that involved cultural, social, and scientific inputs from more than simply a dominant Western European intellectual dialogue.[49]

[47] For defining temporal confines of the Atlantic World, the rise of finance capital, and the development of modernity, see Ian Baucom, *Specters of the Atlantic: Finance Capital, Slavery, and the Philosophy of History* (Durham, NC: Duke University Press, 2005); David Shields, *Oracles of Empire: Poetry, Politics, and Commerce in British America, 1690–1750* (Chicago: University of Chicago, 1990), 13–92; Peter Linebaugh and Marcus Rediker, *The Many-Headed Hydra: Sailors, Slaves, Commoners, and the Hidden History of the Revolutionary Atlantic* (Boston: Beacon, 2000).

[48] Charles Taylor, "Inwardness and the Culture of Modernity," in *Philosophical Interventions in the Unfinished Project of Enlightenment*, eds. Axel Honneth, Thomas McCarthy, Claus Offe, and Albrecht Wellmer (Cambridge, MA: MIT Press, 1992), 88–112, quote on 93.

[49] For examples of material goods and sensory integration, see Wolfgang Schivelbusch, *Tastes of Paradise: A Social History of Spices, Stimulants, and Intoxicants* (New York: Pantheon, 1992), 145–146; Marcy Norton, *Sacred Gifts, Profane Pleasures: A History of Tobacco and Chocolate in the Atlantic World* (Ithaca: Cornell University Press, 2008); David Shields, "The Atlantic World, the Senses, and the Arts," in *The Oxford Handbook of the Atlantic World, C.1450-C.1850*, eds. Nicholas Canny and Philip Morgan (New York: Oxford, 2011), 130–146; Joyce Chaplin, *Subject Matter: Technology, the Body, and Science on the Anglo-American Frontier, 1500–1676* (Cambridge, MA: Harvard, 2001), 148–151; Michael LaCombe, *Political Gastronomy: Food and Authority in the English Atlantic World* (Philadelphia: University of Pennsylvania Press, 2012), 60–62; Richard Cullen Rath, "Hearing Wampum: The Senses, Mediation, and the Limits of Analogy," in *Colonial Mediascapes: Sensory Worlds of the Early Americas*, eds. Matt Cohen and Jeffrey Glover (Lincoln: University of Nebraska Press, 2014), 290–321; Marcy Norton, "Tasting Empire: Chocolate and the European Internalization of Mesoamerican Aesthetics," *American Historical Review* 111, 3 (2006): 660–691; Stephen Shapiro, *The Culture and Commerce of the Early American Novel: Reading the Atlantic World-System* (University Park: Pennsylvania State University Press, 2008), 40–42; Daniela Bleichmar, *Visible Empire: Botanical Expeditions and Visual Culture in the Hispanic Enlightenment* (Chicago: University of Chicago Press, 2012), 64–66, 164–168; Jutta Wimmler, *The Sun King's Atlantic: Drugs, Demons and Dyestuffs in the Atlantic World, 1640–1730* (Leiden: Brill, 2017), 93–99.

During the Atlantic Era, myriad populations of Africans, Native Americans, and Europeans met within colonized Atlantic environments wherein identity construction, racial othering, and adaptation marked bodies and minds with different, assertive, and creolized sensory perceptions. Within this Atlantic cultural milieu, the odor of the other became a vital aspect in the construction of English and broader Western identities as pure and Protestant, phallic on the world's proscenium, cleansed for entrance into the eschaton of modernity. As Denise Albanese has argued, New World ethnography converted "alien beings into evidence" while "at the same moment ... the contemporary European male body is exempted from scrutiny and removed ... to the site from which the possibility of assessment is contemplated."[50]

The positivist swerve of modernity involved an assertion of new sensory regimes that defined the lower sensory past as different from what English and Western culture aimed to become.[51] The modernization process asserted its own history as praxis, through types of ethnographical and religious history that each state used to define their power to rule through a legitimacy narrative that increasingly linked faith, race, and nation. This merging of legitimizing narratives

---

[50] Denise Albanese, *New Science, New World* (Durham, NC: Duke University Press, 1996), 37–91, quote on 39; Michel de Certeau, *The Writing of History* (New York: Columbia, 1988), 6–11, 209–243. For patterns of othering, disease, and the links between racialization in the Atlantic World and the Orient, see Mark Harrison, "'The Tender Frame of Man': Disease, Climate, and Racial Difference in India and the West Indies," *Bulletin of the History of Medicine* 70 (1996): 68–93.

[51] For senses, modernity, and state power, see James Mansell, *The Age of Noise in Britain: Hearing Modernity* (Urbana: University of Illinois Press, 2017); Emily Ann Thompson, *The Soundscape of Modernity: Architectural Acoustics and the Culture of Listening in America, 1900–1933* (Cambridge, MA: MIT Press, 2002); Walter Ong, *Orality and Literacy: The Technologizing of the Word* (London: Methuen, 1982), 110–116; David Howes and Constance Classen, *Ways of Sensing: Understanding the Senses in Society* (New York: Routledge, 2014); Jonathan Crary, *Techniques of the Observer: On Vision and Modernity in the Nineteenth Century* (Cambridge, MA: MIT Press, 1990), 9–19; Chris Otter, *The Victorian Eye: A Political History of Light and Vision in Britain, 1800–1910* (Chicago: University of Chicago Press, 2008); Sophia Rosenfeld, "The Social Life of the Senses: A New Approach to Eighteenth Century Politics and Public Life," in Volume IV of *A Cultural History of the Senses*, eds. Constance Classen and Anne Vila (London: Bloomsbury, 2014), 21–40; Jonathan Crary, *Suspensions of Perception: Attention, Spectacle, and Modern Culture* (Cambridge, MA: MIT Press, 1999), 5–10; Alain Corbin, *Time, Desire, and Horror: Towards a History of the Senses* (Cambridge: Polity, 1995), 13–38; Lewis Mumford, *Technics and Civilization* (New York: Harcourt, Brace and Company, 1934).

centralized the state's hegemonic abilities through both language and biopower, defined here as the ability to manipulate the masses through political categories of exclusion and waste demarcated through subconscious alterations of the five senses.[52] The constructed others of the Atlantic World, in opposition to the progressive and increasingly positivist Western self, set the path of modernity through resisting placement within these corporeal discourses about moral discovery, racial ordering, and scientific advancement.[53]

The Smell of Slavery enters this debate on odor and civilization through espousing a renewed importance to the racial metanarrative. As part of a wider chronological analysis, this monograph defines the space of the subaltern body as a place that has yet to be fully conceptualized as an olfactory figure, essentially due to previous reliance on prejudicial textual hermeneutics of the intermittent imperial archive.[54] This monograph

---

[52] For standard theoretical works on biopolitics, see Giorgio Agamben, *Homo Sacer: Sovereign Power and Bare Life* (Stanford, CA: Stanford University Press, 1998); Michel Foucault, *The Order of Things: An Archaeology of the Human Sciences* (New York: Pantheon, 1971); Michel Foucault, *The Birth of Biopolitics: Lectures at the Collège de France, 1978–79* (Basingstoke: Palgrave Macmillan, 2008). See also Andrea Rusnock, "Biopolitics: Political Arithmetic in the Enlightenment," in *The Sciences in Enlightened Europe*, eds. William Clark, Jan Golinski, and Simon Schaffer (Chicago: Chicago, 1999), 49–68; Sophie Gee, *Making Waste: Leftovers and the Eighteenth-Century Imagination* (Princeton, NJ: Princeton University Press, 2010), 35–41; Sarah Jewitt, "Geographies of Shit: Spatial and Temporal Variations in Attitudes towards Human Waste," *Progress in Human Geography* 35, 5 (2011): 608–626; Paul Kreitman, "Attacked by Excrement: The Political Ecology of Shit in Wartime and Postwar Tokyo," *Environmental History* 23, 2 (2018): 342–366.

[53] For sensory resistance, see Peter Stallybrass and Allon White, *The Politics and Poetics of Transgression* (Ithaca, NY: Cornell University Press, 1986), 27–79; Sun Young Park, *Ideals of the Body: Architecture, Urbanism, and Hygiene in Postrevolutionary Paris* (Pittsburgh, PA: University of Pittsburgh Press, 2018), 294–303.

[54] For more on sensory history, anthropology, and the materialist archive, see Brian Massumi, *Politics of Affect* (Malden, MA: Polity, 2016), 47–82; Stuart Walton, *In the Realm of the Senses: A Materialist Theory of Seeing and Feeling* (Winchester: Zero Books, 2016), 227–279; Lauren Klein, "Speculative Aesthetics," *Early American Literature* 51, 2 (2016): 437–446; Mark Smith, "Producing Sense, Consuming Sense, Making Sense: Perils and Prospects for Sensory History," *Journal of Social History* 40, 4 (2007): 841–858; David Howes, "Can These Dry Bones Live? An Anthropological Approach to the History of the Senses," *Journal of American History* 95, 2 (2008): 442–451; Regina Bendix, "Introduction: Ear to Ear, Nose to Nose, Skin to Skin, The Senses in Comparative Ethnographic Perspective," *Etnofoor* 18, 1 (2005): 3–14; Yannis Hamilakis, "Eleven Theses on the Archaeology of the Senses," in *Making Senses of the Past: Toward a Sensory Archaeology*, ed. Jo Day (Carbondale: University of Southern Illinois Press, 2013), 409–420; Jack Goody, "The Anthropology of the Senses and Sensations," *La Ricerca Folklorica* 45 (2002): 17–28; Michael Bull and Jon Mitchell, "Introduction," in *Ritual, Performance and the Senses*, eds. Michael Bull and

expounds that olfactory language is inherently transgressive, synesthetic, and culturally defined, which made the Atlantic World a confusing and aromatic space for the numerous cultures that shared the private spaces, public discourses, and temporal immensities of the Atlantic Slave Trade and the primary advancement of Settler Colonialism throughout the varied spaces of what would become the Global South.[55]

SENSORY HISTORY, CAPITALISM, AND THE RECOVERY OF THE OTHER

Capitalism was born with slavery, kissing cousins hiding their embrace within a grand concert on Southern Plantations, upon West Indian Isles, in Brazilian Big Houses, and within the European metropole.[56] The cyclical and incestuous symphony grew to incorporate the modern state that supports finance capital, but it was in the African body where capitalism was first trumpeted. The commodifying mechanisms that defined that body as property included the use of European perceptions, and Western discourses about proper aesthetics, that codified the African body as an agricultural tool to be bought and sold. The Roman ruler Vespasian first asserted that money does not smell, but the commodified African body defies that very maxim. A stinking African, formed through hard labor and racist discourse, instituted capitalism by helping to create a later pecuniary system which truly did not smell, a system of numbers in space, of automated personalities who traded human souls on ships of wood and iron. Sensory identities justified the horrors of slavery by marking the African body as something that could be wasted as surplus

Jon Mitchell (New York: Bloomsbury, 2015), 1–10; Paul Stoller, *The Taste of Ethnographic Things: The Senses in Anthropology* (Philadelphia: University of Pennsylvania Press, 1989).

[55] For sensory questions of private and public, see William Tullett, "The Macaroni's 'Ambrosial Essences': Perfume, Identity and Public Space in Eighteenth-Century England," *Journal for Eighteenth-Century Studies* 38, 2 (2015): 163–180; Holly Dugan and Lara Farina, "Intimate Senses/Sensing Intimacy," *Postmedieval* 3, 4 (2012): 373–379; Uri Almagor, "Odors and Private Language: Observations on the Phenomenology of Scent," *Human Studies: A Journal for Philosophy and the Social Sciences* 13, 3 (1990): 253–274.

[56] For capitalism and slavery, see Sven Beckert and Seth Rockman, "Introduction: Slavery's Capitalism," in *Slavery's Capitalism: a New History of American Economic Development*, eds. Sven Beckert and Seth Rockman (Philadelphia: University of Pennsylvania Press, 2016), 1–28; Anthony Kaye, "The Second Slavery: Modernity in the Nineteenth-Century South and the Atlantic World," *The Journal of Southern History* 75, 3 (2009): 627–650.

because of a rhetorical pungency that prescribed the African form as excremental to modernity.[57]

For some scholars of slavery, class was the fundamental determinant for patterns of labor accumulation within the early British Atlantic.[58] Rather than focus on ardently economic structures of the labor market, *The Smell of Slavery* looks at the racial spaces of the British Atlantic as ideological constructs born of embodied perceptions and experiences of emotional fear and sensory disgust.[59] Borrowing from scholars who choose to analyze ideologies of race during these early eras of the Atlantic World, this monograph explores the roots of Atlantic racism in the senses, the body politic, and the public sphere.[60] These ideological aspects of race were obviously present within the history of slavery during later eras of the Atlantic World and into the American Republic.[61] Many

---

[57] For more on religious and scientific traditions regarding black skin in Western Europe, see Dienke Hondius, *Blackness in Western Europe: Racial Patterns of Paternalism and Exclusion* (New Brunswick, NJ: Transaction, 2014); Craig Koslofsky, "Knowing Skin in Early Modern Europe, C. 1450–1750," *History Compass* 12, 10 (2014): 794–806.

[58] Simon Newman, *A New World of Labor: The Development of Plantation Slavery in the British Atlantic* (Philadelphia: University of Pennsylvania Press, 2013); Hilary Beckles, *White Servitude and Black Slavery in Barbados, 1627–1715* (Knoxville: University of Tennessee Press, 1989).

[59] For the chronological debate on labor, race, and slavery, see Trevor Burnard, *Planters, Merchants, and Slaves: Plantation Societies in British America, 1650–1820* (Chicago: University of Chicago Press, 2015); William Pettigrew, *Freedom's Debt: The Royal African Company and the Politics of the Atlantic Slave Trade, 1672–1752* (Chapel Hill: University of North Carolina Press, 2013); Christopher Leslie Brown, *Moral Capital: Foundations of British Abolitionism* (Chapel Hill: University of North Carolina Press, 2006); Trevor Burnard and John Garrigus, *The Plantation Machine: Atlantic Capitalism in French Saint-Domingue and British Jamaica* (Philadelphia: University of Pennsylvania Press, 2016); Robin Blackburn, *The Making of New World Slavery: From the Baroque to the Modern, 1492–1800* (London: Verso, 1996).

[60] For scholars who debate ideologies of race in early timelines, usually within the racial milieu prior to Bacon's Rebellion, see Theodore Allen, *The Invention of the White Race* (London: Verso, 1994); Winthrop Jordan, *White Over Black: American Attitudes Toward the Negro, 1550–1812* (Chapel Hill: University of North Carolina Press, 1968); David Eltis, *The Rise of African Slavery in the Americas* (New York: Cambridge University Press, 2006); Edmund Morgan, *American Slavery, American Freedom: The Ordeal of Colonial Virginia* (New York: Norton, 1975); Anthony Parent, *Foul Means: The Formation of a Slave Society in Virginia, 1660–1740* (Chapel Hill: University of North Carolina Press, 2003), 105–106, 253–265; Rebecca Goetz, *The Baptism of Early Virginia: How Christianity Created Race* (Baltimore, MD: Johns Hopkins University Press, 2012), 86–111.

[61] For racial knowing emerging in later eras, see Robert Parkinson, *The Common Cause: Creating Race and Nation in the American Revolution* (Chapel Hill: University of North Carolina, 2017); Stephen Haynes, *Noah's Curse: The Biblical Justification of American Slavery* (Oxford: Oxford University Press, 2002); Nicholas Guyatt, *Bind Us Apart: How*

of these racialized traits were also clearly and constantly expressed within deep and continuing motifs of segregation and modern American racism that rely on concepts of the pungent other.[62]

To illustrate the roots of racism as central within the establishment of slavery and capitalism, Chapter 1 focuses on the constructions of African odors buried deep within the often gendered and sexualized ethnographical observations of European voyagers, the stereotypes and flat characters of the English theatre, and the fearful texts of the Reformation and English political sphere. This chapter exposes how African bodies became associated to negative scents well before the rise of racial categorizations took hold of English and Western scientific literatures during the eighteenth and nineteenth centuries. The English body was informed by tacit knowledge about how to experience race before significant literature about monogenesis or polygenesis created later standardized racial discourses. This earlier tacit knowledge emerged partially through a process whereby linguistic particulars about odors and foulness were made into universals and became stereotypical on the English stage. Specific scented references to African peoples and places in early ethnographic texts, including those within translations of Leo Africanus and Duarte Lopes, became universal through the creation of flat theatrical characters and within constantly repeated maxims about the washing of African bodies as metaphor for wasteful action within English impressions.[63]

Enlightened Americans Invented Racial Segregation (New York: Basic, 2016), 133–158; Jenna Gibbs, *Performing the Temple of Liberty: Slavery, Theater, and Popular Culture in London and Philadelphia, 1760–1850* (Baltimore, MD: Johns Hopkins University Press, 2014), 177–244.

[62] For social construction in modern American racism, see Tavia Amolo Ochieng' Nyongó, *The Amalgamation Waltz: Race, Performance, and the Ruses of Memory* (Minneapolis: University of Minnesota Press, 2009); Werner Sollors, *Neither Black nor White yet Both: Thematic Explorations of Interracial Literature* (New York: Oxford University Press, 1997).

[63] For introduction to linguistic stereotyping in the Atlantic World, see Stephen Greenblatt, "Learning to Curse: Aspects of Linguistic Colonialism in the Sixteenth Century," in *First Images of America: The Impact of the New World on the Old*, ed. Fredi Chiappelli (Berkeley: University of California Press, 1976), 561–580; Tzvetan Todorov, *The Conquest of America: The Question of the Other* (New York: Harper & Row, 1984), 248–249; Walter Mignolo, *Local Histories/Global Designs: Coloniality, Subaltern Knowledges, and Border Thinking* (Princeton, NJ: Princeton University Press, 2012), 313–338. See also L. H. Roper, *The Torrid Zone: Caribbean Colonization and Cultural Interaction in the Long Seventeenth-Century Caribbean* (Columbia: University of South Carolina Press, 2018).

Different patterns of racial knowledge existed during diverse periods of Western history. For the Early Modern Era and into the Atlantic World, these racial regimes generally consisted of monogenetic, polygenetic, and climatological ideals that ebbed and flowed with variances of popular discourse. Generally, monogenetic traditions defined race through alterations in the body after humanity was first born from Adam and Eve. These monogenetic traditions often demarcated race through culture and religion, as in the tales of the Sons of Noah or the Mark of Cain. At different times, traditions of climatology have also become proportionally dominant within racial discourses. These narratives define race through geography and concepts of skin darkening due to time spent in the scorching suns of the Torrid Zone. By the late eighteenth century, as most scholars agree, polygenetic traditions and associated early forms of Scientific Racism emerged. These virulent traditions came to govern racial knowing in the nineteenth century as pseudoscientists asserted different lines of humanity and subhumanity beyond the singular anthropoid seeding of Adam and Eve that was central to earlier traditions of racial knowledge.[64]

Chapter 2 describes the shifting waves of these trends on the Middle Passage through the sense of smell by providing how blackness became increasingly symbolic and peremptory through the social construction of knowledge regarding how Englishpersons were educated to experience encountering the African. This olfactory analysis pairs with Simon Gikandi's examination of visual aesthetics and the black body in *Slavery and the Culture of Taste* (2011). For Gikandi, ideas of the Western self that emerged during the Enlightenment were supported through opposing understandings of who could not access the identity of the subject. Enlightenment promises of personal sovereignty, citizenship, and private property were only conceptualized through a construction of an inferior

---

[64] For different racial narratives, see Patrick Wolfe, *Traces of History: Elementary Structures of Race* (New York: Verso, 2016); Francisco Bethencourt, *Racisms: From the Crusades to the Twentieth Century* (Princeton, NJ: Princeton University Press, 2013); Albert Memmi, *Racism* (Minneapolis: University of Minnesota Press, 2000); Brian Niro, *Race* (New York: Palgrave Macmillan, 2003); Michael Banton, *Racial Theories* (Cambridge: Cambridge University Press, 2002). See also, syntheses of American racist traditions within Ibram Kendi, *Stamped from the Beginning: The Definitive History of Racist Ideas in America* (New York: Nation, 2016); Jacqueline Jones, *A Dreadful Deceit: The Myth of Race from the Colonial Era to Obama's America* (New York: Basic, 2015).

and undeserving African who could not access those modern ideals.[65] Through supporting Gikandi's use of aesthetics within political and social discussions of slavery, *The Smell of Slavery* therefore advances new timelines for the study of racialization within the Atlantic World, providing that numerous recent studies of the rise of racism have construed a late timeline of the emergence of racial discrimination due to a reliance on political and scientific texts of the late eighteenth century. This monograph applies a wider source base, especially using cultural, religious, and literary texts, to show that racism existed within falsely conscious sensory worlds well before the eighteenth century.[66]

The making and unmaking of racial odors within the Atlantic World involved the application of new sensory skills from Western Europeans who haphazardly tricked their profiteering noses into a false consciousness to smell the African as a pungent other. Unlike many sensory skills, which are individually cultivated through personal routine and repetition for the creation of self-technologies, the racialist sensing of the smell of the other in the Atlantic World had more to do with a subconscious tacit knowledge that disseminated through hegemonic patterns of false consciousness.[67]

---

[65] Simon Gikandi, *Slavery and the Culture of Taste* (Princeton, NJ: Princeton University Press, 2014 [2011]). See also Michelle Wright, *Becoming Black: Creating Identity in the African Diaspora* (Durham, NC: Duke University Press, 2004), 27–65; Frank Wilderson, "Gramsci's Black Marx: Whither the Slave in Civil Society?," *Social Identities* 9, 2 (2003): 225–240; Martha Jones, *Birthright Citizens. A History of Race and Rights in Antebellum America* (Cambridge: Cambridge University Press, 2018), 1–15.

[66] For more on Western philosophy, sovereignty, and the exclusion of African identity, see Peter Park, *Africa, Asia, and the History of Philosophy: Racism in the Formation of the Philosophical Canon, 1780–1830* (Albany: State University of New York Press, 2014), 69–96; Damien Tricoire, "Introduction," in *Enlightened Colonialism: Civilization Narratives and Imperial Politics in the Age of Reason*, ed. Damien Tricoire (Cham: Palgrave MacMillan, 2016), 1–24; Herman Bennett, *African Kings and Black Slaves: Sovereignty and Dispossession in the Early Modern Atlantic* (Philadelphia: University of Pennsylvania Press, 2018).

[67] For sensory skills, see Jenner, "Tasting Lichfield," 647–670; C. M. Woolgar, *The Senses in Late Medieval England* (New Haven, CT: Yale University Press, 2006), 117–146; Jonathan Reinarz, "Uncommon Scents: Smell and Victorian England," in *Sense and Scent: An Exploration of Olfactory Meaning*, eds. Bronwen Martin and Felizitas Ringham (Dublin: Philomel, 2003), 129–148; David Wright, *Understanding Cultural Taste: Sensation, Skill and Sensibility* (Basingstoke: Palgrave Macmillan, 2015); Jonathan Reinarz, "Learning to Use Their Senses: Visitors to Voluntary Hospitals in Eighteenth-Century England," *Journal for Eighteenth-Century Studies* 35, 4 (2012): 505–520; Sarah Knott, "The Patient's Case: Sentimental Empiricism and Knowledge in the Early American Republic," *William and Mary Quarterly* 67, 4 (2010): 645–676; Sarah Maslen, "Researching the Senses as Knowledge," *Senses and Society* 10, 1 (2015): 52–70; Susan Lawrence, "Educating the Senses: Students, Teachers, and Medical Rhetoric in Eighteenth-Century London," in *Medicine and the Five Senses*,

Recent literature on British and French medical traditions related to climate, disease, and race has likewise informed this project toward a connection between miasma theory, these diverse forms of bodily false consciousness, and the idea of moral contagion related to the penetrative sense of smell.[68]

Also vital within the olfactory analysis applied throughout this work was Kathleen Brown's examination of hygiene in the Atlantic World within *Foul Bodies: Cleanliness in Early America* (2009). For Brown, cleanliness became an important material and cultural space for the making of gendered and racial categories. *The Smell of Slavery* expands on Brown's essential explorations through interposing greater emphasis on olfactory experience than upon material goods that marked altering ideals of cleanliness and civilization.[69] In the recent *Smell Detectives: An*

---

eds. W. F. Bynum and Roy Porter (Cambridge: Cambridge University Press, 1993), 154–178; Daniela Hacke and Paul Musselwhite, "Introduction: Making Sense of Colonial Encounters and New Worlds," in *Empire of the Senses: Sensory Practices of Colonialism in Early America*, eds. Daniela Hacke and Paul Musselwhite (Leiden: Brill, 2017), 1–34; Clare Brant, "Fume and Perfume: Some Eighteenth-Century Uses of Smell," *The Journal of British Studies* 43, 4 (2004): 444–463; Emily Francomano, "The Senses of Empire and the Scents of Babylon in the *Libro de Alexandre*," in *Beyond Sight: Engaging the Senses in Iberian Literatures and Cultures, 1200–1750*, eds. Steven Wagschal and Ryan Giles (Toronto: University of Toronto Press, 2018), 189–208.

[68] Seth, *Difference and Disease*, 1–24; Katherine Johnston, "The Constitution of Empire: Place and Bodily Health in the Eighteenth Century Atlantic," *Atlantic Studies* 10, 4 (2013): 443–466. For general works on disease, colonialism, and contagion, see Christopher Hamlin, *More Than Hot: A Short History of Fever* (Baltimore, MD: Johns Hopkins University Press, 2015); Charles Rosenberg, *Explaining Epidemics and Other Studies in the History of Medicine* (Cambridge: Cambridge University Press, 2008 [1992]); S. J. Watts, *Epidemics and History: Disease, Power, and Imperialism* (New Haven, CT: Yale University Press, 1999); Athena Vrettos, *Somatic Fictions: Imagining Illness in Victorian Culture* (Stanford, CA: Stanford University Press, 1995); Alan Bewell, *Romanticism and Colonial Disease* (Baltimore, MD: Johns Hopkins University Press, 2003); Sander Gilman, *Disease and Representation: Images of Illness from Madness to AIDS* (Ithaca: Cornell University Press, 1994); Jo Hays, *The Burdens of Disease: Epidemics and Human Response in Western History* (New Brunswick, NJ: Rutgers University Press, 2009). See also Michael Schoeppner, *Moral Contagion: Black Atlantic Sailors, Citizenship, and Diplomacy in Antebellum America* (Cambridge: Cambridge University Press, 2019); Gerald O'Brien, *Contagion and the National Body: The Organism Metaphor in American Thought* (New York: Routledge, 2018).

[69] Brown, *Foul Bodies*, 42–117. For more on English concerns with climate and bodily alterations, see Joyce Chaplin, "Natural Philosophy and an Early Racial Idiom in North America: Comparing English and Indian Bodies," *William and Mary Quarterly* 54 (1997): 229–252; Karen Kupperman, "Fear of Hot Climates in the Anglo-American Colonial Experience," *William and Mary Quarterly* 41, 2 (1984): 213–240; Trudy Eden, "Food, Assimilation, and the Malleability of the Human Body in Early Virginia," in *A Centre of Wonders: The Body in Early America*, eds. Janet

Olfactory History of Nineteenth-Century Urban America (2017), Melanie Kiechle has also offered an introduction to shifts of olfactory consciousness, medicine, and cleanliness that occurred during the nineteenth century. *The Smell of Slavery* develops on this brief analysis of the racial olfactory through exposing the importance of racialization during earlier eras regarding concerns over consciousness and philosophically determined African emanations. Through reading Brown, Kiechle, and the fundamental analysis of olfactory racism in the nineteenth-century evaluations of Mark Smith in *How Race is Made: Slavery, Segregation, and the Senses* (2006), this monograph explores a materialist analysis of bodies through hegemonic discourse and the languages of phenomenological experience.[70]

The end of Chapter 2 describes how commodification of the African from a subject into an object merged with an unevenly applied and broad miasma theory that marked Africa as a place of filthy substances. Using reports from African coasts and Caribbean islands, the end of Chapter 2 designates how ideas about the stinking tropical climates of Africa and the malignant items that Africans became within discursive commodification processes connected to create an idea that smell marked a cultural disease of indolence. The moralized British middle class, self-congratulatory on the ethical profits of abolitionism, looked to Africa as an ensuing space to be saved. The objects to be protected and cleansed were the miasmic Africans who could nary escape their idleness without white hands washing and guiding their cultures to the developments of capitalist modernity.[71]

Moore Lindman and Michele Lise Tarter (Ithaca: Cornell University Press, 2001), 29–42; Kelly Wisecup, *Medical Encounters: Knowledge and Identity in Early American Literatures* (Amherst: University of Massachusetts Press, 2013), 26–29; Ikuko Asaka, *Tropical Freedom: Climate, Settler Colonialism, and Black Exclusion in the Age of Emancipation* (Durham, NC: Duke University Press, 2017), 139–166.

[70] Kiechle, *Smell Detectives*, 132–135; Smith, *How Race is Made*, 48–65. See also the reading of ideas of culturally determined odors of African bodies within William Tullett, "Grease and Sweat: Race and Smell in Eighteenth-Century English Culture," *Cultural and Social History* 13, 3 (2016): 307–322; and the sensory definitions of living and dead used to assemble racial, gender, and class groups within Elizabeth Freeman, *Beside You in Time: Sense Methods and Queer Sociabilities in the American 19th Century* (Durham, NC: Duke University Press, 2019), 52–86.

[71] For British middle class and moral mission in Africa, see Catherine Hall, *Civilising Subjects: Metropole and Colony in the English Imagination, 1830–1867* (Oxford: Polity, 2002), 332–338; Alison Twells, *The Civilising Mission and the English Middle Class, 1792–1850: The 'heathen' at Home and Overseas* (Basingstoke: Palgrave Macmillan, 2009), 125–142.

OLFACTORY SURVIVALS

Sensory studies often explore interactions of class, community solidarity, and the cultural roles of the socially educated senses.[72] Numerous sensory scholars have similarly exhibited the particular importance of culturally constructed smell for formations of identity, national unity, and resistance.[73] Chapters 3 and 4 of this monograph follow these pathways

---

[72] Peter Denney, "'The Sounds of Population Fail': Changing Perceptions of Rural Poverty and Plebian Noise in Eighteenth-Century Britain," in *Experiences of Poverty in Late Medieval and Early Modern England and France*, ed. Anne Scott (Farnham: Ashgate, 2012), 295–311; Joseph Nugent, "The Human Snout: Pigs, Priests, and Peasants in the Parlor," *Senses and Society* 4, 3 (2009): 283–301; Carl Zimring, "Dirty Work: How Hygiene and Xenophobia Marginalized the American Waste Trades, 1870–1930," *Environmental History* 9, 1 (2004): 80–101; Ellen Stroud, "Dead Bodies in Harlem: Environmental History and the Geography of Death," in *The Nature of Cities*, ed. Andrew Isenberg (Rochester, NY: University of Rochester Press, 2006), 62–76; Alex Rhys-Taylor, "Urban Sensations: A Retrospective of Multisensory Drift," in Volume VI of *A Cultural History of the Senses*, eds. Constance Classen and David Howes (London: Bloomsbury, 2014), 55–75; Richard Clay, "Smells, Bells and Touch: Iconoclasm in Paris during the French Revolution," *Journal for Eighteenth-Century Studies* 35, 4 (2012): 521–533; Daniel Bender, "Sensing Labor: The Stinking Working-Class after the Cultural Turn," in *Rethinking US Labor History: Essays on the Working-Class Experience, 1756–2009*, eds. Donna Haverty-Stacke and Daniel Walkowitz (New York: Continuum, 2010), 243–265.

[73] Bruno Latour, "How to Talk About the Body?: The Normative Dimension of Science Studies," *Body & Society* 10, 2–3 (2004): 205–229; Yi-Fu Tuan, *Passing Strange and Wonderful: Aesthetics, Nature, and Culture* (New York: Kodansha, 1995), 55–58; Kelvin Low, "Presenting the Self, the Social Body, and the Olfactory: Managing Smells in Everyday Life Experiences," *Sociological Perspectives* 49, 4 (2006): 607–631; D. D. Waskul, Phillip Vannini, and Janelle Wilson, "The Aroma of Recollection: Olfaction, Nostalgia, and the Shaping of the Sensuous Self," *Senses and Society* 4, 1 (2009): 5–22; Isabelle Rieusset-Lemarié, "What Taste and Smell Add to the Political Interpretation of the Kantian Aesthetic Judgement by Arendt and Deleuze," *Proceedings of the European Society for Aesthetics* 4 (2012): 412–432; Anthony Synnott, "A Sociology of Smell," *Canadian Review of Sociology* 28, 4 (2008): 437–459; Ivan Illich, "The Dirt of Cities, the Aura of Cities, the Smell of the Dead, Utopia in the Odorless City," in *The Cities Culture Reader*, eds. Malcolm Miles, Iain Borden, and Tim Hall (London: Routledge, 2000), 355–359; Jennifer Brookes, "Science Is Perception: What Can Our Sense of Smell Tell Us About Ourselves and the World Around Us?," *Philosophical Transactions. Series A, Mathematical, Physical, and Engineering Sciences* 368, 1924 (2010): 3491–3502; Mark Smith, "Getting in Touch with Slavery and Freedom," *Journal of American History* 95, 2 (2008): 381–391; Richard Cullen Rath, *How Early America Sounded* (Ithaca: Cornell University Press, 2003), 85–89. See also embodiment within Asia Friedman, "'There Are Two People at Work That I'm Fairly Certain Are Black': Uncertainty and Deliberative Thinking in Blind Race Attribution," *The Sociological Quarterly* 57, 3 (2016): 437–461; Osagie Obasogie, *Blinded by Sight: Seeing Race Through the Eyes of the Blind* (Stanford, CA: Stanford University Press, 2014).

to summarize aromatic confrontations that arose from antipodal African spiritualist traditions, whisper networks, and common winds of subaltern communication within the Atlantic World. To analyze the constant malleability, communication, and transformability of odors in African, Atlantic, and African American communities, *The Smell of Slavery* specifically borrows from James Scott's investigations of "hidden transcripts" and "weapons of the weak" to highlight how subalterns of the Atlantic littoral retained transgressive identities through creating shadow olfactory cultures beneath the unintended veils provided by increasingly wicked forms of racialization.[74]

Because of the relative lack of written sources that come directly from slave societies that existed during the first centuries of New World settlement, much of the second part of *The Smell of Slavery* reads multitemporal narratives into the structures and cultures of slavery rather than focus on the explicitly diachronic developments highlighted within the first part of the monograph. Vital within this transition from a narrative of the development of racial sensory consciousness to structural analysis of resistance is understanding different lenses applied by elites or subalterns to comprehend smell. Essentially, the first part of this book argues that elites and slaveholders developed a false sensory consciousness from popular understandings of odor, which later altered the function of the sensorium and mental understanding of their sensory worlds. The second part implicitly portrays subaltern patterns of smelling as much more ingenuous and less constructed than the false racialization of odor by white elites. Less invaded by the implications of the fetish, subaltern slaves were subjected to intense material odors on the slave ship and experienced those smells through less fabricated understandings of how the nose should function. That deep connection to the material combined with African appreciations for odor from earlier cultural traditions to question the fictitious traditions of European smelling that burgeoned throughout the Atlantic World.[75]

---

[74] James Scott, *Domination and the Arts of Resistance: Hidden Transcripts* (New Haven, CT: Yale University Press, 1990). See also Elizabeth Maddock Dillon, "Atlantic Aesthesis: Books and *Sensus Communis* in the New World," *Early American Literature* 51, 2 (2016): 367–395.

[75] For practice theory and resistance to sensory routinization, see Andreas Reckwitz, "Toward a Theory of Social Practices: A Development in Culturalist Theorizing," *European Journal of Social Theory* 5, 2 (2002): 243–263; Michel de Certeau, *The Practice of Everyday Life* (Berkeley: University of California Press, 2008); Theodore Schatzki, "Introduction: Practice Theory," in *The Practice Turn in Contemporary Theory*, eds. Eike von Savigny, K. Knorr-Cetina, and Theodore R. Schatzki (London: Routledge, 2001), 1–14.

With this theoretical background for aromatic resistance, Chapters 3 and 4 specifically expand upon an important aspect of slave studies that relays forms of sensory resistance forged in the furnaces of diverse creolized cultures.[76] Shane White and Graham White portrayed slaves' outward expression of cultural values as such a form of sensory confrontation in *Stylin': African-American Expressive Culture, from Its Beginnings to the Zoot Suit* (1998). During the nineteenth century, African American sartorial expressions often subverted the enslaver's culture through implicit resistance to the blandness of white linen. African hairstyles may have similarly represented individual struggle, through the shaving of heads or the increased use of styling most likely born of ethnic memory from different African pasts where bare heads, braiding, and the threading of hair was common prior to European slave trading.[77] In *The Sounds of Slavery: Discovering African American History Through Songs, Sermons, And Speech* (2005), White and White continued their discussions of sensory resistance from slaves as dependent on cultural memories from Africa though an analysis of creolized soundscapes. African Americans resisted attempts at domination of their acoustic regimes through the use of calls, songs, ring shouts, and psalms.[78]

---

[76] Peter Charles Hoffer, *Sensory Worlds in Early America* (Baltimore, MD: Johns Hopkins University Press, 2003), 137–166; Lauri Ramey, *Slave Songs and the Birth of African American Poetry* (New York: Palgrave Macmillan, 2008); Mark Smith, *Listening to Nineteenth-Century America* (Chapel Hill: University of North Carolina Press, 2001); Renee Harrison, *Enslaved Women and the Art of Resistance in Antebellum America* (New York: Palgrave Macmillan, 2009); Richard Cullen Rath, "Drums and Power: Ways of Creolizing Music in Coastal South Carolina and Georgia, 1730–99," in *Creolization in the Americas*, eds. David Buisseret and Steven Reinhardt (College Station: Texas A&M University Press, 2000), 99–130; Shane White and Graham White, "Slave Hair and African-American Culture in the Eighteenth and Nineteenth Centuries," *Journal of Southern History* 61 (1995): 45–76.

[77] Shane White and Graham White, *Stylin': African American Expressive Culture from Its Beginnings to the Zoot Suit* (Ithaca: Cornell University Press, 1998), 56–60; Helen Bradley Foster, *New Raiments of Self: African American Clothing in the Antebellum South* (Oxford: Berg, 1997), 18–74.

[78] Shane White and Graham White, *The Sounds of Slavery: Discovering African American History Through Songs, Sermons, and Speech* (Boston: Beacon, 2005), 5–9; Katrina Dyonne Thompson, *Ring Shout, Wheel About: The Racial Politics of Music and Dance in North American Slavery* (Urbana: University of Illinois Press, 2014), 13–24; Ronald Radano, "Black Music Labor and the Animated Properties of Slave Sound," *Boundary* 2 43, 1 (2016): 173–208. Alexander Weheliye, "In the Mix: Hearing the Souls of Black Folk," *Amerikastudien/American Studies* 45, 4 (2000): 535–554; Alexander Weheliye, "Engendering Phonographies: Sonic Technologies of Blackness," *Small Axe* 18, 2 (2014): 180–190.

Peter Charles Hoffer's *Sensory Worlds in Early America* (2003) similarly applied slave culture to examine the sensory implications of earlier African resistance in North America, especially concerning the disobedient sounds and sights of the Stono Rebellion in South Carolina of 1739.[79] Also searching these trajectories regarding rebellious aurality, Richard Cullen Rath's *How Early America Sounded* (2003) explored how African populations in North America and the Caribbean applied music as a form of cultural retention to recollect a sense of African ethnic unity through sensory consciousness. *The Smell of Slavery* expands these analyses of sensory opposition among African Americans and African populations throughout the Atlantic littoral and later American Republic through adding olfactory resistance to studies of the sensory dialectics subsisting between masters and slaves.[80]

To develop these discussions of sensory opposition from slave cultures, Chapter 3 locates an African olfactory that existed prior to the Atlantic Slave Trade. This African sense of the olfactory is purposefully essentialized from many different West, Central, and southern African sources that are linked to combine a narrative regarding the higher appreciation for smells within African religious, aesthetic, and environmental traditions. Many scholars have critiqued the ahistorical use of later sources to articulate previous African or New World slave cultures. However, due to the lack of written texts from many of these historical populations, many scholars choose to use later sources to come to structural understandings of how African ethnicities and slave cultures understood their place in the world and the value of natural environments.[81]

---

[79] Hoffer, *Sensory Worlds*, 145–159. See also Jennifer Lynn Stoever, *The Sonic Color Line: Race and the Cultural Politics of Listening* (New York: New York University Press, 2016), 29–77; Louis Onuorah Chude-Sokei, *The Sound of Culture: Diaspora and Black Technopoetics* (Middletown, CT: Wesleyan University Press, 2015); Richard Cullen Rath, "Echo and Narcissus: The Afrocentric Pragmatism of W. E. B. Du Bois," *Journal of American History* 84, 2 (September, 1997): 461–495.

[80] Rath, *How Early America Sounded*, 53–96; Walter Ong, "African Talking Drums and Oral Noetics," *New Literary History* 8, 3 (1977): 411–429; Richard Cullen Rath, "African Music in Seventeenth-Century Jamaica: Cultural Transit and Transition," *William and Mary Quarterly* 50, 4 (October, 1993): 700–726.

[81] For introductions to archival prejudice in slave studies, see Marlene Daut, *Tropics of Haiti: Race and the Literary History of the Haitian Revolution in the Atlantic World, 1789–1865* (Liverpool: Liverpool University Press, 2015), 1–8; Michel-Rolph Trouillot, *Silencing the Past: Power and the Production of History* (Boston: Beacon, 1995); Diana Taylor, *The Archive and the Repertoire: Performing Cultural Memory in the Americas* (Durham, NC: Duke University Press, 2003), 16–20, 193–236.

Denying that anachronism is a blockade within slave studies, Chapter 3 uses different historical terminologies of the sense of smell to apply both sequentially accurate and chronologically out-of-joint sources to overturn the flaws of the imperial archive that cannot correctly manifest slave consciousness from the chronologically precise sources of the Atlantic World. Despite the horrific odors of the Middle Passage and slavery that are also described at the end of Chapter 3 through expressive slave narratives and affective abolitionist tracts, the African olfactory survived the confines of slavery and the Western desire to create sensory regimes of modernity without African bodily influences. Combining both the fecal experiences of the Middle Passage with ideas of sensory resistance exposes how the languages of odor and excrement can often create pathways to positive struggles within areas where the self and other are unstable, undulating, and undecided.[82]

Daniela Babilon has also recently contributed a reading of race in *The Power of Smell in American Literature: Odor, Affect, and Social Inequality* (2017). This brief analysis of slavery focuses on the slave narratives of Olaudah Equiano and Charles Ball for examples of the way slaves countered emphasis on the smell of the black body through their own particular assertions of the pungent material smells caused by the Middle Passage and slave labor.[83] Chapter 4 expands on these and many other narratives of survival and struggle through reading observations about African spiritualism within Obeah accounts from throughout the Atlantic World and African American responses to interviewers of the Federal Writers Project. This interdisciplinary reading shows how African ethnic traditions about the importance of odor were retained throughout the New World through numerous rituals that included smelling-out as divining, forms of scented herbalism, various olfactory conceptions of the spiritual world, and the survival skills necessary for escaping pursuing

---

[82] For such instability, see Peter Smith, *Between Two Stools: Scatology and Its Representations in English Literature, Chaucer to Swift* (Manchester: Manchester University Press, 2012), 227–259; Warwick Anderson, "Excremental Colonialism: Public Health and the Poetics of Pollution," *Critical Inquiry* 21, 3 (1995): 640–669.

[83] Daniela Babilon, *The Power of Smell in American Literature: Odor, Affect, and Social Inequality* (Frankfurt: Peter Lang, 2017), 29–52, 71–86. For reading of race and whiteness within other artistic descriptions in the Early Republic, see Catherine Kelly, *Republic of Taste: Art, Politics, and Everyday Life in Early America* (Philadelphia: University of Pennsylvania, 2016), 92–118; David Bindman, *Ape to Apollo: Aesthetics and the Idea of Race, 1700–1800* (Ithaca, NY: Cornell University Press, 2002). See also a rendering of literature and materialist resistance within Cristin Ellis, *Antebellum Posthuman: Race and Materiality in the Mid-Nineteenth Century* (New York: Fordham University Press, 2018).

dogs and their wanton masters. Resisting the Anglo-Atlantic literary construction, within plays, sermons, and children's folklore, which asserted
African bodies were inherently pungent objects, these Africans and
African Americans created competing geographies replete with odor.
This conception of the ethnogenetic olfactory exposes how slaves articulated various subjective sensory skills and environmental worlding to
aromatically resist racist conceptions that defined African bodies as pungent matter.[84]

As Babilon's project on affect, event, and odor within American literature shows, in the field of olfactory history the role of fiction has become
a vital point of ingress for scholars wishing to discover the cultural poetics
that informed sensory consciousness. As Emily Friedman has recently
summarized in her analysis of sensory philosophy of the eighteenth century,
the "act of naming" smells within literature is "tied to one's ability to
identify odors, and odorant language seems to trigger both linguistic and
olfactory parts of our brain."[85] Most historical fields waver at using fiction
as a means of conceptualizing the past, deeming the use of such texts and
theories anachronistic or inherently romantic. However, sensory scholars
have rarely concerned themselves with such improvident disciplinary
rigor.[86] These sensory analyses using literature regularly rely on discourse

---

[84] For more on the idea of sensory skills, see "techniques of the body" in Marcel Mauss,
Sociologie et Anthropologie (Paris: Presses Universitaires de France, 1973), 70–88. See
also Tim Ingold, *Being Alive: Essays on Movement, Knowledge and Description*
(London: Routledge, 2011), 214–226; Philippe Descola and Janet Lloyd, *Beyond
Nature and Culture* (Chicago: University of Chicago Press, 2013), 91–111.

[85] Friedman, *Reading Smell*, quote on 6. See also Kerry McSweeney, *The Language of the
Senses: Sensory-Perceptual Dynamics in Wordsworth, Coleridge, Thoreau, Whitman,
and Dickinson* (Montreal: McGill–Queen's University Press, 1998), 98–119; Ann
Jessie Van Sant, *Eighteenth Century Sensibility and the Novel: The Senses in Social
Context* (Cambridge: Cambridge University Press, 2004).

[86] For sensory studies of literature, see Janice Carlisle, *Common Scents: Comparative
Encounters in High-Victorian Fiction* (Oxford: Oxford University Press, 2004);
Janice Carlisle, "The Smell of Class: British Novels of the 1860s," *Victorian Literature
and Culture* 29, 1 (2001): 1–19; Richard Griffiths, "From Sexual Arousal to Religious
Rapture: The Importance of the Sense of Smell in the Writings of Zola and Huysmans," in
Sense and Scent: An Exploration of Olfactory Meaning, eds. Bronwen Martin and
Felizitas Ringham (Dublin: Philomel, 2003), 263–292; Susan Stewart, *Poetry and the
Fate of the Senses* (Chicago: University of Chicago Press, 2002), 28–32; Hugo de Rijke,
"The Point of Long Noses: Tristram Shandy and Cyrano de Bergerac," in *Nose Book:
Representations of the Nose in Literature and the Arts*, eds. Victoria De Rijke,
Lene Oestermark-Johansen, and Helen Thomas (London: Middlesex, 2000), 55–76;
Ralf Hertel, "The Senses in Literature: From the Modernist Shock of Sensation to
Postcolonial and Virtual Voices," in Volume VI of *A Cultural History of the Senses*,
eds. Constance Classen and David Howes (London: Bloomsbury, 2014), 173–194.

theory, specifically on what literary critic Paula Backscheider describes as the "hegemonic apparatus" of modernity that was "used to influence a critical public in order to legitimate" the ideologies of capitalism, nationalism, and progress.[87] As Bruce Smith also summarized: "When it comes to explanations of sensations and affects, truths have the virtue of being accepted once and for all, theories can be tested over time and revised to take account of new research, but fictions are truest to experience."[88]

Following these important trends regarding the use of literature to critique the latently imperial archive of pseudoscientific theory and false sensory consciousness, Chapter 4 ends with a treatment of the character of the Obeah sorcerer within different Western fictions of the nineteenth century. In many of these tales, poems, and novels, Africans emerged again as subjects with different sensory behaviors that could influence the world rather than simply suffer through racism, slavery, and commodification. Smell developed within this field of European literature whereby the African subject aromatically spoke through the pens of diverse authors. The conclusion follows these trajectories into fiction with a reading of nineteenth-century American racism and the repeatedly overburdened sense of smell. Aromatic resistance was common within the Atlantic World; however, dominant later discourses of odor continued to mark black bodies as deeply scented and wasteful to modernity on the eve of Jim Crow.[89]

---

[87] Paula Backscheider, *Spectacular Politics: Theatrical Power and Mass Culture in Early Modern England* (Baltimore, MD: Johns Hopkins University Press, 1993), quote on 65. For more on the importance of interdisciplinary studies to sensory history, see Dee Reynolds and Boris Wiseman, "Introduction: Methods of Aesthetic Inquiry across Disciplines," *Senses and Society* 13, 3 (2018): 261–263. See also the attention to interdisciplinary work in odor studies within Melanie Kiechle, "Preserving the Unpleasant: Sources, Methods, and Conjectures for Odors at Historic Sites," *Future Anterior* 13, 2 (Winter, 2016): 22–32.

[88] Bruce Smith, "Afterword: Senses of an Ending," in *Shakespearean Sensations: Experiencing Literature in Early Modern England*, eds. Katharine Craik and Tanya Pollard (Cambridge: Cambridge University Press, 2013), 208–217, quote on 209.

[89] For the senses and later American identity of the nineteenth century, see Conevery Bolton Valencius, *The Health of the Country: How American Settlers Understood Themselves and Their Land* (New York: Basic, 2003), 116–126; Sarah Keyes, "'Like a Roaring Lion': The Overland Trail as a Sonic Conquest," *Journal of American History* 96, 1 (June, 2009): 19–43; Jay Fliegelman, *Declaring Independence: Jefferson, Natural Language & the Culture of Performance* (Stanford, CA: Stanford University Press, 1993); Sandra Gustafson, *Eloquence Is Power: Oratory and Performance in Early America* (Chapel Hill: University of North Carolina Press, 2000); Sarah Knott, *Sensibility and the American Revolution* (Chapel Hill: University of North Carolina Press, 2009); Hoffer, *Sensory Worlds*, 189–251; Wendy Bellion, *Citizen Spectator: Art, Illusion, and Visual Perception in Early National America* (Chapel Hill: University of North Carolina Press, 2011).

THEORIZING SMELL AND POWER

The Smell of Slavery is driven by engaging more with structures of philosophy than the rigors of disciplinary history as it reads a lengthier account about a plethora of ideas regarding pungency that existed due to false sensory consciousness. In these more philosophical terms, the ability to define the other as dirty, as improper, and as pollution marked the cultures of Western Europe that developed with interchanges betwixt their colonies and the metropole within the Atlantic littoral.[90] Rhetoric of odor and pestilence moved the Western European body out of an epidemic past of plagues and poxes into the cleanliness of civilized modernity through a striking cultural policy of rhetorical deodorization that increasingly defined the other as pungent and infected, often regardless of the relevance of material odors.[91]

Europeans used olfactory language within literature, religion, and politics to define Africans as excremental to appropriate the colonized world both physically and symbolically.[92] The ability to define smells placed the Western self in a position of power over objectified Africans

[90] For studies of excrement and waste in the Early Modern Era, see Julian Yates, *Error, Misuse, Failure: Object Lessons from the English Renaissance* (Minneapolis: University of Minnesota Press, 2003), 67–100; Gail Kern Paster, "The Epistemology of the Water Closet: John Harrington's Metamorphosis of Ajax and Elizabethan Technologies of Shame," in *Material Culture and Cultural Materialisms*, ed. Curtis Perry (Turnhout: Brepols, 2001), 139–158.

[91] Kelvin Low and James McHugh's work on social constructions of odor and East Asia have also been instructive when analyzing discourses on the smell of the other. Kelvin Low, "Ruminations on Smell as a Sociocultural Phenomenon," *Current Sociology* 53, 3 (2005): 397–417; James McHugh, "Seeing Scents: Methodological Reflections on the Intersensory Perception of Aromatics in South Asian Religions," *History of Religions* 51, 2 (2011): 156–177; James McHugh, *Sandalwood and Carrion: Smell in Premodern Indian Religion and Culture* (New York: Oxford, 2013).

[92] For more on disease, pollution, and othering, see Elana Gomel, "The Plague of Utopias: Pestilence and the Apocalyptic Body," *Twentieth-Century Literature* 46, 4 (2000): 405–433; Jack Lennon, *Pollution and Religion in Ancient Rome* (New York: Cambridge University Press, 2014), 167–187; Rob Meens, "'A Relic of Superstition': Bodily Impurity and the Church from Gregory the Great to the Twelfth Century Decretists," in *Purity and Holiness: The Heritage of Leviticus*, eds. Marcel Poorthuis and Joshua Schwartz (Leiden: Brill, 2000), 281–293; Alison Bashford, *Imperial Hygiene: A Critical History of Colonialism, Nationalism and Public Health* (Basingstoke: Palgrave Macmillan, 2004); Warwick Anderson, *Colonial Pathologies: American Tropical Medicine, Race, and Hygiene in the Philippines* (Durham, NC: Duke University Press, 2006); Mark Bradley, "Approaches to Pollution and Propriety," in *Rome, Pollution, and Propriety: Dirt, Disease, and Hygiene in the Eternal City from Antiquity to Modernity*, eds. Mark Bradley and Kenneth Stow (Cambridge: Cambridge University Press, 2012), 11–40.

marked as inherently pungent.[93] Symbolically coding a pollutant is part of the process of social division, creating patterns of labor appropriation through rhetoric about sensory disgust.[94] The right to dirty something, to mark a thing as somehow improper, is a human assertion of ownership. Michel Serres explored this concept in *The Parasite* (1982). Humans or animals who can mark their territory are able to access spaces of power through the associated phenomenological coloration of what can be considered waste. Serres theorized: "The first one who, having shit on a terrain, then decided to say, this is mine, immediately found people who were disgusted enough to believe him. They distanced themselves from his territory, without war or treaty."[95]

---

[93] For more on the use of scents to mark aspects of power and wealth in the Western tradition, see David Potter, "Odor and Power in the Roman Empire," in *Constructions of the Classical Body*, ed. James Porter (Ann Arbor: University of Michigan Press, 1999), 169–189; Jo Day, "Imagined Aromas and Artificial Flowers in Minoan Society," in *Making Senses of the Past: Toward a Sensory Archaeology*, ed. Jo Day (Carbondale, IL: University of Southern Illinois Press, 2013), 286–309; Gregory Aldrete, "Urban Sensations: Opulence and Ordure," in Volume I of *A Cultural History of the Senses*, eds. Constance Classen and Jerry Toner (London: Bloomsbury, 2014), 45–68; Blake Leyerle, "Refuse, Filth, and Excrement in the Homilies of John Chrysostom," *Journal of Late Antiquity* 2, 2 (2009): 337–356.

[94] For more on pollution, the senses, and othering, see Chris Woolgar, "The Social Life of the Senses: Experiencing the Self, Others, and Environments," in Volume II of *A Cultural History of the Senses*, eds. Constance Classen and Richard Newhauser (London: Bloomsbury, 2014), 23–44; Raynalle Udris, "Smell and Otherness in 20th Century Texts: An Ideological Investigation of Scent with Special Reference to European Modernist Texts, French Women's Writings and Beur Literature," in *Sense and Scent: An Exploration of Olfactory Meaning*, eds. Bronwen Martin and Felizitas Ringham (Dublin: Philomel, 2003), 293–322; Emily Walmsley, "Race, Place, and Taste, Making Identities through Sensory Experience," *Etnofoor* 18, 1 (2005): 43–60; Carolyn Korsmeyer, *Savoring Disgust: The Foul and the Fair in Aesthetics* (New York: Oxford, 2011); Iain Fenlon, "Piazza San Marco: Theatre of the Senses, Market Place of the World," in *Religion and the Senses in Early Modern Europe*, eds. Wietse de Boer and Christine Göttler (Leiden: Brill, 2013), 331–36; Jonathan Gil Harris, "Usurers of Color: The Taint of Jewish Transnationality in Mercantilist Literature and the Merchant of Venice," in *The Mysterious and the Foreign in Early Modern England*, eds. Helen Ostovich, Mary Silcox, and Graham Roebuck (Newark: University of Delaware Press, 2008), 124–138; Sander Gilman, *Inscribing the Other* (Lincoln: University of Nebraska Press, 1991), 36–42; Winfried Menninghaus, *Disgust: the Theory and History of a Strong Sensation* (Albany: State University of New York Press, 2003), 35–38, 104–111; William Ian Miller, *The Anatomy of Disgust* (Cambridge, MA: Harvard University Press, 1997); Steven Wagschal, "The Aesthetics of Disgust in Miguel de Cervantes and Maria de Zayas," in *Beyond Sight: Engaging the Sense in Iberian Literatures and Cultures, 1200–1750*, eds. Ryan Dennis Giles and Steven Wagschal (Toronto: University of Toronto Press, 2018), 94–120.

[95] Michel Serres, *The Parasite*, trans. Lawrence Schehr (Baltimore, MD: Johns Hopkins University Press, 1982 [1980 in French]), 142–145, quotes on 144; Babilon, *Power of*

The Smell of Slavery applies these structural and philosophical ponder-
ings to discuss how the rhetorical coding of something as miasmic and
excremental creates ownership. These processes of how marking something through scatological categories was vital for the creation of
a modernity based upon the "black gold" profits of the Atlantic Slave
Trade that remain mechanically, psychologically, and historically linked
to the semiotics of ordure. As Saidiya Hartman described, Africans were
commodified as part of this excremental force within the Atlantic Slave
Trade, which profited most when "transforming humans into waste and
back again through the exchange of gold." As both gold and rhetorical
shit within slave systems, Africans became commodities and forms of
specie to exchange commodities within innovative systems of finance
capital built on the backs of dark laboring bodies and the productive
wombs of African women.[96]

In this Atlantic World of shit and smell, different groups were aromatically classified in opposition to other ethnic, gendered, and class assemblages due to an economic necessity that needed certain bodies to be
defined as excremental, which culminated in the creation of
a progressive tautology that linked "Africa" and "waste" within
a performative hendiadys born of capitalist licentiousness. The African
subject became an object, appropriated as filthy to create levels of ownership through discourse that marked sub-Saharan peoples as unable to
access modernity without the cleanliness of white colonial masters.
Regardless of material odors or patterns of hygiene, potent European
cultural knowledges altered the biological function of the five senses to

---

Smell, 38–40; Julia Kristeva, *Powers of Horror: an Essay on Abjection*, trans. Leon
Roudiez (New York: Columbia University Press, 1982 [1980 in French]), 12–22. For
more recent work on the senses and phenomenology, see Michel Serres, *The Five Senses:
a Philosophy of Mingled Bodies* (London: Continuum, 2009), 17–84; Richard Kearney
and Brian Treanor, "Introduction: Carnal Hermeneutics from Head to Foot," in *Carnal
Hermeneutics*, eds. Richard Kearney and Brian Treanor (New York: Fordham University
Press, 2015), 1–14. See also the reading of environmental responsibility through atmospheric phenomenology within Peter Sloterdijk, *Terror from the Air* (Los Angeles:
Semiotext(e), 2009); Jean-Paul Thibaud, *Aesthetics of Atmospheres* (New York: Taylor
and Francis, 2016), 11–24.

[96] Saidiya Hartman, *Lose Your Mother: A Journey along the Atlantic Slave Route*
(New York: Farrar, Straus and Giroux, 2013), 45–48, quote on 47; Mary Douglas,
Purity and Danger: an Analysis of Concepts of Pollution and Taboo (New York:
Praeger, 1966), 36–37. See also William Cohen, "Locating Filth," in *Filth: Dirt,
Disgust, and Modern Life*, eds. William Cohen and Ryan Johnson (Minneapolis:
University of Minnesota Press, 2005), vii–xxxvii; Michael Thompson, *Rubbish Theory:
The Creation and Destruction of Value* (Oxford: Oxford University Press, 1979).

create an olfactory consciousness made to sense the other as foul. Alongside a search for an ethics of confrontation within studies of slavery, *The Smell of Slavery* exposes that concerns with pungency internalized deep within the Anglo-American subject through a civilizing process that then emitted mistrustful odors out of the Western self and into the freshly dug outhouse of the mass slave grave called the Atlantic World.[97]

---

[97] For counter-narratives to Atlantic racism, see recent examples within Juliet Hooker, *Theorizing Race in the Americas: Douglass, Sarmiento, Du Bois, and Vasconcelos* (New York: Oxford University Press, 2017), 1–24; Britt Rusert, *Fugitive Science: Empiricism and Freedom in Early African American Culture* (New York: New York University Press, 2017).

I

The Primal Scene

Ethnographic Wonder and Aromatic Discourse

A peculiar bit of twentieth-century Haitian folklore tells the story of spiritualism, slavery, and the sense of smell in the context of an African child's dreamworld. The tale summarizes the racial perspectives of a dark-skinned slave boy named Tabou whose mother, who had also birthed a free and light-skinned brother with her master, finds her son solemnly eating peppered fish on the banks of a Hispaniola stream. The child tells his mother that he feels increasingly distanced from his brethren, as many diasporic tales explicate in binaries based on twins and/or siblings. Tabou protests: "I'm so black, and I don't like it a bit. I'd like to turn white like my half-brother." When asked why Tabou hates his blackness, he proclaims because everyone knows "the blacker folks are, the stronger they smell."[1]

To find a cure for this scented blackness, which his mother tells him comes from working on their master's plantation in the hot tropical sun and is not a trait inherent to race, the boy enlists a mermaid and other Vodou spirits to rid himself of the darkness on his skin and the odor associated to that hue. Through different trials, the boy achieves a dreaming state whereby he becomes a French nobleman and finds himself controlling a full retinue of his own African slaves. Nevertheless, particular traits remain within Tabou while at his Parisian court, as both his love of peppered fish and his odor continue to persist.[2]

---

[1] Francois Turenne de Pres, "Tabou: A Haitian Folk Tale," *Phylon (1940–1956)* 7, 4 (1946): 365–372, quotes on 365.
[2] Turenne de Pres, "Tabou," 368–372.

The perseverance of this tale within Haitian folklore represents the importance of discourse on African odors within the history of slavery throughout the Atlantic littoral. How did this fictional slave child come to believe that blackness included an inherited biological odor? What mechanisms in the Atlantic World of slavery, race, gender, and class created an ideal that whiteness was pure and deodorized while blackness contained a pungency that signified inferiority through the act of smelling? How did slaves resist this clearly socially constructed false consciousness and racial phenomenon?

The legend of Tabou generally combines a common Atlantic application of siblings and water spirits to discuss patterns of racialization and resistance.[3] Another more specific moral of the folktale – and there are many in the winding and byzantine story – is that there is not an inherent smell to African bodies, and Tabou should have just washed in the river when in Haiti, because even as a French nobleman he would smell of the odors of the body if he did not bathe and of the stinking fish that he could never refuse. However, more than a morality and childcare tale for twentieth-century Haitian families, the folklore also represents a deep cultural bricolage of smelling that informed many Atlantic slave societies.[4]

The flawed tautology of race and smell, which tied concerns over being unable to remove the darkness of black hue, even with furious washing, to Tabou's engrained belief that one could never wash away the odor of blackness, was formulated diachronically through the advent of racism during the Early Modern Era.[5] Firstly, the tale is deeply reminiscent of

---

[3] For water spirits and resistance, see Henry John Drewal, "Introduction: Charting the Voyage," in *Sacred Waters: Arts for Mami Wata and Other Divinities in Africa and the Diaspora,* ed. Henry John Drewal (Bloomington: Indiana University Press, 2008), 1–18; Marilyn Houlberg, "Magique Marasa: The Ritual Cosmos of the Twins and other Sacred Children," in *Fragments of Bone: Neo-African Religions in a New World,* ed. Patrick Bellegarde-Smith (Urbana: University of Illinois Press, 2005), 13–31; Wyatt MacGaffey, "Twins, Simbi Spirits and Lwas in Kongo and Haiti," in *Central Africans and Cultural Transformations in the American Diaspora,* ed. Linda Heywood (Cambridge: Cambridge University Press, 2002), 211–226.

[4] For introduction to bricolage and creolization, see Mimi Sheller, *Consuming the Caribbean: From Arawaks to Zombies* (London: Routledge, 2008), 174–203; Douglas Chambers, *Murder at Montpelier: Igbo Africans in Virginia* (Jackson: University Press of Mississippi, 2009), 159–187; Sidney Mintz and Richard Price, *The Birth of African-American Culture: An Anthropological Perspective* (Boston: Beacon, 1992).

[5] For introduction to historiography on race and literature within the Early Modern Era, see Lara Bovilsky, *Barbarous Play: Race on the English Renaissance Stage* (Minneapolis: University of Minnesota Press, 2008), 1–36; Jean Feerick, *Strangers in Blood: Relocating Race in the Renaissance* (Toronto: University of Toronto Press, 2010), 3–24;

a scene from *Titus Andronicus* (1594) wherein the Moorish and evil antagonist Aaron summarized a Greek anecdote through the syntax of the Shakespearean pen: "For all the water in the ocean,/ Can never turn the swans blacke legs to white,/ Although shee lave them howrely in the flood."[6] Secondly, Tabou's tale stems from the aforementioned Greek story of the fabulist Aesop, due to the use of the proverb in Jeremiah 13:23: "Can the Ethiopian change his skin, or the leopard his spots?"[7] Lastly, Tabou's belief in the odor of African skin resulted from the rise of European racism, which began during the sixteenth century to introduce categories that later reduced Africans to a defined and separate race with an established foulness and pungency.[8]

The social construction of African odors as a biological inheritance was built upon the dream-work of early modern English popular literature, which formulated racial stereotypes and flat characters for mass consumption. To define this process, this chapter applies Sigmund Freud's concept of *verschiebung*, or displacement, whereby the mind, as in a dream, codes a conception of reality that is not the true material reality in order to displace sexual anxiety of facing the erotic other during a "primal scene" or first encounter.[9] Regardless of the odors encountered or the actual material cleanliness attributed to African peoples, these English and broader European sensory and cultural shifts were so potent as to alter

Francesca Royster, "The 'End of Race' and the Future of Early Modern Cultural Studies," *Shakespeare Studies* 26 (1998): 59–70; Dympna Callaghan, "What's at Stake in Representing Race?" *Shakespeare Studies* 26 (1998): 21–27.

[6] William Shakespeare, *The Most Lamentable Romaine Tragedie of Titus Andronicus* (London: John Danter, 1594), quote on 26–27.

[7] *The Holy Bible Containing the Old Testament and the New* (Cambridge: Roger Daniel, 1648), quote on xviii; Jean Michel Massing, "From Greek Proverb to Soap Advert: Washing the Ethiopian," *Journal of the Warburg and Courtauld Institutes* 58 (1995): 180–201; Anandi Ramamurthy, *Imperial Persuaders: Images of Africa and Asia in British Advertising* (Manchester: Manchester University Press, 2003), 24–62.

[8] For the rise of English racism, see Sujata Iyengar, *Shades of Difference: Mythologies of Skin Color in Early Modern England* (Philadelphia: University of Pennsylvania Press, 2005), 140–169; Kim Hall, *Things of Darkness: Economies of Race and Gender in Early Modern England* (Ithaca: Cornell University Press, 1995), 25–61.

[9] For *verschiebung*, see Jacques Lacan, *Ecrits: A Selection* (New York: Norton, 1977), 158–162; Stephen Greenblatt, *Renaissance Self-Fashioning: From More to Shakespeare* (Chicago: University of Chicago Press, 1980), 222–254; Arthur Little, "'An Essence That's Not Seen': The Primal Scene of Racism in Othello," *Shakespeare Quarterly* 44, 3 (1993): 304–324; Kalpana Seshadri-Crooks, *Desiring Whiteness: A Lacanian Analysis of Race* (London: Routledge, 2000). See also Edward Said, *Orientalism* (New York: Pantheon, 1978); Walter Mignolo, *The Darker Side of Western Modernity: Global Futures, Decolonial Options* (Durham, NC: Duke University Press, 2011).

the function of the Western nose, as cultural fears and the necessities of economic determination transformed the mental readings of nasal encounters to smell the African other as reeking.[10]

VERSCHIEBUNG AFRICANUS

The shifting of English readers and broader society away from ethnographical objectivity concerning African bodies, to be shown through analysis of the works of early modern travelers like the Islamic scholar Leo Africanus and the Portuguese surveyor Duarte Lopes, to race as a social and literary construct denoting African biological inferiority, partially through racial odors, represents an imaginary undertaking in order to discursively construct England as a civilizing community. During the sixteenth century, English literature increasingly focused on the world to be discovered and, through fictional fancy, informed a budding push for expansionism on the eve of capitalism that took on different sensory bounds and rhetoric.[11] That colonialist thrust was apprised not only by explorers and bureaucrats with a plan for empire but also by poets and dramatists working to cure a vast Anglo-Saxon inferiority complex, which increasingly assisted in defining the African through fantasies of both settler occupation and colonial extraction that included portraying the savage other as inherently pungent.[12]

---

[10] For more on the social construction of smelling, see Anthony Synnott, *The Body Social: Symbolism, Self, and Society* (London: Routledge, 1993), 182–205; Rachel Herz, "I Know What I Like; Understanding Odor Preferences," in *The Smell Culture Reader*, ed. Jim Drobnick (Oxford: Berg, 2006), 193–203.

[11] For early modern theatre, the senses, and the rise of capitalism, see Jean Christophe Agnew, *Worlds Apart: The Market and the Theater in Anglo-American Thought 1550–1750* (Cambridge: Cambridge University Press, 1986), 17–46; Richard Newhauser, "John Gower's Sweet Tooth," *The Review of English Studies* 64, 267 (2013): 752–769.

[12] For colonialism, the stage, and race, see Paula Blank, *Shakespeare and the Mismeasure of Renaissance Man* (Ithaca: Cornell University Press, 2006), 80–117; Hall, *Things of Darkness*, 131–136; Emily Bartels, *Speaking of the Moor: From Alcazar to Othello* (Philadelphia: University of Pennsylvania Press, 2008), 65–99; Lemuel Johnson, *The Devil, the Gargoyle, and the Buffoon: The Negro as Metaphor in Western Literature* (Port Washington, NY: Kennikat, 1971), 33–103; Eldred Jones, *Othello's Countrymen; The African in English Renaissance Drama* (London: Fourah Bay College, the University College of Sierra Leone by Oxford University, 1965); Ania Loomba, "The Color of Patriarchy: Critical Difference, Cultural Difference, and Renaissance Drama," in *Women, "Race," and Writing in the Early Modern Period*, eds. Margo Hendricks and Patricia Parker (London: Routledge, 1994), 17–34; Lynda Boose, "'The Getting of a Lawful Race': Racial Discourse in Early Modern England and the Unpresentable Black Woman," in *Women, "Race," and Writing in the Early Modern Period*, eds.

Racial coding of the African through the nose began during the Early Modern Era. To be sure, various cultural others were classified through smelling before the rise of the Atlantic Slave Trade. However, the racial coding of the Early Modern Era was much different due to the manner through which stereotypes developed. This patterning involved the enchanting of cultural motifs about odor into an understanding of inherent and polygenetic smells that could neither be cleansed nor perfumed away.[13] The knowledge of this newly racist English culture was often informed through dialogue between the core and periphery. Rather than encoding biological alterity upon the numerous African nations they encountered, early European travelers to Africa had tried to honestly portray their exotic and fragrant meetings within contact zones. Only later, within the London core, was race categorically stabilized for greater intellectual consumption through a contemptible triangle trade of fictional consciousness. The use of olfactory reading as a lens allows this study to conclude that the proportional transition from religious and ethnographic antiblackness as articulated through cultural, religious, or climatic difference to antiblackness as virulent forms of early polygenetic racism came earlier than most scholars assert and from a core London population rather than the periphery.[14]

Margo Hendricks and Patricia Parker (London: Routledge, 1994), 35–54; Anthony Gerard Barthelemy, *Black Face, Maligned Race: The Representation of Blacks in English Drama from Shakespeare to Southerne* (Baton Rouge: Louisiana State University Press, 1987), 150–162; Ania Loomba, *Gender, Race, Renaissance Drama* (Manchester: Manchester University Press, 1989), 43–47; Francesca Royster, "'Working Like a Dog': African Labor and Racing the Human-Animal Divide in Early Modern England," in *Writing Race Across the Atlantic World: Medieval to Modern*, eds. Philip Beidler and Gary Taylor (New York: Palgrave Macmillan, 2005), 113–134.

[13] For the first assertions of polygenism in the seventeenth-century work of Isaac de La Peyrère, see David Livingstone, *Adam's Ancestors: Race, Religion, and the Politics of Human Origins* (Baltimore, MD: Johns Hopkins University Press, 2008), 26–51. See also the racial role of "sleeping sickness" in the early works of polygenetic scholars in Norris Saakwa-Mante, "Western Medicine and Racial Constitutions: Surgeon John Atkins' Theory of Polygenism and Sleepy Distemper in the 1730s," in *Race, Science, and Medicine, 1700–1960*, eds. Bernard Harris and Ernst Waltraud (London: Routledge, 1999), 29–57.

[14] For racism and the links between core and periphery, see Ann Laura Stoler and Frederick Cooper, "Between Metropole and Colony: Rethinking a Research Agenda," in *Tensions of Empire: Colonial Cultures in a Bourgeois World*, eds. Frederick Cooper and Ann Laura Stoler (Berkeley: University of California Press, 1997), 1–58; Jeremy Adelman, "Mimesis and Rivalry: European Empires and Global Regimes," *Journal of Global History* 10, 1 (2015): 77–98; G. V. Scammell, "Essay and Reflection: On the Discovery of the Americas and the Spread of Intolerance, Absolutism, and Racism in Early Modern Europe," *The International History Review* 13, 3 (1991): 502–521;

This imagined association of pungency to African bodies – a socially constructed olfactory sensation meant to support ideas of European purity and deodorization while displacing English bodies from any association to stench – can be traced to when race was solidified as an increasingly stable notion within seventeenth-century England. Through analyzing this earlier cultural content of the Anglo-Atlantic public sphere, this chapter reconceptualizes the history of race-making in the olfactory realm, reorienting the study of embodied racism in Mark Smith's *How Race is Made* (2006) through offering a wider chronological scope and different causal forces. Smith's analysis focused on the Anglo-American colonial assertion of scented racism starting from the mid-eighteenth century through the pungent racism of twentieth-century Jim Crow.[15] This chapter expands that timeline by emphasizing how the English body of the seventeenth century performed the somatic work of racism well before the ethnic codes of scientists marked the races as derived for placement within European-dominated hierarchies during the Enlightenment. The racial codes that emerged from stereotypes on the London stage allowed metropolitan and colonial actors to remove most Africans from a space where they could access the promises of Christian conversion and Enlightenment ideals of the subject, citizenship, and private property.[16]

The timing of the emergence of these deeply racial ideals of the body is central to a consistent debate within American historiographies of slavery. Many scholars argue that race was created as a justification for forms of earlier bondage.[17] This chapter disputes those claims that primarily focus

Emily Bartels, "Othello and Africa: Postcolonialism Reconsidered," *William and Mary Quarterly* 54, 1 (January, 1997): 45–64.

[15] Mark Smith, *How Race Is Made: Slavery, Segregation, and the Senses* (Chapel Hill: University of North Carolina Press, 2006). For more analysis of cultural ideas of odor and race, see William Tullett, "Grease and Sweat: Race and Smell in Eighteenth-Century English Culture," *Cultural and Social History* 13, 3 (2016): 307–322.

[16] For subject, citizenship, and object in slave studies, see Simon Gikandi, *Slavery and the Culture of Taste* (Princeton, NJ: Princeton University Press, 2011); Stephanie Smallwood, *Saltwater Slavery: A Middle Passage from Africa to American Diaspora* (Cambridge, MA: Harvard University Press, 2008); Orlando Patterson, *Slavery and Social Death: A Comparative Study* (Cambridge, MA: Harvard University Press, 1982).

[17] For more on the contours of this debate, see David Brion Davis, "Constructing Race: A Reflection," *William and Mary Quarterly* 54 (January, 1997): 7–18; Alden Vaughan, "The Origins Debate: Slavery and Racism in Seventeenth-Century Virginia," *The Virginia Magazine of History and Biography* 97, 3 (1989): 311–354; John Coombs, "The Phases of Conversion: A New Chronology for the Rise of Slavery in Early Virginia," *William and Mary Quarterly* 68, 3 (2011): 332–360; Douglas Bradburn and

on class and the violence of indentured servitude, siding with scholars who articulate that earlier forms of English racism, which existed well before the most significant rise of the slave trade, created the impetus for fresh and burgeoning racial classifications.[18] Taking a longer temporal approach, *The Smell of Slavery* connects with much recent scholarship that also debates whether Anglo-Atlantic slavery was essential for the rise of capitalism during the eighteenth century.[19] Developing these arguments another step, this chapter argues that the racial necessities for primitive accumulation were embodied within cultural motifs and the English language well before the rise of standard forms of economic capitalism emerged within the Atlantic World. Anglo-Atlantic culture of the seventeenth century

John Coombs, "Smoke and Mirrors: Reinterpreting the Society and Economy of the Seventeenth-Century Chesapeake," *Atlantic Studies* 3, 2 (2006): 131–157; Russell Menard, "From Servants to Slaves: The Transformation of the Chesapeake Labor System," *Southern Studies* 16 (1977), 355–390; Lorena Walsh, *Motives of Honor, Pleasure, and Profit: Plantation Management in the Colonial Chesapeake, 1607–1763* (Chapel Hill: University of North Carolina Press, 2012), 1–24, 135–142; Simon Newman, *A New World of Labor: The Development of Plantation Slavery in the British Atlantic* (Philadelphia: University of Pennsylvania Press, 2013), 245–248.

[18] For slave studies with race as primary to the rise of slavery, see Winthrop Jordan, *White Over Black: American Attitudes Toward the Negro, 1550–1812* (Chapel Hill: University of North Carolina Press, 1968); Heather Miyano Kopelson, *Faithful Bodies: Performing Religion and Race in the Puritan Atlantic* (New York: New York University, 2016), 4–6, 107–125; Kathleen Brown, *Good Wives, Nasty Wenches, and Anxious Patriarchs: Gender, Race, and Power in Colonial Virginia* (Chapel Hill: University of North Carolina Press, 1996); David Eltis, *The Rise of African Slavery in the Americas* (New York: Cambridge University Press, 2006); Edmund Morgan, *American Slavery, American Freedom: The Ordeal of Colonial Virginia* (New York: Norton, 1975); Anthony Parent, *Foul Means: The Formation of a Slave Society in Virginia, 1660–1740* (Chapel Hill: University of North Carolina Press, 2003), 105–106, 253–265; Rebecca Goetz, *The Baptism of Early Virginia: How Christianity Created Race* (Baltimore, MD: Johns Hopkins University Press, 2012), 86–111.

[19] For more on links between capitalism and slavery, see Trevor Burnard, *Planters, Merchants, and Slaves: Plantation Societies in British America, 1650–1820* (Chicago: University of Chicago Press, 2015); William Pettigrew, *Freedom's Debt: The Royal African Company and the Politics of the Atlantic Slave Trade, 1672–1752* (Chapel Hill: University of North Carolina Press, 2013); Trevor Burnard and John Garrigus, *The Plantation Machine: Atlantic Capitalism in French Saint-Domingue and British Jamaica* (Philadelphia: University of Pennsylvania Press, 2016); Michael Guasco, *Slaves and Englishmen: Human Bondage in the Early Modern Atlantic World* (Philadelphia: University of Pennsylvania Press, 2014), 11–40; Edward Baptist, *The Half Has Never Been Told: Slavery and the Making of American Capitalism* (New York: Basic, 2014); Walter Johnson, *River of Dark Dreams: Slavery and Empire in the Cotton Kingdom* (Cambridge, MA: Harvard University Press, 2013); Caitlin Rosenthal, *Accounting for Slavery: Masters and Management* (Cambridge, MA: Harvard University Press, 2018), 121–156.

prepared the English body for the coming of capitalism through ordering sensory behaviors in such a way as to trace the outlines of racialized bodies before the establishment of the economic basis of capitalism and slavery during more concrete stages of primitive accumulation.[20]

Racial knowledge lives in the bones, in the muscles, in the nasal passages. The common sense and tacit knowledge that African peoples smelled was initially a marking of cultural otherness and disgust described by travelers, but during the seventeenth century olfactory othering altered from descriptions of cultural oddness to increased attributions of biological racism through the machinations of popular literature upon the imagined English nation and broader European community. In early modern England, categories of racial construction combined to create forms of value for whiteness against what was deemed a wasteful, pungent, and polluted blackness.[21] Well before Francois Bernier, Carolus Linnaeus, Johann Blumenbach, and Georges-Louis Leclerc, Comte de Buffon fixed racial hierarchies within Enlightenment philosophical and scientific languages, English and Western bodies were experiencing those categories as sensory reactions to implicitly understand the perceived difference of Africans.[22] Using linguistic and phenomenological analysis of racism, this chapter therefore revises the timeline of the later rise of

---

[20] For debates on the idea that racism emerged only during the Enlightenment, see Robert Bernasconi, "Who Invented the Concept of Race? Kant's Role in the Enlightenment Construction of Race," in *Race*, ed. Robert Bernasconi (Malden, MA: Blackwell, 2001), 11–36; Pierre Boulle, "Francois Bernier and the Origins of the Modern Concept of Race," in *The Color of Liberty: Histories of Race in France*, eds. Sue Peabody and Tyler Edward Stovall (Durham, NC: Duke University Press, 2003), 11–27; William B. Cohen, *The French Encounter with Africans: White Response to Blacks, 1530–1880* (Bloomington: University of Indiana Press, 1980), 35–59; Maghan Keita, *Race and the Writing of History: Riddling the Sphinx* (Oxford: Oxford University Press, 2000), 15–26.

[21] For whiteness in Early Modern England, see Iyengar, *Shades of Difference*, 103–172; Peter Erickson, "'God for Harry, England and Saint George': British National Identity and the Emergence of White Self-Fashioning," in *Early Modern Visual Culture: Representation, Race, Empire in Renaissance England*, eds. Peter Erickson and Clark Hulse (Philadelphia: University of Pennsylvania Press, 2000), 315–345; Ian Smith, *Race and Rhetoric in the Renaissance: Barbarian Errors* (New York: Palgrave Macmillan, 2009), 46–57.

[22] For more on the debate regarding Enlightenment science and the nomenclature of race, see Siep Stuurman, "Francois Bernier and the Invention of Racial Classification," *History Workshop Journal* 50 (2000), 1–21; Nicholas Hudson, "From 'Nation' to 'Race': The Origin of Racial Classification in Eighteenth-Century Thought," *Eighteenth-Century Studies* 29, 3 (1996): 247–264; Richard Popkin, "The Philosophical Basis of Eighteenth-Century Racism," *Studies in Eighteenth-Century Culture* 3 (1973): 245–262. See also the link between nation, climate, geography, and race within medical discourse in Suman Seth, *Difference and Disease: Medicine, Race,*

racism asserted by a number of scholars. Through the analysis of somatic experience and intersensorial language that included odor, this chapter asserts that by the middle of the seventeenth century racism was a significant marker of biological inferiority for many English readers in the metropole and for the countless rapacious slaveholders throughout the colonies.[23]

AFRICAN CULTURAL AROMAS AND THE ETHNOGRAPHIC IMAGINATION

Most European readings of skin color were often racially illegible prior to the discovery of the New World. Because religion dominated the sensory consciousness of most premodern Europeans, the odors of pungency and aroma were usually defined through narratives of the Catholic Church. Skin color was consequently often considered a marker of religious weakness rather than any form of long-standing biological inheritance. For example, the medieval romance *The King of Tars* included a tale of a formless black mass birthed by a white woman and her Saracen lover. After baptism, the lump of black mass became human, white, and Christian. The Saracen father, also upon baptism alongside his child, could become pure and white with the water of Christ. The interiority of Christian whiteness could mark a dark body as white on a previously dark exterior because race was not yet a permanent categorization of the other.[24] Within similarly religious-focused traditions used to describe

and the Eighteenth-Century British Empire (Cambridge: Cambridge University Press, 2018), 167–207.

[23] For more analysis of the rise of Anglo-Atlantic racism as part of later eras, see George Boulukos, *The Grateful Slave: The Emergence of Race in Eighteenth-Century British and American Culture* (Cambridge: Cambridge University Press, 2008); Robert Parkinson, *The Common Cause: Creating Race and Nation in the American Revolution* (Chapel Hill: University of North Carolina Press, 2017); Roxann Wheeler, *The Complexion of Race: Categories of Difference in Eighteenth-Century British Culture* (Philadelphia: University of Pennsylvania Press, 2000); Renato Mazzolini, "Skin Color and the Origin of Physical Anthropology (1640–1850)," in *Reproduction, Race, and Gender in Philosophy and the Early Life Sciences*, ed. Susanne Lettow (Albany, NY: State University of New York Press, 2014), 131–162; Caitlin Fitz, *Our Sister Republics: The United States in an Age of American Revolutions* (New York: Liveright, 2016), 80–115; C. A. Bayly, "The British and Indigenous Peoples, 1760–1860: Power, Perception, and Identity," in *Empire and Others: British Encounters with Indigenous Peoples, 1600–1850*, eds. M. J. Daunton and Rick Halpern (Philadelphia: University of Pennsylvania Press, 1999), 19–41.

[24] Katie Walter, "The Form and the Formless: Medieval Taxonomies of Skin, Flesh, and the Human," in *Reading Skin in Medieval Literature and Culture*, ed. Katie Walter

suspicious places in the Middle East, upon the African continent, and cultivated by African peoples, it was also often difficult for many Renaissance thinkers to negatively conceptualize different human groups within Africa because the cosmographical descriptions of the areas focused on religious discussions of transient characters like the Queen of Sheba and Prester John in the Maghreb, Middle East, and North Africa.[25]

Sir John Mandeville's often cited and frequently read *Travels*, which were first disseminated throughout Europe during the fourteenth century and had been collected from numerous sources of different levels of repute, exposed Western Europeans to different areas of the world through many of these religiously inspired and wondrous myths. The multifarious forms of Mandeville's text summarized non-European spaces that included many intelligent species who could wear scented skins that kept animals away from attacking, a tree that could change odor every hour, and a group of pygmies that lived only on the smell of apples.[26] The geographical and temporal ambiguity within Mandeville's texts led many Europeans to later place several of these aromatic myths in different global areas, occasionally among the many peoples they hoped to mark as culturally inferior. Despite the increased contact with Africans in Europe, many images in art and on maps consistently used older portrayals of Africans as from mythical and monstrous areas. Homologizing

(New York: Palgrave Macmillan, 2013), 119–140; Annemette Kirkregaard, "Questioning the Origins of the Negative Image of Africa in Medieval Europe," in *Encounter Images in the Meeting Between Africa and Europe*, ed. Mai Palmberg (Uppsala: Africa Institute, 2001), 20–36. See also Katharine Gerbner, *Christian Slavery: Conversion and Race in the Protestant Atlantic World* (Philadelphia: University of Pennsylvania Press, 2018), 74–90.

[25] Jean Michel Massing, "The Image of Africa and the Iconography of Lip-Plated Africans in Pierre Decelier's World Map of 1550," in *Black Africans in Renaissance Europe*, eds. T. F. Earle and K. J. P. Lowe (Cambridge: Cambridge University Press, 2005), 48–69; Lorraine Daston and Katharine Park, *Wonders and the Order of Nature, 1150–1750* (New York: Zone, 1998); Matteo Salvadore, *The African Prester John and the Birth of Ethiopian-European Relations, 1402–1555* (London: Taylor and Francis, 2017), 114–115; Victoria Brownlee, *Biblical Readings and Literary Writings in Early Modern England, 1558–1625* (Oxford: Oxford University Press, 2018), 67–70.

[26] John Block Friedman, *The Monstrous Races in Medieval Art and Thought* (Syracuse, NY: Syracuse University Press, 2000), 26–36; John Mandeville, *The Voyages and Travels of Sir John Mandevile, Knight* (London: A. Wilde, 1722); Rosemary Tzanaki, *Mandeville's Medieval Audiences* (Aldershot: Ashgate, 2003); Edward Tyson and Michael van der Gucht, *Orang-Outang, Sive, Homo Sylvestris, or, The Anatomy of a Pygmie Compared with That of a Monkey, an Ape, and a Man To Which Is Added, A Philological Essay Concerning the Pygmies, the Cynocephali, the Satyrs and Sphinges of the Ancients: Wherein It Will Appear That They Are All Either Apes or Monkeys, and Not Men, As Formerly Pretended* (London: Thomas Bennet and Daniel Brown, 1699), 18–20.

the non-European other was provoked by Mandeville wonders and became a pattern that often continued into the imaginations of later Europeans and within their colonialist canons.[27]

Religious and mythical connotations that infused later racism were often a part of these pre-Modern European worldviews. As part of these religious beliefs, poor odors were often attributed to Jewish populations prior to the Early Modern Era.[28] Jews were often considered so stinking due to supposed past religious malevolence that they were believed to cure their signifying poor odors through the drinking of Christian blood or through the mixing of Christian fluids within Passover breads.[29] Beliefs in the odors of the religiously other continued well into the seventeenth century, often informing later traditions of racism against African bodies that would emerge with greater force the more Europeans found profit from the shores of Africa.[30]

Nonetheless, biological racism was not yet a fixed category within most sixteenth-century European ethnography.[31] During the Renaissance, in

---

[27] Francesc Relaño, *The Shaping of Africa: Cosmographic Discourse and Cartographic Science in Late Medieval and Early Modern Europe* (Aldershot: Ashgate, 2002); John Gillies, *Shakespeare and the Geography of Difference* (Cambridge: Cambridge University Press, 1994), 54–55.

[28] Kenneth Stow, "Was the Ghetto Cleaner . . . , " in *Rome, Pollution, and Propriety: Dirt, Disease, and Hygiene in the Eternal City from Antiquity to Modernity*, eds. Mark Bradley and Kenneth Stow (Cambridge: Cambridge University Press, 2012), 169–181; Mark Smith, "Transcending, Othering, Detecting: Smell, Premodernity, Modernity," *Postmedieval* 3, 4 (2012): 380–390; Colin Kidd, *The Forging of Races: Race and Scripture in the Protestant Atlantic World, 1600–2000* (Cambridge: Cambridge University Press, 2006), 61–75; Joshua Trachtenberg, *The Devil and the Jews: The Medieval Conception of the Jew and Its Relation to Modern Antisemitism* (Philadelphia: Jewish Publication Society of America, 1983), 49–50; Benjamin Braude, "Michelangelo and the Curse of Ham: From a Typology of Jew-Hatred to a Genealogy of Racism," in *Writing Race Across the Atlantic World: Medieval to Modern*, eds. Philip Beidler and Gary Taylor (New York: Palgrave Macmillan, 2005), 79–92.

[29] Bruce Baum, *The Rise and Fall of the Caucasian Race: A Political History of Racial Identity* (New York: New York University Press, 2006), 32–33.

[30] For arguments on earlier forms of anti-blackness, see Benjamin Isaac, *The Invention of Racism in Classical Antiquity* (Princeton, NJ: Princeton University Press, 2004), 17–23; Peter Biller, "Proto-racial Thought in Medieval Science," in *The Origins of Racism in the West*, eds. Miriam Eliav-Feldon, Benjamin Isaac, and Joseph Ziegler (Cambridge: Cambridge University Press, 2009), 157–180; Joseph Ziegler, "Physiognomy, Science, and Proto-Racism, 1200–1500," in *The Origins of Racism in the West*, eds. Miriam Eliav-Feldon, Benjamin Isaac, and Joseph Ziegler (Cambridge: Cambridge University Press, 2009), 181–199; Jeremy Lawrance, "Black Africans in Renaissance Spanish Literature," in *Black Africans in Renaissance Europe*, eds. T. F. Earle and K. J. P. Lowe (Cambridge: Cambridge University Press, 2005), 70–93.

[31] For early anthropology and race, see Surekha Davies, *Renaissance Ethnography and the Invention of the Human: New Worlds, Maps and Monsters* (Cambridge: Cambridge

much of Europe, black skin was increasingly considered a negative trait. However, that classification did not mean that the person with that hue was stereotypically considered fundamentally inferior.[32] During the Renaissance, many portrayals of Africans living within England were positive, offering a subject that could reach religious, civic, and moral potential. There were significant possibilities for Africans to enter English communities. Many Africans could intermarry and assimilate into English society. Within sixteenth-century England, and in broader Western Europe, many portrayals of Africans in literature and art therefore remained constructive. This allowed many African peoples to achieve significant social mobility in their adopted countries.[33]

Even as race augmented as a marker of cultural and religious difference for many groups, the cultures of the English Renaissance had yet to fully code the black body as a marker of biological inferiority. For those who could read the Old Testament, positive portrayals of darker-skinned Africans persisted and were consistently cited. The story of the eunuch Ebed-Melech, in Jeremiah 38:7, summarized the inherent ingenuity and bravery of the Ethiopian in rescuing Jeremiah from Babylonian dungeons through the use of a pulley.[34] Black bodies portrayed in art frequently

University Press, 2016), 23–46. See also Margaret Hodgen, *Early Anthropology in the Sixteenth and Seventeenth Centuries* (Philadelphia: University of Pennsylvania Press, 1964), 295–353; Antonio Barrera-Osorio, *Experiencing Nature: The Spanish American Empire and the Early Scientific Revolution* (Austin: University of Texas Press, 2006); Antonello Gerbi, *Nature in the New World: From Christopher Columbus to Gonzalo Fernandez De Oviedo* (Pittsburgh, PA: University of Pittsburgh Press, 1985); P. E. H. Hair, "Attitudes to Africans in English Primary Sources on Guinea Up to 1650," *History in Africa* 26 (1999): 43–68.

[32] For more on race in the Renaissance, see Peter Erickson, "Representations of Blacks and Blackness in the Renaissance," *Criticism* 35, 4 (1993): 499–528; Peter Mark, *Africans in European Eyes: The Portrayal of Black Africans in Fourteenth and Fifteenth Century Europe* (Syracuse, NY: Syracuse University Press, 1974), 70–98; Jack D'Amico, *The Moor in English Renaissance Drama* (Tampa, FL: University of South Florida Press, 1991), 7–40; Frank Snowden, *Before Color Prejudice: The Ancient View of Blacks* (Cambridge, MA: Harvard University Press, 1983), 99–108; Frank Snowden, *Blacks in Antiquity; Ethiopians in the Greco-Roman Experience* (Cambridge, MA: Belknap, 1970), 178–204.

[33] Imtiaz Habib, *Black Lives in the English Archives, 1500–1677: Imprints of the Invisible* (Aldershot: Ashgate, 2008), 116–145; Anu Korhonen, "Washing the Ethiopian White: Conceptualising Black Skin in Renaissance England," in *Black Africans in Renaissance Europe*, eds. T. F. Earle and K. J. P. Lowe (Cambridge: Cambridge University Press, 2005), 94–112.

[34] Robert Allen, *A Treatise of Christian Beneficence, and of That Like Christian Thankefulnese Which Is Due to the Same: The Which, As They Are Duties of Singular Account with God, so Are They of As Necessarie Use to All Christians, for the Keeping of*

focused on the Black Magi tradition, which became an allegory that asserted both the strangeness of Africa and the fear of encountering the other. This Magi, or ruler, would usually be portrayed in a white crowd signifying difference as a questioning of the crowd's piety rather than later assertions of racial superiority.[35] Similarly racially ambiguous, consistent discussions of national variance within ethnographic texts that summarized Africans shows how vital characteristics of culture and nationality were to travelers within Africa. The consistent mixing of metaphors and anecdotes about varying peoples of the world were key aspects of early modern ethnographical travel, not markers of biological racism upon specific populations.[36]

Even as portrayals remained positive from metropolitan education about religious figures, some travelers were progressively informed by a growing Islamic and Old Testament contention regarding the inferiority of dark-skinned peoples. Many of these tales focused on the biblical tradition of Noah's sons related to the settlement of racial populations throughout the globe after the flood. In many interpretations of the story, the lineage of Noah's son Ham were cursed with black skin and curly hair because Ham had seen his father's naked body and possibly remarked negatively about his father's corporeal form in public. William McKee Evans has written of the shifting location of the biblical character of Ham to African territories and the belief that the inferiority of black skin came partly from medieval Arabic sources that spread with greater force throughout Europe during the later Middle Ages.[37]

Faith and a Good Conscience, As Are Fire and Water for Common Use and Comfort to the Naturall Life of All Men (London: John Harison for Thomas Man, 1600), 62–63.

[35] Paul Kaplan, *The Rise of the Black Magus in Western Art* (Ann Arbor: UMI Research, 1985), 43–62; Joseph Leo Koerner, "The Epiphany of the Black Magus Circa 1500," in Book I of Volume III of *The Image of the Black in Western* Art, eds. David Bindman, Henry Louis Gates, and Karen Dalton (Cambridge, MA: Belknap, 2010), 7–92.

[36] Philip Morgan, "Encounters Between British and 'Indigenous' Peoples, c. 1500–1800," in *Empire and Others: British Encounters with Indigenous Peoples, 1600–1850,* eds. M. J. Daunton and Rick Halpern (Philadelphia: University of Pennsylvania Press, 1999), 43–78. See also the rise of whiteness as anathema to Africa described within Geraldine Heng, *The Invention of Race in the European Middle Ages* (Cambridge: Cambridge University Press, 2018), 181–256.

[37] What is clear in discussion of Ham's skin color and national origin in the sixteenth century is that there was much debate on the topic. Rather than solely a signifier for racial Africans, Ham's origin tale was also often used as a metaphor for confused lineage. Elliot Tokson, *The Popular Image of the Black Man in English Drama, 1550–1688* (Boston: G. K. Hall, 1982), 10–16; William McKee Evans, "From the Land of Canaan to the Land of Guinea: The Strange Odyssey of the 'Sons of Ham'," *American Historical*

Though there was no significant link between race and slavery, or between Ham and Africa, in the Quran, although a cultural link frequently existed within Islamic and Arab societies between race and slavery linguistically.[38] During the Medieval Era of what many scholars consider "racism without race," Islamic society emerged as the most genealogically defined. As James Sweet summarized, "The Muslim world expected blacks to be slaves."[39] Middle Eastern civilizations, which dominated the intellectual centers of the world for centuries, later disseminated partially racialized cultures to Iberian travelers and Europe during the Renaissance. This scholarly culture of Islam seemed to include an assertion that black bodies had possibly inherent odors. For example, the eleventh-century Baghdad Christian physician Ibn Botlan, in "The Art of Making Good Purchases of Slaves," had summarized that black slaves "have the whitest teeth and this because they have much saliva. Unpleasant is the smell emitted from their armpits and coarse is their skin."[40]

The wondrous and religious traditions of Mandeville and Prester John, the cultural conducts of sensory anti-Semitism, European concepts of the Curse of Ham, and these Arabic customs of stinking Africans all were present when European travelers began their journeys to African shores starting during the fifteenth century. Nevertheless, even with these many possible pre-texts for streamlining racism, within most early European ethnographic texts on Africa focus remained upon wonder and cultural bartering. Most of these works, like the narrative of John Leo Africanus,

Review 85, 1 (1980): 78–102; Elizabeth Fox-Genovese and Eugene Genovese, *The Mind of the Master Class: History and Faith in the Southern Slaveholders' Worldview* (Cambridge: Cambridge University Press, 2005), 521–525. For a recent reading of the Curse of Ham regarding the act of witnessing and the ability of the subaltern to speak, see Bénédicte Boisseron, *Afro-Dog: Blackness and the Animal Question* (New York: Columbia University Press, 2018), 157–193. See also Terence Keel, *Divine Variations: How Christian Thought Became Racial Science* (Stanford, CA: Stanford University Press, 2018), 113–136.

[38] For the blackness of Ham as it changed over time, see Benjamin Braude, "The Sons of Noah and the Construction of Ethnic and Geographical Identities in the Medieval and Early Modern Periods," *William and Mary Quarterly* 54, 1 (1997): 103–142; David Whitford, *The Curse of Ham in the Early Modern Era: The Bible and the Justifications for Slavery* (Farnham: Ashgate, 2009), 101–102; David Goldenberg, *The Curse of Ham: Race and Slavery in Early Judaism, Christianity, and Islam* (Princeton, NJ: Princeton University Press, 2003), 195–200.

[39] James Sweet, "The Iberian Roots of American Racist Thought," *William and Mary Quarterly* 54, 1 (1997): 143–166, quotes on 143, 147.

[40] Sweet, "Iberian Roots," 143–166, quote on 151; Murray Gordon, *Slavery in the Arab World* (New York: New Amsterdam, 1989), 102–103.

an Islamic scholar from different areas throughout the Mediterranean, focused on different cultural totems and taboos. Transnational ethnographic texts like that of Africanus separated African peoples by their languages, diets, and cultural traditions of occasionally oiled skins, perfumed ceremonies, and stinking weeds. Direct aromatic encounters rarely produced racial codes; instead, they marked distinct ethnicities and social constructs.[41]

Many Iberian ethnographical texts described the smells of different African nations as distinct cultural productions. Portuguese explorer Duarte Lopes' *Report of the Kingdome of Congo* (1597), initially collected in 1591 by Fillipo Pigafetta and later to be included in the widely distributed fourth edition of the English compendium *Purchas' Pilgrims* (1626), summarized the smell of specific African bodies as originating from the odors of copper powder and palm oil that the "Anziques" nation used to anoint their bodies. In summarizing the use of this oil, Lopes retained a fantastical ear for wondrous stories. During his ambassadorship to Congo's King Alvaro II, which began in 1578, he noted a certain type of African wolf that "smell this oyle a farre off" and would steal vials of palm oil between their teeth and flee into the night.[42] The importance of scented body oils as a cultural material was also summarized earlier within Alvise Cadamosto's letters sent from African outposts by the Venetian slave trader to Henry the Navigator during the 1450s. In one letter, probably referencing Mali, Cadamosto also summarized the "Azaneques" people who covered their mouths with linen to prevent people from smelling their breaths. These ethnic groups were classified as stinking by Cadamosto through their use of pungent fish oil to cover their bodies.[43]

Dutch explorer Pieter de Marees' *Description and Historical Account of the Gold Kingdom of Guinea* (1602), disseminated through multiple translations after initial release in Dutch during the early seventeenth century, described similar African pungency through cultural traditions,

[41] Heng, *The Invention of Race*, 36–42, 75–81.

[42] Duarte Lopes, *A Report of the Kingdome of Congo, a Region of Africa* (London: John Wolfe, 1597), quotes on 33–34, 88–89; Samuel Purchas, Jerome Horsey, William Methold, Jirjis ibn al-'Amīd Makīn, Thomas Erpenius, William Stansby, and Henry Featherstone, *Purchas His Pilgrimage, or, Relations of the World and the Religions Observed in All Ages and Places Discovered, from the Creation Unto This Present* (London: William Stansby for Henrie Fetherstone, 1626), 763–764.

[43] Richard Major, *The Life of Prince Henry of Portugal Surnamed the Navigator and Its Results: Comprising the Discovery, Within One Century, of Half the World* (London: Asher, 1868), 254–255.

even with his perceptions attuned to what he deemed uncivil. He noted the towns near the coast of Guinea "stink like carcasses because of the rubbish which they throw out on the road in heaps."[44] The second edition of Spanish Jesuit Alonso de Sandoval's *De Instauranda Aethiopum Salute* (1647) similarly distinguished the "rudeness, nudity and bad odor" of Africans. Sandoval noted the specific "bad odor in the mouth" of explicit nations.[45] Like Lopes before him, Sandoval, who analyzed African cultures and peoples from his base in Cartagena de Indias, also leaned on early interpreters, like Mandeville, when describing the wondrous people of Africa, relating tales of one group, the "Astomos," who had no mouth with which to eat and consequently lived through the sustenance of smell alone; they "uphold the smell of fruit and flowers" as their only alimentary nourishment.[46]

Portuguese Jesuit Manuel Alvares's *Ethiopia Minor and a Geographical Account of the Province of Sierra Leone* summarized many accounts of voyages into sub-Saharan Africa from the sixteenth century while on his own Catholic mission to the region from 1607 to 1617. Alvares's collection similarly defined odors that came from cultural rituals and African technology rather than biological concepts of race. He discussed the fragrant process for tarring boats for river travel within Sierra Leone, the use of strong-smelling foods as a mark of African cultures near Ethiopia, and, while among the "Sousos" people, probably ancestors to the Susu of modern Guinea, he noted the cultural skills of the nation of Putases who "sniff their noses, as one does when sniffing scent" while people of this community encountered each other during their everyday state of affairs.[47]

These many accounts of Africa described diverse African groups as part of different nations with diverse culturally created odors. Many of these ethnically categorized odors may have allowed for an expansion of

---

[44] Pieter de Marees, *Description and Historical Account of the Gold Kingdom of Guinea (1602)*, trans. A. van Dantzig and Adam Jones (Oxford: Published for the British Academy by Oxford University Press, 1987), quote on 77.

[45] Alonso de Sandoval, *De Instauranda Aethiopum Salute* (Madrid: A. de Paredes, 1647), quotes on xxii and 18.

[46] Sandoval, *De Instauranda Aethiopum Salute*, quote on 320.

[47] Manuel Alvares, *Ethiopia Minor and a Geographical Account of the Province of Sierra Leone (c.1615)*, trans. P. E. H. Hair (Liverpool: University of Liverpool, 1990), Part One, Ch. 4, quotes on 6–7, Part Two, Ch. 4, quotes on 4–6, Appendix, "Of the Province of the Sousous: Single Chapter," quotes on 7–8; P. E. H. Hair, "Heretics, Slaves and Witches-As Seen by Guinea Jesuits C. 1610," *Journal of Religion in Africa* 28, 2 (1998): 131–144.

signifiers to be attributed to skin color. However, these olfactory signifiers were originally culturally demarcated by foreign travelers, whereby ethnic descriptions persisted because English texts, foreign texts, and translations of foreign texts into English were consistently informed by an Aristotelian and Galenic conception of difference that was based on geographical variance whereby skin was black due to the heat of the sun's rays.[48]

With a common cultural understanding that blackness was a geographical or climatological trait rather than biologically determined, the writings of late sixteenth- and early seventeenth-century travelers consistently articulated smells as created solely through cultural totems rather than through inherent bodily odors. Leo Africanus' *Geographical Historie of Africa* (1600) described the nations of Africa using these cultural differences through summaries of ritual practice and the aromas of different geographical locales.[49] He summarized the state of "Maraco" as "greene every where, and most fertile of all things, which serve for foode, or which delight the senses of smelling or seeing."[50] Poor smells of these areas and their built environments were also described using cultural foundations. Thus, the people who lived near Mount Dedes on the plains of Todga, in present-day southern Morocco, smelled poorly because of the "stinking smell" of the goats who wandered their villages.[51] The people of Tegassa, near Tunis, similarly lived in a stinking part of Africa, though it was the "extreme ... smell of their fishes" that caused the pungent odors of their villages.[52]

---

[48] For Anglo-Atlantic arguments linking skin color to climate, see Roger Williams, *A Key into the Language of America* (London: Gregory Dexter, 1643), 50–52; Levinus Lemnius and Thomas Newton, *The Touchstone of Complexions* (London, 1633 [1576]), 62–65. For more on the importance of climate as a marker of skin color in early modern and Atlantic literature, see Mary Floyd-Wilson, "Temperature, Temperance, and Racial Difference in Ben Jonson's 'The Masque of Blackness'," *English Literary Renaissance* 28, 2 (1998): 183–209; Molly Murray, "Performing Devotion in *The Masque of Blacknesse*," *Studies in English Literature 1500–1900* 47, 2 (2007): 427–449; Katy Chiles, *Transformable Race: Surprising Metamorphoses in the Literature of Early America* (New York: Oxford University Press, 2014), 31–63.

[49] For Africanus and historical methodology, see Tokson, *Popular Image of the Black Man*, 16–18; Hair, "Attitudes to Africans," 52–53.

[50] Leo Africanus and John Pory, *A Geographical Historie of Africa, Written in Arabicke and Italian by John Leo a More, Borne in Granada, and Brought Up in Barbarie* (London: George Bishop, 1600 [1550]), 56–65, quotes on 64–65.

[51] Africanus, *Geographical Historie*, quotes on 106–108.

[52] Africanus, *Geographical Historie*, quote on 187–188.

Africanus, a Muslim from Christian Grenada who was originally named Al-Hassan Ibn Mohammed Al-Wezaz Al-Fasi and became John Leo Africanus when baptized by Pope Leo X in Rome, pressed ethnographical texts that described each African nation as a separate culture. As Natalie Davis has described, Africanus frequently tricked the Christians in the areas where he lived into thinking him a Catholic through the application of *taqiyya*, or the denouncement of Islamic faith to protect the body during duress. He was therefore a transgressive figure, a trickster bound to nothing, and it was his transgressive forms that marked his identity.[53] As part of this trickster distinctiveness, Africanus kept a keen sensory lens for cultural wonder in worldly environments and amongst the peoples he encountered.[54] However, when the work was sent to publisher John Pory, the terms within the 1550 Latin text for each African nation were often covered over by the use of the term "Moor" to describe most national groups living in Africa.[55] The metropolitan English core turned the variation, culturally defined through odor among other sensory observations, into a common other through a process of amanuensis that shifted particularities of culture into progressively more symbolic and stereotypical orders.[56]

BLACK SMELLS ON THE POPULAR PROSCENIUM

On the early Atlantic periphery, European ethnographers, travelers, and explorers often wrote of other peoples they encountered as different fruits from the same tree. The internal conceptualization of the European and opposing racial others were only later born through forms of what Colin Kidd has described as "ethnic theology," an identity apart from national origin that only arose during the later periods of the Early Modern Era, especially through the racialized exegesis of the stories of Noah, Ham, and

---

[53] Natalie Zemon Davis, *Trickster Travels: A Sixteenth-Century Muslim between Worlds* (New York: Hill and Wang, 2006).

[54] Davis, *Trickster Travels*, 266–269.

[55] Emily Bartels, "Making More of the Moor: Aaron, Othello, and Renaissance Refashionings of Race," *Shakespeare Quarterly* 41, 4 (1990): 433–454; Eldred Jones, *The Elizabethan Image of Africa* (Charlottesville, VA: Published for the Folger Shakespeare Library by the University Press of Virginia, 1971), 21–37.

[56] For similarities between othering of different races in early modern England, see Emily Bartels, "Imperialist Beginnings: Richard Hakluyt and the Construction of Africa," *Criticism* 34, 4 (Fall, 1992), 517–538, 522–526; Jesús López-Peláez Casellas, "'Race' and the Construction of English National Identity: Spaniards and North Africans in English Seventeenth-Century Drama," *Studies in Philology* 106, 1 (2009): 32–51.

Canaan. As this new biological identity based in concepts of European superiority formed, it needed a linguistic other as a formulaic counter; thus rose the African, as the other, as marked within European literature rather than from the perspectives of those on the periphery who had perceived the human similarities between themselves and the different indigenous peoples of the Atlantic World.[57]

Significant populations of Africans lived in England during the 1500s. Most of these Africans came from previous stops on the European mainland, and a significant portion lived with Sephardic Jews while settled in England.[58] This population had grown quickly enough to lead Elizabeth I to draft laws to remove the black presence from her kingdom during the late sixteenth century.[59] Nonetheless, for most Englishpersons the conception of the African did not come from the rare occurrence of encountering a Moorish court ornament, musician, or envoy. It did not come from the sporadic incidence of stumbling upon Africans on the streets of London or on ships in the ports of Liverpool or Plymouth. Rather, the conception of the African came through popular culture, out of what Jean Feerick has termed the shifting categories of race defined within "textual moments" articulated by English writers.[60]

Later fears of encountering Africans caused by these popular narratives increasingly created the tension necessary to define increasingly permanent racial differences. The popular theater became the essential space for marking these embodied experiences for how to encounter the racial other. The stage, either on the home isle or performing English plays in

[57] Colin Kidd, *British Identities before Nationalism: Ethnicity and Nationhood in the Atlantic World, 1600–1800* (Cambridge: Cambridge University Press, 1999), 11–12, 290–291.

[58] Onyeka, *Blackamoores: Africans in Tudor England, Their Presence, Status and Origins* (London: Narrative Eye, 2013), 1–18, 107–128.

[59] Emily Bartels, "Too Many Blackamoors: Deportation, Discrimination, and Elizabeth I," *Studies in English Literature, 1500–1900* 46, 2 (2006): 305–322; Laura Hunt Hume, *Strangers Settled Here Amongst Us: Policies, Perceptions, and the Presence of Aliens in Elizabethan England* (London: Routledge, 2003); Carole Levin and John Watkins, *Shakespeare's Foreign Worlds: National and Transnational Identities in the Elizabethan Age* (Ithaca, NY: Cornell University Press, 2009), 9–13; Leslie Fiedler, *The Stranger in Shakespeare* (New York: Stein and Day, 1972), 139–198.

[60] Jean Feerick, *Strangers in Blood: Relocating Race in the Renaissance* (Toronto: University of Toronto Press, 2010), quote on 21. For biographies of African men and women in England of the Tudor Era, see Miranda Kaufmann, *Black Tudors: The Untold Story* (London: Oneworld, 2018).

the colonies with the "intimate distance" of a perceived common Englishness, was the central area for creating what could or could not remain a part of what Elizabeth Dillon has termed the "performative commons." This discursive popular domain included textual spaces where identity was negotiated and debated by both performers and onlookers, while providing the discursive cultural space for acts of performative resistance.[61]

Emerging from the deep sexual fear of encountering the cultural other on the periphery, racial stereotypes from the popular stage recurrently pooled within the olfactory membranes. Literary descriptions of cultural scents of the other were referenced as both pungent and aromatically sensuous. Analysis of the term "foul" in its early modern contexts shows that what may seem an implicit reference to moral constitution was, during the era of Shakespeare, a synesthetic assertion of odor. Similarly, the aforementioned proverb "to wash a blackamoor white" contained implicit synesthetic concerns with odor that have been overlooked within the analysis of the axiom, used especially as analogy to the concept of striving in vain. These explicit and implicit textual references highlight how the literary use of smell linked African bodies to pungency in order to free England of its Roman and Renaissance label as a barbarian backwater. The shift from cultural descriptions of odor to stereotypical narratives of blackness that included inherent and biological smells occurred within the popular literature, religious debates, and political wrangling of seventeenth-century England.[62]

The term "foul" had many more linguistic implications than simply signifying a negative demeanor or moral malevolence. For many Englishpersons, the word inherently meant "scent," partially because odor was linked so strongly to marking the stenches of sin within classical and Christian traditions. "Foul" comes from the original Latin *pus*, implying stink, as in putridity. It retained much of this meaning prior to metaphorical attributions on the later English stage to ideas such as foul

---

[61] Elizabeth Maddock Dillon, *New World Drama: the Performative Commons in the Atlantic World, 1649–1849* (Durham, NC: Duke University Press, 2014), quotes on 13–16; Jacques Rancière, *Dissensus: On Politics and Aesthetics*, trans. Steve Corcoran (London: Continuum, 2010), 135–137; Jacques Rancière, *The Politics of Aesthetics: the Distribution of the Sensible*, trans. Gabriel Rockhill (London: Continuum, 2004), 32–50.

[62] For senses and the English stage, see Jonathan Gil Harris, *Untimely Matter in the Time of Shakespeare* (Philadelphia: University of Pennsylvania, 2009), 125–128; Jonathan Gil Harris, "The Smell of Macbeth," *Shakespeare Quarterly* 58, 4 (2007): 465–486; Jennifer Waldron, *Reformations of the Body: Idolatry, Sacrifice, and Early Modern Theater* (Basingstoke: Palgrave Macmillan, 2013), 55–84.

play. The use of the term "foul" in modern parlance elicits moral disquiet, the movement beyond an ethical boundary, even the penalty for breaking that principled limit. During the time of Shakespeare, "foul" usually also meant "pungent"; the term meant "odor" not in the sense of a specifically stinking item, as "pungent" implies today, but "pungent" in the connected moral, ethical, religious, and intersensorial sense. Thus, when English writers summarized the foul "blackamoor" or African they referenced not only the moral foulness of supposed paganism but also a specific and universalizing African odor that was associated to blackness as both implicitly anti-Christian and increasingly racially coded.[63]

These references to "foul" appeared often within the increasingly racialized literatures of early modern England. Thomas Heywood's *The Four Prentices of London* (1615), performed as early as the 1590s, described the foulness of an "Aethiop" as a metaphor for becoming the other when wearing burnt cork as blackface.[64] Francis Bacon's *New Atlantis* (1626) included the tale of a pious hermit who "desired to see the Spirit of Fornication; and there appeared to him a little foul ugly Aethiop."[65] Shakespeare's *Antony and Cleopatra* (1607) had similarly used the olfactory informed reference of foulness to portray Cleopatra as a "foul Egyptian" who "hath betrayed" the noble Antony.[66] Likewise, the duplicitousness of women was portrayed as "foul and blacker than/ The Night, or sun-burnt African," in English Bishop Henry King's poem "The Defense."[67] Additionally, Lady Mary Wroth's *Urania* (1621)

---

[63] For "foul" on the stage, see Natasha Korda, *Shakespeare's Domestic Economies: Gender and Property in Early Modern England* (Philadelphia: University of Pennsylvania, 2002), 85–86; Hristomir Stanev, *Sensory Experience and the Metropolis on the Jacobean Stage (1603–1625)* (Farnham: Ashgate, 2014), 160–161; Lemuel Johnson, *Shakespeare in Africa (& Other Venues): Import & the Appropriation of Culture* (Trenton, NJ: Africa World, 1998), 80–92; Anne Mangum, *Reflection of Africa in Elizabethan and Jacobean Drama and Poetry* (Lewiston, NY: Edwin Mellen Press, 2002), 41–50; Holly Dugan, "*Coriolanus* and the 'Rank-Scented Meinie': Smelling Rank in Early Modern England," in *Masculinity and the Metropolis of Vice, 1550–1650*, eds. Amanda Bailey and Roze Hentschell (New York: Palgrave Macmillan, 2010), 139–159.

[64] Thomas Heywood and Mary Ann Weber Gasior, *The Four Prentices of London: A Critical, Old-Spelling Edition* (New York: Garland, 1980 [1615]), quotes on 60–61.

[65] Jordan, *White over Black*, quote on 17.

[66] William Shakespeare, "Antony and Cleopatra," in *The Arden Shakespeare: Complete Works*, ed. Richard Proudfoot (London: Thomson Learning, 2007), 121–160, quote on 150.

[67] Henry King and Lawrence Mason, *The English Poems of Henry King* (New Haven: Yale University Press, 1914), quote on 40.

involved a complex plot that worked to subvert gender categories through the application of racial embodiment using similar language. Within this intricate work, the term "foul" introduced a discussion on the immortality of the manipulations of skin color that might have affected the categories of nobility central to the play.[68]

Similar synesthetic use of the term was applied within Shakespeare's most racially analyzed plays, *Titus Andronicus* (1594) and *Othello* (1603). Throughout his canon, and especially as a part of these dramas, Shakespeare often explored everyday experience through a mixed style that linked the high culture of literature with the low culture of the common audience.[69] Part of this mixed style often involved imposing upon his audiences a new "material logic" that relayed how to sense what was being performed on stage as a means to overcome the barrier between what could not be understood through spoken language alone.[70]

Titus Andronicus (1594) represents forms of English stereotypes about the Moor within a play about violence, race, language, and the role of the barbarian within ancient Rome.[71] The production's indispensable character, Aaron, is an evil dark-skinned prisoner of the Roman general Titus Andronicus who starts the play returning from conquering the Goths and their barbarian Queen Tamora. After family squabbling and numerous murders, Tamora vows revenge on Titus. Tamora's lover, the Moor Aaron, persuades Tamora's two sons to violently rape Lavinia, the daughter of Titus. This scene, one of the most horrific in Shakespeare's catalogue, shapes the violent contours of the play, which concludes with Tamora's consumption of her two convicted rapist sons within a pie baked by Titus. The racial contexts of the play involve the affair between Tamora and Aaron, which produced a mixed-race child that Aaron must

---

[68] Kim Hall, "'I Rather Would Wish to be a Black-Moor': Beauty, Race, and Rank in Lady Mary Wroth's 'Urania'," in *Women, "Race," and Writing in the Early Modern Period*, eds. Margo Hendricks and Patricia Parker (London: Routledge, 1994), 178–194; Mary Wroth and Simon van de Pass, *The Countesse of Mountgomeries Urania* (London: Augustine Mathewes for John Marriott and John Grismand, 1621), 29–30, 144.

[69] Erich Auerbach, *Mimesis: The Representation of Reality in Western Literature* (Princeton, NJ: Princeton University Press, 2003 [1953]), 201–231, 312–313. Unlike the publication dates for other texts, which generally reference print dates except when noted, the in-text publication dates for Shakespeare's texts reference initial performances.

[70] Catherine Richardson, *Shakespeare and Material Culture* (Oxford: Oxford University Press, 2011), 193–196.

[71] For an introduction to race and *Titus Andronicus*, see Francesca Royster, "White-Limed Walls: Whiteness and Gothic Extremism in Shakespeare's *Titus Andronicus*," *Shakespeare Quarterly* 51, 4 (2000): 432–455.

keep secret by murdering the midwife and fleeing into the Roman forests. To save his child once captured, Aaron reveals Tamora's plot to destroy Titus's family, and for his honesty he is buried to die of starvation.[72]

Aaron is undoubtedly an evil character within a violent and tragic play. Scholars have debated the importance of his race to the performance and have generally agreed that his dark hue would have been essential to the drama's meaning for early modern spectators. Numerous times within the play, Shakespeare references the "foul" actions set in motion by Aaron. Specifically, when the mutilated Lavinia is revealed, her brother Marcus proclaims: "O, why should nature build so foul a den,/ Unless the Gods delight in tragedies."[73] As Virginia Vaughn described, the play was partially based on the seventeenth story of Italian polymath and Bishop Matteo Bandello's collected novels of 1554, which tells the story of similar Moorish-induced love triangles with parallel levels of intense violence. The original story ends with a suicide by the malicious Moor when he has accomplished his most dastardly deceits. For Bandello, the moral is that "men should not make use of slaves of this sort, for ... they are seldom found faithful and are mostly full of all manner of filth and uncleanness and stink at all seasons like buck-goats."[74]

Shakespeare also often used African stories to influence the writing of many of his works.[75] Through this authorial acquainting, the bard penned *Othello* as a play that questioned and possibly reinforced categories about Africa, race, honor, and gender through the common trope of the false

[72] For more on the racial complexity of *Titus Andronicus*, see Ian Smith, "Those 'slippery customers': Rethinking Race in *Titus Andronicus*," *Journal of Theatre and Drama* 3 (1997): 45–58; Jean Feerick, "Botanical Shakespeares: The Racial Logic of Plant Life in *Titus Andronicus*," *South Central Review* 26, 1–2 (2009): 82–102; Jeannette White, "'Is Black so Base a Hue': Shakespeare's Aaron and the Politics and Poetics of Race," *CLA Journal* 40, 3 (1997): 336–366; Carolyn Sale, "Black Aeneas: Race, English Literary History, and the 'Barbarous' Poetics of *Titus Andronicus*," *Shakespeare Quarterly* 62, 1 (2011): 25–52.

[73] William Shakespeare, "Titus Andronicus," in *The Arden Shakespeare: Complete Works*, ed. Richard Proudfoot (London: Thomson Learning, 2007), 1125–1218, quote on 1127.

[74] Virginia Mason Vaughan, *Performing Blackness on English Stages, 1500–1800* (Cambridge: Cambridge University Press, 2005), quotes on 43–44; Matteo Bandello and John Payne, Volume V of *The Novels; Now First Done into English Prose and Verse* (London: Villon Society, 1890), 277–278.

[75] Wole Soyinka, "Shakespeare the Living Dramatist," in *Shakespeare and Race*, eds. Catherine M. S. Alexander and Stanley Wells (New York: Cambridge University Press, 2000), 82–100; Diana Adesola Mafe, "From Ògún to Othello: (Re)Acquainting Yoruba Myth and Shakespeare's Moor," *Research in African Literatures* 35 (2004): 46–61; Rosalind Johnson, "Parallels between Othello and the Historical Leo Africanus," *Bim* 18, 70 (1986): 9–34.

cuckold.[76] Many argue *Othello* is also a play about the assertion of English identity that was meant, in part, to cure Anglo-Saxon concerns with inferiority.[77] The essential narrative follows from the coupling of Othello, a Moorish general, and Desdemona, a white Venetian. The antagonist Iago tricks Othello into believing that Desdemona has committed adultery, thus leading to the final climactic scene where Othello murders his perceived adulteress wife. Scholars have debated the racial contexts of the play since the time of Samuel Taylor Coleridge and the early Shakespearean critics.[78] Most agree that the play is motivated, but not driven, by a racial conception of Othello that early modern English audiences generally shared.[79]

Consequently, when Iago referenced Othello's thoughts of being cuckolded through a synesthetic allusion to the foulness of Desdemona's possible betrayal, Shakespeare continued to inform early modern England as to the duplicitous scents of foul sensuality: "Ay, there's the

[76] For introduction to *Othello* and gender, see Patricia Parker, "Fantasies of Race and Gender: Africa, Othello, and Bringing to Light," in *Women, "Race," and Writing in the Early Modern Period*, eds. Margo Hendricks and Patricia Parker (London: Routledge, 1994), 84–100.

[77] Michael Neill, "'Mulattos,' 'Blacks,' and 'Indian Moors': Othello and Early Modern Constructions of Human Difference," *Shakespeare Quarterly* 49, 4 (1998): 361–374; Dennis Austin Britton, *Becoming Christian: Race, Reformation, and Early Modern English Romance* (New York: Fordham University Press, 2014), 112–141; Ian Smith, "Barbarian Errors: Performing Race in Early Modern England," *Shakespeare Quarterly* 49, 2 (1998): 168–186; Ian Smith, *Race and Rhetoric in the Renaissance: Barbarian Errors* (New York: Palgrave Macmillan, 2009), 97–121; Martin Orkin, "Othello and the 'Plain Face' Of Racism," *Shakespeare Quarterly* 38, 2 (1987): 166–188; Philip Armstrong, *Shakespeare's Visual Regime: Tragedy, Psychoanalysis, and the Gaze* (Houndmills: Palgrave, 2000), 57–90; Mark Burnett, *Constructing Monsters in Shakespeare's Drama and Early Modern Culture* (New York: Palgrave Macmillan, 2014), 95–124.

[78] For Othello, race, national origin, and keyword analysis, see Shaul Bassi, *Shakespeare's Italy and Italy's Shakespeare: Place, "Race," Politics* (New York: Palgrave Macmillan, 2016), 43–62; Patricia Parker, *Shakespearean Intersections: Language, Contexts, Critical Keywords* (Philadelphia: University of Pennsylvania Press, 2018), 210–272; Phyllis Natalie Braxton, "Othello: The Moor and the Metaphor," *South Atlantic Review* 55, 4 (1990): 1–17.

[79] For more on *Othello* and race, see Ian Smith, "We Are Othello: Speaking of Race in Early Modern Studies," *Shakespeare Quarterly* 67, 1 (2016): 104–124; Michael Neill, "Unproper Beds: Race, Adultery, and the Hideous in *Othello*," *Shakespeare Quarterly* 40, 4 (1989): 383–412; Arthur Little, *Shakespeare Jungle Fever: National-Imperial Re-Visions of Race, Rape, and Sacrifice* (Stanford, CA: Stanford University Press, 2000), 68–101; Janet Adelman, "Iago's Alter Ego: Race as Projection in *Othello*," *Shakespeare Quarterly* 48, 2 (1997): 125–144; Ben Saunders, "Iago's Clyster: Purgation, Anality, and the Civilizing Process," *Shakespeare Quarterly* 55, 2 (2004): 148–176.

point: as, to be bold with you,/ Not to affect many proposed matches/ Of her own clime, complexion, and degree,/ Whereto, we see, in all things nature tends;/ Foh! one may smell in such, a will most rank/ Foul disproportion, thoughts unnatural."[80] Also referencing the foulness of African odors within the play, Shakespeare implicitly renders a cultural summary of African religious fetishes and the fear of Christian Europe to the spiritual other.[81] When Brabantio, the father of Desdemona, first learned of Othello's wishes upon his daughter he used the olfactory terminology to describe Othello as a "foul thief," who had "enchanted" his daughter with a mixture of African sexuality and implicit tribal witchcraft, proclaiming that he had "practiced on her with foul charms" and "abused her delicate youth with drugs or minerals."[82] Each reference to "foul" triggered sensations within the English audience that linked the low culture of foul smells with the high culture of using "foul" to describe morality, further connecting smells to bodies through the synesthetic hearing of specific terms.[83]

Such an understanding of mixed narrative was also present within the olfactory descriptions applied within *The Tempest* (1610).[84] That specific production centers on the political manipulations of Prospero, who hopes

[80] William Shakespeare, "Othello," in *The Arden Shakespeare: Complete Works*, ed. Richard Proudfoot (London: Thomson Learning, 2007), 941–978, quotes on 933–935.

[81] For more on the disparagement of African religions and racism, see Peter Mark, "Fetishers, 'Marybuckes' and the Christian Norm: European Images of Senegambians and Their Religions, 1550–1760," *African Studies Review* 23, 2 (September, 1980): 91–99.

[82] Shakespeare, "Othello," quotes on 946–948.

[83] For Shakespeare, keywords, and ideology, see Jonathan Lamb, *Shakespeare in the Marketplace of Words* (Cambridge: Cambridge University Press, 2017), 1–32; Parker, *Shakespearean Intersections*, 1–31; Guido Giglioni, "Sense," in *Renaissance Keywords*, ed. Ita Mac Carthy (New York: Routledge, 2017), 13–30; Patricia Parker, *Shakespeare from the Margins: Language, Culture, Context* (Chicago: University of Chicago Press, 1996), 20–55; Ayesha Ramachandran, *The Worldmakers: Global Imagining in Early Modern Europe* (Chicago: University of Chicago Press, 2016), 10–32; Arthur Greene, *Five Words: Critical Semantics in the Age of Shakespeare and Cervantes* (Chicago: University of Chicago Press, 2013), 107–142; William Empson, *The Structure of Complex Words* (London: Penguin Books, 1995 [1951]), 19–34.

[84] For introductions to race and *The Tempest*, see Alden Vaughan and Virginia Mason Vaughan, *Shakespeare's Caliban: A Cultural History* (Cambridge: Cambridge University Press, 1991), 4–12, 32–36; Peter Platt, *Reason Diminished: Shakespeare and the Marvelous* (Lincoln: University of Nebraska Press, 1997), 169–187; Fiedler, *Stranger in Shakespeare*, 234–244; Thomas Cartelli, "Prospero in Africa: *The Tempest* as Colonialist Text and Pretext," in *Shakespeare Reproduced: The Text in History and Ideology*, eds. Jean Howard and Marion O'Connor (New York: Methuen, 1987), 99–115.

to restore his daughter, Miranda, to her perceived rightful royal station. To produce her correct residence, Prospero conjures a storm to trap his political rivals, including his brother Antonio, upon an island. On that isle, Prospero's political rivals encounter mysterious and magical scenes that force political agreements with Prospero. Many of those passages involved the confusing figure of Caliban. For many scholars, the racially ambiguous oddity Caliban represents the cacophonous confusion and possible resistance that Europeans met when encountering the shores of both Africa and the New World.[85]

Jodi Byrd has recently traced how the court jester Trinculo's attribution of a "fish" smell to Caliban in *The Tempest* represents the monstrosity of the racial other, even as the commodified language used to signify dried market fish and "strange" odors may also indicate capital, marine ambiguity, and veiled subaltern power.[86] As with the characters of Othello and Aaron, Caliban's portrayal within *The Tempest* marks a moment in early modern England when numerous categories of human, climate, and race were originally being debated.[87] These deliberations, prompted by ethnographical observations and global discoveries, involved European metropoles of the early seventeenth century taking the culturally defined ethnographies of the peripheries and creating universalizing stereotypes on the stage and page.[88] The material cultures that Shakespeare applied,

[85] John Demaray, *Shakespeare and the Spectacles of Strangeness:* The Tempest *and the Transformation of Renaissance Theatrical Forms* (Pittsburgh, PA: Duquesne University Press, 1998), 53–61; Jonathan Bate, "Caliban and Ariel Write Back," in *Shakespeare and Race*, eds. Catherine Alexander and Stanley Wells (New York: Cambridge, 2000), 165–176; Jan Kott, *The Bottom Translation: Marlowe and Shakespeare and the Carnival Tradition* (Evanston, IL: Northwestern University Press, 1987), 84–106.

[86] Jodi Byrd, *The Transit of Empire: Indigenous Critiques of Colonialism* (Minneapolis: University of Minnesota Press, 2011), quote on 55; Burnett, *Constructing Monsters*, 125–153. See also colonialism, metaphors, dependency, and *The Tempest* within Octave Mannoni, *Prospero and Caliban: The Psychology of Colonization* (Ann Arbor: University of Michigan Press, 2008 [1950]).

[87] Julián Jiménez Heffernan, *Shakespeare's Extremes: Wild Man, Monster, Beast* (New York: Palgrave Macmillan, 2015), 109–150; Mary Floyd-Wilson, *English Ethnicity and Race in Early Modern Drama* (Cambridge: Cambridge University Press, 2003), 67–86; John Gillies, *Shakespeare and the Geography of Difference* (Cambridge: Cambridge University Press, 1994), 24–28.

[88] For more on Shakespeare and sensation, see Kenneth Gross, *Shakespeare's Noise* (Chicago: University of Chicago Press, 2001), 88–118; Katharine Craik, *Reading Sensations in Early Modern England* (Basingstoke: Palgrave Macmillan, 2007); Lowell Gallagher and Shankar Raman, "Introduction," in *Knowing Shakespeare: Senses, Embodiment and Cognition*, eds. Lowell Gallagher and Shankar Raman (Basingstoke: Palgrave Macmillan, 2010), 1–29; Michael Neill, "'Noises, Sounds, and Sweet Airs': The Burden of Shakespeare's *Tempest*," *Shakespeare Quarterly* 59, 1 (2008):

both on the stage as tangible objects and through using specific terms to signal to his audiences physical perceptions, contributed to alterations within English sensory consciousness, increasingly trained to experience the other in newly racist ways.[89]

Because of these increasing allocations of inherent race to black characters on the English stage, Englishpersons came to a greater belief that blackness naturally smelled. This attribution was part of a racialized knowledge that increasingly became embodied throughout the seventeenth century. The intense racial marking applied in Lewis Machin and Gervase Markham's *The Dumbe Knight* (1608) represents such a reiterative semantic manacle between dirt and blackness. The authors used the pungent term "sooty" to describe resistance to an arranged marriage for Philocles, the dumb knight. Pleading to the King of Cyprus, the protagonist Philocles summarized disdain for the proposed bride: "But not me my thrice royall soveraigne./ I'le rather wed a sooty blackamoore,/ A Leaper, monster, Incubus or hagge,/ A wretch deformd in nature, loath'd of men/ Then her that hath bemonster'd my pure soule,/ Her scorne and pride had almost lost her life,/ A maid so faulted, seldome proves' good wife."[90] In the translation of Italian humourist Trajano Boccalini's *New-Found Politicke* (1626), Englishpersons would have been commonly aware enough of these racialized and gendered tropes to understand the metaphor applied by Boccalini regarding the stench of the Moor to portray the disdain for three women being allowed to enter an academic organization within ancient Greece. These "Poeticall Ladies of

---

36–59; Patricia Parker, "Rude Mechanicals," in *Subject and Object in Renaissance Culture*, ed. Margreta De Grazia (Cambridge: Cambridge University Press, 2002), 43–82; Holly Dugan, "Shakespeare and the Senses," *Literature Compass* 6, 3 (2009): 726–740; Colleen Kennedy, "Performing and Perfuming on the Early Modern Stage: A Study of William Lower's The Phaenix in Her Flames," *Early English Studies* 4 (2011): 1–33; Richard Altick, "Hamlet and the Odor of Mortality," *Shakespeare Quarterly* 5, 2 (Spring 1954): 167–176; Danielle Nagler, "Towards the Smell of Mortality: Shakespeare and Ideas of Smell 1588–1625," *Cambridge Quarterly* 26, 1 (1997): 42–58.

[89] For more on Shakespeare, language, and material knowledge, see Jonathan Dollimore, *Radical Tragedy: Religion, Ideology, and Power in the Drama of Shakespeare and His Contemporaries* (Chicago: University of Chicago Press, 1984); Karen Newman, "'And Wash the Ethiop White': Femininity and the Monstrous in *Othello*," in *Shakespeare Reproduced: The Text in History and Ideology*, eds. Jean Howard and Marion O'Connor (New York: Methuen, 1987), 143–162; Ian Smith, "White Skin, Black Masks: Racial Cross-Dressing on the Early Modern Stage," *Renaissance Drama* 32 (2003): 33–68; Dennis Kezar, "Shakespeare's Addictions," *Critical Inquiry* 30, 1 (2003): 31–62.

[90] Lewis Machin and Gervase Markham, *The Dumbe Knight* (London: Nicholas Okes, 1608), quotes on 19–20.

Parnassus" read sonnets to the "Academicall Corporation" that "offended *Apolloes* divine nostrills worse than the stinke of a - Blackamore."[91] Such commonsensical uses of the dirtiness and smell of blackness, in such an obvious manner referenced through the increasingly common political allegory of ancient Greece, imply the consistent use of racist tropes within the common transnational European culture of the early seventeenth century that increasingly asserted normative whiteness as pure and blackness as dirty and stinking.[92]

English culture continued with a seventeenth-century racializing program through often defining African nations as overly sexual and jealous of their women.[93] The intensive sexual anxiety of encountering Africans was portrayed in Robert Heath's *Clarastella* (1650). This collection of literature included a brief poem entitled "To a Lascivious Blackamoore Woman." In that selection, Heath composed: "'Tis Night in thine, in my face day: but yet/ Should wee joyn; wee might mongrel twilight get;/ A Tawny-moore that would of both partake:/ Haunt me not Shade! I'l no new monster make."[94] The child of miscegenation, for Heath, was a "new monster" that the dark-skinned woman hoped to create through a form of sexual trickery against her pure English lover. Richard Brome's play *The English Moor, or the Mock-Marriage* (1659), possibly performed as early as 1637, likewise exposed such anxiety when a wife was painted black and a crowd instantly believed her to be offering sexual favors.[95] A similar sexual apprehension caused by the temptation of an African woman can be found in nonconformist preacher and politician William Greenhill's *Sound-Hearted Christian* (1670). In that sermon, Greenhill stated: "if a man be in love with a Blackamore, it may be she hath a good feature, but she is black … [T]he world is but

[91] Trajano Boccalini, William Vaughan, John Florio, and Thomas Scott, *The New-Found Politicke* (London: Francis Williams, 1626), quote on 201–202.
[92] For more on whiteness in Shakespeare, see Kim Hall, "'These bastard signs of fair': Literary Whiteness in Shakespeare's Sonnets," in *Shakespeare and Race*, eds. Catherine Alexander and Stanley Wells (New York: Cambridge, 2000), 64–83.
[93] Carolyn Prager, "'If I Be Devil': English Renaissance Response to the Proverbial and Ecumenical Ethiopian," *Journal of Medieval and Renaissance Studies* 17, 2 (Fall, 1987): 257–279.
[94] Robert Heath, *Clarastella: Together with Poems Occasional, Elegies, Epigrams, Satyrs* (London: Moseley, 1650), quotes on 1–2.
[95] Richard Brome, *Five New Playes, Viz. The English Moor, or the Mock-Marriage. The Love-Sick Court, or the Ambitious Politique: Covent Garden Weeded. The New Academy, or the New Exchange. The Queen and Concubine* (London: A. Crook and H. Brome, 1659), 36–40.

a Blackamore, an evil thing, and it's full of corruption."⁹⁶ This understanding of the sexuality of the other, usually arising from sources
within the relatively objective ethnography previously analyzed, changed the English mind to induce a racist defense mechanism that was
articulated as universalizing on the stage and through the pen.⁹⁷

Within the combative cultural sphere of the theatre, analogously denoting a growing commonsensical olfactory racism that relied on removing
the sexual connection between black and white bodies, was the play *Lust's
Dominion* (1657), usually attributed to Thomas Dekker and possibly
performed in decades prior. The performance centers upon the machinations of an evil and murderous Moorish character Eleazar, who gained
power in the court of the King of Fez, earning his role as Prince through
malicious politicking.⁹⁸ The brutal Moor feigned love to the Queen
Mother to get closer to the King and murdered the Queen Mother's son
Philip. In a dramatic conclusion to the play, Eleazar then kills the Queen
Mother and the King through a vain attempt to gain the throne. His plans
are dashed as he himself is run through. The internal evil, in this final
failure, was previously linked to his internal odors and race. Philip, pre-
paring for his unsuccessful contest, had proclaimed: "Ambition plumes
the Moor, whilst black despair,/ Offering to tear from him the diadem/
Which he usurps, makes him to cry at all,/ And to act deeds beyond
astonishment;/ But Philip is the night that dark his glories:/ This sword,
yet reeking with his negro's blood,/ Being grasp'd by equity and this strong
arm,/ Shall through and through."⁹⁹ The play, especially as a text that
came to modernity without a specifically defined author, represents an
early modern England that had set for the Moor an evil level of sexual
jealousy and offered the African's internal flowing blood as pungent. As
scholars have often portrayed, throughout the Early Modern Era the
general understanding of what moderns call "race" shifted from the idea
of bloodlines within a specific family, or the Greco-Roman idea of *gens*, to
a more virulent idea that race was a marker of difference at a biological

---

⁹⁶ William Greenhill, *The Sound-Hearted Christian, or, A Treatise of Soundness of Heart
    with Several Other Sermons* (London: Crouch, 1670), quotes on 318–319.
⁹⁷ Joel Fineman, *Shakespeare's Perjured Eye: The Invention of Poetic Subjectivity in the
    Sonnets* (Berkeley: University of California Press, 1986), 42–46.
⁹⁸ For this debate on authorship, see Arthur Freeman and Janet Ing Freeman, *John Payne
    Collier: Scholarship and Forgery in the Nineteenth Century* (New Haven, CT: Yale
    University Press, 2004), 130–133.
⁹⁹ Christopher Marlowe and George Robinson, *The Works of Christopher Marlowe*
    (London: W. Pickering, 1826 [1657]), 268–270, quote on 270.

level that defined one group as less human than another. This shift to universalizing categories of race, whether from these genealogical customs or broader religious and climatological knowledges, occurred within the public sphere, whereby popular performances alerted English audiences to the perceptual difference of the other through increasingly stereotypical terminologies of darkness and pungency as something that could no longer be washed away through religious conversion.[100]

TORTURED SKIN UPON THE SCOURED BLACKAMOOR

The foul and increasingly biological African odors that consistently appeared within popular texts and on the stage were also linguistically tied through implicit metaphorical and synesthetic links to the axiomatic tradition, from roots within Jeremiah 13:23, that one could not "wash the blackamoor white." Originally from a Greek proverb, the idea of not being able to change black skin to white became a rhetorical tool for humanist disputants of the sixteenth century. From the Renaissance to the early seventeenth century, many in Europe applied the phrase to visual art and poetry. Political discourses from the later English Civil War also used many references to washing blackamoors to describe the evils of different political factions and their ineffectual attempts to usurp power. The implicit links between hopelessly washing and black skin grew to encompass more than simply a visual metaphor amongst these political and social disputants. The implication of washing tied the blackamoor not only to a darker hue but also to a murkier scent, a stinking spoor linked to blackness that was increasingly being used to define a separate and pungent race.

One of the most substantial early modern references to this proverb came from English emblem book author, poet, and illustrator Geffrey Whitney, who applied the metaphor both visually and textually within his *A Choice of Emblemes and Other Devises* (1586). Beneath a heading where an image of a dark-skinned man in a tub was being furiously washed by two fully clothed and clean white men, Whitney summarized: "Leave of with paine, the blackamore to skowre,/ With washinge ofte, and

---

[100] For general shifts from climatology to modern racism, see Kwame Anthony Appiah, "Race," in *Critical Terms for Literary Study*, eds. Frank Lentricchia and Thomas McLaughlin (Chicago: University of Chicago Press, 1995), 274–287; A. J. Hoenselaars, *Images of Englishmen and Foreigners in the Drama of Shakespeare and His Contemporaries: A Study of Stage Characters and National Identity in English Renaissance Drama, 1558–1642* (Rutherford, NJ: Fairleigh Dickinson University Press, 1992), 15–25.

wipinge more then due."[101] The use of the metaphor within such religious and rhetorical texts increased the presence of the image and repetitive terms for the abortive washing of the blackamoor into the general public.

Michael Drayton's poetic reimagining within *The True Chronicle History of King Leir, and His Three Daughters, Gonorill, Ragan, and Cordella* similarly relayed the metaphor in 1605, emphasizing through the words of the neglected Cordelia: "As easy is it for the Blackamoore,/ To wash the tawny colour from his skin,/ Which all oppose against the course of nature,/ As I am able to forget my father."[102] Pamphlet author and courtesy essayist Joseph Swetnam expanded the comparison to describe the fault of marrying a widow compared to the fruitlessness of trying to wash a blackamoor white in his *Araignment of Lewd, Idle, and Unconstant Women* (1615). He summarized, through the pseudonym Thomas Tell-Troth, that in taking on a widow the "unfortunate" husband must make the woman "forget her former corrupt and disordered behaviour, the which if thou take upon thee to doe, thou hadst even as good undertake to wash a Blackamore white."[103] The fable was revitalized from ancient roots as part of a newfangled literature of English racialization.

The return of the Greeks and Romans to literary prominence also ignited interest for the Aesop fable and its derivative proverb within the Old Testament. English Puritan Henry Burton's *Truth's Triumph over Trent* (1629) applied the phrase as part of a Reformation text to describe the perceived vanity of Aristotelian scholars who chose allegiance with the Counter-Reformation when stating: "They but wash the Blackamore, when they thinke to have Aristotle to be our adversary."[104] Welsh poet George Herbert's *Remains* (1652) used the metaphor through a list of common allegories meant to convey the idea of certainty to English audiences. He noted, "Of a pigs taile you can never make a good shaft/ The Bathe of the Blackamoor hath sworne not to whiten."[105] During

---

[101] Geffrey Whitney, *A Choice of Emblems and Other Devises: For the Most Part Gathered Out of Sundrie Writers* (Leyden: Francis Raphelengius, 1586), quote on 57.

[102] Michael Drayton and Thomas Heywood, *The True Chronicle History of King Leir, and His Three Daughters, Gonorill, Ragan, and Cordella* (London: Simon Stafford for John Wright, 1605), quotes on 18–19.

[103] Joseph Swetnam, *The Araignment of Lewd, Idle, Froward, and Unconstant Women* (London: George Purslowe for Thomas Archer, 1615), quotes on 59–60.

[104] Henry Burton, *Truth's Triumph over Trent, or, The Great Gulfe Betweene Sion and Babylon* (London: Sparke, 1629), quote on 250–252.

[105] George Herbert and Barnabas Oley, *Herbert's Remains, or, Sundry Pieces of That Sweet Singer of the Temple* (London: Timothy Garthwait, 1652), quotes on 154–155.

FIGURE I.I Print of "Pears Soap Advertisement based on Aesop's fable, 1884." This advertisement appeared in *The Graphic* on December 18, 1884. Courtesy of the British Library

the mid-seventeenth century, the use of this metaphor took on new intensity within numerous political debates of the English Civil War and the Restoration. The proportional growth in the use of the allegory provides implicit evidence of a growing racial sentiment in England that was marked by the inability to wash away black skin and associated implications of dark scents.[106] The constant and repetitive assertion of these phrases from a fable implies moments when race became something increasingly certain within English sensory consciousness. These maxims burgeoned within English popular culture, to such an extent that much later advertising involved the use of the blackamoor fable, as within the Pears Soap Advertisements of the later Victorian Era (see Figure I.I).

Denying the inherent fraternity of mankind, earlier English authors had allegorized the meanings of whiteness and blackness upon a scale of

[106] For more examples, see John Goodwin and George Glover, *Hybristodikai: The Obstructours of Justice* (London: Henry Cripps and Lodowick Lloyd, 1649), 67–70; John Cook, *Monarchy, No Creature of Gods Making* (Waterford, Ireland: Peter de Pienne, 1651), 88–98.

increased certainty as racialized textual moments became increasingly common and clarified on the stage and page. For example, English non-conformist cleric Anthony Burgess's *Spiritual Refining* (1652) offered a long discourse on the blackamoor metaphor and the possibilities of baptism, cleanliness, and purity. In doing, Burgess continued the wider cultural project of defining race through his use of the axiom to discuss the very inability to baptize or clean the dark-skinned body: "Doe not thou then rest in thy Baptism, doe not presume upon that; for unlesse thereby thou art taught to loath thy self for sinne: unlesse thou art washed from filthy sinnes and lustfull wayes, this washing is no more to thee, than the washing of a Blackamoor, which leaves him as deformed as he was."[107] This use of the metaphor within this specific text works in two ways: first, to assert the hollowness of believing that baptism, without an unsoiled life, would enter one into heaven; and second, more subversively and subconsciously, to demarcate a commonsense proclamation of race through the inability of any blackamoor to achieve religious cleanliness.[108]

Throughout the seventeenth century, these assertions of the inability of other races to achieve religious purity or an equal space as part of civic life became increasingly common. For Jewish populations in England, odors were also increasingly linked to something different than within religious cultures that could be transcended through conversion. English polymath and natural philosopher Thomas Browne's popular *Psuedodoxia Epidemica* (1646), repeatedly published and frequently noted in contemporary works, submitted absurdist summaries of Judaism with an understanding of the natural "stink" of Jews that had existed as a religious trope from earlier eras.[109] For Presbyterian theologian John Weemes in the

---

[107] Anthony Burgess, *Spiritual Refining: Or, A Treatise of Grace and Assurance* (London: A. Miller for Thomas Underhill, 1652), quotes on 377–378.

[108] Religious metaphor was vital elsewhere in the making of race as a deeply scented phenomenon, especially as blackamoors often appeared in numerous plays and literature as stereotypical references to demons and devils. Stage productions commonly used the figure of a Moorish boy to tie these devil and demons to blackness. For example, in Richard Carpenter's *The Pragmatical Jesuit* (1665), a "Blackamoor Boy" was represented as the puppet of the pungent Lucifer who worked to subvert London politics. Richard Carpenter, *A New Play Call'd The Pragmatical Jesuit New-Leven'd A Comedy* (London: N. R., 1665), 2–3.

[109] Mary Campbell, *Wonder & Science: Imagining Worlds in Early Modern Europe* (Ithaca: Cornell University Press, 1999), 85–96; Thomas Browne, Edward Dod, Andrew Crooke, William Wordsworth, and Thomas Dunham Whitaker, *Pseudodoxia Epidemica, or, Enquiries into Very Many Received Tenents, and Commonly Presumed Truths* (London: Edward Dod, 1658), 255–257.

earlier 1630s, the Mark of Cain had fallen upon Jewish bodies as a consistently pungent and generational signifier of an original evil. The Mark of Cain, like the Curse of Ham, implied that a religious act of the past, as with Cain's murder of Abel, marked specific races to suffer upon the earth. For Weemes, as a "judgment upon their bodies" for their ancestor's mortal action, God marked the "posteritie" of Jewish populations with a "leprosie" that provided a perpetually "loathsome and stinking smell" and an associated "stinking breath." As Geraldine Heng has summarized, these anti-Semitic tropes helped to establish England as the first racial state of the West, whereby racism asserted greater force through sensory feelings of disgust against Jewish bodies that, like Africans, were increasingly understood as unable to be cleansed.[110]

Religious and cultural definitions of odor frequently took on these increasing associations between the stereotypes of subaltern bodies and the pungency of a past evil. Racialism mixed cultural thoughts about smell and increasingly biological concerns with pungent difference to create a varied and mixed brand of English racism out of the London core. As part of these sensory definitions, Lord Mayor's Pageants paraded Africans throughout the streets of London as a marker of English imperial superiority throughout the seventeenth century.[111] These African bodies marched with markers of an idealized and romantic wilderness past. Many times, scent was inherently associated to these marches through

---

[110] John Weemes, *A Treatise of the Foure Degenerate Sonnes viz. the Atheist the Magician the Idolater and the Jew* (London: Thomas Cotes, 1636), quotes on 329–331; Geraldine Heng, *England and the Jews: How Religion and Violence Created the First Racial State in the West* (Cambridge: Cambridge University Press, 2019), 71–73. See also sensory performances of racism against Jews within Elizabeth Krimmer, "Jewish Ears and Aryan Dirndls: National Socialist Racial Ideology and Jewish Identity," in *Sentient Performativities of Embodiment: Thinking alongside the Human*, eds. Lynette Hunter, Elisabeth Krimmer and Peter Lichtenfels (Lanham, MD: Lexington, 2016), 247–266.

[111] Tracey Hill, *Pageantry and Power: A Cultural History of the Early Modern Lord Mayor's Show, 1585–1639* (Manchester: Manchester University Press, 2010), 4–6. Catherine Molineaux has recently shown how these shows informed later popular representations of Africans in the British public sphere through images of Africans on shop signs, trading cards, and board games. Catherine Molineux, *Faces of Perfect Ebony: Encountering Atlantic Slavery in Imperial Britain* (Cambridge, MA: Harvard University Press, 2012). For a reading of later parades, see the nineteenth-century performances in London as similarly racialized within Sadiah Qureshi, *Peoples on Parade: Exhibitions, Empire, and Anthropology in Nineteenth Century Britain* (Chicago: University of Chicago Press, 2011), 4–12, and the cultural performances of Mardi Gras in Joseph Roach, *Cities of the Dead: Circum-Atlantic Performance* (New York: Columbia University Press, 1996).

the floral and animal attributes of the floats on parade and the metaphorical attribution of strong odors like "cloves" near African bodies, as within the pageantry of 1680.[112] These pageants also frequently involved much metaphorical attribution of sensory allegory outside of the specific traits of the African body, whereby different races of women would also dress as specific senses, with roses and violets marking their bodies through diverse sensory allegories.[113] During the London performances of 1681, songs were sung to perfumers and traders who used smell to grow the English empire through taking the products of the periphery and making new antiseptic and counteractive scents for English bodies to find ever greater purity. Nearby African figures rode on many different animals, representing difference indicated through fresh sensory signs and stereotypical wardrobes portrayed to the London onlookers.[114]

Within the aesthetic constructions of race within pageants, plays, and political pamphlets, the African became a deeply sensuous and olfactory character for English sensoriums. As another aspect of these suspicious odors, many painted references to black bodies during the seventeenth century also took on the trope of the "Smoking Moor," wherein the character in portraiture would be set in a smoky room, smoking, or clouded in what seemed to be fragrant airs. These explicit references to the "Smoking Moor," and the "dark lady" of Shakespearean sonnets

---

[112] Thomas Jordan, John Playford, and Henry Playford, *London's Glory, or, The Lord Mayor's Show: Containing an Illustrious Description of the Several Triumphant Pageants, on Which Are Represented Emblematical Figures, Artful Pieces of Architecture, and Rural Dancing; with the Speeches Spoken in Each Pageant; Also, Three New Songs ... with Their Proper Tunes; Performed on Friday, October XXIX. 1680; at the Proper Cost and Charges of the Right Worshipful Company of Merchant-Taylors* (London: John and Henry Playford, 1680), 8–9, Courtesy of the Huntington Library, San Marino, CA; F. W. Fairholt, *Lord Mayors' Pageants: Being Collections Towards a History of These Annual Celebrations, with Specimens of the Descriptive Pamphlets Published by the City Poets* (London: Percy Society, 1843), 66–67, 83, and 102.

[113] Thomas Dekker, *The Magnificent Entertainment Giuen to King Iames, Queene Anne his wife, and Henry Frederick the Prince, upon the day of his Maiesties Tryumphant passage (from the Tower) through his Honourable Ctie (and chamber) of London, being the 15. of March. 1603. As well by the English as by the strangers: with the speeches and songes, deliuered in the seuerall pageants* (London: T. C. for Tho. Man the Younger, 1604), 19–20.

[114] Thomas Jordan, *London's Joy, or, The Lord Mayors Show: Triumphantly Exhibited in Various Representations, Scenes, and Splendid Ornaments, with Divers Pertinent Figures and Movements* (London: John and Henry Playford, 1681), 5–8, Courtesy of the Huntington Library, San Marino, CA; David Worrall, *Harlequin Empire: Race, Ethnicity and the Drama of the Popular Enlightenment* (London: Pickering & Chatto, 2007), 34–38.

mentioned at the start of this work, further linked African bodies to a deeply embodied and increasingly conspiratorial sensuality that was to be both feared and sneered at with a nose attuned to sensory disgust.[115]

PURITY IN THE METROPOLE

The smell of the African body is an overburdened imaginary. That imaginary infected the symbolic and embodied discourses of the Atlantic World enough that later children's folklore of twentieth-century Haiti involved concerns over the inherent smell of African bodies. That aromatic acridity attributed to Africa was rarely encountered by the gourmands of Fleet Street or in the gardens of Parliament. Rather, the odor of African bodies formulated through the ear by word of mouth, through the eye by the spectacle of "Africans" as a darkened other on a stenchful stage, and through encounters with exotic sensations defined as African within London parades. The multisensory image of the African as an olfactory and cultural other in ekphrastic travel narratives of the early English empire could not help but transfer into the plays of the early modern English stage as the polymath writers of the Globe, Phoenix, and Rose read travel narratives and wondered of the world beyond their curtained stages.[116]

It was there, upon those draped prosceniums, where generally absent African bodies were marked in the imaginary as stenchful for the English masses. These invented literary ideals of race and nation became symbolic as English advances within the later slave trade continued marking the other as a colorful figure with stained skin, vibrant odors, animated dances, and queer noises. These slave trade developments, though small compared to Spain and Portugal prior to 1650, increased rapidly

[115] Johnson, *Shakespeare in Africa*, 106–110; David Bindman, "The Black Presence in British Art: Sixteenth and Seventeenth Centuries," in Book I of Volume III of *The Image of the Black in Western Art*, eds. David Bindman, Henry Louis Gates, and Karen Dalton (Cambridge, MA: Belknap, 2010), 235–270; Anne Lafont, "How Skin Color Became a Racial Marker: Art Historical Perspectives on Race," *Eighteenth-Century Studies* 51, 1 (Fall, 2017): 89–113; Carmen Fracchia, *"Black but Human": Slavery and Visual Arts in Hapsburg Spain, 1480–1700* (Oxford: Oxford University Press, 2019), 56–90. See also later ideas of conspiracy within Adrian Wisnicki, *Fieldwork of Empire, 1840–1900: Intercultural Dynamics in the Production of British Expeditionary Literature* (New York: Routledge, 2019), 133–146.

[116] For more on stereotypes on the early modern English stage, see Travis Curtright, *Shakespeare's Dramatic Persons* (Madison Teaneck, NJ: Fairleigh Dickinson University Press, 2017), 96–111; Matthieu Chapman, *Anti-Black Racism in Early Modern English Drama: The Other "Other"* (New York: Routledge, 2017).

thereafter, in part justified through the sensory coloration of the black body as pungent. Embodied racism stereotyped in the core attempted to cure the constant and continuing shock of encountering the peripheral other. European minds offered sensory alterations as a curative through creating secular sensory worlds based upon new definitions of race, class, and gender. Englishpersons came to find within fresh patterns of racialization a new means of control for categorizing and classifying the odor of the African other. Through this process, the English metropole created race through stage productions that oversimplified ethnicity in Africa to the flat characters of the "foul" Moor or stinking African for these simple productive tropes and static types.[117]

Racist associations created through reading texts of the English print industry, or simply living within a culture of interpersonal osmosis where those texts had cultural capital, educated the common sailor and slave trader later encountering Africans of a belief that the English nose could detect the inferiority of the other through the smell of universalized blackness. This new olfactory prejudice of the West was born within a broad process whereby capitalism replaced the common enchantment of the world that the Catholic Church had applied to dominate European social life before the Reformation. In order for capitalism to rise, new categories of suppression were created out of imagined existences of racial superiority that puddled within the racialized subconscious. These categories encoded in the deep recesses of the human senses as part of a cultural construction that transcended concerns with religious faith to increasingly became embodied, uncanny, and persistent.[118]

---

[117] For disenchantment and capitalism, see Keith Thomas, *Religion and the Decline of Magic* (New York: Scribner, 1971). Stephen Greenblatt, *Shakespearean Negotiations: The Circulation of Social Energy in Renaissance England* (Berkeley: University of California Press, 1988), 112–127.

[118] For more debates on the secularization of the body in early modern Europe, see Jennifer Elizabeth Waldron, *Reformations of the Body: Idolatry, Sacrifice, and Early Modern Theater* (New York: Palgrave Macmillan, 2013), 8–13; Natalie Zemon Davis, "The Sacred and the Body Social in Sixteenth-Century Lyon," *Past & Present* 90 (1980): 40–70; Alexandra Walsham, "The Reformation and 'The Disenchantment of the World' Reassessed," *The Historical Journal* 51, 2 (2008): 497–528; Eamon Duffy, *The Stripping of the Altars: Traditional Religion in England, C.1400-C.1580* (New Haven, CT: Yale University Press, 1992), 262–266, 427–430.

2

Triangle Trading on the Pungency of Race

Thomas Herbert, an English traveler near the Cape Verde Islands during the early seventeenth century, linked the malevolent scents of the underworld to Africa when he wrote that the "Aethiopian" inhabitants of the islands lived as "idolaters" whose weather during Herbert's time spent off the West African coast "had no wind" and "was very sulphurous and raging hot, so that (albeit we had ... Awnings to shade us, and were almost naked) we could enjoy no rest, nor eate, drinke, lie still, or what else without excessive sweating day and night."[1] For Herbert and many other English travelers during the colonizing centuries to follow, the corrupt airs off the African coast were considered hot, hellish, and stinking, often emerging from a land of increasingly commodified and objectified beings from the Torrid Zone who were progressively part of the very cause of diseased miasmas that emerged from deep within the Dark Continent.[2]

---

[1] Thomas Herbert and William Marshall, *A Relation of Some Yeares Travaile Begunne Anno 1626. Into Afrique and the Greater Asia, Especially the Territories of the Persian Monarchie: and Some Parts of the Orientall Indies, and Iles Adiacent. Of Their Religion, Language, Habit, Discent, Ceremonies, and Other Matters Concerning Them. Together with the Proceedings and Death of the Three Late Ambassadours: Sir D.C. Sir R.S. and the Persian Nogdi-Beg: As Also the Two Great Monarchs, the King of Persia, and the Great Mogol* (London: P. William Stansby and Jacob Bloome, 1634), quotes on 6–8. For airs and climate in British Medicine of the late seventeenth century, see Suman Seth, *Difference and Disease: Medicine, Race, and the Eighteenth-Century British Empire* (Cambridge: Cambridge University Press, 2018), 30–56.

[2] Mark Harrison, "'The Tender Frame of Man': Disease, Climate, and Racial Difference in India and the West Indies," *Bulletin of the History of Medicine* 70 (1996): 68–93; Katherine Johnston, "The Constitution of Empire: Place and Bodily Health in the

For one of the original examiners of hurricanes and wind patterns in the Atlantic World, Ralph Bohun, the smell of the Atlantic African coast similarly and repeatedly extended such "putrid and sulpherous exhalations" that breathed "out in such venomous Blasts, that they breed Pestilentiall Feavers, and other diseases in the inhabitants."[3] Like Herbert decades before, Bohun's *Discourse Concerning the Origine and Properties of Wind* (1671) provided a reminder of the feverish and odoriferous spaces of Africa that increasingly emerged because place and people were gradually interconnected as both diseased and pungent.[4] Many of these racialized texts about odor, wind, and miasma combined throughout the Early Modern Era to link Africa and smells to such a force that Western Europeans felt justified to occupy the African continent during the nineteenth century through an attempt to turn what they understood as wasted land of an improvident and stinking peoples into cleanly European spaces of progress.[5]

The wide-ranging miasma theory that defined much of olfactory ideology for the Early Modern Era, as summarized within the introduction through the works of scholars like Robert Boyle, demarcated that

Eighteenth Century Atlantic," *Atlantic Studies* 10, 4 (2013): 443–466. For more on English concern with climate and bodily alterations in their colonies, see Joyce Chaplin, "Natural Philosophy and an Early Racial Idiom in North America: Comparing English and Indian Bodies," *William and Mary Quarterly* 54 (1997): 229–252; Karen Kupperman, "Fear of Hot Climates in the Anglo-American Colonial Experience," *William and Mary Quarterly* 41, 2 (1984): 213–240; Trudy Eden, "Food, Assimilation, and the Malleability of the Human Body in Early Virginia," in *A Centre of Wonders: The Body in Early America*, eds. Janet Moore Lindman and Michele Lise Tarter (Ithaca: Cornell University Press, 2001), 29–42; Kelly Wisecup, *Medical Encounters: Knowledge and Identity in Early American Literatures* (Amherst: University of Massachusetts Press, 2013), 26–29; Ikuko Asaka, *Tropical Freedom: Climate, Settler Colonialism, and Black Exclusion in the Age of Emancipation* (Durham, NC: Duke University Press, 2017), 139–166; Alan Bewell, *Romanticism and Colonial Disease* (Baltimore, MD: Johns Hopkins University Press, 2003), 194–241.

[3] Ralph Bohun, *A Discourse Concerning the Origine and Properties of Wind with an Historicall Account of Hurricanes and Other Tempestuous Winds* (Oxford: W. Hall for Tho. Bowman, 1671), quotes on 203–204.

[4] For general introduction to miasma theory and increasing links between smell and disease in the Early Modern Era, see S. J. Watts, *Epidemics and History: Disease, Power, and Imperialism* (New Haven, CT: Yale University Press, 1999), 22–37; Donald Beecher, "An Afterword on Contagion," *in Imagining Contagion in Early Modern Europe*, ed. Claire Carlin (Basingstoke: Palgrave Macmillan, 2005), 243–260; Annick Le Guérer, *Scent, the Mysterious and Essential Powers of Smell* (New York: Turtle Bay, 1992), 39–50.

[5] For more on the bad airs off African coasts in later decades, see Emanuel Bowen, *Particular Draughts of Some of the Chief African Islands in the Mediterranean, As Also in the Atlantic and Ethiopic Oceans. Complete Atlas, or, Distinct View of the Known World* (London: William Innys and Joseph Richardson, 1752), 46–48.

decaying objects provided odors that were the primary vectors for disease.[6] Suman Seth's *Difference and Disease* (2018) defined the British medical obsession with such consequential airs and climates during the eighteenth century through an essential reading of the colonial works of William Hillary and Hans Sloane that similarly related understandings of wind as tied to cultural ideas of illness and race. Seth's analysis offered that the colonial surveyor Hillary, as with many British scientists within the West Indies of the eighteenth century, recognized that understanding local medical geographies was vital for the treatment of different diseases. The emergence of these fresh forms of tropical medicine throughout the British Empire generally followed traditions regarding an influence of smell within bad airs and an understanding that climate linked particular bodies to specific localized diseases and the treatments to cure those ailments.[7]

Emily Senior's *Caribbean and the Medical Imagination, 1764–1834* (2018) has also recently articulated how these scientific literatures of miasma and race often informed English literary output regarding colonial projects on West Indian islands, especially concerning the climatological language of early analyst of the slave trade James Grainger, as outlined in his verse epic *The Sugar Cane* (1764).[8] This chapter expands

---

[6] For more on the roots of these ideas of decay, geography, and miasma within medicine, see Andrew Wear, "Place, Health, and Disease: The Airs, Waters, Places Tradition in Early Modern England and North America," *Journal of Medieval and Early Modern Studies* 38, 3 (2008), 443–465, and the works of Montaigne on odor and disease within Helene Cazes, "Apples and Moustaches: Montaigne's Grin in the Face of Infection," in *Imagining Contagion in Early Modern Europe*, ed. Claire Carlin (Basingstoke: Palgrave Macmillan, 2005), 79–93.

[7] Seth, *Difference and Disease*, 65–87. For connections to odor, see the smell of patient's breath analyzed within William Hillary, W. Clarke, Robert Collins, and L. Hawes, *Observations on the Changes of the Air and the Concomitant Epidemical Diseases in the Island of Barbadoes: To Which is Added a Treatise on the Putrid Bilious Fever commonly called the Yellow Fever and such other Diseases as are Indigenous or Endemial in the West India Islands or in the Torrid Zone* (London: L. Hawes, W. Clarke and R. Collins, 1766), 184–185. See also the reading of early American diets and levels of susceptibility to specific diseases like malaria and yellow fever within Dale Hutchinson, *Disease and Discrimination: Poverty and Pestilence in Colonial Atlantic America* (Gainesville: University Press of Florida, 2016), 101–147, and the importance of the yellow fever and miasma to alterations in medical procedures within Stephen Coss, *The Fever of 1721: The Epidemic That Revolutionized Medicine and American Politics* (New York: Simon and Schuster, 2017), 66–70.

[8] Emily Senior, *The Caribbean and the Medical Imagination, 1764–1834: Slavery, Disease and Colonial Modernity* (Cambridge: Cambridge University Press, 2018), 23–54; Jim Egan, "The 'Long'd-for Aera' of an 'Other Race': Climate, Identity, and James Grainger's 'The Sugar-Cane'," *Early American Literature* 38, 2 (2003): 189–212; Steven Thomas,

on these analyses of disease, climatology, and literary criticism to expose the importance of smell to understandings of corrupt airs, miasma theory, and British patterns of olfactory racialization throughout the Atlantic World. This examination specifically adds to investigations of excrement, putrefaction, and decay to argue that Atlantic racialization involved a shift from understanding that waste matter decomposed into bad smells that caused disease to a consideration that certain races released specifically viral odors that infected not only susceptible European bodies but also the morals and cultures of the superficially enlightened West.[9]

Within the racialized environments of the Atlantic World, the African body became an excess object as part of broadly understood and frequently applied olfactory miasma theory, producing smells as a decaying and commodified item removed of subject status and made into a thing that produced wasteful spaces and smells upon the earth when not in the control of white masters.[10] Throughout the Early Modern Era, defining

---

"Doctoring Ideology: James Grainger's *The Sugar Cane* and the Bodies of Empire," *Early American Studies: An Interdisciplinary Journal* 4, 1 (2006): 78–111.

[9] Seth's discussion of decay in the works of Richard Mead, James Lind, and John Pringle offers that British physicians understood that the body weakened due to both internal decay and the intake of external putrefied material. Seth, *Difference and Disease*, 123–166. See also Pratik Chakrabarti, *Materials and Medicine: Trade, Conquest and Therapeutics in the Eighteenth Century* (Manchester: Manchester University Press, 2014), 157–170; Mark Harrison, *Medicine in an Age of Commerce and Empire: Britain and Its Tropical Colonies, 1660–1830* (Oxford: Oxford University Press, 2011), 38–44, 93–108, 259–263. For olfactory references in primary selections from the later eighteenth century, see the idea of stenchful swamps as creating disease in James Lind, *An Essay on Diseases Incidental to Europeans in Hot Climates* (London: J. Murray, 1792), 50, 72, 152; the smell of fevered patients within John Pringle, *Observations on the Diseases of the Army* (London: Pringle, 1753), 183–184; the connection between Hippocratic ideas of odor and the smell of West Indian disease environments within Benjamin Moseley, *A Treatise on Tropical Diseases: And on the Climate of the West-Indies* (London: T. Cadell, in the Strand, 1787), 379–382; the discussion of smell and the causes of illness within Salomon van Monchy, *An Essay on the Causes and Cure of the Usual Diseases in Voyages to the West Indies ... in answer to the questions proposed by the Society of Sciences in Holland ... To which Essay the Prize was adjudged. Translated from the Dutch Philosophical Transactions* (London: T. Becket and P. A. De Hondt, 1762), 41–46; and the smell of breath and bile of diseased patients within Colin Chisholm and John Lining, *An Essay on the Malignant Pestilential Fever Introduced into the West Indian Islands from Boullam, on the coast of Guinea, as it appeared in 1793 and 1794 to which is annexed, a description of the American Yellow Fever, Which prevailed at Charleston in 1748, in a letter from Dr. John Lining* (Philadelphia, PA: Thomas Dobson, 1799), 133, 260.

[10] For English traditions of controlling excess through the ideal of the virtuous mean, or common moral moderation, see Joshua Scodel, *Excess and the Mean in Early Modern English Literature* (Princeton, NJ: Princeton University Press, 2002), 12–31; the ideas of senses in peril when encountering marvels of other places on the globe within

Africa as such a scented place of darkly foul bodies that were commodified as objects turned the continent from a place of wonder and cultural construction to a rhetorically defined wasteland that Europeans believed they had to cure and save. Africa became a pungent and inefficient abyss, whereby Europeans of the later nineteenth century entered as conquering heroes into the heart of an overpowering and sulfuric darkness.[11] By the nineteenth century, these links between disease, odor, and African bodies turned the entire continent of Africa into a rhetorically defined profligate space that had to be saved by cleanly, godly, and positivist Europeans.[12] Discursive patterns regarding odor and disease increased during the nineteenth century to mark black bodies for medical service in this grand game of empire that constructed ideas defining the black body as both

---

Dieter Bitterli, "Strange Perceptions: Sensory Experience in the Old English 'Marvels of the East'," in *The Five Senses in Medieval and Early Modern England*, eds. Annette Kern-Stähler, Beatrix Busse, and Wietse de Boer (Leiden: Brill, 2016), 137–162; and the reading of the threats of New World tobacco as creating excesses of sensation within the eighteenth-century novel in Emily Friedman, *Reading Smell in Eighteenth-Century Fiction* (Lewisburg, PA: Bucknell University Press, 2016), 25–50.

[11] For increasing English metropolitan concerns with bad airs, see the role of miasma in Jan Golinski, *British Weather and the Climate of Enlightenment* (Chicago: University of Chicago Press, 2011), 137–178; Margaret DeLacy, *Contagionism Catches On: Medical Ideology in Britain, 1730–1800* (Cham: Springer, 2017), 88–92, 141–147; Philip Curtin, *Death by Migration: Europe's Encounter with the Tropical World in the Nineteenth Century* (New York: Cambridge University Press, 2003), 60–67; James Riley, *The Eighteenth-Century Campaign to Avoid Disease* (Basingstoke: Macmillan, 1987), 12–19; Vladimir Janković, *Confronting the Climate: British Airs and the Making of Environmental Medicine* (New York: Palgrave Macmillan, 2010), 15–17; Thomas Ford, *Wordsworth and the Poetics of Air* (Cambridge: Cambridge University Press, 2018); Candace Ward, *Desire and Disorder: Fevers, Fictions, and Feeling in English Georgian Culture* (Lewisburg, PA: Bucknell University Press, 2007); Mark Jenner, "Civilization and Deodorization? Smell in Early Modern English Culture," in *Civil Histories: Essays Presented to Sir Keith Thomas*, eds. Peter Burke, Brian Howard Harrison, Paul Slack, and Keith Thomas (Oxford: Oxford University Press, 2000), 127–144; Carla Mazzio, "The History of Air: *Hamlet* and the Trouble with Instruments," *South Central Review* 26, 1–2 (2009): 153–196; Leah Knight, *Reading Green in Early Modern England* (Farnham: Ashgate, 2014), 37–60.

[12] For more on moral, medical, and capitalist quests into Africa, see Megan Vaughan, *Curing Their Ills: Colonial Power and African Illness* (New York: John Wiley & Sons, 2013); Deborah Joy Neill, *Networks in Tropical Medicine: Internationalism, Colonialism, and the Rise of a Medical Specialty, 1890–1930* (Stanford, CA: Stanford University Press, 2012); Pratik Chakrabarti, *Medicine and Empire, 1600–1960* (Basingstoke: Palgrave Macmillan, 2014), 122–140; Philip Curtin, *Disease and Empire: The Health of European Troops in the Conquest of Africa* (Cambridge: Cambridge University Press, 1998), 60–66.

inherently immune to diseases like yellow fever while also being inherently diseased from diverse medical, religious, and mythical pasts.[13]

The idea that the continent of Africa was inherently poisonous because of stench was a common element of many English political documents from the nineteenth century and contributed to the idea that climate altered social morality to create indolent bodies within African societies.[14] In Joseph Corry's *Observations upon the Windward Coast of Africa* (1807), which partially involved travel on the slave ship *Andersons*, the explorer's feverish condition was autobiographically determined to have arisen from the "intense heat" of Africa that constantly created "malignant nervous fevers" due to the filling of African atmospheres with "animalculae and corrupted matter." For Corry, the miasma of decaying animal parts caused African fevers to penetrate vulnerable white bodies.[15] In surgeon Alexander Bryson's *Report on the Climate and Principal Diseases of the African Station* (1847), the airs off the coast of Sierra Leone were also deemed so detrimental to English bodies during the summer months that ships had to anchor well off of the West African shoreline. The perceived threat of "marsh effluvia" emanating from the swamps caused the African atmosphere to "smell" even "at a considerable distance" from the shoreline.[16]

---

[13] For more on these debates on medicine, climate, and race, see Sharon Block, *Colonial Complexions: Race and Bodies in Eighteenth-Century America* (Philadelphia: University of Pennsylvania Press, 2018), 10–34; Rana Hogarth, *Medicalizing Blackness: Making Racial Differences in the Atlantic World, 1780–1840* (Chapel Hill: University of North Carolina Press, 2017), 17–80; Stephen Snelders, *Leprosy and Colonialism: Suriname Under Dutch Rule, 1750–1950* (Manchester: Manchester University Press, 2017); Andrew Curran, *The Anatomy of Blackness: Science & Slavery in an Age of Enlightenment* (Baltimore, MD: Johns Hopkins University Press, 2011), 117–166; Urmi Engineer Willoughby, *Yellow Fever, Race, and Ecology in Nineteenth-Century New Orleans* (Baton Rouge: Louisiana State University Press, 2017).

[14] For moral climatology, see David Livingstone, "Race, Space and Moral Climatology: Notes Toward a Genealogy," *Journal of Historical Geography* 28, 2 (2008): 159–180. See also the discussion of dirt-eating as a racial and tropical disease within Hogarth, *Medicalizing Blackness*, 81–103, and the general application of climate theory in discussions of American racism within Curran, *Anatomy of Blackness*, 167–215.

[15] Joseph Corry, *Observations upon the Windward Coast of Africa, the Religion, Character, Customs, &c. of the Natives; with a System upon which they may be Civilized, and a Knowledge Attained of the Interior of this Extraordinary Quarter of the Globe; and upon the Natural and Commercial Resources of the Country made in the years 1805 and 1806. With an Appendix, Containing a Letter to Lord Howick, on the most Simple and Effectual means of Abolishing the Slave Trade* (London, G. and W. Nicol, 1807), quotes on 121–122.

[16] Alexander Bryson, *Report on the Climate and Principal Diseases of the African Station* (London: Clowes, 1847), quotes on 4–6, 224–226.

For doctor and British politician Thomas Hutchinson near the Bight of Biafra during the 1850s, the heights of this "fever miasma" that troubled many travelers could rise to possibly 2,000 feet above the ground. According to the Anglo-Irish traveler, "as soon as we come within the sphere of the germination of malaria, our olfactory nerves frequently make us sensible of its presence. Walking along pathways through the bush-wood, and far away from what we are apt to consider as the indispensables of decomposition, we occasionally become conscious of a 'steamy vapour,' which flies up with an intensity sufficient to bring on an attack of ague ... in the course of a few hours."[17] As the progressions of many English travelers, explorers, and surveyors like Hutchinson portray, these smells of the African coast progressively represented a rhetorically constructed idea that all things African – bodies, landscapes, and social spaces – inherently smelled, and it was up to Europeans to medically cure the land of its feverish pungency.[18]

The sensorial processes that turned the African subject into a commodified and pungent object signifying a requisite conscription into modernity accelerated during the Atlantic Slave Trade, which burgeoned a broader English consciousness based upon multiple biopolitical and sensory forces that culturally constructed an uncanny and subconscious knowledge that English bodies smelled less pungent than the bodies of the African other. The construction of racial smells was biologically malleable because of a tacit knowledge that defined inferiority partly through olfaction. English olfactory consciousness involved rousing environmental and cultural references to odor, as within travel narratives of the sixteenth and seventeenth centuries, to later describe spaces of the Atlantic World that defined blackness as inherently scented.[19] Africans

[17] Thomas Hutchinson, *Impressions of Western Africa: With Remarks on the Diseases of the Climate and a Report on the Peculiarities of Trade up the Rivers in the Bight of Biafra* (London: Longman, Brown, Green, Longmans, & Roberts, 1858), quote on 199, 229–230.

[18] For philosophy on the construction of Africa and Africans as indolent and unreasonable, see V. Y. Mudimbe, *The Invention of Africa: Gnosis, Philosophy, and the Order of Knowledge* (Bloomington: Indiana University Press, 1988), 1–23; Susan Buck-Morss, *Hegel, Haiti, and Universal History* (Pittsburgh: University of Pittsburgh Press, 2012), 111–119; Teshale Tibebu, *Hegel and the Third World: The Making of Eurocentrism in World History* (Syracuse, NY: Syracuse University Press.

[19] For cultural adaptability as a dominant concern in the Atlantic World, see Thomas Benjamin, *The Atlantic World: Europeans, Africans, Indians and Their Shared History, 1400–1900* (Cambridge: Cambridge University Press, 2009); Kevin Hutchings, *Romantic Ecologies and Colonial Cultures in the British Atlantic World, 1770–1850* (Montreal: McGill–Queen's University Press, 2009).

became a miasma that lingered like a deviant cloud over the continent of Africa, creating a darkness that shaped a medical pall upon the white colonialists who traveled to African shores and a hovering mist that fashioned a cultural disease of profligacy among the inhabitants of the Dark Continent. The English nose was threatened by objects that smelled. Over time, smell would be increasingly attributable to alterations in moral constitutions as well, whereby objects that smelled were increasingly deemed able to alter the moral probity of the Western self.[20]

COLONIZED NOSES

For most Western Europeans prior to the 1600s, Africans were part of a single human race that shared a lineage that began with Adam and Eve. In the highly devout times, most Westerners could not conceptualize that Africans were not human. As Chapter 1 noted, most Englishpersons believed that the foremost explanations for dark skin was due to the hot sun, tropical climates, or past ancestral sinfulness. Throughout the Enlightenment, a period that saw many advances in scientific and political thought, many Western Europeans increasingly came to believe that there were multiple races with different origins that were often considered subhuman. This belief is called polygenetic racism, or the idea that different races emerged from more than one original human coupling. Throughout the 1700s and 1800s, this belief in polygenesis became a popular form of racial thinking, climaxing within languages of Scientific Racism throughout much of the nineteenth-century Atlantic World.[21]

---

[20] For transnational concerns with miasma and disease, see Julyan Peard, *Race, Place, and Medicine: The Idea of the Tropics in Nineteenth-Century Brazil* (Durham, NC: Duke University Press, 2000), 49–54; Hugh Cagle, *Assembling the Tropics: Science and Medicine in Portugal's Empire, 1450–1700* (Cambridge: Cambridge University Press, 2018), 6–10. For race and geography, see Frank Barrett, *Disease & Geography: The History of an Idea* (Toronto: York University Press, 2000); Sari Altschuler, *The Medical Imagination: Literature and Health in the Early United States* (Philadelphia: University of Pennsylvania Press, 2018), 121–159.

[21] For monogenetic traditions and the emergence of polygenesis, see Richard Popkin, *The Third Force in Seventeenth-Century Thought* (Leiden: Brill, 1992); Robert Sussman, *The Myth of Race: The Troubling Persistence of an Unscientific Idea* (Cambridge, MA: Harvard University Press, 2014), 11–63; Colin Kidd, *The Forging of Races: Race and Scripture in the Protestant Atlantic World, 1600–2000* (Cambridge: Cambridge University Press, 2006).

The English entered the Atlantic in larger numbers during the eighteenth century educated by a fragrant conception they had learned through popular culture and literature: that African bodies smelled pungent. It was vital that the structures of such overpowering tacit knowledge and racial common sense were broadly incorporating. The olfactory rules that defined Africans as stinking were part of a body knowledge that had little to do with material reality and more to do with a space of racial domination that included enough nasal wiggle room to define domination through ever-changing forms of false sensory consciousness.[22] Through marginalizing and defining the excremental other, English bodies demarcated their identity as lacking in odor and primed for the cleanliness of modernity. Hygiene became the marker of who could access the mythical Protestant eschaton to be formed on the earth, a new Babel for the uncontaminated, and the black body could never be cleansed because it was progressively deemed biologically inferior.[23]

The olfactory social construction central to this analysis does not denote that the smells of African bodies were not perceived by English noses. Rather, smells grew out of a sensory metaphor introduced to the British linguistic episteme as symbolic, which subsequently informed the biological function of the colonial sensorium through falsely conscious manipulations of perception. Tacit knowledge of the body and the languages of the educated mind created the sensory experience of smelling through a vast and multivalent semiotic system that incorporated ideas of blackness from religion, race, and other European cultural traditions to mark the African as stinking. This was not a forced sensory skill, every colonist pressing themselves to smell the African body as scented. Rather, the sin of embodied racist semantics marked Africans as scented through cultural education and the exchange of ideas within the Republic of Letters, which thereafter modified the everyday and essentially subconscious perceptions of many European noses to smell Africans as a separate race.[24]

---

[22] For the similarly adaptable role of pseudoscience in the assertion of socially constructed bourgeois racial ideals, see the analysis of phrenology in Steven Shapin, "Homo Phrenologicus: Anthropological Perspectives on a Historical Problem," in *Natural Order: Historical Studies of Scientific Culture*, eds. Barry Barnes and Steven Shapin (Beverly Hills, CA: Sage, 1979), 41–72.

[23] For more on cleanliness and race, see Kathleen Brown, *Foul Bodies: Cleanliness in Early America* (New Haven, CT: Yale University Press, 2009); Alison Bashford, *Imperial Hygiene: A Critical History of Colonialism, Nationalism and Public Health* (Basingstoke: Palgrave Macmillan, 2004).

[24] For embodied racial knowing, see Alexis Shotwell, *Knowing Otherwise: Race, Gender, and Implicit Understanding* (University Park: Pennsylvania State University Press, 2011),

Throughout the Early Modern Era, previous beliefs attributing the cause of black skin to the climate of Africa deteriorated as the idea that blackness was an inherited trait of infection, born of religious punishment, or due to different polygenetic human origins began to take firmer hold of racial narratives and their olfactory components. Although most sixteenth- and early-seventeenth-century accounts of Africa focused on cultural conceptions, some Englishpersons were gradually informed through the pronouncements of the African "natural infection" that caused blackness through a mark "polluted with the same blot" in George Best's narrative of English privateer and merchant Martin Frobisher's African travels published in 1578. Though not proportionally dominant within discourse at that time, a belief that Africans had a "natural infection" or were inherently different biologically began to perpetuate into later analyses of both cultural difference and scientific knowledge.[25]

Over time, the root ideals of polygenesis became popular as the masses and metropolitan elites informed each other to attribute natural smells, rather than cultural odors, to African bodies. These ideas of different human origins, articulated from diverse source into the theories of polygenism within Isaac de La Peyrère's Latin edition of *Prae-Adamitae* (1655), were frequently so intellectually mobile as to fit within existing religious narratives that would otherwise have excluded their narrative illogicality with standard biblical interpretations. Specifically, early polygenetic scholars often were able to manipulate the monogenetic story of

14–15, 34–36; Constance Classen, "The Odor of the Other: Olfactory Symbolism and Cultural Categories," *Ethos* 20, 2 (1992): 133–166; Mark Smith, *How Race Is Made: Slavery, Segregation, and the Senses* (Chapel Hill: University of North Carolina Press, 2006), 96–114; Will Jackson and Emily Manktelow, "Introduction: Thinking With Deviance," in *Subverting Empire: Deviance and Disorder in the British Colonial World*, eds. Will Jackson and Emily Manktelow (Basingstoke: Palgrave Macmillan, 2015), 1–21; Jonathan Reinarz, *Past Scents: Historical Perspectives on Smell* (Urbana: University of Illinois Press, 2014), 85–112.

[25] George Best, *A True Discourse of the Late Voyages of Discouerie, for the Finding of a Passage to Cathaya, by the Northvveast, vnder the conduct of Martin Frobisher Generall Deuided into Three Bookes* (London: Henry Bynnyman, 1578), quotes on 29–30; Karen Newman, "'And Wash the Ethiop White': Femininity and the Monstrous in *Othello*," in *Shakespeare Reproduced: The Text in History and Ideology*, eds. Jean Howard and Marion F. O' Connor (New York: Methuen, 1987), 143–162; Alden Vaughan and Virginia Mason Vaughan, "Before Othello: Elizabethan Representations of Sub-Saharan Africans," *William and Mary Quarterly* 54, 1 (1997): 19–44.

creation through arguing that different races existed before the serpentine betrayal in the Garden of Eden.[26]

As described earlier, the scent descriptions throughout most of the travel narratives of Africa during the sixteenth and seventeenth centuries focused upon cultural ideals and rarely discussed inherent odors of the body. However, by the middle of the seventeenth century, parts of the English core had turned these cultural descriptions into stereotypes and flat characters on the stage and within political and religious discourse. Once coded in the core, these semantic links between odor and blackness surfaced on the whitecaps of the Atlantic World with a force driven by material incentives that connected slavery and primitive accumulation within the ambitious scheme of capitalist modernity. Slaveholders, traders, and surveyors defined the African as naturally pungent through continuing discourses of cleanliness, odor, and biological difference that emerged from the proscenium to change the very function of the English nose within the colonies.[27]

Following many of these informal ideas about natural odors, English traveler and sugar investor Richard Ligon, who left England for Barbados due to political intrigues of the English Civil War, was among the first colonials to reference the stink of African bodies within the New World. Barbados was the primary English colony established in the West Indies. Settled by English sailors in 1627 and originally applying indentured labor for tobacco manufacturing, the colony quickly switched to import large numbers of African slaves during the middle of the seventeenth century to solidify a growing sugar economy. The sugar revolution of Barbados, starting essentially during the 1640s, turned the English colony into a manufacturing center for sugarcane, pulled from the ground on the backs of constantly imported African slaves, quickly nearing 100,000 by 1700.[28]

---

[26] David Livingstone, *Adam's Ancestors: Race, Religion, and the Politics of Human Origins* (Baltimore, MD: Johns Hopkins University Press, 2008), 26–51; Norris Saakwa-Mante, "Western Medicine and Racial Constitutions: Surgeon John Atkins' Theory of Polygenism and Sleepy Distemper in the 1730s," in *Race, Science, and Medicine, 1700–1960*, eds. Bernard Harris and Ernst Waltraud (London: Routledge, 1999), 29–57.

[27] For coding and decoding of race, see Joshua Glasgow, *A Theory of Race* (New York: Routledge, 2009); Anthony Marx, *Making Race and Nation: A Comparison of the United States, South Africa, and Brazil* (Cambridge: Cambridge University Press, 1999); Stuart Hall, *The Fateful Triangle: Race, Ethnicity, Nation* (Cambridge, MA: Harvard University Press, 2017), 31–79.

[28] For debates on early Barbados settlement, see Larry Dale Gragg, *Englishmen Transplanted: The English Colonization of Barbados, 1627–1660* (Oxford: Oxford University Press, 2003); Hilary Beckles, *White Servitude and Black Slavery in Barbados, 1627–1715* (Knoxville: University of Tennessee Press, 1989); Richard Dunn,

Ligon first published his obscure though celebrated *A True and Exact History of the Island of Barbadoes* in 1657, based upon his time on the island from 1647 to 1650. Part literature and part history, Ligon's text offers a view of English colonial culture within the West Indies at a time of formation and colonial elevation. Such a foundational stage, borne on the backs of slaves, included the metropolitan information that African bodies inherently smelled. The abstruse surveyor wrote of his specific concern for the natural smell of black bodies invading his drinking supply while visiting plantations on Barbados. He was greatly concerned upon one day seeing "the Negroes washing themselves in the Ponds, in hot weather; whose bodies have none of the sweetest savours."[29] As compared with the rest of his narrative, this reference to the lack of the "sweetest savors" inherently meant that the stereotypically termed "Negroes" on the island lacked the naturally pleasant smell of white bodies. Implicitly because of these miasmic odors, Ligon concluded that these bathing ponds never had "any thing that lives or moves." Due to the concern of such pungent pollutants entering his drinking supply, Ligon questioned slaveholders on the island who assured him that, before the water made its way from the ponds to the drinking streams, the island's sweltering heat evaporated out the African olfactory mist. Among the first to note the inelasticity of African race and smell in the Atlantic World, Ligon wrote of the naturalness of these foul odors as linked to Africans who "had a mark set upon" them by God, "which will hardly ever be wiped off."[30]

As alluded to within Chapter 1, such a discourse of naturalness and the inability of washing is directly reminiscent of the political and religious discourses of coterminous decades in the metropole, where "washing the blackamoor white" was a commonly applied political maxim. As with Ligon's implicit notation, many European travelers often cited this metaphorical axiom through more explicit terminology within discussions of diverse philosophical concerns, as within explorer Willem Bosman's use of the metaphor to discuss the "unnecessary task" or "wash an Ethiopian" when discussing the traits of the African parrot on the Gold

Sugar and Slaves: Rise of the Planter Class in the English West Indies, 1624–1713 (New York: Norton, 1972); Russell Menard, *Sweet Negotiations: Sugar, Slavery, and Plantation Agriculture in Early Barbados* (Charlottesville: University of Virginia Press, 2006).

[29] Richard Ligon, *A True and Exact History of the Island of Barbados*, ed. Karen Ordahl Kupperman (Indianapolis, IN: Hackett, 2011 [1657]), quote on 75–76.

[30] Ligon, *True and Exact History*, quotes on 104–106.

Coast.[31] These aromatic, often benign, and well-trodden political comparisons born out of religious proverbs were made into more malignant cultural weapons on the clashing waves of the Middle Passage.[32] The stale and reeking smells of African laborers defined through these metaphors and axioms were separated from the considerations of the purity of white sugar and white bodies, even as white hands could control the satisfying bodies of African females and write, like Ligon, about the links between sweet fleshes of African women and the sugars of Barbadian fruit.[33]

Scottish translator John Ogilby's disseminations on specific African nations continued to exemplify how colonial accounts gradually took on even more of the scented core ideologies about internal and natural odors. Taking his cue from many cultural descriptions of the Dark Continent and the West Indies, Ogilby's *Africa* (1670) described a group of African peoples living on an island south of Ethiopia as "low of Stature, with short Curl'd Hair like Wool ... [T]hey smell very ranck, when ... warm; they are by nature barbarous, cruel, and revengeful." Ogilby's account, using traits that were determined "by nature," increasingly offered that Africa inherently smelled pungent and was inhabited by peoples who were sensed as biologically different due to natural conditions and not simply due to fluctuating cultural constructs of aroma.[34]

As within the writings of numerous English travelers and surveyors, many French scholars of the Enlightenment era, often applying socially constructed doctrines of race through ideas of blood nobility that predated polygenism, created similarly strict racial hierarchies that regularly relayed olfactory notes.[35] These Continental and ancestral odors tied

---

[31] Willem Bosman and G. Brown Goode, *A New and Accurate Description of the Coast of Guinea, Divided into the Gold, the Slave, and the Ivory Coasts* (London: James Knapton and Dan. Midwinter, 1705), 27–28.

[32] For another relatively benign use of the metaphor, see Anonymous, *The Accomplish'd Sea-Mans Delight* (London: Harris, 1686), 127–129.

[33] For sweetness and Ligon, see Keith Albert Sandiford, *The Cultural Politics of Sugar: Caribbean Slavery and Narratives of Colonialism* (Cambridge: Cambridge University Press, 2000), 30–32. Keith Albert Sandiford, *Theorizing a Colonial Caribbean-Atlantic Imaginary: Sugar and Obeah* (New York: Routledge, 2011), 75–99.

[34] John Ogilby, *Africa: Being an Accurate Description of the Regions of Ægypt, Barbary, Lybia, and Billedulgerid, the land of Negroes, Guinee, Æthiopia and the Abyssines* (London: Johnson, 1670), quotes on 612–613.

[35] For more on French racial ideals, see Tzvetan Todorov, *On Human Diversity: Nationalism, Racism, and Exoticism in French Thought* (Cambridge, MA: Harvard University Press, 1993), 90–170; Phillip Sloan, "The Idea of Racial Degeneracy in Buffon's *Histoire Naturelle*," in *Studies in Eighteenth-Century Culture*, ed. American Society for Eighteenth-Century Studies (Cleveland, OH: The Press of Case Western Reserve University, 1971),

English perceptions to discourse from other nations within an increasing transnational assertion that the African body was an inherently scented biological other. As a part of the English printing of French Jesuit missionary Guy Tachard's *Relation of the Voyage to Siam* (1688), the traveler's journeys along African coasts to Asia recorded an encounter with a Dutch settler in southern Africa who similarly relayed his olfactory encounter with an African population. For this settler, the "Hotentots" of the region had an "insupportable . . . smell" that arose from their deeply pungent habits of wearing sheep-skin clothes prepared with cow dung and "a certain grease" that let off fragrant vapors. As with English traditions, other European encounters with African peoples often began with these cultural ideas of smell emerging from direct sensory meetings on the periphery. For Tachard's transmission of the thoughts of this anonymous Dutch traveler, smell was uncivilized and pungent, while arriving from distinct cultural components. For later French travelers in the Atlantic World, as with the English, these peripheral concerns with culturally particular odors increasingly became biological and were ethnographically deemed universal and eternal.[36]

French traveler, Native American ethnographer, architect, and slave-owner Monsieur Antoine-Simon Le Page du Pratz – also influenced by increasing Enlightenment concerns with defining race as something that emerged from spaces other than culture and environment – determined in 1758 of his travels in Louisiana of the 1720s and 1730s that slaves "ought not to be placed so near your habitation as to be offensive, I mean by that the smell which natural to some nations of negroes, such as the *Congos,* the *Angolas,* the *Aradas,* and others. On this account it is proper to have in their camp a bathing place formed by thick planks."[37] As Shannon Dawdy

293–322; Guillame Aubert, "The Blood of France: Race and Purity of Blood in the French Atlantic World," *William and Mary Quarterly* 61 (July 2004): 439–478; William B. Cohen, *The French Encounter with Africans: White Response to Blacks, 1530–1880* (Bloomington: University of Indiana Press, 1980), 60–120.

[36] Guy Tachard, *A Relation of the Voyage to Siam performed by six Jesuits, sent by the French King, to the Indies and China, in the year, 1685: with their Astrological Observations, and their Remarks of Natural Philosophy, Geography, Hydrography, and History* (London: T. B. for J. Robinson and A. Churchil; S. Crouch, 1688), quotes on 67–69.

[37] M. Le Page Du Pratz, Volume II of *The History of Louisiana, The Western Parts of Virginia and Carolina Containing a Description of the Countries that lye on bothe sides of the River Missisipi with an account of the Settlements, Inhabitants, Soil, Climate, and Products* (London: T. Beckbt and P. A. Db Hokdt, 1763 [1758 in French]), quote on 262, Du Pratz's italics. See also Patricia Galloway, "Rhetoric of Difference: Le Page Du Pratz on African Slave Management in Eighteenth-Century Louisiana," *French Colonial History* 3, 1 (2003): 1–15.

has described, Du Pratz often overlooked African influences within the growing creolized cultures of New France due to the surveyor's racialized lens that dismissed black bodies as inherently other.[38] Both representing this dismissal of cultural influence and asserting forms of early French biological racism, Du Pratz continued to inform planters: "[T]hat you may be as little incommoded as possible with their natural smell, you must have the precaution to place the negro camp to the north or northeast of your house, as the winds that blow from these quarters are not so warm as the others, and it is only when the negroes are warm that they send forth a disagreeable smell." Throughout a more categorized minutiae regarding his architectural and spatialized racism, Du Pratz persisted: "[N]egroes that have the worst smell are those that are the least black; and what I have said of their bad smell, ought to warn you to keep always on the windward side of them when you visit them at their work; never to suffer them to come near your chi'dren, who, exclusive of the bad smell, can learn nothing good from them, either as to morals, education, or language."[39] For slaves to breed crops out of Louisiana bayous, their stench – what the later French traveler to Martinique Thibault de Chanvalon called the "odeur de Caraibe" – had to be controlled as a threat to both the white body and childhood morality to allow for masters and overseers to continue turning dark mud into white sugar and snowy cotton through ambidextrous black workhands.[40]

During analogous decades, English culture was asserting what Tachard, Du Pratz, and Chanvalon emphasized through Francophone racial sentiments. In the New World, these cultural traditions of race

---

[38] Shannon Lee Dawdy, "'A Wild Taste': Food and Colonialism in Eighteenth-Century Louisiana," *Ethnohistory* 57, 3 (2010): 389–414.

[39] Du Pratz, Volume II of *The History of Louisiana*, quotes on 262–263. For more on architecture and the avoidance of bad smells, see the Jamaican plantations summarized in Louis Nelson, *Architecture and Empire in Jamaica* (New Haven, CT: Yale University Press, 2016), 205–206.

[40] Thibault de Chanvalon, *Voyage à la Martinique contenant diverses observations sur la physique, l'histoire naturelle, l'agriculture, les mœurs et les usages de cette isle, faites en 1751 et dans les années suivantes. Lu à l'Académie royale des sciences de Paris en 1761* (Paris: Bauche, 1763), quote on 44. See also connections between smell, race, and disease concerning Blumenbach, Chanvalon, and the toughness of skin for wild persons within James Prichard, *Researches into the Physical History of Man* (London: Arch, 1813), 345–349. For metaphors of white sugar to ideas of whiteness in the later Atlantic World, see Daniel Rood, *The Reinvention of Atlantic Slavery: Technology, Labor, Race, and Capitalism in the Greater Caribbean* (New York: Oxford University Press, 2017), 42–63.

construction were increasingly used to justify legal codes that marked Africans as inherently made for slavery.[41] Many of these Enlightenment attitudes and legal strictures were often guided by European conceptions of the wild man, often found within yet-to-be-enclosed European forests of the Early Modern Era. One example of this stereotypical figure was Lord Peter, discovered in 1726. Peter was believed able to find truffles in his forest dwellings quite easily, as he had a powerful sense of smell gained from his apparently intuitive past. For Richard Nash, "The wild man is not safely 'other' than the citizen – but is instead one of those troubling, necessary hybrids in part constitutive of an emergent public sphere – that has required us to shuffle back and forth between high and low culture, bourgeois and plebian spaces, the savage and the civilized." The ideal of the wild man often placed much burden on discussions of who could be deemed human, or what peoples were reckoned as able to access citizenship.[42]

Africans, increasingly considered from tyrannical lands of wild peoples, were denied their subject status as human through an increasingly scientific language that included olfactory othering. Slave studies have been attuned to this removal of Africans from subject status to commodified objects through mixed narratives of biological difference, labor needs in the New World, and ideologies of cultural and intellectual inferiority. The aesthetics and science of odor were also vital in this movement from subject status to the hardening of African peoples into stereotypically scented, material, and inferior things.[43] This framing

---

[41] For colonial law and race, see A. L. Higginbotham, *In the Matter of Color: Race and the American Legal Process; the Colonial Period* (Oxford: Oxford University Press, 1980); Kirsten Fischer, *Suspect Relations: Sex, Race, and Resistance in Colonial North Carolina* (Ithaca: Cornell University Press, 2002), 98–130.

[42] Richard Nash, *Wild Enlightenment: The Borders of Human Identity in the Eighteenth Century* (Charlottesville: University of Virginia Press, 2003), 15–66, quote on 101; Julia Douthwaite, *The Wild Girl, Natural Man, and the Monster: Dangerous Experiments in the Age of Enlightenment* (Chicago: University of Chicago Press, 2002), 60–73; Constance Classen, "The Sensory Orders of 'Wild Children'," in *The Varieties of Sensory Experience: A Sourcebook in the Anthropology of the Senses*, ed. David Howes (Toronto: University of Toronto Press, 1991), 47–60; Hayden White, "The Forms of Wildness: Archaeology of an Idea," in *The Wild Man Within: An Image in Western Thought from the Renaissance to Romanticism*, eds. Edward Dudley and Maximillian Novak (Pittsburgh: University of Pittsburgh Press, 1973), 3–38.

[43] For the rise of liberalism as justified through othering of Africans, see Simon Gikandi, *Slavery and the Culture of Taste* (Princeton, NJ: Princeton University Press, 2011); Uday Mehta, "Liberal Strategies of Exclusion," in *Tensions of Empire: Colonial Cultures in a Bourgeois World*, eds. Frederick Cooper and Ann Laura Stoler (Berkeley:

connects narratives of the Atlantic World beyond the normal temporal confines attributed to that historical region. Ending historical understandings of the Atlantic World with an era of Republican revolutions, or even emancipation, abuses the fact that Atlantic forms of racism continued to infiltrate into the later Scramble for Africa.[44]

ODOR AND PSEUDOSCIENCE

The discursive operations of natural philosophers who would come to be called scientists were, and continue to be, located within culture. The cultures of science, like all discourse, can alter the function of the body through the manipulations of what Pierre Bourdieu has defined as the habitus, the milieu that defines the proper emotions, perceptions, and bodily gestures within a society, in part created through discussions of what can be considered tasteful.[45] During the eighteenth century, numerous scientists, including many within the Royal Society, continued linking African racial traits to smells through a linguistic and conceptual tautology that mutually reinforced smell and race as linked aspects of ideology.

University of California Press, 1997), 59–86; Michelle Wright, *Becoming Black: Creating Identity in the African Diaspora* (Durham, NC: Duke University Press, 2004), 27–65.

[44] For the role of the Great Chain of Being in these discussions of natural philosophy and the subject, see Chiara Bottici, *Imaginal Politics: Images Beyond Imagination and the Imaginary* (New York: Columbia University Press, 2014), 26–30; Richard Bradley, W. Mears, and John Cole, *A Philosophical Account of the Works of Nature: Endeavouring to Set Forth the Several Gradations Remarkable in the Mineral, Vegetable, and Animal Parts of the Creation, Tending to the Composition of a Scale of Life: to Which Is Added, an Account of the State of Gardening, As It Is Now in Great Britain, and Other Parts of Europe: Together with Several New Experiments Relating to the Improvement of Barren Ground, and the Propagating of Timber-Trees, Fruit-Trees: with Many Curious Cutts* (London: W. Mears, 1721).

[45] Pierre Bourdieu, *Distinction: A Social Critique of the Judgement of Taste* (Cambridge, MA: Harvard University Press, 1984), 190–192; Alan Petersen, *The Body in Question: A Socio-Cultural Approach* (London: Routledge, 2007), 50–52; David Inglis, *A Sociological History of Excretory Experience: Defecatory Manners and Toiletry Technologies* (Lewiston, NY: Edwin Mellen Press, 2001), 30–45, 128–132, 156–160. For social construction in fields of science, see Andrew Pickering, *Science As Practice and Culture* (Chicago: University of Chicago Press, 1992), 6–10; Thomas Kuhn, *The Essential Tension: Selected Studies in Scientific Tradition and Change* (Chicago: University of Chicago, 1977), 128–147; Steven Shapin, *The Scientific Revolution* (Chicago: University of Chicago Press, 1996), 55–64; Pamela Smith, *The Business of Alchemy: Science and Culture in the Holy Roman Empire* (Princeton, NJ: Princeton University Press, 1994); Theresa Levitt, *The Shadow of Enlightenment: Optical and Political Transparency in France, 1789–1848* (Oxford: Oxford University Press, 2009); Steven Shapin and Simon Schaffer, *Leviathan and the Air-Pump: Hobbes, Boyle, and the Experimental Life* (Princeton, NJ: Princeton University Press, 2011).

Many of these olfactory notations increasingly combined ideas of disease and odor to further commodify the African body as an object that released miasma. Specifically, for many scientists, odor was frequently linked as a signifier of a generational leprosy that many in the Royal Society believed caused a darkening of skin. Earlier religious ties between uncleanness and leprosy within Leviticus knotted with the growing scientific faith that this illness, or the "true plague" of leprosy, caused African skin's dark hue. During the eighteenth century, these ideals merged even more with concerns regarding diseased odors emerging from black bodies. In 1744, a later colonial member of the Royal Society, John Mitchell of Virginia, who became famous for his analysis of blistering on African skins and cartographic works on North America, articulated these connections between leprosy, race, and smell. Mitchell summarized that the "perspirable matter of black or tawny people is more subtile and volatile in it's nature; and more acrid, penetrating, and offensive, in it's effects; and more of the nature, and more apt to degenerate to a contagious miasma, than the milder effluvia of Whites." For Mitchell, from this inherently sweatier skin "proceeded the first seeds of the measles and small-pox, with the *African* or true plague. From hence likewise proceeds the rank smell, or peculiar *Fetor*, of dark-skinned people."[46] Such discourses on leprosy linked narratives of race, promiscuity, sexually transmitted diseases, and odor throughout the greater Atlantic World as the languages of science transcended the national boundaries of racialist practitioners and their diffusive and misleading diagnoses.[47]

For Mitchell, the African body produced miasma that both signified and caused disease through the passages of the European sinuses. For many earlier scholars, these odors emerged from sicknesses born of religious curses that began with the lineages of Ham or the Mark of Cain. For

---

[46] John Mitchell, "Causes of the Different Colours of Persons in Different Climates," in *The Philosophical Transactions of the Royal Society (From the Year 1743 to the Year 1750)* (London: Royal Society, 1756): 926–949, quote on 946, emphasis in original; Edmund Berkeley and Dorothy Smith Berkeley, *Dr. John Mitchell: The Man Who Made the Map of North America* (Chapel Hill: University of North Carolina Press, 1974).

[47] Kristin Block, "Slavery and Inter-Imperial Leprosy Discourse in the Atlantic World," *Atlantic Studies: Global Currents* 14 (April, 2017): 243–262; Rod Edmond, *Leprosy and Empire: a Medical and Cultural History* (Cambridge: Cambridge University Press, 2009); Carole Rawcliffe, *Leprosy in Medieval England* (Woodbridge: Boydell, 2006). For more on earlier religious connotations of leprosy and miasma theory in Iberian literatures, see Ryan Giles, "The Breath of Lazarus in the *Mocedades de Rodrigo*," in *Beyond Sight: Engaging the Sense in Iberian Literatures and Cultures, 1200–1750*, eds. Ryan Dennis Giles and Steven Wagschal (Toronto: University of Toronto Press, 2018), 17–30.

others, disease was deemed common enough among Africans for the assertion of increasingly biological chronicles related to stereotypes about the medical inferiority of the African body. The eighteenth century saw these trans-Atlantic racial, olfactory, and medical categorizations increasingly involve comparisons between other subjected peoples. In the *London Magazine* of 1750, the idea that African bodies smelled continued to grow as part of such an additive hierarchy of the numerous subjects for the emerging British Empire. Therein, an anonymous author declared that "the people called Negroes" are the "most remarkably distinct from the rest of the human species …. [A] great difference between Negroes and all other Blacks, both in Africa and the East Indies, lies in this, that the former smell most abominably when they sweat, whereas the latter have no bad smell even when they are sweating."[48] Through the racial notions of those in the Royal Society that made their way to these more popular printings, the tracks of racism were also quickly taking on more intense polygenetic imprints, which separated groups of humans into different types rather than considering ethnicities simply culturally distinct as part of a singular humanity within different aromatic geographies.[49]

English physician, botanist, and traveler Patrick Browne's *Civil and Natural History of Jamaica* (1756), researched through ten years spent on the island, asserted that humanity was accordingly separated into four distinct groupings that followed permanent ancestral patterning. One of the classifications was determined as "Africanus, niger, crinibus crispis. The African, or Negro." Such hurried and overdetermined grouping based on the curliness of African hair, the *crinibus crispis*, assisted with pulling ever more physical traits into a racialized space beyond skin color, where Anglo-Atlantic consciousness could link Africans to an imagined inferiority based on vague, informal, and maneuverable stereotypes like hair, miasma, and smell.[50] This discursive flexibility allowed for olfactory racism to propagate as an invasive viral dialogue within the languages of capital and empire, tying all "blacks" of colonial empires to subaltern status while also dividing different racialized groups upon hierarchies of

---

[48] Peter Fryer, *Staying Power: The History of Black People in Britain* (London: Pluto, 1984), quote on 152–153.

[49] For Royal Society and race, see Cristina Malcolmson, *Studies of Skin Color in the Early Royal Society: Boyle, Cavendish, Swift* (Burlington, VT: Ashgate, 2013), 65–92, 113–146.

[50] Patrick Browne and Georg Dionysius Ehret, *The Civil and Natural History of Jamaica in Three Parts* (London: Osborne and Shipton, 1756), quotes on 489–490.

identity and ladders of citizenship as a way to manipulate categories of ethnic prominence and rights to labor and land.

Representatively, numerous authors wrote long discourses on the classifications of all the peoples, plants, and animals of the world to categorize and survey spaces of the globe for continued policies of Settler Colonialism and extractive cameralism.[51] The first edition of British geographers Daniel Fenning and Joseph Collyer's *New System of Geography* (1765) continued constructing these domineering categories through hierarchies of smell within descriptions of the "Hottentots" of southern Africa specifically through what "renders them ... disagreeable." These inherently distinct traits included: "their wooly hair to be matted together with fat and dirt; their offensive smell, arising from their uncleanly customs; and their abominable lousiness."[52] Throughout the long eighteenth century, descriptions of cultural traits of using grease and oils to cover bodies progressively took on permanent racial tones that melded pungent grease in hair with irreversible biological qualities also perceived through the imperious sense of smell.

In the Atlantic World, the rubbish odors marking the slave body within medical fictions and false forms of science meant that Africans were consistently equated with waste: a categorization of the surplus that marked savagery and indolence upon African cultures, only to be possibly altered into proper labor through the hands of unpolluted and appropriately aromatic white hands. These ideas of savagery, odor, and racialization continued to define the profitable dialogues about Africans throughout the colonial empires of European slavery within the New World. Many English colonists in North America argued that the offensive smell of African Americans would help in the process of silk cultivation due to the "negro" stench being offensive to silkworms. The botanical artist Mark Catesby applied these prejudicial discourses on scenting in 1754 when describing the Native Americans of the Carolinas and Florida as possessing "nothing of the rankness" of African slaves. Such belief in the poor smells of Africans continued beyond the American Revolution. To many British travelers, the 1780s American South featured the "rank offensive smell" of African American slaves. Much of the

---

[51] For more on hybrids, racial surveying, and categorizing, see Bruce Thomas Boehrer, *Animal Characters: Nonhuman Beings in Early Modern Literature* (Philadelphia: University of Pennsylvania Press, 2010), 164–190.

[52] Daniel Fenning and Joseph Collyer, *A New System of Geography, or a General Description of the World* (London: Crowder, 1765), quote on 364.

discussion of slave smells during this era in the American colonies focused on odor characterized through a medical understanding of "skin scent" that harkened back to the work of Mitchell and the scientific narratives of the Royal Society. Such a focus on "skin scent" buttressed earlier forms of racism, while also portraying that antiblackness was becoming a specific form of scientific racialization that focused ardently on embodied forms of difference articulated through the tacit knowledge of the Anglo-American sensorium.[53]

For English colonial ambitions outside of the North American mainland, Jamaica had been settled during a difficult and long progression after the clearing of Barbados during the seventeenth century. The much larger island provided greater spaces for English colonists to profit but also presented a mountainous and mixed terrain that allowed for slaves to resist and often form Maroon communities on the many diverse ecological spaces of the landmass.[54] The diversity of land, labor, resistance, and freedom on the island prompted enough English colonial concern to perpetuate a constant desire to survey and comprehend slave cultures and how white hands could better manage black laboring bodies. The Jamaican official Edward Long's multivolume *History of Jamaica* (1774) involved such an analysis of profit, race, and space during an era when discourses of revolution and abolitionism were both beginning to multiply from slaves, free blacks, and white moralists throughout the Atlantic World.

As part of this survey, Long's examination took on the ideology of scented African bodies as a racial inheritance that trapped Africans as part

---

[53] Smith, *How Race Is Made*, 5–16, quotes on 5, 7, and 11; Mark Catesby, *The Natural History of Carolina, Florida, and the Bahama Islands: Containing the Figures of Birds, Beasts, Fishes, Serpents, Insects and Plants: Particularly the Forest-Trees, Shrubs, and Other Plants, Not Hitherto Described, or Very Incorrectly Figured by Authors. Together with Their Descriptions in English and French. To Which Are Added, Observations on the Air, Soil, and Waters: with Remarks Upon Agriculture, Grain, Pulse, Roots, &C. To the Whole Is Prefixed a New and Correct Map of the Countries Treated of* (London: Marsh, Wilcox, Stichall, 1754), viii.

[54] For introductions to Jamaican slavery, see Richard Dunn, *A Tale of Two Plantations: Slave Life and Labor in Jamaica and Virginia* (Cambridge, MA: Harvard University Press, 2014); Sasha Turner, *Contested Bodies: Pregnancy, Childrearing, and Slavery in Jamaica* (Philadelphia: University of Pennsylvania Press, 2017), 45–67; Trevor Burnard, *Mastery, Tyranny, and Desire: Thomas Thistlewood and His Slaves in the Anglo-Jamaican World* (Chapel Hill: University of North Carolina Press, 2004); Vincent Brown, *The Reaper's Garden: Death and Power in the World of Atlantic Slavery* (Cambridge, MA: Harvard University Press, 2008); Brooke Newman, *A Dark Inheritance: Blood, Race, and Sex in Colonial Jamaica* (New Haven, CT: Yale University Press, 2019).

of an animal past, often noting his reading of many Enlightenment discourses on the causes of different racial hierarchies. Long's investigation specifically described various African peoples, noting a "covering of wool, like the bestial fleece," the "roundess of their eyes," the "black colour of the lice which infect their bodies," and a "bestial or fetid smell, which they all have in a greater or less degree; the Congo's, Arada's, Quaqua's, and Angola's, particularly the latter, who are likewise the most stupid of the Negro race, are the most offensive; and those of Senegal (who are distinguished from other herds by greater acuteness of understanding and disposition) have the least noxious odour." As with earlier French scholars who defined the first contours of polygenesis, Long's nascent and specific understanding of polygenism may have emerged from his belief in the odors of these explicit African nations rebirthed in the New World.[55]

Long separated his conceptions of the civilized or malleable nature of African nations according to how pungent he believed the scents that emanated from particular dark bodies and creolized communities. Regardless of portraying these ethnic differentiations that were important for planters who wanted slaves from specific ports due to an understanding of specific nations' agricultural expertise, Long also generally homogenized African peoples into a single race through summarizing that the "scent in . . . them is so excessively strong, especially when their bodies are warmed either by exercise or anger, that it continues in places where they have been near a quarter of an hour."[56] Long was often considered a recluse by English gentlemen but found in his West Indian surveys a space to assert his whiteness and English identity as racially superior.[57] As part of this personal pursuit of distinctiveness, he was often so puzzled by the odor emanating from African bodies, which he could never fully relate to the backbreaking work of the tropical sugar fields and arduous rum economy, that he asserted African peoples in Jamaica were often also confused by the odor. As part of his own

---

[55] Edward Long, Volume II of *The History of Jamaica, or, General Survey of the Ancient and Modern State of That Island with Reflections on Its Situation, Settlements, Inhabitants, Climate, Products, Commerce, Laws, and Government* (London: Lowndes, 1774), quotes on 352–353; Seth, *Difference and Disease*, 208–212, 237–240.

[56] Long, *History of Jamaica*, quote on 353.

[57] Trevor Burnard, "West Indian Identity in the Eighteenth Century," in *Assumed Identities: The Meanings of Race in the Atlantic World*, eds. John Garrigus and Christopher Morris (College Station, TX: Published for the University of Texas at Arlington by Texas A&M, 2010), 71–87.

confusion, he attributed an African origin tale of the goat among some nations, articulated by the aforementioned traveler Willem Bosman during the seventeenth century, as a way certain groups explained the pungency that emanated from their bodies. Long particularly summarized a slave's account of a female spirit who anointed African bodies with an odor to attract goats for sustenance. When the African nation she daubed with the perfume asked for more of the fragrance, she became incensed and, in her deceitful manner, "with a box of very foetid mixture … communicated it to their posterity; and to this day, they remain ignorant of the trick put upon them, but value themselves on possessing the genuine perfume; and are so anxious to preserve it undiminished, that they very carefully avoid the rain, and every thing that might possibly impair the delicious odor."[58] Here, though prejudicially marking African odors through his limited knowledge of ethnic belief systems, the Jamaican surveyor also portrayed African bouquets as an inherent cultural survival that slaves believed connected their communities to a long-standing spiritual past.[59]

The surveyor continued his nascently polygenetic digest through dismissing cultural differences or hygiene as important aspects for creating the particular odors of slaves and free Africans, regarding that the "rancid exhalation, for which so many of the Negroes are remarkable does not seem to proceed from uncleanliness, nor the quality of their diet." He focused on a specific anecdote to describe the force of these inherent odors compared to any remaining concerns over cultural cleanliness: "I remember a lady, whose waiting-maid, a young Negroe girl, had it to a very disagreeable excess. As she was a favorite servant, her mistress took great pains, and the girl herself spared none, to get rid of it." He continued to summarize that the slave girl "constantly bathed her body twice a day, and abstained wholly from salt-fish, and all sorts of rank food. But the attempt was similar to washing the Black-a-moor white; and, after a long course of endeavors to no purpose, her mistress found there was no remedy but to change her for another attendant, somewhat less odoriferous."[60] Long's anecdote exemplifies two defining aspects of the discourse of African

---

[58] Long, *History of Jamaica*, quotes on 425–426; Bosman, *New and Accurate Description*, xiii–xiv, 237–239.

[59] For more on gender, othering, and sensory aesthetics in the slave trade, see Stephanie Camp, "Early European Views of African Bodies: Beauty," in *Sexuality and Slavery: Reclaiming Intimate Histories in the Americas*, eds. Daina Ramey Berry and Leslie Maria Harris (Athens: University of Georgia Press, 2018), 9–32.

[60] Long, *History of Jamaica*, quotes on 425–426.

odors described within the Atlantic littoral: first, subconsciously attributing his own belief about racial odors to a metaphor that ironically was partially the cause of those perceptions; and second, noticing how a slave woman could possibly manipulate her own scents to free her purposefully stinking body from a master.

Supportive of these repetitious and cyclical racial manifestations that marked Africans as scented with the works of Long and within the American Colonies, the English core received new scientific justification within an intellectual interchange of racial information with the pungent periphery, further authorizing English consciousness in the metropole to believe in the foul scents of the African bodies they rarely encountered. For example, aforementioned and celebrated Irish novelist Oliver Goldsmith's *A History of the Earth and Animated Nature* (1774) found in the mass of information arriving to English ports a way to create hierarchies of humanity based on the presence of olfactory putrefaction among different outlying nations. Goldsmith described the beauty of specific peoples of Africa, especially those of Mozambique, as not containing any odor but said that the "Negroes" of Guinea possessed an "insupportable scent" to go along with the signifying nature of their "extreme ugliness."[61] Goldsmith's texts represent an English culture of the late eighteenth century that increasingly racialized, supported by a growth of pseudoscientific justifications born from earlier cultural ideas related to the performative stereotypes of the stage and within the literatures of the Atlantic World and her fresh novelistic, ekphrastic, and epistolary tendencies toward polygenism.[62]

Often throughout the Atlantic World, these fragrant and often informal literary categorizations would frequently become comparative and gendered. While in Barbados during the 1790s, English physician George Pinckard noted in a letter an informal conversation he had with a soldier's wife from north of the River Tweed that focused upon the smell of African women dancing. When asked if there were any women as pretty in the Scottish Highlands, she replied "whether or not – they smell better."[63] In late-eighteenth-century Britain, the gendered performances of the sense of smell also included the famous fencing master, dandy, macaroni, and

---

[61] Oliver Goldsmith, *A History of the Earth and Animated Nature: In Eight Volumes* (Dublin: Christie, 1813 [1774]), quote on 164.

[62] Daniel O'Quinn, *Entertaining Crisis in the Atlantic Imperium, 1770–1790* (Baltimore, MD: Johns Hopkins University Press, 2011), 243–301.

[63] George Pinckard, *Notes on the West Indies* (London: Longman, Hurst, Rees, and Orme, 1806), quote on 268.

minstrel Julius Soubise, a freedman who would often tantalize his audiences noses by playing up odors as way to perform his foppish African character. Soubise became well known for his assortment of nosegays, flowers, and perfumes, all meant to perform the character of the fop as a privileged space for black celebrity in Britain of the 1760s and 1770s.[64] Regardless of how the smells of these gendered characters were materially constructed, odors consistently functioned to other African bodies as objects of sexual desire and racial inferiority for consistently emerging assertions of English and French whiteness on the stage and page.[65]

Even when considered fair, many of the smells of slavery and blackness often created much hardship for female slaves always under threat of rape throughout the Atlantic World. Buffon's particular medical analysis of the Caribbean slave Genevieve involved attributing to her a "sugary-breathed" scent that included later discussions of the woman's thighs, buttocks, and breasts through decidedly desirous terms.[66] The smell of female slaves in the Brazilian Big Houses described by Gilberto Freyre were also believed to often trail with *catinga* or *budum*, terms denoting the scents of Africans with an implicit link to sexual desire or potency.[67] These general attributions of odor to female African bodies illustrate that links between scent and race were discursive elements within the demography of all European colonial slave systems in the Atlantic littoral, often correlated through a transnational, multilingual, and scientific epistolary culture that educated bodies to sense race through specific sensory traditions.[68]

[64] F. O. Shyllon, *Black People in Britain 1555–1833* (London: Oxford University Press for the Institute of Race Relations, 1977), 42–44; Monica Miller, *Slaves to Fashion: Black Dandyism and the Styling of Black Diasporic Identity* (Durham, NC: Duke University Press, 2009), 57–70.

[65] For more on whiteness in English culture, see Mary Brewer, *Staging Whiteness* (Middletown, CT: Wesleyan University Press, 2005), 1–17; Katharine Tyler, *Whiteness, Class and the Legacies of Empire: On Home Ground* (Basingstoke: Palgrave Macmillan, 2012), 175–222.

[66] Curran, *Anatomy of Blackness*, 99–101; Julia Douthwaite, *The Wild Girl, Natural Man, and the Monster* (Chicago: University of Chicago Press, 2002), 73–75.

[67] James Lorand Matory, *Black Atlantic Religion: Tradition, Transnationalism, and Matriarchy in the Afro-Brazilian Candomblé* (Princeton, NJ: Princeton University Press, 2005), 154–156; Gilberto Freyre, *The Masters and the Slaves: a Study in the Development of Brazilian Civilization* (Berkeley: University of California Press, 1986), 279, 346, 480–483.

[68] For a summary of earlier Iberian attitudes to Africans, see the reading of idioms about blackness and other religiously inspired language about dark skin within Eileen MacGrath Grubb, "Attitudes Towards Black Africans in Imperial Spain," *Legon Journal of the Humanities* 1 (1974): 68–90, and the anecdotes about the smell of João de Sa Panasco, a slave to the court of Portuguese King John III in the sixteenth century,

Within what would become the spaces of modern Latin America, ideas of racial odor grew alongside concepts also associated with Catholic religiosity and Church assertions of Iberian blood nobility, *limpieza de sangre*.[69] Part of what occasionally defined black men as the "devil" throughout early-nineteenth-century Latin American colonies was the fetid smell associated with the black body as linked to the sulfur of perdition. These religious narratives of hell, blackness, and brimstone often connected to the widely distributed Atlantic literatures of American academic and Presbyterian minister Samuel Stanhope Smith, which regarded that the curliness of African hair could be attributed to the radiating heat of the devil's hands placed upon black heads.[70] The folklore of what would become the nation of Uruguay also defined black bodies as having an "odor like a chimney," while transnational South America legends of the later nineteenth century defined the devil within black men due to the bituminous smell that was said to surround their bodies. Similarly prejudicial, black women were considered to smell like the dirty crow within some Colombian myths, a pungent sentiment also summarized in a common contemporary Brazilian poetic axiom: "being black is not a dishonor/ it is a very natural thing/ but they give off a certain odor/ that no one can stand."[71]

within Francisco Bethencourt, *Racisms: From the Crusades to the Twentieth Century* (Princeton, NJ: Princeton University Press, 2013), 90–92.

[69] María Elena Martínez, "The Black Blood of New Spain: Limpieza De Sangre, Racial Violence, and Gendered Power in Early Colonial Mexico," *William and Mary Quarterly* 61, 3 (2004): 479–520; Maria Elena Martínez, *Genealogical Fictions: Limpieza de Sangre, Religion and Gender in Colonial Mexico* (Stanford, CA: Stanford University Press, 2008); Rebecca Earle, "The Pleasures of Taxonomy: Casta Paintings, Classification, and Colonialism," *William and Mary Quarterly* 73, 3 (2016): 427–466; Verene Stolcke, "Invaded Women: Gender, Race, and Class in the Formation of Colonial Society," in *Women, "Race," and Writing in the Early Modern Period*, eds. Margo Hendricks and Patricia Parker (London: Routledge, 1994), 272–286; Rachel Sarah O'Toole, *Bound Lives: Africans, Indians, and the Making of Race in Colonial Peru* (Pittsburgh: University of Pittsburgh Press, 2012), 161–165.

[70] Alexander Caldcleugh, Edward Francis Finden, W. Daniel, John Murray, and Charles Roworth, *Travels in South America, During the Years 1819–20–21: Containing an Account of the Present State of Brazil, Buenos Ayres, and Chile* (London: John Murray, 1825), 86–88; Samuel Stanhope Smith and Henry Home, *An Essay on the Causes of the Variety of Complexion and Figure in the Human Species* (Edinburgh: American Philosophical Society, 1787), 37–40; Samuel Stanhope Smith, *An Essay on the Causes of the Variety of Complexion and Figure in the Human Species: To Which Are Added, Animadversions on Certain Remarks Made on the First Edition of This Essay* (Frederickton, New Brunswick: J. Simpson and Company, 1810), 90–91.

[71] Paulo de Carvalho-Neto, "Folklore of the Black Struggle in Latin America," *Latin American Perspectives* 5, 2 (1978): 53–88, quotes on 56, 73–74; Patricia de

Throughout the eighteenth century, a fortified transnational ideal defined that African bodies inherently smelled. Informal patterns of early polygenism and continuing religious monogenism informed the hardened arrangements of Scientific Racism during the nineteenth century, even as abolitionism worked to remove the horrors of the Atlantic Slave Trade and the continuance of slavery after the trade was initially abolished in 1807. Invigorated olfactory beliefs were not simply a cultural mixture of describing the scents of religious fetish and African agricultural goods. Rather, sensory references became something more akin to a biological certainty and perpetuated through a scientifically imbued racialism that defined the African body as an entity that produced miasma upon the land. This expanding rhetorical aspect of sensory colonialism – that African bodies produced wasteful and diseased smells that could infect both the bodies and minds of Westerners – tied the commodified African object as a savage upon a Dark Continent that had to either be healed, cleansed, and cured by the burdened white hands of European modernity or continue to stay restrained within the unscratched fields of the tropical world.[72]

AROMATIC SIGNS OF PROFLIGACY

As Nancy Stepan determined: "the history of racial science is a history of a series of accommodations of the sciences to the demands of deeply held convictions about the 'naturalness' of the inequalities between human races."[73] The rise of the Enlightenment created greater impetus to promote ideas of ethnic legitimacy to rule that increasingly used categories of human and nonhuman to define race and inferiority. This evocative discursive push, existing partly from the seventeenth century, established a questioning of the older orders of religious identity and introduced new ideas of citizenship and nationality that culminated within polygenetic racial dialogues of exclusion during a nineteenth century that

Santana Pinho, *Mama Africa: Reinventing Blackness in Bahia* (Durham, NC: Duke University Press, 2010), 105–111.
[72] For more on medicine and the black body in later American slavery, see Katherine Bankole, *Slavery and Medicine: Enslavement and Medical Practices in Antebellum Louisiana* (New York: Garland, 1998), 109–118; William Etter, *The Good Body: Normalizing Visions in Nineteenth-Century American Literature and Culture, 1836–1867* (Newcastle: Cambridge Scholars, 2010), 21–85.
[73] Nancy Stepan, *The Idea of Race in Science: Great Britain, 1800–1960* (Hamden, CT: Archon, 1982), 47–110, quote on xx–xxi.

asserted white as a signifier for the citizen and black as inherently tied to land and bonded labor.[74]

New and emerging philosophies and fictions of science and medicine discursively defined the African body as a scented spectacle in need of racial uplift, supporting justifications for Western adventures into the later Scramble for Africa. British physician J. P. Schotte's analysis of fevers in sub-Saharan Africa in *A Treatise on the Synochus Atrabiliosa* (1782) summarized that Africans had a different pungency than Europeans because they lived in an environment where their bodies had grown to resist the "foul and nasty vapours" of pestilence and miasma that would disturb European travelers to the region.[75] Like with the notations on airs and sulfur that began this chapter, Africa was increasingly defined as a space that intrinsically smelled because the people who lived in the "Heart of Darkness" were considered scented and excremental to senses of European modernity. During the late eighteenth century, traditions of polygenetic racism congealed within these European intellectual circles.

As noted, polygenesis is the belief that different groups of humans come from more than one original stock and therefore are separated by their biological makeup at an original point rather than distinct due to disease, sin, or climatological malformations, as in earlier monogenetic and culturally defined racial traditions. One of the leading early scholars of polygenesis was Henry Home, Lord Kames, who advanced a stadial history of racial evolution within his *Sketches of the History of Man* (1774). Therein, Kames described how "the black colour of negroes, thick lips, flat nose, crisped woolly hair, and rank smell, distinguish them from every other race of men." For Kames, whose writings on politics, race, and nation influenced many early American politicians including John Adams, the distinguished African was dissimilar biologically, which cyclically manifested within Kames' many considerations that Africans were also culturally inferior and pungent.[76]

---

[74] Ivan Hannaford, *Race: The History of an Idea in the West* (Washington, DC: Woodrow Wilson Center, 1996), 8–15.

[75] Philip Curtin, *The Image of Africa: British Ideas and Action, 1780–1850* (Madison: University of Wisconsin Press, 1964), quote on 84–85; Johann Peter Schotte, *A Treatise on the Synochus Atrabiliosa: A Contagious Fever, Which Raged at Senegal in the Year 1778 ... By J.P. Schotte, M.D* (London: Scott, 1782), 103–112.

[76] Henry Home, Lord Kames, Volume I of *Sketches of the History of Man* (Edinburgh: W. Creech, 1774), quotes on 12–13; Edward Cahill, *Liberty of the Imagination: Aesthetic Theory, Literary Form, and Politics in the Early United States* (Philadelphia: University of Pennsylvania, 2012), 26–27, 41–55.

The racialized understandings of Buffon, generally still settled within fields of monogenesis, similarly entered Anglo-Atlantic understandings of race and smell through the different publications of his thirty-six volume *Histoire Naturelle*. This seminal work, published in different editions from 1749 to 1804, offered frequent summaries of the black body for diverse readers. For the curiously inclined, the publication of the fourth volume provided a summary of the manners and countenances of the different peoples of the world. That edition, originally in French in 1753 and translated in many English editions thereafter by William Smellie and J. S. Barr, proffered that the people of "Guinea are extremely ugly, and have an insufferable stench; those of Sofala and Mozambique are handsome, and have no bad smell." For Buffon, such inherent odors provided the impetus to question the racial derivation of Africans beyond the use of sight alone. The cataloguer provided that these variances in odor made it "necessary then to divide the black into different races, and, in my opinion, they may be reduce to two principles ones, that of the Negroes and that of the Caffres."[77] Such scientific assurances of race proposed by Enlightenment scholars such as Buffon, and Blumenbach within his later doctoral work on phrenology, smell, and the geographical varieties of human races, increasingly melded with previous public conceptions of the stage and from the pulpit that sub-Saharan bodies smelled. This violent olfactory discourse perpetuated a triangle trade in pseudoscientific racism that continued to feed a colonial mindset buttressed upon a profitable eighteenth-century slave system that resisted consistent slave rebellions and the rising moralist tendencies of abolitionism.[78]

English printings of French traders Monsieur de Saugnier and Pierre-Raymond de Brissons's *Voyages to the Coast of Africa* (1792), summarizing trading, shipwreck, and capture by indigenous Senegalese in the 1780s, similarly represents such a colonial reimaging of African scents once those stereotypes formed within European cores. Rather than ethnographically summarize African cultural traits that smelled, the authors

---

[77] Georges Louis Leclerc de Buffon and J. S. Barr, *Barr's Buffon. Buffon's Natural History: Containing A Theory of the Earth, A General History of Man, Of the Brute Creation, and Of Vegetables, Minerals* (London: H. D. Symonds, 1797), quotes on 275–277.

[78] Johann Friedrich Blumenbach, K. F. H. Marx, P. Flourens, Rudolph Wagner, and John Hunter, *On the Natural Varieties of Mankind = De Generis Humani Varietate Nativa* (New York: Bergman, 1969 [1775]); Abigail Leslie Swingen, *Competing Visions of Empire: Labor, Slavery, and the Origins of the British Atlantic Empire* (New Haven, CT: Yale University Press, 2015), 5–8; Susan Dwyer Amussen, *Caribbean Exchanges: Slavery and the Transformation of English Society, 1640–1700* (Chapel Hill: University of North Carolina Press, 2007), 232–235.

described that the female slaves who served the Arab populations of North Africa had a "naturall … ill smell." The traders continued to note that the "negresses … exhale a scent sufficient to disgust a man of the least delicacy" choosing instead "to sleep in the open air, than to remain in the same tent with a negress." The travelers also described specific North African women using similar nasal stereotypes learned from centuries of European narratives about scented superiority: "it is impossible for imagination to form a more disgusting and revolting idea than the appearance and smell of a Moorish woman."[79] Rather than listing only ethnographic traits, by the late eighteenth century writers within European cores had informed colonial travelers enough to alter ethnographic objectivity to descriptions of inherent and "natural" inferiority through pungent and scientific racialization breeding even stronger reactions of sensory disgust.

Over time, previous ideas of the wild man integrated with perceptions of the "savage" as concepts defining modernity through opposition set a standardized form of the hybrid other as the regular inhabitant of colonial spaces.[80] Those who followed traditional liberalism from the proto-evolutionary ideas of the Great Chain of Being, the ideologies of John Locke, and the body politic of Thomas Hobbes frequently defined civilization as inherently surpassing and contrasting to these forms of savagery that were susceptible to spectacles of the lower senses that Europeans believed they had moved past. Through what Stephanie Martens calls an "aboriginalism" that focuses upon the "Far-Away-Long-Ago Fallacy," many scholars began to define the other as part of a historical world already transcended. European scholars often applied this philosophy of the past by asserting ideals of cultural evolution through analyzing Africans, and their sensory worlds, as valuable for the study of cultures within the European past.[81]

[79] Pierre-Raymond de Brisson and Saugnier, *Voyages to the Coast of Africa Containing an Account of Their Shipwreck on Board Different Vessels, and Subsequent Slavery, and Interesting Details of the Manners of the Arabs of the Desert, and of the Slave Trade, As Carried on at Senegal and Galam* (London: G. G. J. and J. Robinson, 1792), quotes on 98–99, 472.

[80] Felicity Nussbaum, *The Limits of the Human: Fictions of Anomaly: Race, and Gender in the Long Eighteenth Century* (Cambridge: Cambridge University Press, 2003), 189–212.

[81] Stephanie Martens, *The Americas in Early Modern Political Theory: States of Nature and Aboriginality* (New York: Palgrave Macmillan, 2016), quotes on 32–35; Richard Ashcraft, "Leviathan Triumphant: Thomas Hobbes and the Politics of Wild Men," in *The Wild Man Within; An Image in Western Thought from the Renaissance to Romanticism*, eds. Edward Dudley and Maximillian Novak (Pittsburgh, PA: University of Pittsburgh Press, 1973), 141–182; P. J. Marshall and Glyndwr Williams, *The Great*

Late-eighteenth-century European accounts of Africa often continued to include cultural connotations about the filth and odor of environments that furthered links between biological inferiority, smell, and these European narratives of African cultural suspension. Like a hideous dream, European travelers to Africa portrayed the environments of the Dark Continent through phantasmagoric representations of cultures and peoples lost to time and European notions of progressive civilization. These mixed connotations of cultural and biological inferiority were raised again when the ship *Sandown* entered the region of Rionunez near the coast of modern Guinea in July of 1793. The log of Commander Samuel Gamble relayed how "The Banks" were "swampy and Oozey overrun with Mangroves and noxious weeds, full of rivulets & Creeks, the Slime and filth of which at low water is very disagreable especialy in the night. This Country appears to be at variance with Mankind." This inconsistency with "Mankind" was noted by many English sailors, who found in African smells the vast otherness that marked the carnal worlds of Africa as primitive and antique through discursive fields of culture, biology, and environment. These lands, as Gamble implied, grew overrun with a natural vegetation that was not maintained or harvested by the African populations that lived in the very filth, pestilence, and odor provided by miasmic marshes and their zymotic airs.[82]

Throughout the Atlantic World, the idea that Africa persisted as a wide-ranging diseased space was linked with ideas of the African body as a vessel of medical inferiority. In many cases, odor was included within discourse to mark the African body not only as a diseased part of the human family but also as exterior to the anthropological domicile inhabited by Europeans. To be sure, the Atlantic racial milieu was inherently illogical. However, racism

---

Map of Mankind: Perceptions of New Worlds in the Age of Enlightenment (Cambridge, MA: Harvard University Press, 1982), 204–222; Antonello Gerbi, *The Dispute of the New World: The History of a Polemic, 1750–1900* (Pittsburgh, PA: Pittsburgh University Press, 1973), 325–441; Susanne Lettow, "Generation, Genealogy, and Time: The Concept of Reproduction from *Histoire Naturelle* to *Naturphilosophie*," in *Reproduction, Race, and Gender in Philosophy and the Early Life Sciences*, ed. Susanne Lettow (Albany: State University of New York Press, 2014), 21–44; Christopher Loar, *Political Magic: British Fictions of Savagery and Sovereignty, 1650–1750* (New York: Fordham University Press, 2014), 51–55, 193–194: Peter Burke, "America and the Rewriting of World History," in *America in European Consciousness, 1493–1750*, ed. Karen Kupperman (Chapel Hill: University of North Carolina Press, 1995), 33–51; Michael Adas, *Machines As the Measure of Men: Science, Technology, and Ideologies of Western Dominance* (Ithaca: Cornell University Press, 1989), 122, 315, 397.

[82] Bruce Mouser and Samuel Gamble, *A Slaving Voyage to Africa and Jamaica: The Log of the Sandown, 1793–1794* (Bloomington: Indiana University Press, 2002), quote on 52.

became so embodied and supported through its own internal logic that manifested and justified itself so effectively that many uncanny racial contours waded into the subconscious place of disgust where reason goes to slumber. Also informing Thomas Jefferson's own racial olfactory highlighted in the preface to this book, the Atlantic interchange of knowledge about odors continued to become more scientific and standardized around the turn of the nineteenth century. The American doctor Benjamin Rush summarized often what much of the medical establishment believed about the different racial derivation of Africans in the *Transactions of the American Philosophical Society* (see Figure 2.1).

FIGURE 2.1 Print of portrait of Benjamin Rush, by Charles Willson Peale, 1818. Courtesy of the National Independence Historical Park

Despite remnants of the climatological understanding of race that once again arose in the wake of the Henry Moss incident of the 1790s, whereby an American black man with vitiligo was said to have been washed into a white man, Rush understood that race was not something that could be altered by the environment within a single lifetime or washed away through hygienic modification.[83] Following the pseudoscientific work of Mitchell and the Royal Society, Rush came to believe that generational leprosy deemed evident in Africa caused the smell that remained as a part of African progeny not afflicted with the disease. Rush generally presented that diseases emerged from a weakened psychology or impaired condition that could be caused by many different external forces, including miasma and even institutions of social control that could impose undue stress upon the mind and body.[84] Probably applying transnational understandings of leprosy, odor, and race from both Mitchell and Swedish scientist Franz Swediaur, Rush expanded the idea that leprosy created the blackened skins and odors of African peoples when correlating the specific aspects of a diseased body to the African race. For Rush, patients directly afflicted with a form of leprosy believed to cause black skin "exhale perpetually a disagreeable smell, which I can compare to nothing but the smell of a mortified limb." Rush emphasized this diseased body as a racial stereotype when comparing this specific disease symptom of darkened appendages to a certain "smell" which "continues with a slight modification in the African to this day."[85]

---

[83] Winthrop Jordan, *White Over Black: American Attitudes Toward the Negro, 1550–1812* (Chapel Hill: University of North Carolina Press, 1968), 517–518; Kariann Akemi Yokota, *Unbecoming British: How Revolutionary America Became a Postcolonial Nation* (Oxford: Oxford University Press, 2010), 192–225; Charles Martin, *The White African American Body: A Cultural and Literary Exploration* (New Brunswick, NJ: Rutgers University Press, 2002), 32–43.

[84] For background on Rush, anti-slavery motivations, and medicine, see Eric Herschthal, "Antislavery Science in the Early Republic: The Case of Dr. Benjamin Rush," *Early American Studies: An Interdisciplinary Journal* 15, 2 (2017): 274–307; Donald D'Elia, "Dr. Benjamin Rush and the Negro," *Journal of the History of Ideas* 30, 3 (1969): 413–422.

[85] Benjamin Rush, "Reasons for Ascribing the Colour of Negroes to Leprosy," *The Monthly Magazine and American Review* 2, 4 (April, 1800): 298–301, quote on 298; Franz Swediaur, *The Philosophical Dictionary, or, The Opinions of Modern Philosophers on Metaphysical, Moral, and Political Subjects* (London: G. G. J. and J. Robinson and for C. Elliot, 1786), 160–161. For another link between illness, smell, and the darkening of skin, see the reading of malignant fevers in John Huxham, *An Essay on Fevers, and their Various Kinds, as Depending on Different Constitutions of the Blood* (London: S. Austen, 1750), 98–100.

Diagnoses of generational leprosy, miasmic extremities, and cultural variance from "Mankind" all combined to define Africa and its stereotypically pungent peoples as wasteful and excremental to modernity. This lack of ability to reach the civilized spaces of the modern subject was often attributed through a discursive hawser tied rigidly between bad airs and morally pregnable constitutions. For Rush, as in an earlier oration he provided to the American Philosophical Society in 1786, human decency could be altered by the different "species of airs" that affected the "moral faculty," as with certain atmospheres that could create a "serenity of mind." For Rush, Greek peoples had particularly broiling temperaments and were rarely serene because of the often volcanic and sulfurous winds that sprang forth from the many vents of the Mediterranean littoral.[86]

The field of moral climatology that linked medical ideas of airs and beliefs about personal behavior emerged from a deep history of Galenic humors and psychological determinations during the late eighteenth century to mark the lungful breathed in certain regions with moral productions and a propensity to create patterns of social welfare or public evil.[87] Broad discourses on climatology that also marked racial codes articulated how moral distemper could be caused by moving from one climate to another, altering into a broadly applied and universalizing motif of climatology and miasma theory that asserted generational and cultural effects upon nation and temperament that arose from living within specific racialized climates. Odor had justified slavery, and, within the grand process of colonialism within Africa that quickened during the nineteenth century, the olfactory sciences increasingly came to be categorized as another validation for the intrusion of white hands upon dark bodies and scented lands. Floating atmospherics hardened into conscious columns, building a metahistorical pantheon that tied together centuries of thought about smell, from the Galenic nose as a vulnerable hollow tube to the later threatening African spores that rose from racialized bodies. False sciences demarcated deceitful categories of the races through mendacious

---

[86] Benjamin Rush, *An Oration, Delivered before the American Philosophical Society, held in Philadelphia on the 27th of February, 1786; Containing an Enquiry into the Influence of Physical Causes upon the Moral Faculty* (Philadelphia: Charles Cist, 1786), quotes on 26–27. For more on Rush's influence on medical training in the Early Republic, see Altschuler, *Medical Imagination*, 21–35.

[87] For more on moral climatology, see Livingstone, "Race, Space and Moral Climatology," 159–180; Eric Thomas Jennings, *Curing the Colonizers: Hydrotherapy, Climatology, and French Colonial Spas* (Durham, NC: Duke University Press, 2006), 8–22.

sensory consciousness born within the racialized public spheres of the Atlantic World.[88]

THE REVERSE MIDAS: ODOR AND THE SCRAMBLE
FOR AFRICA

Resisting abolitionist rhetoric, numerous Atlantic planters and slave traders continued to espouse the idea that Africans were naturally less than fully human and consequently in need of paternal care and white social ordering. Cultural forms of polygenesis also entered popular narratives, as within the anonymous English engraving entitled "The Rabbits," of 1792. The graphic piece, which adorns the cover of this work, included an African man selling rabbits on a street corner in London. The print portrays a gloriously clad white woman disgusted by the stink of the rabbits. In her confrontation with the vendor in the representation, she hears him proclaim: "If Blacke Man take you by Leg so – you smell too."[89] This wording can entail that all the black man touches – defined through the use of the racialized term "Mungo" within the print – would become noxious. This disgustingly inverse formulation of a black Midas proposes that odor was also important in the creation of a cultural motif whereby Africans were believed incapable of creating their own modern societies, as all that darkness touched would turn to excremental waste and miasmic decay.

Throughout the early nineteenth century, temporalization of race also increased, as Western Europeans justified their ascension to world dominance through historical narratives of cultural periodization that defined certain groups as intellectually imprisoned within former periods of development. As a part of this historical ideal, the concept of the atavistic Torrid Zone linked darkened bodies with being infected by living in part of the world where questions of morality and aptitude were infused with

[88] For more on the idea that race created inherited behavioral conditions, see the reading of comportment in Block, *Colonial Complexions*, 110–118, and the idea of moral improvement as a racial quest within Bruce Dain, *Hideous Monster of the Mind: American Race Theory in the Early Republic* (Cambridge, MA: Harvard University Press, 2009), 40–80. See also associations between specific races and particular labors within Jonathan Robins, *Cotton and Race Across the Atlantic: Britain, Africa, and America, 1900–1920* (Rochester, NY: University of Rochester Press, 2016).

[89] "The Rabbits," Robert Sayer and Company, Printed October 8, 1792. Courtesy of National Maritime Museum, Greenwich, London, Michael Graham-Stewart Slavery Collection; Gretchen Gerzina, *Black London: Life before Emancipation* (New Brunswick, NJ: Rutgers University Press, 1995), 10–11.

categorizations of race, odor, and disease. Race became "atmospheric," as Fanon has prompted, because racialized bodies were deemed to emanate racialized matters of waste contained within small pieces of effluvium. The atmospherics of race, throughout the world of colonization, were then consequently used to create fear of disease among racialized bodies forced to live what within what were considered wasteful and contagious spaces.[90]

Within these narratives of race and the positivist inheritance of white nations, the traits of the African body were continuously assembled through scientific languages, blended through fact and fiction within medical tracts that seemed assertive but were as falsely advantageous as the colonial mindset that supported their methods. As part of the justification for the European intrusion into Africa, different African nations were consequently and unceasingly summarized as statically in the past and part of a landscape that was marked during ancient eras but was no longer being cultivated. These temporalized narratives portrayed lost cultures that may have been eager to work but had failed to change the landscape enough to find pathways into modernity. For many Western Europeans, Africans were thus laborers, trapped in the past, in need of capitalism to scratch the land through fresh European instruction. As with discussions of the naturalness of slavery, stories of scent were not lost in these accounts that coincided with the rise of capitalism and the beginnings of what would become the Scramble for Africa that turned contact zones into spaces of European colonialist hegemony.[91]

Many of these ideas of African profligacy and laziness persisted from concepts of labor and power within the Atlantic World. Within historian Robert Renny's *An History of Jamaica* (1807), readers encountered a common discourse on the rise of slavery in Africa due to the nature of the climate, which naturally bred "sloth" and "indolence." Though unwilling to classify the African as either human or subhuman in a text partially meant to bring attention to the plight of the enslaved, Renny

---

[90] Frantz Fanon, *The Wretched of the Earth*, trans. Richard Philcox (New York: Grove, 2007), 30–40; Christina Sharpe, *In the Wake: On Blackness and Being* (Durham, NC: Duke University Press, 2016), 108–112.

[91] For more on race and torrid landscapes as justifications for colonialism, see Mary Louise Pratt, "Scratches on the Face of the Country; or, What Mr. Barrow Saw in the Land of the Bushmen," *Critical Inquiry* 12, 1 (1985): 119–143; Zine Magubane, "Simians, Savages, Skulls, and Sex: Science and Colonial Militarism in Nineteenth-Century South Africa," in *Race, Nature, and the Politics of Difference*, eds. Donald Moore, Jake Kosek, and Anand Pandian (Durham, NC: Duke University Press, 2003), 99–111.

portrayed Africa as environmentally determined to include slavery due to a warm and bountiful landscape that would otherwise have turned possible workers into wasteful consumers.[92] Both the disease of profligacy and the propensity for medical illness that defined racial inferiority continued to mark the African body and the continent of Africa as an olfactory other well into the nineteenth century. These medical designations, as with Rush from earlier decades, found readily apparent links to the odors of Africans and Africa that continued to be perceived throughout the Atlantic World. Nomenclature was also often used as hegemonic assertion of the spaces of Africa and the pungency that derived from the continent. When a large-scale fever broke out in the West Indies from approximately 1815 to 1816, the "horrid stench" of the ship holds and ill patients of all nationalities was attributed to the "pestiferousness" of miasmic airs off the West African coast. These "sulphuric" airs were believed to have emerged from putrid waters off the African shore. Following the standard and still popular miasma theory of the day, English doctors defined the illness as the "African fever."[93]

Many of these Atlantic concerns with the miasma emerging from black bodies, African airs, and emanating diseases from the Torrid Zone transferred to concerns with European settlement within Africa during the middle of the nineteenth century. In Commodore George Collier's reports from the Gold Coast, metropolitan politicians read often of the horrid stench of the waters that supplied African populations and European settlements. Collier specifically wrote in 1820 of the "damps" that "are so extraordinary and so very penetrating" to English bodies. He also believed that these "exhalations from the earth are so powerful and continual, that nothing" could "resist their destructive effects" upon African societies. In Collier's estimation, the miasmas that emerged near European forts destroyed naval stores, white bodies, and African subjects' desire to work the land.[94]

The bad airs off Sierra Leone, for Collier within his later reports of 1821, were similarly of "a vapor which" he "could but compare to gas

[92] Robert Renny, *An History of Jamaica: With Observations of the Climate, Scenery, Trade, Productions, Negroes, Slave Trade . . .: To Which Is Added an Illustr. of the Advantages Which Are Likely to Result, from the Abolition of the Slave Trade* (London: Cawthorn, 1807), quotes on 160–161.

[93] David East, *Western Africa, Its Condition, and Christianity, the Means of Its Recovery* (London: Houlston & Stoneman, 1844), 380–394.

[94] *Reports from Commodore Sir George Collier, Concerning the Settlements on the Gold and Windward Coast of Africa. Ordered by the House of Common, to be Printed 25 May 1820* (London: House of Commons, 1820), quotes on 6–8. Courtesy of the John Carter Brown Library.

from coal." Upon surveying the region and the African populations nearby, Collier concluded that the unhealthfulness of the winds arose because of a lack of cultivated vegetation in the area. He was therefore pleased to find that the inhabitants of Free Town had taken his advice to clear vegetable matter from their streets. At the Fort of Dix Cove, Collier's desire for African populations to clear their putrid waters and control the emergence of effluvia and vapors ran against indigenous concerns over a sacred alligator who lived within a nearby swamp. For Collier, these fetishes and the lack of a desire to clean the water supplies and vegetal waste were cultural contagions that Africans had to overcome to cure the miasmas that hung over their ability to progress into a decidedly European and capitalist form of modernity.[95]

In his report of 1822, Collier elaborated on his concerns with African pungency and labors. Writing of the island of Fernando Po, Collier similarly surveyed that the "damps and vapours" customarily "generate fever and destroy European life." For Collier, the African populations in the region could cure these physical ills, which did take many European and African lives, if only they would work until the "island became cleared of wood and would be more healthful."[96] The increasingly shared racial motif of climate and labor upon which Collier and other bureaucrats progressively relied was also summarized quite succinctly in a *Report on Captured Negroes in Tortola* (1825) that articulated prospects for the application of African apprentices on the eve of larger emancipation debates within the British Empire. Resisting religious justifications for African freedom, British Major Thomas Moody argued: "In every climate where men can exist without much labour, the habits of steady agricultural industry are less generally found, because the stimulus of necessity has then very little power."[97]

[95] George Collier, "Second Annual Report of Sir George R. Collier," in *Further Papers Relating to the Suppression of the Slave Trade: Copies or Extracts of all Communications received by the Lords Commissioners of the Admiralty, from the Naval Officers stationed on the Coast of Africa, or in the West Indies, since the 1st of January 1820; Relative to the State of the Slave Trade* (London: House of Commons, 1821), 40–77, quotes on 67–68. Courtesy of the John Carter Brown Library.

[96] George Collier, "Extract from a Report from Commodore Sir G. R. Collier on the Coast of Africa, dated 27th December 1821," in *Further Papers Relating to the Slave Trade Viz, Communications to the Admiralty, and Instructions to Naval Officers, Ordered by the House of Commons, to be printed, 22 April 1822* (London: House of Commons, 1822), 15–31, quote on 26. Courtesy of the John Carter Brown Library.

[97] Thomas Moody, "Separate Report of Major Thomas Moody, Royal Engineers, late Commissioner, stating his Reasons, why he could not sign or approve of the Report of his Colleague, dated London, 2d March, 1825," in *Further Papers Relating to Captured*

The idea that tropical climates created indolence emerged from a capitalist ideology that defined the African body as an object that produced diseased miasmas, which was believed to cyclically affect laziness upon societies. These ideas of odor, labor, and social disease informed debates upon later colonialism that attempted to justify dominion over Africa in the nineteenth century. As part of these discursive shifts, pro-slavery British bureaucrat James MacQueen summarized the necessity of capitalism to cure the laziness and scented ills of the African race within Sierra Leone in an 1831 letter to Charles, Earl Grey. MacQueen asked: "How much more difficult and dangerous then, my Lord, must it be to abrogate ... society in the Tropical World ... where the colour of the skin and the smell of the one race separate the races by almost impassable barriers – where barbarous manners prevail amongst one class, and where, above all, from the ideas, the pursuits, the wants and the inclinations – from the influence of climate and habits amongst the most numerous class – these are disinclined to labour, and more especially disinclined to engage in every species of agricultural labour."[98] For these many diplomats, the homogenized other of the lazy and reeking African later merged with the composite other of all non-Westerners in the great game of New Imperialism with rules that demarcated savage bodies as inferiorly scented and lacking proper capitalist work ethic.

Within the metropole, such figurations moved from the periphery to visual codification within the new graphic culture of print and political comics within the English public sphere. In the comic "Free Labor: Or the Sunny Side of the Wall," from 1833, Africans in the Caribbean were deemed profligate and culturally miasmic, through the imagery of rum and dirtied clothes, and unable to feed or clothe themselves without their slave masters. One freedman in the background of the comic reaches for the last fruit on a nearby tree and is guided by another African to burn down the sapling as "climbing" would be too much work, signifying to English readers a discourse on indolent consumption over Protestant cultivation common within the racialized languages of the Atlantic World (see Figure 2.2).

Negroes: VIZ: Return to an Address of The Honourable House of Commons, dates the 7th March 1825; -for Reports of Commissioners Relating to Captured Negroes, Apprentices, &c Ordered by the House of Commons, to be Printed 16 March 1825 (London: House of Commons, 1825), 49–152, quote on 67. Courtesy of the John Carter Brown Library.

[98] James MacQueen, "Letter to the Right Honourable Earl Grey," *Blackwood's Edinburgh Magazine* 29 (March, 1831): 454–466, quote on 463.

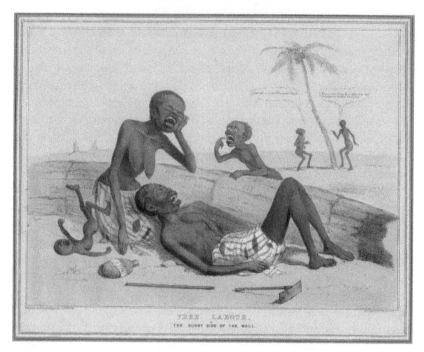

FIGURE 2.2 Print of "Free Labour: Or The Sunny Side of the Wall." Included within London. Thos. McLean 26 Haymarket. 1833. June 19th. John Carter Brown Library. Political Cartoons. Accession Number: 72–149. Courtesy of the John Carter Brown Library

The celebrated British explorer Bedford Pim followed these traditions of African profligacy to shape later English concerns with race through his writings regarding Afro-Caribbean populations during the 1860s. Despite his discoveries in Central American interiors that would lead to later establishments in pursuit of what would become the Panama Canal, Pim's work in *The Negro and Jamaica* (1866) may have been more detrimental to race relations than his explorations were ornamental within the grand narrative of Western progress. Guided much by his reading of Richard Burton's *A Mission to Gelele, King of Dahome* (1864), Pim described his understanding of the inherent savagery and evil of black bodies set free on Jamaica during the earlier 1830s. In a work that quoted numerous other racially motivated authors to explore the supposed savagery and hostile nature of African peoples, Pim offered the use of olfactory language to link an internal rankness of the African body and the traits of barbarity and indolence that were used to continue further domination of the Western European over African nations and diasporic populations during the later nineteenth century.[99]

Written in the wake of racial rebellion in Jamaica at Morant Bay in 1865, Pim's narrative classified malicious acts that were often found throughout histories of Africa and could only be constrained in a future colonial world of stronger white hands upon black bodies. To Pim, the "idle" and "miscreant" Africans of Jamaica could never reach civilization on their own merits. For Pim, this was because Africans were inherently trapped within the climatological and cultural backwardness of "practising fetish worship, grisgris, murder, rapine, and cannibalism" that was "flourishing" in Africa's "rankest luxuriance."[100] Pim wrote elsewhere of other forms of this "rankest" African culture and the smells of the African body that signified indolence. In *Dottings on the Roadside, in Panama, Nicaragua, and Mosquito* (1869), while he surveyed areas for European railroads across Central America, Pim summarized his discontent for the "African bouquet" that permeated the region. Struck by this intense odor, Pim portrayed himself as a hero due to his ability to persevere when faced with such deeply pungent sensory worlds. Within an egotistical narrative, Pim also discussed the desires of a mixed-race woman to continue to dance with him, while also defining the odor of the African bodies in Jamaica as under the control of a "rotten" form of infectious "niggerdom" that affected the West Indian body politic to its "core."[101] Through Pim, and the many racists before him, the tentacles of Atlantic racialism combined into a hideous monster whereby the odor of African bodies signified not only biological inferiority but also contributed to a cultural infection that stalled the positive alteration of the lucrative landscape.

---

[99] For background on Pim, see Marc Flandreau, *Anthropologists in the Stock Exchange: A Financial History of Victorian Science* (Chicago: University of Chicago Press, 2016), 281–287.

[100] Bedford Pim, *The Negro and Jamaica: Read Before the Anthropological Society of London, February 1, 1866, at St. James's Hall, London* (London: Trübner, 1866), quote on 14; Richard Francis Burton, *A Mission to Gelele, King of Dahome: With Notices of the so Called "Amazons," the Grand Customs, the Yearly Customs, the Human Sacrifices, the Present State of the Slave Trade, and the Negro's Place in Nature* (London: Tinsley Brothers, 1864). For more on British moral mission in Jamaica and Morant Bay, see Catherine Hall, *Civilising Subjects: Metropole and Colony in the English Imagination, 1830–1867* (Oxford: Polity, 2002), 380–433. See also cannibalism and discourse in the Atlantic World within Jared Staller, *Converging on Cannibals: Terrors of Slaving in Atlantic Africa, 1509–1670* (Athens: Ohio University Press, 2019).

[101] Bedford Pim, *Dottings on the Roadside, in Panama, Nicaragua, and Mosquito* (London: Chapman and Hall, 1869), quotes on 219–221.

Throughout the Early Modern Era, Europeans increasingly defined Africa as a place of disease and odor and consistently portrayed the peoples arriving to New World plantations as similarly pungent and savage.[102] The conception of Africa as a wasteland that caused people to become indolent emerged out of interchange between the peripheries and the London metropole, which searched Africa for spaces of new wealth to accumulate. To find new areas to accrue monies from African and Atlantic shores, Western Europeans of the nineteenth century defined Africans as primitive through the sense of smell, applying whiteness through a sense of scenting that discursively marked black bodies and minds as profligate and incapable of the modern application of mercantilist, cameralist, and capitalist cultivation.

CORE, PERIPHERY, STENCH

As the Conclusion to this book will outline in further detail, the nose also became vital on the eve of the American Civil War to cure the race crisis caused by the emergence of a mixed-race class of slaves and free blacks in the United States. Because slaveholders raped their slaves for centuries, mixed-race children became an often-concerning population group for white masters and emerging Herrenvolk political culture. As Mark Smith has argued, one way to cure this racial crisis of the sense of sight, whereby slaves and free blacks could increasingly pass as white and into white society, was to increasingly rely on the other four senses to define racial others.[103] This racial crisis led to much concern over what society would look and smell like when freedom arrived. Because of these apprehensions, renewed discourses on African odors became common during the later Antebellum Era, as within Charles Van Allen's "Suggestions upon

---

[102] Within the nineteenth-century United States, race, odor, and disease also linked within racialized geographies of cholera and yellow fever. Altschuler, *Medical Imagination*, 105–120. For a medical reading of yellow fever causes that focuses on contagion, see Thomas Apel, *Feverish Bodies, Enlightened Minds: Science and the Yellow Fever Controversy in the Early American Republic* (Stanford, CA: Stanford University Press, 2017), 35–64. See also Timothy Choy, "Air's Substantiations," in *Lively Capital: Biotechnologies, Ethics, and Governance in Global Markets*, ed. Kaushik Sunder Rajan (Durham, NC: Duke University Press, 2012), 121–154; Projit Bihari Mukharji, "The 'Cholera Cloud' in the Nineteenth Century 'British World': History of an Object-Without-an-Essence," *Bulletin of the History of Medicine: Organ of the American Association for the History of Medicine and of the Johns Hopkins Institute of the History of Medicine* 86, 3 (2012): 303–332.

[103] Smith, *How Race Is Made*, 62–76.

Animal Odor" of 1856 that summarized how common it was to encounter the smell of Africans and African Americans in the South. This "peculiar odor" that was so distinguishable "from the white race" and would not "easily yield to a due application of soap and water" was part of consistent debate in the Old South amongst both polygenetic and monogenetic racial scholars as to the variances of humankind.[104]

Within British actress Fanny Kemble's *Journal of a Residence on a Georgian Plantation in 1838–1839* (1863), such concerns with a frighteningly amalgamated society also took on scented comparison and olfactory concern. Surveying her husband's plantation in Georgia, Kemble noted the extreme dirtiness of the footmen who worked as slave servants in the central house. The way the servants waited on the table was "not … particularly agreeable" to Fanny due to the "personal offensiveness" of odor that the "Southerners you know insist … is inherent with the race, and it is one of their most cogent reasons for keeping them as slaves." The smell of African bodies turned Kemble's relatively progressive nose into a racial critic in her sojourning Southern environs, leading her to assert that "freeing of the blacks might prove a rather odoriferous process than the contrary."[105]

Continuing such an increasingly common Western tradition of olfactory racism that infected popular considerations and academics alike was French scientist Georges Pouchet, a comparative anatomist whose *De la Pluralité des Races Humaines* (1858) was published in English as *The Plurality of the Human Race* (1864). The systematic work explored how to clarify links between polygenetic studies of anatomy and cultural studies in the growing field of anthropology. Within his racialist analysis, Pouchet applied these dual academic lenses to articulate differences within both physiological and cultural aspects of human societies. For one of his decisive physiological variances, Pouchet highlighted the "peculiar smell of the Negro. This is so strong, that it even impregnates for some time a place where a Negro may only have been remained for a few hours and it

---

[104] Charles Van Allen, "Suggestions upon Animal Odor," *Southern Medical and Surgical Journal* 12 (1856): 360–366; John Van Evrie, *Subgenation: The Theory of the Normal Relation of the Races: an Answer to "Miscegenation"* (New York: John Bradburn, 1864), 13–17; Melanie Kiechle, *Smell Detectives: An Olfactory History of Nineteenth-Century Urban America* (Seattle: University of Washington Press, 2017), 130–135.

[105] Fanny Kemble, *Journal of a Residence on a Georgian Plantation in 1838–1839* (London: Longman, Green, Longman, Roberts & Green, 1863), quotes on 21–25; Diane Roberts, *The Myth of Aunt Jemima: Representations of Race and Region* (London; New York: Routledge, 1994), 94–96.

is so characteristic, that it alone constitutes a grave presumption in matters of slave-trading."[106] These "matters of slave-trading" focused on
how black bodies were easily tracked throughout the wilderness due to
an odor that was deemed "quite independent of age." This tracking was
becoming increasingly simplified as the "American race" of white men
and women reached such a "sensitive perfection" as to be able search out
fleeing slaves due to the supposedly universal pungency of the black body.
Pouchet followed this digest on hunting slaves through their smell by
summarizing that these odors did not come from sweat, could not be
washed away with bathing, and were deeply ingrained within the black
body. Consequently, he asserted stereotypical black odors as justification
for his belief in the polygenetic derivation of the human races through an
axiom regarding the different smells of animal species like the jackal and
the dog, turning his belief in polygenesis even more into discussions of the
supposed subhumanity signaled by African scents.[107]

The raw material of cultural ethnography about Africa and Africans
was originally sent from the periphery to the core. English and French
writers then took that raw material and coded sensory stereotypes for the
consumption of the Atlantic masses. For all their genius, these writers
took a vast and diverse ethnographic corpus from the likes of Leo
Africanus, Duarte Lopes, and Samuel Purchas and created flat racial
stereotypes necessary for theatrical and narrative production. These colonialist productions of the metropole expanded a consumer revolution of
material goods that also entered embodied racism into a vast and increasingly scientific Republic of Letters. That network involved the exchange of
pseudoscientific information that linked freshly racialized knowledge
through an epistolary, performative, and interactive culture of the literate
elite who circulated ideals and prejudices through scientific debate, religious discourse, and personal correspondence.[108]

---

[106] Georges Pouchet, *The Plurality of the Human Race*, trans. Hugh J. C. Beavan (London:
Longman, Green, Longman, and Roberts, 1864), quotes on 54–56.

[107] Pouchet, *Plurality*, 54–56. For more on polygenesis in later American contexts, see
Robert Entman, *The Black Image in the White Mind* (Chicago: University of Chicago
Press, 2010 [1971]), 71–96; Jessica Blatt, *Race and the Making of American Political
Science* (Philadelphia: University of Pennsylvania Press, 2018). See also foundational
forms of later racialism within Robert Knox, *The Races of Men: a Philosophical Enquiry
into the Influence of Race Over the Destinies of Nations* (London: Renshaw, 1862).

[108] For the early modern Republic of Letters, see Beth Fowkes Tobin, *Colonizing Nature:
The Tropics in British Arts and Letters, 1760–1820* (Philadelphia: University of
Pennsylvania Press, 2011); Peter Mancall, *Hakluyt's Promise: An Elizabethan's
Obsession for an English America* (New Haven, CT: Yale University Press, 2010),

Inundated with letters, the eighteenth-century Atlantic World functioned as an interconnected system that circulated the standards of the elite through conscious acts of reading and writing that informed the body how to function.[109] This horrendous triangle trade thereafter was perpetuated throughout the Atlantic World through a racially informed slave system supported by popular beliefs of natural olfactory inferiority that no cleansing could possibly cure. Therein, the African body was framed as a temporal and biological object to justify the rise of a form of capitalism based upon Western imperialism in Africa and the continued use of slave bodies throughout the New World. Within this ultimate cultural conception, the entire continent of Africa became an objectified commodity that produced miasmas. To cure these multifarious ills, Europeans scrambled to African shores with curative justifications based within Christian moralism and ethical discourses centering upon capitalist agronomy and the profits to be earned from imposing colonial experiments.

As Chapters 3 and 4 will portray, African diasporic populations throughout the Atlantic World would not simply internalize such racial olfactory discourses without resistance. African American slaves often became adept at understanding the disdain that slaveholders had for the supposed odor of the African. As one slave told his industrial labor master, W. B. Morgan, in antebellum Anderson County, Kentucky:

236–240; Richard Brown, *Knowledge Is Power: The Diffusion of Information in Early America, 1700–1865* (New York: Oxford University Press, 1989), 65–81, 110–131; Norman Fiering, "The Transatlantic Republic of Letters: A Note on the Circulation of Learned Periodicals to Early Eighteenth-Century America," *William and Mary Quarterly* 33, 4 (1976): 642–660; Ian Steele, *The English Atlantic, 1675–1740: An Exploration of Communication and Community* (New York: Oxford University Press, 1986); Lindsay O'Neill, *The Opened Letter: Networking in the Early Modern British World* (Philadelphia: University of Pennsylvania Press, 2015), 78–112; Konstantin Dierks, *In My Power: Letter Writing and Communications in Early America* (Philadelphia: University of Pennsylvania Press, 2011), 141–188; Michael Warner, *The Letters of the Republic: Publication and the Public Sphere in Eighteenth-Century America* (Cambridge, MA: Harvard University Press, 2010), 34–72.

[109] For literacy and the sensory alterations of the body, see Elizabeth Spiller, *Reading and the History of Race in the Renaissance* (Cambridge: Cambridge University Press, 2014), 1–10; the readings of insects, the soul, and the mind within Kate Tunstall, "The Early Modern Embodied Mind and the Entomological Imaginary," *in Mind, Body, Motion, Matter: Eighteenth-Century British and French Literary Perspectives*, eds. Mary Helen McMurran and Alison Conway (Toronto: University of Toronto Press, 2016), 202–229; the education of civil manners within David Shields, *Civil Tongues & Polite Letters in British America* (Chapel Hill: University of North Carolina Press, 1997), 6–10; and racial seeing within literature in William Cohen, *Embodied: Victorian Literature and the Senses* (Minneapolis: University of Minnesota Press, 2009), 65–85.

"White folks don't like to smell a live nigger."[110] Knowing the olfactory disdain of their masters' false sensory perceptions, groups of Africans, slaves, and free blacks would often retaliate, survive, and persist through different understandings of the sense of smell. Through exposing the transgressive possibilities of smelling as African agency and using smells to fill gaps within the poor medical establishment provided by masters, slaves found creative olfactory spaces for everyday opposition to the dreadful systems of slavery in the Americas and the colonialism that dotted the laboring landscapes of what would only later become the decolonized Global South.

[110] *Federal Writers' Project: Slave Narrative Project, Vol. 7, Kentucky, Bogie-Woods* (Washington, DC: Library of Congress, 1936), quote on 119.

3

Ephemeral Africa

Essentialized Odors and the Slave Ship

The opening epigraph of James Scott's *Domination and the Arts of Resistance* (1990) introduces an Ethiopian proverb to exemplify the concepts of "hidden transcripts" and "weapons of the weak," two notions now essential to understanding subaltern resistance. In this adage, a nobleman walks in front of an Ethiopian serf: "When the great lord passes the wise peasant bows deeply and silently farts."[1] African slaves in the Atlantic littoral applied similarly rebellious ideas about odor as both "hidden transcripts" and "weapons of the weak" to respond to the conditions of different slave systems. These various spiritual attentions to olfactory components of daily life within diverse African pasts created creolized understandings of odor within the Atlantic World. For most African ethnic groups forced into the Atlantic Slave Trade from West, Central, and southern African nations, the olfactory frequently inhabited a space between the living and the dead, whereby ghosts, spirits, and religious practitioners in the material world could detect each other through the sense of smell.[2]

For Scott, a hidden transcript implies the inherent lower-class critique of class or colonial power that is kept "behind the back" of the socially

---

[1] James Scott, *Domination and the Arts of Resistance: Hidden Transcripts* (New Haven, CT: Yale University Press, 1990), quote on v. See also Randy Browne, *Surviving Slavery in the British Caribbean* (Philadelphia: University of Pennsylvania Press, 2017), 6–8.

[2] For more on ideas of specters and fetishes within European ideas of African spiritualism, see Monique Allewaert, *Ariel's Ecology: Plantations, Personhood, and Colonialism in the American Tropics* (Minneapolis: University of Minnesota Press, 2013), 119–135; Agnes Kedzierska Manzon, "Humans and Things: Mande Fetishes as Subjects," *Anthropological Quarterly* 86, 4 (2013): 1119–1152.

dominant populace. A hidden transcript is a way to speak truth to power through methods that the prevailing leadership cannot perceive, because that class does not attribute enough intellectual ingenuity to the dominated to believe that group could formulate a significant language of resistance. This "backstage discourse consisting of what cannot be spoken in the face of power" has frequently been represented through the assertion that carnivalesque uses of odor, pungent material culture, and fecal matter against the dominant class are a common structural element of subaltern struggle.[3]

Within these clashes, the use of the fecal, polluted material, and odors often resists what literary critic Warwick Anderson has called the "somatic disciplining" that came with rising colonial forces and their domineering "poetics of pollution" in what would become the Global South.[4] Critical backstage uses of odor, like all hidden transcripts, can reify against dominant classes within cultural transcripts that speak truth to power in open forums of the public sphere. Within the Atlantic littoral, partly because of the acculturated sensory environs of Europeans that judged smell as increasingly biological, the cultural odors created by Africans persisted as forms of quotidian ethnic retention that rose from the mire of bondage as veiled forms of everyday resistance.[5]

Through exhibiting a diversity of smells and ideas about smelling that were individual, ethnic, and often idiosyncratic, Africans throughout the Atlantic littoral asserted themselves as subjects against Western attempts to make the African into a commodified, miasmic, and pungent object. As a part of this process, minor acts of cultural retention that asserted forms of sensory individuality could gather into a broader discourse of resistance that involved the retention of generally conceived African sensory understandings. The commodification process applied by European slave traders worked to homogenize ideas about African bodies, to make the

---

[3] Scott, *Domination and the Arts of Resistance*, x–xii, 4–10, quote on xii; M. M. Bakhtin, *Rabelais and His World* (Cambridge, MA: MIT Press, 1968); Marlene Ringgaard Lorensen, *Dialogical Preaching: Bakhtin, Otherness and Homiletics* (Gottingen: Vandenhoeck & Ruprecht, 2013), 13–19, 95–115; Michael Bristol, *Carnival and Theater: Plebeian Culture and the Structure of Authority in Renaissance England* (New York: Methuen, 1985), 72–87.

[4] Warwick Anderson, "Excremental Colonialism: Public Health and the Poetics of Pollution," *Critical Inquiry* 21, 3 (1995): 640–669, quotes on 640, 644.

[5] Dipesh Chakrabarty, "Open Space/Public Place: Garbage, Modernity and India," *South Asia: Journal of South Asian Studies* 14, 1 (1991): 15–31; J. D. Esty, "Excremental Postcolonialism," *Contemporary Literature* 40, 1 (1999): 22–59; Stephen Greenblatt, "Filthy Rites," *Daedalus* 111, 3 (1982): 1–16.

stereotypical and commodified object partly through hackneyed but resilient ideas about biological odor and race. Resistance arose from Africans and African Americans asserting their antagonistically subject status partly through both individual preservation and cultural appreciation for smells.[6]

Many Africans in the Atlantic World also directly resisted the idea of pungent bodies and fragrant cultures within their written texts. The brief history of Africa provided within Olaudah Equiano's *Interesting Narrative* (1789) suggested such a contradiction through a summary of the table manners of many African groups, who before tasting food "always wash our hands: indeed our cleanliness on all occasions is extreme; but on this it is an indispensable ceremony."[7] Other abolitionists, slaves, and free blacks also found olfactory assertions of racist masters ridiculous through the inclusion of material scrutiny against slaveowners within written descriptions of laboring lives. Although sources are limited, rich cultural memory remains that Africans and their descendants in the Atlantic World often attributed poor odors to traders and their masters, while defending their own olfactory cultures through rhetoric that included accusing masters of not providing the materials necessary for European ideals of cleanliness. For example, John Andrew Jackson, an escaped slave, healer, and abolitionist who had fled South Carolina in 1846, specifically portrayed that slaves were not allowed to clean their bodies, and because they "are not allowed a change of clothes, but only one suit for summer, and the perspiration is so great that they smell rank ... they are robbed of comfort and cleanliness by the cruelty and avarice of their masters."[8] Slaves often used these sensory terms to describe their masters and the work regime that slavery created as demonic. The hell of living in slavery frequently

[6] For introduction to ideas of sensory resistance and odor, see Constance Classen, "Other Ways to Wisdom: Learning through the Senses across Cultures," *International Review of Education* 45, 3 (1999): 269–280; Peter Stallybrass and Allon White, *The Politics and Poetics of Transgression* (Ithaca: Cornell University Press, 1986), 27–79.

[7] Olaudah Equiano, *The Interesting Narrative of the Life of Olaudah Equiano, or, Gustavus Vassa, the African* (Norwich: S. P., 1794), quote on 9–10. For more on Equiano and resistance, see Shaun Regan, "Learning Not to Curse: Swearing, Testimony, and Truth in Olaudah Equiano's *The Interesting Narrative*," *The Eighteenth Century* 54, 3 (2013): 339–358; Stefan Wheelock, *Barbaric Culture and Black Critique: Black Antislavery Writers, Religion, and the Slaveholding Atlantic* (Charlottesville: University of Virginia Press, 2016).

[8] John Andrew Jackson, *The Experience of a Slave in South Carolina* (London: Passmore & Alabaster, 1862), quotes on 22–23.

became a deeply sensory experience for those subjected to the specific toil of the cotton fields of the Deep South. In response, many former slaves wrote of their masters producing the sensory domains of hell.[9]

As later postcolonial scholars have also portrayed, nearly everything within colonized spaces was often degraded by the colonizer through abusive materiality and the rhetoric of sensory semantics and scientific discourse, which was often resisted through subaltern psychological modifications and the creation of different sensory expectations. As Albert Memmi proclaimed in his essential *The Colonizer and the Colonized* (1965): "[T]he colonized's devaluation ... extends to everything that concerns him: to his land, which is ugly, unbearably hot, amazingly cold, evil smelling; such discouraging geography that it condemns him to contempt and poverty, to eternal dependence."[10]

African ethnic sensory retention throughout the diaspora, which resisted such colonial degradation and attempts to create dependency, has often been considered a cultural and romantic triumph.[11] However, understanding specific African ethnic sensory understandings of perception is not directly demonstrable from documentation from the slave trade era. In order to explore smelling, this chapter therefore applies particular structural ideas about smelling to construct a broader and inclusive African past, a pan-African motif of sensing that focuses on specific West, Central, and southern African histories of smelling in order to conceptualize a clearer understanding of the nasal cultures of the Dark Continent that were taken upon the Middle Passage.[12]

---

[9] For more on how African slaves in the American South described their subjection in sensory terms, see Edward Blum, "'It Is True in More Senses than One, That Slavery Rests upon Hell!' Embodiment, Experience, and Evil in African American Discussions of Slavery and Slaveholders," *The Journal of Religion* 97, 3 (2017): 301–322; Daphne Brooks, *Bodies in Dissent: Spectacular Performances of Race and Freedom, 1850–1910* (Durham, NC: Duke University Press, 2006), 66–130.

[10] Albert Memmi, *The Colonizer and the Colonized* (New York: Orion, 1965 [1957 in French]), quote on 67. For more on Caribbean forms of inward and psychological resistance, see Richard Burton, *Afro-Creole: Power, Opposition, and Play in the Caribbean* (Ithaca: Cornell University Press, 1997), 48–50.

[11] For examples of romantic agency, see Floyd Merrell, *Capoeira and Candomblé: Conformity and Resistance in Brazil* (Princeton, NJ: Markus Wiener, 2005), 12–15; Charles Joyner, *Down by the Riverside: A South Carolina Slave Community* (Urbana: University of Illinois Press, 2009 [1985]).

[12] For studies of archival prejudice, see Carolyn Steedman, *Dust* (Manchester: Manchester University Press, 2001), 5–10; Natalie Zemon Davis, *Fiction in the Archives: Pardon Tales and Their Tellers in Sixteenth-Century France* (Stanford, CA: Stanford University Press, 1987), 1–6; Carlo Ginzburg, *The Cheese and the Worms: The Cosmos of a Sixteenth-Century Miller* (Baltimore, MD: Johns Hopkins University Press, 1980);

This broad understanding of a pan-African olfactory past does not deny that there were significant ethnic and linguistic differences regarding smelling amongst the diverse African nations, ethnogenetic assemblages, and creolized communities within the Atlantic littoral. Rather, these differences are vital, but overemphasis on those differences would habitually prevent understanding an expansive history of smelling due to the sparsity of source materials regarding specific African ethnic concepts of odor. The examples used in this chapter to explore African considerations of smelling in the past offer individual ethnic identifications of smell to grasp a fuller understanding of African diasporic concepts of smell and resistance within the New World, while revealing the obvious consideration that ethnic identity was not pan-African during nearly all eras of the Atlantic Slave Trade.[13]

Many Africanist scholars also often claim that the use of African cultural motifs from after the slave trade should not be used as a way to analyze past philosophies, as it possibly traps Africans within a colonialist understanding that Africa remained static while European colonies conquered the globe through forward cultural achievements.[14] However, while understanding these concerns, *The Smell of Slavery* explores the use of many twentieth-century and modern African cultural rituals of smelling to appreciate anachronism as an academic weapon against the

Ann Laura Stoler, *Along the Archival Grain: Epistemic Anxieties and Colonial Common Sense* (Princeton, NJ: Princeton University Press, 2009), 105–140.

[13] For slave studies and archival prejudice, see Marlene Daut, *Tropics of Haiti: Race and the Literary History of the Haitian Revolution in the Atlantic World, 1789–1865* (Liverpool: Liverpool University Press, 2015), 1–8; Michel-Rolph Trouillot, *Silencing the Past: Power and the Production of History* (Boston: Beacon, 1995); Jenny Sharpe, *Ghosts of Slavery: A Literary Archaeology of Black Women's Lives* (Minneapolis: University of Minnesota Press, 2003); Diana Taylor, *The Archive and the Repertoire: Performing Cultural Memory in the Americas* (Durham, NC: Duke University Press, 2003), 16–20, 193–236; Sibylle Fischer, *Modernity Disavowed: Haiti and the Cultures of Slavery in the Age of Revolution* (Durham, NC: Duke University Press, 2004); Ifeoma Kiddoe Nwankwo, *Black Cosmopolitanism: Racial Consciousness and Transnational Identity in the Nineteenth-Century Americas* (Philadelphia: University of Pennsylvania Press, 2005), 8–10; James Epstein, *Scandal of Colonial Rule: Power and Subversion in the British Atlantic During the Age of Revolution* (Cambridge: Cambridge University Press, 2012), 228–265; Wendy Anne Warren, "'The Cause of Her Grief': The Rape of a Slave in Early New England," *Journal of American History* 93, 4 (2007): 1031–1049; Marisa Fuentes, *Dispossessed Lives: Enslaved Women, Violence, and the Archive* (Philadelphia: University of Pennsylvania Press, 2016).

[14] For pan-Africanism and debates on the archive, see Akinwumi Ogundiran, "The End of Prehistory? An Africanist Comment," *American Historical Review* 118, 3 (2013): 788–801; Paul Lovejoy, "Identifying Enslaved Africans in the African Diaspora," in *Identity in the Shadow of Slavery*, ed. Paul Lovejoy (London: Continuum, 2000), 1–29.

standard temporal structures of colonized archives that overly appreciated the sensory changes introduced by European colonization. Following the linear timeline of the history of slavery and the whiggish histories of the Enlightenment and abolitionism does not suffice for understanding the cultural complexities of African survivals within the diaspora and changing cultural patterns upon the African continent.[15] Within this chapter, structural and anachronistic use of modern ritual is therefore paired with the few references that remain from African experiences of odor within Africa during the era of the Atlantic Slave Trade. These rhizomatic connections across time and space allow for appreciation of common and resistant African understandings of odor that were, during the time of slavery in the Atlantic World, ethnically oriented and never static.[16]

As the anecdote about the Jamaican slave girl described by surveyor Edward Long in Chapter 2 exemplifies, African slaves within the Atlantic World could mobilize odor as a multivalent weapon of the weak against their masters.[17] Chapter 3 expands upon that reference to explore African ideas about odor prior to crossing upon the stenchful and torturous Middle Passage. Chapter 4 continues this analysis to portray how Africans and African Americans throughout the Atlantic littoral contributed olfactory traditions to assert medical and spiritual agency and create rival geographies in a spatial game against their master's judgmental noses.[18] This analysis of the retention and recreation of cultural ideas

---

[15] Michelle Wright, *Physics of Blackness: Beyond the Middle Passage Epistemology* (Minneapolis: University of Minnesota Press, 2015), 37–72; Michael Gomez, *Exchanging Our Country Marks, The Transformation of African Identities in the Colonial and Antebellum South* (Chapel Hill: University of North Carolina Press, 1998), 8–13; Joseph Miller, "Retention, Reinvention, and Remembering: Restoring Identities through Enslavement in Africa and under Slavery in Brazil," in *Enslaving Connections: Changing Cultures of Africa and Brazil during the Era of Slavery*, eds. José Curto and Paul Lovejoy (Amherst, NY: Humanity, 2004), 81–121.

[16] For the power of anachronism to disrupt an archive, see Jacques Derrida, *Archive Fever: A Freudian Impression* (Chicago: University of Chicago Press, 1996), 27–29; Steedman, *Dust*, 66–82.

[17] Edward Long, Volume II of *The History of Jamaica, or, General Survey of the Ancient and Modern State of That Island with Reflections on Its Situation, Settlements, Inhabitants, Climate, Products, Commerce, Laws, and Government* (London: T. Lowndes, 1774), 425–426.

[18] For introduction to work on African medical traditions, see Jonathan Roberts, "Medical Exchange on the Gold Coast During the Seventeenth and Eighteenth Centuries," *Canadian Journal of African Studies* 45, 3 (2011): 480–523; Robert Martin Baum, *Shrines of the Slave Trade: Diola Religion and Society in Precolonial Senegambia* (New York: Oxford University Press, 1999), 8–23; George Harley, *Native African Medicine, with Special Reference to its Practice in the Mano Tribe in Liberia* (London:

about odor in the New World continues the project of recentering the African as the driving force for modernity within studies of capitalism, commodification, and colonial subjugation.[19]

CLEANLY AFRICANS AND FALSELY CONSCIOUS SMELLS

Despite generally spreading ideas about African bodies and their inherent odors, many early modern European travelers to Africa noted often of the cleanliness procedures that some Africans applied as fragments of different ethnic traditions. James Welsh's early voyages to Benin in 1588 and 1590 recorded the abundance of the "stores of soaps" that smelled like "beaten violets" that the West Africans he encountered used for their daily washing.[20] Richard Jobson's voyages up the River Gambra, the modern Gambia River, chronicled originally in the *Golden Trade* (1623), also entailed specific cultural and ecological encounters with intense African odors. While surveying the African landscape with his nose, Jobson noted the importance of laundering for the nations he encountered, distinguishing the importance of using large "gowrdes" for the "washing of clothes." The West Africans that Jobson described used many different herbs and plants to scent their bodies and found European garlic an interesting olfactory substance that they chose to use as a perfume rather than as a foodstuff.[21]

Frank Cass, 1970); Abayomi Sofowora, *Medical Plants and Traditional Medicine in Africa* (Ibadan: John Wiley & Sons, 1982); Bep Oliver-Bever, *Medicinal Plants in Tropical West Africa* (Cambridge: Cambridge University Press, 1986).

[19] Chris Uroh, "Looking Through a Broken Mirror: Blackness, Shared Memory, Shared Identity and Shared Destiny," in *Africa, Brazil, and the Construction of Trans-Atlantic Black Identities*, eds. Barry Boubacar, Elisee Akpo Soumonni, and Livio Sansone (Trenton, NJ: Africa World, 2008), 127–146; Michael Gomez, *Reversing Sail: A History of the African Diaspora* (Cambridge: Cambridge University Press, 2008), 162–215. See also Toby Green, *A Fistful of Shells: West Africa from the Rise of the Slave Trade to the Age of Revolution* (Chicago: University of Chicago Press, 2019), 384–392.

[20] John Hamilton Moore, *A New and Complete Collection of Voyages and Travels: Containing All That Have Been Remarkable from the Earliest Period to the Present Time ...: Comprehending an Extensive System of Geography, Describing, in the Most Accurate Manner, Every Place Worthy of Notice, in Europe, Asia, Africa, and America* (London: Alexander Hogg, 1778), quotes on 335–336. See also water cultures and critique of masters within Kevin Dawson, *Undercurrents of Power: Aquatic Culture in the African Diaspora* (Philadelphia: University of Pennsylvania Press, 2018), 14–40.

[21] Richard Jobson, *The Golden Trade; or, A Discovery of the River Gambra, and the Golden Trade of the Aethiopians* (Devonshire: Speight and Walpole, 1904 [1623]), 166–175, quotes on 168.

While surveying the coastal establishments near Guinea in 1666, the French sailors of Sieur Villault's voyage to West Africa described comparable cleanliness customs of both perfuming and washing. Through an often disturbing tale that presented children of the region as having flat noses because their mothers worked too hard in the fields and birthed more rectangular and smooth faces, the English translation of *A Relation of the Coasts of Africk Called Guinee* (1670) summarized how these Guinean women also washed their children each day with palm oils.[22] Prior to offering fetishizes upon altar rituals observed by the French sailors, these West African ethnic groups would "wash also their faces" with "particular care."[23] After funerals where fetishes and donations were placed alongside and within the grave of the honored dead, the Guinea nations that Villault observed would then rinse in preparation for a funeral feast. As well, the male nobles of the nearby Fetu region, in modern Ghana, washed and were kept "neat against night" by groups of women who, like the rest of the citizenry, would retain "great veneration" for their cleanly leaders.[24] Although Villault became famed in later European literature for his shattering of fetishes and handing out crosses to African nations, reading against the grain of his Christian worldview portrays African cultures he encountered as attuned to both cleanliness and perfuming. As these encounters exemplify, during this primary period of the Early Modern Era, as outlined in Chapter 1, travelers to Africa still focused on cultural odors and could often consequently find in African ethnic customs an appreciation for hygiene and aroma.[25]

The aforementioned Scottish translator John Ogilby's *Africa* (1670) similarly described a group of Africans near the Gold Coast region of Insoko, possibly near Begho in the Bono trading state, who "wash every morning and evening from head to foot" and "count it a great shame to Break Wind in the presence of any" person near them.[26] English merchant and mariner William Wilkinson's *Systema Africanum* (1690) likewise described the importance of washing within different African nations near Guinea. Often confusing and possibly merging Islamic practices of the wandering marabout with descriptions of traditional West African

---

[22] Nicolas Villault, *A Relation of the Coasts of Africk Called Guinee* (London: John Starkey, 1670), 148–150.

[23] Villault, *Relation*, quotes on 168–169.   [24] Villault, *Relation*, quote on 224–225.

[25] Villault, *Relation*, 194–195.

[26] John Ogilby, *Africa: Being an Accurate Description of the Regions of Ægypt, Barbary, Lybia, and Billedulgerid, the land of Negroes, Guinee, Æthiopia and the Abyssines* (London: Johnson, 1670), quotes on 446–466.

spiritualism, Wilkinson described the roles of different "priests" in the region who would travel to heal the sick, some with "simples" and herbals and others with spiritual "charms."[27] William Smith, who traveled to Africa in 1726, also offered a summary of the scented cleanliness of the people he observed on the islands off the Central African coast due to the abundance of palm oil soap and the industry for soap boiling common in the region, at that time run by the Portuguese.[28]

Even as English and French travelers to Africa encountered complex cultures that used various forms of soap and cleansing procedures, smell penetrated the concerns of the metropole to create many bodies within the later Atlantic World that constantly sensed the internally recognized and pungent inferiority of African bodies. Well into the era of European colonialism, general sensory discourse based on a false consciousness about the inherent smell of Africans was able to displace the material reality faced by many particular travelers who found something much more fragrant in the Heart of Darkness than simply the scents of the sub-human. In the metropole and on the periphery, writers generally discussed Africa as a place of odor and profligacy; however, many other travelers sensed directly with their noses something much more hygienically complex.

Although sources are limited, many African societies used oils and soaps for scenting and cleanliness prior to sustained European contact with their specific nations. During the voyage of English explorers Dixon Denham and Hugh Clapperton to areas in the Eastern Soudan in the 1820s, the observers often encountered many West and Central African cultures that similarly used an abundance of soap. While surveying areas for future European industrial entrances in the kola nut business, the travelers offered that the Africans they encountered in Bornou used lathers that included a "pleasant smell."[29] In the Western tradition of the civilizing process, soap became a commodity meant to conscript savage populations into modernity. These prejudicial narratives of odor and soap persisted within European metropolitan discourse, even though the actual

---

[27] William Wilkinson, *Systema Africanum: or a Treatise, Discovering the Intrigues and Arbitrary Proceedings of the Guiney Company* (London: Parliament, 1690), quotes on 24–25.

[28] Moore, *New and Complete Collection*, 483–484.

[29] Dixon Denham, Hugh Clapperton, Walter Oudney, and Abraham Salamé, *Narrative of Travels and Discoveries in Northern and Central Africa: In the Years 1822, 1823, and 1824* (London: John Murray, 1826), quote on 175.

material conditions within most of Africa already included soap, perfume, and cleanliness procedures from diverse ethnic pasts.

While considering his own body cleanly during his 1850s travels through different regions of Northern and Western Africa, the German explorer Henry Barth was also provided soap from his African companions, who traded their "native" commodity for the scented cloves that Barth carried with him on a specific journey into what is modern Nigeria.[30] At the Mendi Mission in Sierra Leone during the 1850s, the British traveler George Thompson similarly wrote of attention to cleanliness and scents within specific African cultures. The nations that were living in the area of southern Sierra Leone, where Thompson and his fellow English missionaries worked, generally "wash their hands before and after eating."[31] In *Western Africa* (1856), John Leighton Wilson, one of the first missionaries to West Africa from the United States as part of his service on the American Board of Commissioners for Foreign Missions, similarly described the importance of cleanliness during his earlier travels among the Kru of the Gold Coast in service of the American government, at that time choosing a place to establish the Liberian colony. He noted the importance of "washing and oiling their persons" and the great attention paid to the "care of their bodies" to remove "distressing odors."[32] As these American and English travelers displayed through their exchanges and encounters, the attention to soaping and cleaning the savage African had much more to do with the social and false construction of an African natural odor understood by many Europeans than with significant realities of material cleanliness that had always been part of African ethnic assemblages.

Partially because African traditions already included vast cleanliness procedures, the introduction of material Western soap was not able to deceitfully domesticate the African into European social formations because discourses of polygenesis defined the other of the African with an inherently different biology and pungency. The social construction of

[30] Heinrich Barth, Volume II of *Travels and Discoveries in North and Central Africa: Being a Journal of an Expedition Undertaken under the Auspices of H. B. M.'s Government, in the Years 1849–1855* (New York: Harper & Brothers, 1857), quote on 154–155.

[31] George Thompson, *Thompson in Africa, or, An Account of the Missionary Labors, Sufferings, Travels, Observations, &C. of George Thompson, in Western Africa, at the Mendi Mission* (Cleveland, OH: D. M. Ide, 1852), quote on 218–219.

[32] J. Leighton Wilson, *Western Africa; Its History, Condition, and Prospects* (London: S. Low, 1856), quotes on 124–126.

racial odors in the metropole included vast discursive power to define Africans as more stereotypically pungent than references to Africans' actual and material soaps, which were often considered aromatic and cleanly by those who traveled to truly visit sub-Saharan regions. As Anne McClintock described concerning the "commodity racism" of the nineteenth century West: "What could not be incorporated into the industrial formation ... was displaced on to the invented domain of the 'primitive', and thereby disciplined and contained."[33] The bourgeois Western European men and women of the nineteenth century claimed modernity through justifying the causes of colonial rule, a prerogative that often created structures of false sensory knowledge that reproduced racialized colonialism upon commodified colonial objects regardless of material realities.[34]

ANACHRONISTIC TRANSGRESSION

There are few references from African writers that describe a cultural appreciation for odors and perfumes from the peak era of the slave trade during the seventeenth and eighteenth centuries. To analyze African olfactory culture, research methods accordingly must highlight these references. However, in order to conceptualize a greater understanding of African olfactory philosophies during this era, vitality arises from reading against the temporal grain and relying on anachronistic sources. For direct and contemporary slave trade accounts, Equiano can again be instructive. His account of West Africa during his remembered childhood of the mid-eighteenth century focused often on the importance of smell in different aspects of his Igbo youth.[35] As the celebrated abolitionist described from his later English study, for the Igbo the "principal luxury is in perfumes," often made through the mixing and beating of

---

[33] Anne McClintock, "Soft-Soaping Empire: Commodity Racism and Imperial Advertising," in *Travellers' Tales: Narratives of Home and Displacement*, ed. George Robertson (London: Routledge, 1994), 131–154, quote on 140.

[34] David Theo Goldberg, *Racist Culture: Philosophy and the Politics of Meaning* (Oxford: Blackwell, 1993), 1–13; Wendy Brown, *Regulating Aversion: Tolerance in the Age of Identity and Empire* (Princeton, NJ: Princeton University Press, 2006), 3–13.

[35] For debates on Equiano's African origins, see Paul Lovejoy, "Autobiography and Memory: Gustavus Vassa, Alias Olaudah Equiano, the African," *Slavery & Abolition* 27, 3 (2006): 317–347; Vincent Carretta, *Equiano the African: Biography of a Self-Made Man* (Athens: University of Georgia Press, 2005); Alexander Byrd, "Eboe, Country, Nation, and Gustavus Vassa's 'Interesting Narrative'," *William and Mary Quarterly* 63, 1 (2006): 123–148.

odoriferous woods into powders later mixed for a fragrance filled with a "powerful odour." To access other aromas, Equiano described how different West African trees, most importantly various versions of the palm, were often tapped to release gallons of scented liquid into gourds that were strategically placed to fill during overnight hours.[36]

Prejudicial European sources like Ogilby's *Africa* (1670) are also important as a guide for understanding smelling within African societies during the era of the slave trade. The Scottish translator relayed how women in the Insoko region of what is now southern Nigeria used many different perfumes made of herbs and the parts of civet cats to scent their daily lives.[37] Many other populations in the South and West African regions that Ogilby described used smelling within spiritual contests whereby the wearing of specifically dirty and stinking garments warded off both evil spirits and carnivorous animals. Regarding southern African regions, Ogilby specifically recorded a narrative that centered on the wearing of an "ornament"-covered dress that included "guts of beasts" and sometimes encompassed the sartorial application of smelly "roots" taken from the bottom of rivers. To the north of these regions, in what was deemed the apocryphal, ancient, and sometimes utopian kingdom of Monomotapa and is probably today within modern Zimbabwe, the King in the region performed his power through perfuming the lights that were used to illuminate the path of his carried arrival.[38]

These references portray different West, Central, and southern African concepts of odor from the peak eras of Atlantic slavery. Together, they suggest that smelling was an important aspect of many different African societies before those cultures were creolized or altered through ethnogenesis within the New World.[39] Paired with summaries of some European

---

[36] Equiano, *Interesting Narrative*, quotes on 9–10.   [37] Ogilby, *Africa*, 464–466.

[38] Ogilby, *Africa*, quotes on 590–592, 596–598.

[39] A significant literature informs slave studies through describing how masters in the New World desired specific African national populations for different labor needs. This monograph understands those desires but must analyze odor through different ethnogenetic and creolized perspectives in order to articulate a common African desire for olfactory retention in the New World. For important works on different African ethnic groups in the Atlantic littoral and the importance of skilled labor that determined many purchases, see Peter Wood, *Black Majority: Negroes in Colonial South Carolina from 1670 Through the Stono Rebellion* (New York: Norton, 1976); Daniel Littlefield, *Rice and Slaves: Ethnicity and the Slave Trade in Colonial South Carolina* (Urbana: University of Illinois Press, 1991 [1981]); Daniel Domingues da Silva, *The Atlantic Slave Trade from West Central Africa: 1780–1867* (Cambridge: Cambridge University Press, 2017), 73–99; David Eltis and David Richardson, "The 'Numbers Game' and Routes to Slavery," in *Routes to Slavery: Direction, Ethnicity, and Mortality in the Transatlantic Slave Trade,*

travelers, these later narratives portray many different African ethnic patterns of olfactory appreciation. Whether for imbuing royal carriages, perfuming bodies, or making aromatic religious rituals, odor was a vital facet of many African societies before and during the slave trade. When nineteenth-century European travelers entered Africa in greater numbers, they consistently offered similar discussions of perfume and religious odors that can be used to correspondingly elaborate on African ideas of smelling during earlier eras.[40]

In his *Journal of a Residence in Ashante* (1824), Joseph Dupuis, an envoy from Great Britain who spent many years in North and West Africa, described olfactory religious rituals that are akin to the scented descriptions within Ogilby's earlier accounts. Odor was often deemed a transferal point within many of these West African traditions, whereby the ability to be smelled-out by medicine men meant a certain contact with a form of evil or internal spiritual weakness. As Dupuis described, during a great ceremony meant to honor the "Asante" chieftain, symbolic evil spirits danced toward the ruler and held their noses closed to signify the elder's olfactory impermeability.[41] Also submitting a description of the importance of odor as a spiritual vector during their travels to the Eastern Soudan during the 1820s, the aforementioned English voyagers Denham and Clapperton encountered a story regarding their desire to meet with the Sultan of Sego, within the borders of what is modern Mali. They recorded how the Sultan was told to be fearful of encountering the medical equipment of the Western doctors. This leader consequently "feared they had charms which would kill him, either by sight or smell." A West African cultural past had taught this leader that the odors of medical charms could invade the body and inflict harm. Such a fear was predicated

eds. David Eltis and David Richardson (London: Frank Cass, 1997), 1–15; Phillip Morgan, "The Cultural Implication of the Atlantic Slave Trade: African Regional Origins, American Destinations, and New World Developments," in *Routes to Slavery: Direction, Ethnicity, and Mortality in the Transatlantic Slave Trade*, eds. David Eltis and David Richardson (London: Frank Cass, 1997), 122–145.

[40] For English missionaries, religious judgment, and race during the nineteenth century, see Steven Maughan, *Mighty England Do Good: Culture, Faith, Empire, and World in the Foreign Missions of the Church of England, 1850–1915* (Grand Rapids, MI: Eerdmans, 2014); Brian Stanley, *Christian Missions and the Enlightenment* (Grand Rapids, MI: Eerdmans, 2001); Peter Edgerly Firchow, *Envisioning Africa: Racism and Imperialism in Conrad's Heart of Darkness* (Lexington: University of Kentucky Press, 2000).

[41] Joseph Dupuis, *Journal of a Residence in Ashantee, Comprising Notes and Researches Relative to the Gold Coast, and the Interior of Western Africa; Chiefly Collected from Arabic Mss. and Information Communicated by the Moslems of Guinea* (London: Colburn, 1824), 42–44.

on centuries of olfactory concern within diverse formulae of African ethnic medicines.[42]

The *Memoirs of William G. Crocker* (1860) likewise described a West African attention to the sense of smell within religious and medical rituals. Crocker, of Massachusetts, was a Baptist missionary in the Bassa region near Liberia during two expeditions from 1835 until his death in 1840. As part of his missionary activity, he described a West African practitioner, Sante Will, who used a "bowl of water in which were some herbs" to wash himself and bathe what was deemed a troubled married couple. This ceremony of matrimonial counseling involved the use of what Crocker described as "grisgri" charms and a "heterogeneous mass of dismal looking things" that were used in preparation for the bathing ceremony.[43]

Although dreary and languid to explore, the sources of Scientific Racism regarding Africa and Africans of the late nineteenth century that were partly inspired by the increasingly medical language of earlier sources also deliver references to the olfactory columns that upheld the psychological architecture of African spiritual cultures in the earlier Atlantic World.[44] The use of smelling-out became an important topic to these later scholars of Scientific Racism, who argued that primitive man was led to his primitive gods through his primitive nose. However, buried beneath the prejudicial association between odors and the primeval is a deep attention to odor among southern African nations that is at the positive root what seems to be a continental context for shared African beliefs within cultural value systems for smell. Reading between the lines of the racial treatises of the *American Phrenological Journal and Life Illustrated* from 1865 provides a summary of such practices of smelling-out witches as a traditional southern African skill through the racially termed "Kaffir" peoples. Like the seventeenth-century Guinea nations who sniffed out each other's morality summarized by traveler Manuel Alvares in Chapter 1, doctors of the southern African populations

---

[42] Denham, Clapperton, Oudney, and Salamé, *Narrative*, quotes on 94–96.

[43] *Memoir of William G. Crocker: Late Missionary in West Africa among the Bassas, Including a History of the Bassa Mission*, ed. Rebecca Stetson Medbery (Boston: Gould and Lincoln, 1860), quotes on 123–125.

[44] For Africa and Scientific Racism, see Helen Tilley, *Africa As a Living Laboratory: Empire, Development, and the Problem of Scientific Knowledge, 1870–1950* (Chicago: University of Chicago Press, 2011); Jeannette Jones, *In Search of Brightest Africa: Reimagining the Dark Continent in American Culture, 1884–1936* (Athens: University of Georgia Press, 2010).

analyzed by the xenophobic journal "profess to be able to 'smell out' the person they say bewitched the sick people." This nation, as with many African cultures during the Atlantic Slave Trade, believed most illness came from witchcraft, and the way to find witches was to smell-out their poison, bags of bewitching goods, or scented illnesses upon infirm bodies.[45]

These often-inimical nineteenth-century descriptions of African odors provide knowledge of the profound appreciation for smelling within a continuity of different African ethnic traditions. In British poet and Egyptologist Gerald Massey's *The Natural Genesis* (1883), a southern African proverb relayed similar aspects of olfactory spirituality. The adage proposed: "My Grandfather's root, bring sleep on the eyes of the lion and leopard and hyena: make them blind that they cannot find us: cover their noses that they cannot smell us out." While Massey was popular among Social Darwinist scholars through linking the increased use of the nose to primitive humans, he also left to scholars important links between different African languages and the sense of smell that show, partly through this proverb, the deep attention to the olfactory herbalism within southern African traditions of the curative mimosa-root and the spiritualism of smelling-out.[46]

Anthropologist Robert Rattray's analysis of the West African Asante during the 1920s also involved direct attention to the idea of smelling within African religious traditions. During ethnographical studies, Rattray summarized the "Ashanti"/Asante belief in the smell of spirits and the odors of ghosts. These spirits often had enough olfactory sensibility within the spiritual world that the Asante frequently presented spills of their wine to the ground to please

[45] Anonymous, "A Kaffir Witch Doctor," *The American Phrenological Journal and Life Illustrated: A Repository of Science, Literature, and General Intelligence* 41, 6 (June, 1865): quote on 189; Manuel Alvares, *Ethiopia Minor and a Geographical Account of the Province of Sierra Leone (c.1615)* (Liverpool: University of Liverpool Press, 1990), Appendix, "Of the Province of the Sousous: Single Chapter," 7–8. See also, Constance Classen, "The Witch's Senses: Sensory Ideologies and Transgressive Femininities from the Renaissance to Modernity," in *Empire of the Senses: The Sensual Culture Reader*, ed. David Howes (New York: Berg, 2005), 70–84.

[46] Gerald Massey, *The Natural Genesis, or, Second Part of A Book of the Beginnings, Containing an Attempt to Recover and Reconstitute the Lost Origines of the Myths and Mysteries, Types and Symbols, Religion and Language, with Egypt for the Mouthpiece and Africa As the Birthplace* (London: Williams and Norgate, 1883), 75–83, quotes on 386–387. See also, Theophilus Hahn, *Tsuni-Goam: The Supreme Being of the Khoi-Khoi* (London: Trübner & Company, 1881), 81–82.

their ghostly sensoriums.⁴⁷ Similarly, modern phenomenologist P. R. McKenzie has described the centrality of the natural and aromatic within West African religious traditions of the nineteenth century through a reading of how the spirit Orisha could be detected through the sensations of the Yoruba. In certain altar traditions observed in 1855 by Egba pastor Thomas King, the Yoruba practiced the burning of sacred charms to present an aroma that was meant to please the powerful deity.⁴⁸

Understanding that the olfactory is not primitive and can have its own aesthetic history is an important acknowledgement necessary to overcome the prejudice of scientific racists and can assist with uncovering a new sensory archive for the subaltern and racialized bodies of the Atlantic World. As noted, the literature on African smelling-out traditions within the historical settings of the Atlantic Slave Trade is limited.⁴⁹ Historically, using anachronistic sources was problematic for histories of Africa and the Atlantic Slave Trade, as such primary source work could aid in the creation of a rhetorically defined "static Africa" that was understood as unable to change without Western capitalist intrusion. However, anachronistic application of later sources to earlier histories is only problematic if value judgments are asserted through a Western understanding of time consciousness and progressive civilization. If passing and riverine time do not inherently mean progress, then it may not be specifically judgmental to equate African spiritualism of later eras to understand the earlier African past and the spiritualism of slaves within the Atlantic littoral.⁵⁰

As cases of smelling-out, personal African narratives, and European narratives of either soaping or "savagery" portray, many African

---

⁴⁷ R. S. Rattray and J. G. Christaller, *Ashanti Proverbs: The Primitive Ethics of a Savage People* (Oxford: Clarendon, 1969 [1916]), 36–38.

⁴⁸ P. R. McKenzie, *Hail Orisha!: A Phenomenology of a West African Religion in the Mid-Nineteenth Century* (Leiden: Brill, 1997), 38–47, 250–251.

⁴⁹ For examples, see Karen Elizabeth Flint, *Healing Traditions: African Medicine, Cultural Exchange, and Competition in South Africa, 1820–1948* (Athens: University of Ohio Press, 2008), 114–116; Geoffrey Parrinder, *West African Psychology: A Comparative Study of Psychological and Religious Thought* (Cambridge: James Clarke & Company, 2002), 164–165. Although far afield from slave trade regions, see also the tragic case of smelling-out and subsequent torture of the supposed witch Mamatiwane within *Pondoland: Unsettled Conditions in Pondoland; Case of 'smelling-out' (witchcraft) leading to torture of a woman at instigation of Chief Sigcan*, folio 610, 1891–1892, South Africa, DO 119/118.

⁵⁰ For more debates on static Africa, see Walter Rodney, *How Europe Underdeveloped Africa* (Fahamu, Kenya: Pambazuka, 2012), 135–136, 249–250; Toyin Falola, *The Power of African Cultures* (Rochester, NY: University of Rochester Press, 2008), 52–59.

conceptions of odor during the slave trade often involved formations of fair and foul smells that could emerge from different constructs of work, perfume, ritual practice, and witchcraft. Various conceptions of herbalism, witchcraft, divining, and smelling the natural world should not be dismissed as anachronistic to earlier African cultures, as the evidence that exists for the history of those societies is often clouded in the etic and oppressive languages of colonial powers and their archives of suppression.[51]

Within the Atlantic World to be explored through narratives of aromatic resistance and the ethnogenetic olfactory in Chapter 4, the use of odor in rituals often involved similar survivals of aromatic appreciation for animals and spirituality. In a print relaying African rituals of the Water Mama in Paramaribo of 1833, such appreciation is represented through the familiars, mixing bowl, clothing, and necromancy also portrayed throughout the many African travel narratives described earlier in this chapter (see Figure 3.1).[52] Such visually relayed survivals represent that African spiritualism and sensory consciousness were reborn in the New World through continued connection to a version of the sensorium that was much different and materially engaged for Africans than Europeans succumbing to false sensory consciousness of racialized subterfuge and the fetishized influences of bourgeoise consciousness.

LITERATURE AND THE AFRICAN OLFACTORY

As with reading against the temporal grain of Massey's transmission of southern African folklore within his anthropological and Social Darwinist texts, some twentieth-century West African folktales and oral history can also provide attention to emic considerations of African concentrations on odor in the different cultural and temporal settings of the Atlantic World.[53] Animal metaphors are common in tales of odor that permeate redolent African oral traditions, as with the potent sense of smell

---

[51] For more historical references to smelling-out, see Geoffrey Parrinder, *West African Religion, A Study of the Beliefs and Practices of Akan, Ewe, Yoruba, Ibo, and Kindred Peoples* (London: Epworth, 1961), 169–171; E. E. Evans-Pritchard, *The Zande Trickster* (Oxford: Clarendon, 1967), 82–83.

[52] For more on Mami Wata and this image, see Browne, *Surviving Slavery*, 138–139; Mei-Mei Sanford, "Living Water," in *Osun across the Waters*, eds. Joseph Murphy and Mei-Mei Sanford (Bloomington: Indiana University Press, 2001), 237–250.

[53] For introductions to traditional West African spiritualisms, see Patrick McNaughton, *The Mande Blacksmiths: Knowledge, Power, and Art in West Africa* (Bloomington: University of Indiana Press, 1988), 8–18; Timothy Insoll, "Introduction: Shrines,

FIGURE 3.1 Print of "A Spiritual Healer, Paramaribo, Suriname, ca. 1831."
Source: Pierre Jacques Benoit, *Voyage a Surinam ... cent dessins pris sur nature
par l'auteur* (Bruxelles, 1839), plate xvii, fig. 36. Courtesy of the John Carter
Brown Library

regarding talking elephants in "The Tail of the Elephant Queen" that
focuses upon treating siblings with reverence.[54] In the tale of "Spider
Finds a Fool," about the importance of trust within economic relation-
ships, the odor of a stinking mouse is commonly used as a signifier of
a mistrusting relationship.[55] As well, West African folklore often includes
a narrative regarding a greedy tortoise that desires to switch heads with
a ram. The story frequently portrays the overindulgence in the smell of
food as a gluttonous sensory skill.[56] Many tales of the important West
African spider character Ananse also portray the interplay of odor, space,
and death within different spiritual customs.[57]

   Substances and Medicine in Sub-Saharan Africa: Archaeological, Anthropological, and
   Historical Perspectives," *Anthropology and Medicine* 18, 2 (2001): 145–166.
[54] Jack Berry and Richard Spears, *West African Folktales* (Evanston, IL: Northwestern
   University Press, 1991), 161–163.
[55] Berry and Spears, *West African Folktales*, 32–34.
[56] Hugh Vernon-Jackson and Patricia Wright, *West African Folk Tales* (Mineola, NY:
   Dover, 2003), 15–18.
[57] Berry and Spears, *West African Folktales*, 90–91, 101–102.

These stories are also educative in the spiritual worlds of ghosts and aroma. In the story "The River's Judgement," which moralizes upon mothers who should not be jealous of their daughters, the smell of local recipes is a common element of a ghost's memory that creates a remembered heartache between a mother and her offspring.[58] Ritual customs are also often portrayed in these folktales through different African spiritual practices.[59] In the animal metaphors applied within "The Young Man Who Was Carried Off by a Lion," a metaphorically human figure of a lion attempts to "smell-out" a traveling African boy.[60] Herbalism is also common in these West African narratives, as with the bin of simples and the odor of the *mateva* palm in the folklore of "Ngomba's Basket," concerning the traits of marital jealousy.[61]

One of Bedford Pim's sources for much of his discussions of the racialized African body in Chapter 2 was the orientalist scholar Richard Burton, a traveler within West Africa who studied much in Dahomey, present day Benin. While working in West Africa during the 1850s and 1860s, Burton translated many West African proverbs for English readers. For one of his adages, he bastardized a transliteration of a maxim about stinking ants (*ahoho*) in order to assert the continued reliance on racialized smells and British concerns with civilizing the African. Burton recorded the proverb: "Nnipa iniara de anka gwarre-a, von hu ye, cwam; na ahoho se oko da so, na ne hu bon." He was provided a vernacular meaning: "Everybody who washes himself with lemon juice, becomes sweet-scented: therefore the Ahoho said he would go upon (the lemon tree) and live there, but still he stinks." To misleadingly clarify for his English readers, Burton drew a direct comparison between the proverb and the Christian maxim of unnecessarily "washing the Ethiopian" central to earlier English literary racialization when noting: "These negroes wash themselves from head to foot at least once a day, and after washing rub their bodies with lime-juice to remove the bouquet of Afrique. The Ahoho is a red ant of peculiarly ill savour ... The meaning is, 'No remedy will affect innate and inveterate vices.'"[62]

[58] Berry and Spears, *West African Folktales*, 60–62.
[59] Raouf Mama and Imna Arroyo, *"Why goats smell bad" and Other Stories from Benin* (North Haven, CT: Linnet, 1998).
[60] Paul Radin, *African Folktales* (Princeton, NJ: Princeton University Press, 1970), quotes on 161–164.
[61] Radin, *African Folktales*, 266–268.
[62] For racial connotations of this proverb, see Richard Francis Burton, *Wit and Wisdom from West Africa, or a Book of Proverbial Philosophy, Idioms, Enigmas, and Laconisms*

Later English literature also signifies significant openings to read against the temporal grain for discovering African traditional medicine and an appreciation for odor that can reach past the racial connotations of bastardized concepts of African smells portrayed by both Pim and Burton. In Elspeth Huxley's *The Flame Trees of Thika* (1959), a deep appreciation for the odors of Africa defines the setting and background of a miasmic narrative of remembrance within British colonial Kenya. In the autobiographical novel, the uncleanness and dirtiness of hyenas is attributed partly to their space as a "haunt of dead men's spirits." The scented charms of the *mundu-mugos*, or good witch doctors, are ever-present throughout the narrative of childhood and romance under the umbrella of colonial control. In one instance, a witch doctor protects an antelope from pythons through the use of scented charms and a paste that Elspeth placed upon the animal's body. These witch doctors "carried ... two or three long gourds with stoppers made of cows' tails, and some smaller gourds, the size of snuff bottles, containing all sorts of powders and medicines, hanging by fine chains from his neck." In Huxley's tale, different African bodies are classified as smelling "much stronger and more musky, almost acrid." However, Huxley took space to often remind the reader that Europeans "smelt just as strong and odd to Africans." For the English author of early-twentieth-century Kenya, even in spaces far afield from the more focused spaces of the Atlantic Slave Trade, the continental context of odors within Africa were remembered through mostly positive associations to different variations of the *mundu-mugos* and their spiritual and material medicines.[63]

From the perspective of novelist Chinua Achebe, smell was also a common element of spiritual practice during the British colonial decades within late-nineteenth- and early-twentieth-century Nigeria. In his celebrated *Things Fall Apart* (1958), during a funeral for the elder and secondary character Ezeudu, the sense of smell was used a potent signifier that a powerful and pungent one-armed spirit had entered the area of dancing ceremonies. One *egwugwu*, or representative of the ancestral spirit, was always followed by a "sickly odour" that "hung in the air wherever he went, and flies went with him." Following Igbo traditions, Achebe wrote of how the "air was full of dust and the smell of gunpowder.

(London: Tinsley Brothers, 1865), quotes on 99–100; Rattray and Christaller, *Ashanti Proverbs*, 132–133.

[63] Elspeth Huxley, *The Flame Trees of Thika: Memories of an African Childhood* (London: Penguin, 1962 [1959]), quotes on 10–11, 166–167, 186–188.

It was then that the one-handed spirit came, carrying a basket full of water. People made way for him on all sides and the noise subsided. Even the smell of gunpowder was swallowed in the sickly smell that now filled the air."[64]

Achebe's African trilogy commonly applied the tenants of African spiritualism to critique forms of colonial power. Throughout the African trilogy are masked spirits, ceremonies of traditional West African religious practice, and consistent use of the descriptions of airs, smells, and washing. Achebe's *Arrow of God* (1964), also references the "smelling-out" practices of West African medicine men. When the Igbo ruler and chief priest Ezeulu returns after being taken prisoner by the colonial leadership, he questions a medicine man regarding tribal politics. When the medicine man, Akuebue, responds that he does not know whether a contestant to Ezeulu's power committed poisoning, Ezeulu responds that "I can smell a poisoner as clearly as I can a leper."[65] These literary descriptions within the celebrated works of Achebe offer a multitemporal link to African pasts where odor and smelling-out vitalized aspects of religious practice. These olfactory worlds remained important for social organizations in an Atlantic World of fellow Igbo like Equiano and the many Igbo slaves that were proportionally dominant in many times and spaces of the British Atlantic.[66]

Like within the fiction told through Achebe's celebrated narratives, some present African nations also include sensoriums where smelling is applied momentously within everyday life and leisure. Susan Rasmussen has shown how smelling and tasting in modern Tuareg society of Northern Africa and Berber spaces in Nigeria involves the intermingling of sensory understandings with a sense of social cohesion and medical traditions.[67] W. E. A. van Beek has similarly applied the olfactory to show how the cultures of the Kapsiki/Higi of North-Eastern Nigeria use smell to set apart and laud those wealthy men associated with agricultural profit and cow dung.[68] Kathryn Geurts's analyses of the importance of animism within modern West African cultural traditions has also argued that

[64] Chinua Achebe, *The African Trilogy* (New York: Everyman's Library, 2010), quotes on 79–87.

[65] Achebe, *The African Trilogy*, quotes on 455–457.

[66] For background, see Douglas Chambers, *The Igbo Diaspora in the Era of the Slave Trade: An Introductory History* (Glassboro, NJ: Goldline & Jacobs, 2014).

[67] Susan Rasmussen, "Matters of Taste: Food, Eating, and Reflections on 'the Body Politic' in Tuareg Society," *Journal of Anthropological Research* 52, 1 (1996): 61–83.

[68] W. E. A. van Beek, "The Dirty Smith: Smell as a Social Frontier among the Kapsiki/Higi of North Cameroon and North-Eastern Nigeria," *Africa* 62 (1992): 38–58.

African cultures teach a much different sensory hierarchy that includes a higher appreciation for olfactory learning and the sensations of the nose.[69] In his analysis of "choreographic modalities" to show that the categories of cultural retention in the New World often included similarly deep sensory aspects related to the natural environments of Africa, Robert Farris Thompson has also described: "The slang term 'funky' in black communities originally referred to strong body odor ... The black nuance seems to derive from the Ki-Kongo *lu-fuki*, 'bad body odor,' and is perhaps reinforced by contact with *fumet*, 'aroma of food and wine,' in French Louisiana."[70] The Ki-Kongo traditions described by Thompson adhere to the idea that the smell of a hardworking elder of the community is frequently considered to carry good luck. Funkiness, partly of odor, means a return to the fundamental essence of earthiness important to cultural constructs that began in Africa but permeated into later African American mystical and musical cultures.[71]

Similarly, in many twentieth-century regions of the Congo, as with those analyzed by ethnographer Anita Jacobson-Widding during the 1970s, ceremonial songs frequently related to smell diviners or *nganga ngombo*. These songs often also involved inducing nightly visitations from strong-smelling ghosts. Among these Congo peoples, the use of smell-diviners was common for the routines of herbalism and within spiritual healing ceremonies where a diviner acclimated to the intensity of the spiritual world through the smelling of strong powders and plants. Once acclimated, the diviner frequently entered a preternatural space and tremors would take over their body.[72] Also relevant are Victor Turner's anthropological studies of ritual among the Ndembu of twentieth-century Zambia, who used smell as a marker of disease and gathered numerous stinking roots to cure diseases. Turner particularly noted the

---

[69] Kathryn Linn Geurts, *Culture and the Senses: Bodily Ways of Knowing in an African Community* (Berkeley: California, 2002). See also Mariane Ferme, *The Underneath of Things: Violence, History, and the Everyday in Sierra Leone* (Berkeley: University of California Press, 2007), 190–192; Paul Stoller, *The Taste of Ethnographic Things: The Senses in Anthropology* (Philadelphia: University of Pennsylvania Press, 1989), 8–25.

[70] Robert Farris Thompson, *Flash of the Spirit: African and Afro-American Art and Philosophy* (New York: Random House, 1983), 117–131, quote on 104.

[71] Thompson, *Flash of the Spirit*, 104–105.

[72] Anita Jacobson-Widding, *Red – White – Black as a Mode of Thought: A Study of Triadic Classification by Colours in the Ritual Symbolism and Cognitive Thought of the Peoples of the Lower Congo* (Uppsala: Uppsala, 1979), 69–71, 290–291; Christopher Fennell, *Crossroads and Cosmologies: Diasporas and Ethnogenesis in the New World* (Gainesville: University Press of Florida, 2010), 6–14, 43–67.

Central and south-eastern African ethnic belief that precise menstrual distresses could be cured through herbal concoctions: "The bitterness (*kulula*) of the *mwala* root can kill the disease ... The woman should drink its medicine to make her stomach smell very much. The disease will smell it and die because of its stink."[73] Within the late-twentieth-century Beng culture of the Ivory Coast, gender was also important to olfactory components related to the soul inherited through the matriclan. Therein, odors signified the positive form of the idea of "substance" that creates legitimacy for assorted rulers.[74] Ceremonial songs, plants, powders, and beliefs regarding gendered categorizations that related ideologies of odor persisted within many earlier African societies and arrive to modernity often through these continuing motifs within relatively contemporary cultural performances.

Reading against concerns with anachronism due to a lack of sources and a domineering European archive provides how many of these olfactory ritualized patterns also informed earlier structural tendencies within African diasporic retention of ways of smelling in the Atlantic World. As Wyatt MacGaffey understood in *Religion and Society in Central Africa* (1986), ritualization was central within historical African belief systems, often educating African cultures through social roles performed in specific ways.[75] As Chapter 4 will further articulate – in combination with the many references in this chapter from the era of the slave trade regarding perfumes and cleanliness – ethnobotanists have also linked various strong-smelling herbs, barks, and powders from the era of the slave trade to African religious practices within the New World.[76] Combining these many olfactory references from the era of the trade with numerous later olfactory components of African spirituality and environmental awareness portrays plenteous and deeply engaged aromatic African cultures that

---

[73] Victor Turner, *The Forest of Symbols: Aspects of Ndembu Ritual* (Ithaca: Cornell University Press, 1967), quote on 314. For more on Turner and African ethnic rituals, see Mark Mathuray, *On the Sacred in African Literature: Old Gods and New Worlds* (Basingstoke: Palgrave Macmillan, 2009), 8–10, 38–39.

[74] Alma Gottlieb, "Witches, Kings, and the Sacrifice of Identity or The Power of Paradox and the Paradox of Power among the Beng of Ivory Coast," in *Creativity of Power: Cosmology and Action in African Societies*, eds. William Arens and Ivan Karp (Washington, DC: Smithsonian Institution, 1989), 245–272.

[75] Wyatt MacGaffey, *Religion and Society in Central Africa: The BaKongo of Lower Zaire* (Chicago: University of Chicago Press, 1986), 88–90.

[76] For examples, see Tinde van Andel, Sofie Ruysschaert, Kobeke Van de Putte, and Sara Groenendijk, "What Makes a Plant Magical?: Symbolism and Sacred Herbs in Afro-Surinamese *Winti* Rituals," in *African Ethnobotany in the Americas*, eds. Robert Voeks and John Rashford (New York: Springer, 2013), 246–284.

resisted the appropriation of the land that was knotted to a toughened form of chattel slavery falsely justified, in part, through various scented beliefs of race and progress. Throughout numerous New World slave communities, the use of specific traditions, including smelling-out for divining purposes, using smell for ecological knowledge and sensory worlding, and expending scented objects to heal sick brethren, helped to provide agency for slaves trapped in the body-grinding machines of these different racist, fetishized, and profitable slave economies.

EXPERIENCING ODOR IN THE ATLANTIC WORLD

The smell of African medicine and religion, and even of fecal matter, marks a significant aspect of resistance through the sensorium. This chapter has worked to explore African concepts of smelling that entered upon the Atlantic World through the Middle Passage. It has attempted to do so through using both an essentialized Africa from the era of the slave trade and anachronist sources from later eras in order to deconstruct the prejudicial remnants of the colonized archive. This application of essentialism and anachronism is an important historical methodology because of what the colonized archive supported for centuries of the Atlantic Slave Trade. Through these methods, it becomes clear that African cultures used diverse historical understandings of odor to retain diverse sensory cultures in the New World despite the commodifying force of European sensory modernity, the profiteering of the slave trade, and the still repressive and demonstrably chronological archives of the modern academy.

However vital these olfactory references were to the retention, survival, and combinations of African sensations in the New World, in most cases of slavery and transport within the Atlantic World, slaves died on diseased ships, in burdensome cane fields, or under the duress of oppressive tropical heat. Their bodies would putrefy and stink even worse than the sweat produced from their labor. Slaves beneath decks trembled without tenderness, sloshing in the pungent musk of their own watery, salted, shitty, and deadly filth. As the naturalist Alexander Garden described from South Carolina of the common odors of the slave ship during the 1750s: "I have never yet been on board one, that did not smell most offensive and noisome, what for filth, putrid air, putrid dysenteries, (which is their common disorder) it is a wonder any escape with life."[77]

---

[77] Alexander Garden to Stephen Hales, circa 1758–1760, quoted in Edmund Berkeley and Dorothy Smith Berkeley, *Dr. Alexander Garden of Charles Town* (Chapel Hill:

Even before being taken into the stinking holds of the slave ship, many Africans faced the terrible odors of the slave system during their journeys from the African interior to the shore. While being taken on a coffle to the coast of West Africa during the middle of the eighteenth century, the future American slave Jeffrey Brace summarized the pungency he was forced to reside upon when trapped within a riverine craft full of "filth and stinking fish."[78] Being paired as a commodity with the fish of slave traders who moved Africans like Brace to the coast placed the captive in constantly changing and deleterious sensory worlds. Before reaching his destination in Connecticut, where he would later serve in the American Revolution and become remembered as an American military hero, Brace was trapped in constantly changing and horribly new sensory domains of waste and filth. A specifically cruel master at a later seasoning stop on the Middle Passage provided only dirty water for Jeffrey and his fellow slaves to ingest. Brace recalled how the slaves at the three-months seasoning were "obliged to lie down in filthy brooks to drink." These rivulets were often full of "the excrements from their necessary houses" that would be "sucked in as we drank." Such vile drinking water was probably partly to also attribute to the "maggots" that ate at the ropes and chains that held Jeffery's ankles together with other bonded men and women.[79]

Like Brace, Equiano portrayed the entire commodification process as one that took him from a pleasantly scented world of West Africa, with its odoriferous gourds, constructed perfumes, and peppered meals, to the pungency and effluvia of many different topographies of the slave trade. Below deck, Equiano remembered the "loathsomeness and stench" of the

---

University of North Carolina Press, 1969), quote on 124. For more on the smell of slave ships, see Trevor Burnard, *Planters, Merchants, and Slaves: Plantation Societies in British America, 1650–1820* (Chicago: University of Chicago Press, 2015), 85–86; Marcus Rediker, *The Slave Ship: A Human History* (New York: Penguin, 2008), 218–220; Saidiya Hartman, *Lose Your Mother: A Journey Along the Atlantic Slave Route* (New York: Farrar, Straus and Giroux, 2013), 47–50, 139–144; David Brion Davis, *Inhuman Bondage: The Rise and Fall of Slavery in the New World* (Oxford: Oxford University Press, 2006), 92–96.

[78] Boyrereau Brinch and Benjamin Franklin Prentiss, *The Blind African Slave, or Memoirs of Boyrereau Brinch, Nick-Named Jeffrey Brace Containing an Account of the Kingdom of Bow-Woo, in the Interior of Africa, with the Soil, Climate and Natural Productions, Laws and Customs Peculiar to That Place; With an Account of His Captivity, Sufferings, Sales, Travels, Emancipation, Conversion to the Christian Religion, Knowledge of the Scriptures, Etc.; Interspersed with Strictures on Slavery, Speculative Observations on the Qualities of Human Nature, with Quotations from Scripture* (St. Alban's, VT: Harry Whitney, 1810), quotes on 71–72.

[79] Brinch, *Blind African Slave*, quotes on 110–111.

many bodies piled and "crying together." Unable to eat due to the intense odors, Equiano hoped for death to arrive as a "last friend" that would end his miserable experiences. While anchored off the sweltering African coast waiting to begin the journey of the Middle Passage after traders worked to fill their holds completely, Equiano noticed that the "stench of the hold" became only more "pestilential." Bodies trapped together with heaving lungs made the "perspirations" so full of "loathsome smells" that the air became "unfit for respiration" and caused many deaths, to the detriment of the "purchasers." In a most horrific memory, Equiano also noted how the "necessary tubs" below deck, probably for feces or dirtied from the cleaning of the holds that were full of fecal matter, often may have been places wherein African children fell and nearly "suffocated" or drowned, with waste water lining their overflowing lungs.[80]

In the slave port of Charleston, South Carolina, the smell of dead Africans who had faced these pungent episodes of the Middle Passage often became damaging not only to those in slave holds waiting to be seasoned on Sullivan's Island and then sold upon market but also to the various inhabitants of the town, when the air of death hung low after a slave trader illegally dumped his dead cargo in the Cooper River in 1769.[81] Slave ships were commonly sensed off shore by inhabitants of Atlantic ports, frequently due to the wafted stench emanating from the holds. George Pinckard, introduced in Chapter 2 as an English physician under the command of Scottish politician Ralph Abercromby, also described the horrid stench that remained "offensive to European olfactories" even after the commodity holds in a slave ship at Bridgetown, Barbados, was thoroughly scoured during the 1790s. Well after the "cleaning and airing" of the ship, the sailors "could not subdue the stench created" by slaves "sleeping together in such crowded heaps."[82]

Abolitionists used these disturbing realities of stench and odor beneath the decks of slave ships to present their cases to Parliament and the English populace during their moralizing attempts to abolish the slave trade during the late eighteenth century. Celebrated at the start this work, abolitionists including Alexander Falconbridge and John Newton wrote persuasively

---

[80] Equiano, *Interesting Narrative*, quotes on 48–54.
[81] Peter McCandless, *Slavery, Disease, and Suffering in the Southern Lowcountry* (Cambridge: Cambridge University Press, 2011), 44–45.
[82] George Pinckard, *Notes on the West Indies* (London: Longman, Hurst, Rees, and Orme, 1806), quotes on 234. See also James Walvin, *The Trader, the Owner, the Slave: Parallel Lives in the Age of Slavery* (London: Cape, 2007), 58–62; John Newton, *The Journal of a Slave Trader (John Newton) 1750–1754* (London: Epworth Press, 1962), 80–110.

about the suffering beneath decks, including the miasma of death and pungency.[83] Many other abolitionist leaders, including English politicians William Wilberforce, Granville Sharp, and Anglo-African writers such as Equiano, applied religious motives and olfactory language to similarly justify arguments working to end the slave trade. Through these means, many Europeans worked heroically to defeat the slave systems their ancestors instituted.[84]

Whether anomalies or standard practices, the experience of slaves in the dirty holds showed that the entire slave trade was an increasingly pungent and filthy practice. As also noted in the Preface, plantations also often smelled of evil acts by slaveholders, who often beat their laborers to such an extent as to similarly cause death and associated odors of decay. On Nevis in 1817, a case of significant abuse regarding the slaveholder and clergyman Henry Rawlins caused the sick bays of the plantation to smell of "putrefaction" after Rawlins had his slave Creole Jack whip a fellow slave named Congo Jack until the latter laborer was unconscious after what some testimonies noted was a deafening amount of whip cracks. Suffering from wounds and probably receiving washing from a "sick nurse" who treated his bloodied back and fevered conditions, Congo Jack lived only a few days before succumbing to his wounds, days he still spent guided by the master's whim as he was forced to continue his work sifting through molasses in the very boiling house where he was beaten.[85]

For the abolitionist Thomas Clarkson observing the outlines of the slave system that both Creole Jack and Congo Jack suffered through, slave ship holds were full of such "heat, stench, and corrupted air" that they created a "dying state" for nearly all the slaves held below decks. So many slaves were packed together in the common slave ship that many bodies would be brought up "quite dead from suffocation" as others were hazarded to death by the poisoned air before they could rise from their hellish holds. In his famous analysis of the ship *Brookes*, Clarkson used quantitative measures to describe these cramped spaces provided for

---

[83] See also Niel Douglas, *The African Slave Trade: or, a Short View of the Evidence, Relative to That Subject Produced before the House of Commons in 1791* (Edinburgh: J. Guthrie, 1792), 32–34.

[84] For introductions to British suppression of slave trade, see Marika Sherwood, *After Abolition: Britain and the Slave Trade Since 1807* (London: I. B. Tauris, 2007); Peter Grindal and Andrew Lambert, *Opposing the Slavers: The Royal Navy's Campaign against the Atlantic Slave Trade* (London: I. B. Tauris, 2016).

[85] *Further Papers Relating to the Treatment of Slaves in the Colonies: St. Christopher's* (London: House of Commons, 1818), quotes on 6–7. Courtesy of the John Carter Brown Library.

individual slaves, who lived within suffocating quarters "for want of room and air."[86] Often, rains upon the Middle Passage would only increase the suffering of slaves below decks of ships like the *Brookes*. During storms, sailors would frequently place tarps upon and above their decks to protect the holds. However, this process trapped pungent and diseased air beneath the holds, increasing the tightness of lungs and inducing suffocating embolisms within the bodies beneath.[87]

As the British tried to suppress the slave trade during the early nineteenth century, some European captains hoping to still profit from the trade in slaves from African coasts packed their holds even tighter, to the detriment of the figures below deck and the noses that smelled those tightly crammed consequences. In a *Report on African Forts* presented to the House of Commons, a letter from Naval Commander Sir James Yeo dated November 7, 1816, summarized that part of the poor condition of British forts was because the Spanish and Portuguese trade in slaves from the Gold Coast had quadrupled since the abolition of the slave trade by the British in 1807. The newly gluttonous forces from Iberia often would "fill their ships beyond any former precedent; as a proof of which, His Majesty' ship *Barin* ... captured the Portuguese brig *San Antonio*, only 120 tons, with 600 slaves." During her passage, the *San Antonio* lost thirty of these African slaves, and "in the midst" of the remaining cargo upon capture the British sailors identified "putrid corpses" and a "horrid stench" that suggested the odors of a plague.[88]

Similar repulsions continued as the British attempted to subvert the Iberian and French trade on the West African coast during the years to follow. On the French slave ship *Rodeur* during January of 1819, slaves taken above the stinking holds quickly ran to the edges of the

[86] Thomas Clarkson, *The Cries of Africa to the Inhabitants of Europe, or, A Survey of that Bloody Commerce called the Slave-Trade* (London: Harvey and Darton, and W. Phillips, 1822), quotes on 30–31. See also David Barnes, "Cargo, 'Infection,' and the Logic of Quarantine in the Nineteenth Century," *Bulletin of the History of Medicine: Organ of the American Association for the History of Medicine and of the Johns Hopkins Institute of the History of Medicine* 88, 1 (2014): 75–101.

[87] Sean Kelley, *The Voyage of the Slave Ship Hare: A Journey into Captivity from Sierra Leone to South Carolina* (Chapel Hill: University of North Carolina Press, 2016), 92. For social construction of comfort and the *Brookes*, see J. Y. Chu, "Boxed In: Human Cargo and the Technics of Comfort," *International Journal of Politics, Culture and Society* 29, 4 (2016): 403–421. See also the slave ship and modern racism within Simone Browne, *Dark Matters: On the Surveillance of Blackness* (Durham, NC: Duke University Press, 2015), 32–50.

[88] *Report from the Select Committee on Papers Relating to the African Forts* (London: House of Commons, 1817), quotes on 6–7. Courtesy of the John Carter Brown Library.

deck and flung themselves consistently into the waiting ocean. Those that were captured during their attempts at suicide were beaten, shot, or hanged as punishment for asserting their subject and human agency to take their own lives. The filth below deck had created such a desire for suicide due, in part, to an outbreak of diseased blindness that affected all upon the ship, whereby both slaves and sailors lost their sight to ophthalmia during the start of their aborted Middle Passage voyage.[89]

March of 1821 near the River Bonny saw British officials encounter similar horrors when observing the Spanish ship *Anna Maria*. The aforementioned Commodore George Collier described the dismay uncovered when investigating the ship. He noted how the "tonnage of the *Anna Maria* is under 200; yet she had on board nearly 300 living souls!" These tight packings of rooms only two feet and eleven inches high made the slaves intensely hot, whereby they were found "[c]linging to the gratings to inhale a mouthful of fresh or pure air, and fighting with each other for a taste of water, showing their parched tongues, and pointing to their reduced stomachs" to portray oncoming famine. Collier compared the scene to that of a "morning market" for hogs that became so "appalling and distressing" that slaves had to be told to "cease at the maddening act of self-destruction which had occurred to some by throwing themselves overboard, a prey to the sharks in attendance, rather than endure a continuance of that misery." Fighting with the common enemy of rats for bodily space and pure air within corrupted and stinking spaces also developed into a common event throughout the Atlantic World. These experiences, of rodents, maggots, filth, and stench affectively taught Africans who survived the Middle Passage that understandings of miasma, odor, and atmospherics would become an important aspect of critiquing the very masters and traders who controlled the amount of oxygen, breath, and stench to be allowed below the thousands of decks concealing the millions of bodies of the capitalized and commodifying Atlantic Slave Trade.[90]

---

[89] Clarkson, *Cries of Africa*, 35–37.

[90] "Copy of the Declaration of Captors of the Spanish Schooner 'Anna Maria,' detained by His Majesty's Ship Tartar, in March 1821, in the River Bonny, on the Coast of Africa, dated the 26th March 1821," in *Further Papers Relating to the Slave Trade: Copies of Papers Relating to the Portuguese Schooner Brig "Gaviao," and the Spanish Schooner "Anna Maria"* (London: House of Commons, 1822), quotes on 25. Courtesy of the John Carter Brown Library. See also James Walvin, *Crossings: Africa, the Americas and the Atlantic Slave Trade* (London: Reaktion Books, 2013), 94–96.

IDENTITY AND THE FLUX

Once in slavery, the menacing smells of profit did not cease. The sweat of labor, regardless of the racialized and constructed observations of white masters, could always smell pungent.[91] To cure these ills, slaveholders often perfumed slave bodies to portray healthfulness for sale. Although most colonials accepted European core beliefs about odor through a growing exchange of racial inscription, some later American and Atlantic markets tried to linguistically and materially control these smells for the marketing of commodified bodies. In order to make their products more attractive, many slave traders attempted to change their slaves' smells by using violet smelling oils to make their bodies both shiny and fragrant. The oil chosen was commonly palm oil cultivated from African trees. In Georgia of the 1790s, a scented compound applied to slave bodes was also often made of gunpowder, lime juice, and palm oil.[92] Different oils for slave bodies smelled pleasant within European descriptions and also frequently scented white bodies that incorporated their aromas into soap.[93]

Because of the intense and often pungent horrors of the slave trade, resistance to slavery from African populations was often based upon an amalgamation of both personal agencies to revolt and a biological survival response triggered under oppressive conditions. Specific slave resistance upon the ships of European traders often led to wider forms of defiance and protected many African populations within Africa.[94] While sitting in the holds of these slave ships, African men and women were often forced to defecate upon the places where they would later sleep. Though travelers like Pinckard deemed these habits as "filthy," such defecation of normal excrement or the bloody flux might very well have been a form of

---

[91] Robert DuPlessis, *The Material Atlantic: Clothing, Commerce, and Colonization in the Atlantic World, 1650–1800* (Cambridge: Cambridge University Press, 2016); Kathleen Brown, *Foul Bodies: Cleanliness in Early America* (New Haven, CT: Yale University Press, 2009), 98–117; Hartman, *Lose Your Mother*, 47–50.

[92] Pinckard, *Notes on the West Indies*, 238.

[93] Ghillean Prance and Mark Nesbitt, *The Cultural History of Plants* (New York: Routledge, 2005), 340–341. For the smell of this oil as that of violet, see Hans Sloane, Michael van der Gucht, John Savage, Caspar Georg Carl Reinwardt, and Roland Napoléon Bonaparte, *A Voyage to the Islands Madera, Barbados, Nieves, S. Christophers and Jamaica* (London, B. M. for the Author, 1707), 115–116.

[94] David Richardson, "Shipboard Revolts, African Authority, and the Atlantic Slave Trade," *William and Mary Quarterly* 58, 1 (2001): 69–92; Claudius Fergus, "'Dread of Insurrection': Abolitionism, Security, and Labor in Britain's West Indian Colonies, 1760–1823," *William and Mary Quarterly* 66, 4 (2009): 757–780.

resistance, forcing masters to protect their slaves from disease by airing and cleaning their holds at a higher frequency.[95] The olfactory dialectic, in this sense, is quite complex and alarming. The very act of defecating on oneself, read through the violent horrors of the slave trade, could very well be an act of agency against slave traders who needed to protect the health of their cargo for sale at market. Often slave ship captains would use vinegar to clean their decks and holds to prevent the greater effects of these possible acts of resistance and to keep their cargoes at healthful and profitable capacities.[96] Other captains, even after using bricks as scrubbing cleaners for their decks and holds, would often still grumble about the smell of their ships that could signal infections amongst their commodified products.[97]

Slaves understood European beliefs in miasma theory through their own constant and historical use of odors within ethnic rituals and social customs. The value of odor within African societies provided slaves an understanding that Europeans prized cleanliness and believed that smell was disease to such an extent that those in bondage would create odors as a way to resist, often through the use of bodily ejaculate that signaled to European traders a need to clean, scrub, and vinegar the slave holds. In an even more absurdist game of olfaction, labor, and resistance, could the suicide of slave, meant to smell of death as the body putrefied, be a similar cause of olfactory class consciousness meant to protect the community by creating forms of ephemeral distance? In the slave narrative of Charles Ball, who after servitude became a hero of the War of 1812, a slave's suicide began to smell. The former laborer that Charles encountered hung with chains still upon his body and presented a pungency that "assailed" Charles' nostrils.[98] In the Atlantic World, masters tried to prevent slave suicides through denying ritual burials for laborers' bodies and often performing the slave body as a part of necromantic rituals meant to scare living workhands. Overcoming the fear of necromancy through suicide could therefore possibly represent a brave act that was partially

---

[95] Pinckard, *Notes on the West Indies*, 234–235.

[96] Bruce Mouser and Samuel Gamble, *A Slaving Voyage to Africa and Jamaica: The Log of the Sandown, 1793–1794* (Bloomington: University of Indiana Press, 2002), 56–57.

[97] Sowande' Mustakeem, *Slavery at Sea: Terror, Sex, and Sickness in the Middle Passage* (Urbana: University of Illinois Press, 2016), 58–64.

[98] Charles Ball, *Slavery in the United States: A Narrative of the Life and Adventures of Charles Ball, a Black Man, Who Lived Forty Years in Maryland, South Carolina and Georgia, As a Slave* (Pittsburgh, PA: J. T. Shryock, 1854), quotes on 335–337; Ras Michael Brown, *African-Atlantic Cultures and the South Carolina Lowcountry* (Cambridge: Cambridge University Press, 2012), 140–141, 169–173.

meant to throw death and the smells of decay back at the master and his reekingly peculiar institution.[99]

There is no denying that the Middle Passage was a sea of death constructed through a commodification of the African body meant to remove most ethnic diversity and cultural pasts. Slaves were often tricked into their African coffles, trapped on ships, and sorted as pecuniary objects. The filth beneath ships manifested the pains of nutritional depravation, the smell of feces, and the constant tactile and alimentary attendance of shit and illness. Groping together, often sightless, the noses and lungs of trapped slaves tied odor to the Middle Passage at her first stages. Constant attention to the horrors and smells makes us remember, forces a remembrance, that the Middle Passage and the hollow men who ran its windward tracts wore fecal morals on their very sleeves.[100]

Remembering the pungent and decrepit horrors that caused significant circumstances of social death also triggers redolent narratives of slave agency and subaltern resistance. The choices regarding odor, either from those in power who coded African bodies or among those who threw smell rhetorically or materially as decoded messages of freedom from the oppressed, represent that the environmental use of volatile materials and "excremental language" is frequently an "inherent index of self/other instability."[101] The Atlantic World was such a place of semantic, discursive, and embodied volatility regarding sensory alterations and identity fluctuations, whereby the field of odor became a contentious arena to define self and other, subject and object, and fair and foul within a grand and disturbingly human game of capitalism, racism, and resistance.

---

[99] Vincent Brown, "Spiritual Terror and Sacred Authority in Jamaican Slave Society," *Slavery and Abolition* 24, 1 (2003): 24–53; Mustakeem, *Slavery at Sea*, 106–130; Richard Price, "Dialogical Encounters in a Space of Death," in *New World Orders: Violence, Sanction, and Authority in the Colonial Americas*, eds. John Smolenski and Thomas Humphrey (Philadelphia: University of Pennsylvania Press, 2005), 47–65.

[100] Mustakeem, *Slavery at Sea*, 55–75; *The Mirror of Misery, or, Tyranny Exposed* (New York: Wood, 1814), 9–12.

[101] Esty, "Excremental Postcolonialism," 47–51. For "fecal habitus," see Martin Weinberg and Colin Williams, "Fecal Matters: Habitus, Embodiments, and Deviance," *Social Problems* 52, 3 (2005): 315–336.

4

"The Sweet Scent of Vengeance"

Olfactory Resistance in the Atlantic World

French novelist and religious provocateur Eugene Sue's *Atar-Gull: Or, The Slave's Revenge* (1831) depicted the "sweet scent of vengeance" taken by a slave on the body of an old, insane, and ill planter who entrusted the medicine man with healing his sickened body. Seeking revenge for the death of his father in Africa, the slave concocted a plan whereby he earned the trust of his owner, Tom Will, enough to become his personal caretaker. Once in control of Tom's body, Atar Gull, a former African prince turned healer, slowly wrought the Jamaican planter from the aromatic beauty of previously florid plantation wealth of "perfumed aloes" and his bodily rights to the slave woman "sweet Jenny" to the demised and poor man he became upon a pungent and tortured European sickbed.[1]

During the nineteenth century, fresh forms of European literature advanced increasing attention to African subjects of the Atlantic World. In many narratives, American and European authors provided significant spiritual agency to African and African American characters that had been considerably absent within many Western European aesthetic traditions during the previous two centuries. Specific to literature about the Caribbean, these darker characters often appeared as feared and wayward spiritual conjurers who upset standard ways of sensing the world.[2] For

---

[1] Eugène Sue, *Atar-Gull: Or, The Slave's Revenge*, trans. William Henry Herbert (New York: H. L. Williams, 1846 [1831 in French]), quotes from 85–94. See also Christopher Miller, *The French Atlantic Triangle: Literature and Culture of the Slave Trade* (Durham, NC: Duke University Press, 2008), 274–299.

[2] Alan Richardson, "Romantic Voodoo: Obeah and British Culture, 1797–1807," in *Sacred Possessions: Vodou, Santería, Obeah, and the Caribbean*, eds. Margarite Fernandez Olmos and Lizabeth Paravisini-Gebert (New Brunswick, NJ: Rutgers

example, Atar Gull, a character who had witnessed the tortures of the Middle Passage, became a subject and agent on his Jamaican plantation, poisoning cattle and using snakes to threaten and murder his owner's daughter. Through a series of manipulations, the slave wrested control of the care of his master from a sequence of physicians. The slave healer, later positioned in France after Tom Will's journey to mourn the deaths of his offspring and brokenhearted wife, then drives his master to madness and death through scented herbal concoctions forced down his owner's sweltering and crusted throat.[3]

The representative European sickroom for Tom Will, originally portrayed as a pleasurably fragrant arena, included a "morbid atmosphere" amused by the "odor of draughts, drugs" and "lotions" that Atar Gull used to spitefully treat his master. Atar Gull was such a trusted and skilled medicine man for much of his owner's life that he had earned the respect of many planters on Jamaica and French aristocrats he conversed with once serving in Europe. The confidence game that the slave perpetuated led the European friends of Tom Will to praise the healer's loyalty after his master died, enough admiration that Atar Gull became the inheritor of his master's remaining property and received scientific awards for his great skill at keeping his master alive for such a considerable period of time. However, the slave healer remained vengeful he could not keep his master flourishing longer, as he desired to use his scented charms and poisons to continue to torture his master's body as a symbolic and dialogic punishment against the oppression slavery had wrought upon black bodies throughout the Atlantic World.[4]

As the character of Atar Gull represents, the darkness of the Middle Passage would not, as masters generally hoped, swallow and completely consume the cultures of Africa. During the nineteenth century, European writers noticed the subjective agency of slaves within different texts of the colonized archive and created romantic and rebellious characters that

University Press, 1997), 171–194; Laura Doyle, *Freedom's Empire: Race and the Rise of the Novel in Atlantic Modernity, 1640–1940* (Durham, NC: Duke University Press, 2008), 183–204 and 255–282; Candace Ward, "'Duppy Knows Who fi Frighten': Laying Ghosts in Jamaican Fiction," in *Transnational Gothic: Literary and Social Exchanges in the Long Nineteenth Century*, eds. Monika Elbert and Bridget Marshall (Burlington, VT: Ashgate, 2013), 217–236.

[3] Sue, *Atar-Gull*, 85–90. For more on finding agency within literary texts about Africans from earlier eras, see Cassander Smith, *Black Africans in the British Imagination: English Narratives of the Early Atlantic World* (Baton Rouge: Louisiana State University Press, 2017), 113–114.

[4] Sue, *Atar*-Gull, quotes from 90–94.

represented specific aspects of slave culture and sensory beliefs that differed from dominant Western European sensory worlds. The increased attention to the olfactory in Atar Gull's treatment of Tom Will proposes such a threatening and ephemeral attention to scent within various slave societies. Disrupting the common function of the senses allowed for an escape from Western sensory routinization. Such disorder remains a central aspect of Caribbean philosophy and within understandings of African resistance to both slavery and later forms of European colonialism.[5]

Because slaveholders often focused their attention on turning African humans into working laborers and tradeable objects, assertions of subjecthood from African persons in the New World were inherently resistant to the slave system.[6] Christopher Fennell has recently portrayed how the retention of specific "core symbols" from African ethnic pasts represents the maintenance of traditions and resistance to dehumanization throughout the Atlantic World.[7] Although the retention of core symbols partially created grand revolutionary moments like those at Stono in 1739, New York City of 1741, and Saint-Domingue throughout the 1790s, most preservation of African ethnic pasts involved forms of internalized or interpersonal daily resistance. African traditions of smelling, whether from the era of the slave trade or read anachronistically back upon African

[5] For corporeal resistance and the history of later Afro-Caribbean philosophy, especially through the works of C. L. R. James, see Paget Henry, *Caliban's Reason: Introducing Afro-Caribbean Philosophy* (London: Routledge, 2000), 21–62.

[6] For slave studies and sensory resistance, see Shane White and Graham White, *Stylin': African American Expressive Culture from Its Beginnings to the Zoot Suit* (Ithaca: Cornell University Press, 1998); Shane White and Graham White, *The Sounds of Slavery: Discovering African American History Through Songs, Sermons, and Speech* (Boston: Beacon, 2005); Peter Charles Hoffer, *Sensory Worlds in Early America* (Baltimore, MD: Johns Hopkins University Press, 2003), 133–149; Helen Bradley Foster, *New Raiments of Self: African American Clothing in the Antebellum South* (Oxford: Berg, 1997), 18–74; Lauri Ramey, *Slave Songs and the Birth of African American Poetry* (New York: Palgrave Macmillan, 2008); Renee Harrison, *Enslaved Women and the Art of Resistance in Antebellum America* (New York: Palgrave Macmillan, 2009); Richard Cullen Rath, "Drums and Power: Ways of Creolizing Music in Coastal South Carolina and Georgia, 1730–99," in *Creolization in the Americas*, eds. David Buisseret and Steven Reinhardt (College Station, TX: Texas A&M University Press, 2000), 99–130; Shane White and Graham White, "Slave Hair and African-American Culture in the Eighteenth and Nineteenth Centuries," *Journal of Southern History* 61 (1995): 45–76; Walter Ong, "African Talking Drums and Oral Noetics," *New Literary History* 8, 3 (1977): 411–429; Richard Cullen Rath, "African Music in Seventeenth-Century Jamaica: Cultural Transit and Transition," *William and Mary Quarterly* 50, 4 (October, 1993): 700–726.

[7] Christopher Fennell, *Crossroads and Cosmologies: Diasporas and Ethnogenesis in the New World* (Gainesville: University Press of Florida, 2010), 6–14, 43–67.

ethnic customs, involved an increased and greater appreciation for the sense of smell in both spiritual and worldly spaces of these common forms of everyday rebellion.[8]

This chapter shows how these olfactory aspects of West, Central, and southern Africa made their way across the Middle Passage to be reborn as creolized, ethnogenetic, and essentialized scents of Africa that planters feared as signals of agency.[9] Specifically, slaves and free blacks in the Atlantic littoral engaged African appreciation for odors through retaining traditions of smelling-out disease, understanding the importance of scenting in their new environments, resisting the master's use of dogs, considering the importance of scent in the formulae for poisons, and consistently believing in the importance of producing smells for cultural rituals, personal agency, and herbal medicines.[10]

As part of a greater historiographical trajectory, this chapter therefore asserts the importance of African survivals in the analysis of slave resistance within the Atlantic World. Alongside scholars such as Londa Schiebinger, Michael Gomez, Stephanie Camp, Joseph Miller, Maureen Warner-Lewis, Gwendolyn Hall, John Thornton, and Jason Young, this chapter shows how African survivals, especially concerning olfactory medicine and spiritualism, allowed Africans in the New World fresh spaces to assert their own forms of identity. This analysis of smell expands on these earlier analyses of survivals and cultural rebirth through extending how phenomenological and sensory traditions persisted across the Middle Passage, further highlighting the interpretive vitality of survivals and psychological

---

[8] For more on charms, fetishes, and the assertion of African identity, see Monique Allewaert, *Ariel's Ecology: Plantations, Personhood, and Colonialism in the American Tropics* (Minneapolis: University of Minnesota Press, 2013), 173–182; Monique Allewaert, "Swamp Sublime: Ecologies of Resistance in the American Plantation Zone," *Publications of the Modern Language Association* 123, 2 (2008): 340–357.

[9] For debates on ethnogenesis and creolization, see James Sidbury, *Becoming African in America: Race and Nation in the Early Black Atlantic* (Oxford: Oxford University Press, 2007); Gunvor Simonsen, "Belonging in Africa: Frederik Svane and Christian Protten on the Gold Coast in the Eighteenth Century," *Itinerario* 39, 1 (2015): 91–115; Richard Price, "On the Miracle of Creolization," in *Afro-Atlantic Dialogues: Anthropology in Diaspora*, ed. Kevin Yelvington (Santa Fe, NM: School of American Research, 2006), 115–147; Michelle Wright, *Becoming Black: Creating Identity in the African Diaspora* (Durham, NC: Duke University Press, 2004), 229–232.

[10] For more on the senses and slavery, see Mark Smith, "Getting in Touch with Slavery and Freedom," *Journal of American History* 95, 2 (2008): 381–391; Mark Smith, *Listening to Nineteenth-Century America* (Chapel Hill: University of North Carolina Press, 2001); Katrina Dyonne Thompson, *Ring Shout, Wheel About: The Racial Politics of Music and Dance in North American Slavery* (Urbana: University of Illinois Press, 2014), 13–24.

resistance beyond that usually understood through more stable ideas of material retention and agricultural expertise.[11] These ephemeral spaces of individual resistance could grow to incorporate large transnational zones of broader informal resistance and allow for greater fluidity of movement among the oppressed cultures of the Atlantic littoral.[12] Olfactory and deterritorializing responses within these rival and ephemeral geographies were hard to identify and troublesome to white planters who could not perceive the olfactory complexity of African cultures because they defined most African odors as a cultural or biological inferiority.[13] Thus, African slaves' uses of odor became weapons of the weak, to which the elites of colonial culture were partially anosmiac due to their stereotypical and blindingly racist olfactory mindfulness.[14]

[11] Stephanie Camp, *Closer to Freedom: Enslaved Women & Everyday Resistance in the Plantation South* (Chapel Hill: University of North Carolina Press, 2004); Jason Young, *Rituals of Resistance: African Atlantic Religion in Kongo and the Lowcountry South in the Era of Slavery* (Baton Rouge: Louisiana State University Press, 2007); Michael Gomez, *Exchanging Our Country Marks: The Transformation of African Identities in the Colonial and Antebellum South* (Chapel Hill: University of North Carolina Press, 1998); Maureen Warner-Lewis, *Central Africa in the Caribbean: Transcending Time, Transforming Cultures* (Kingston: University of the West Indies Press, 2003); Michael Gomez, "African Identity and Slavery in the Americas," *Radical History Review* 75 (1999): 111–120; Joseph Miller, "Retention, Reinvention, and Remembering: Restoring Identities through Enslavement in Africa and under Slavery in Brazil," in *Enslaving Connections: Changing Cultures of Africa and Brazil during the Era of Slavery*, eds. José Curto and Paul Lovejoy (Amherst, NY: Humanity, 2004), 81–121; Gwendolyn Midlo Hall, *Slavery and African Ethnicities in the Americas: Restoring the Links* (Chapel Hill: University of North Carolina Press, 2005); John Thornton, *A Cultural History of the Atlantic World, 1250–1820* (Cambridge: Cambridge University Press, 2012); Londa Schiebinger, *Secret Cures of Slaves: People, Plants, and Medicine in the Eighteenth-Century Atlantic World* (Stanford, CA: Stanford University Press, 2017); Susan Scott Parrish, "Diasporic African Sources of Enlightenment Knowledge," in *Science and Empire in the Atlantic World*, eds. James Delbourgo and Nicholas Dew (London: Routledge, 2008), 281–310.
[12] See especially Ernesto Bassi, *An Aqueous Territory: Sailor Geographies and New Granada's Transimperial Greater Caribbean World* (Durham, NC: Duke University Press, 2017), 3–11; John Savage, "Slave Poison/Slave Medicine: The Persistence of Obeah in Early Nineteenth-Century Martinique," in *Obeah and Other Powers: The Politics of Caribbean Religion and Healing*, eds. Diana Paton and Maarit Forde (Durham, NC: Duke University Press, 2012), 149–171.
[13] For sensory performances as disruptive, see Rupert Cox, Andrew Irving, and Christopher Wright, "Introduction: the Sense of the Senses," in *Beyond Text?: Critical Practices and Sensory Anthropology*, eds. Rupert Cox, Andrew Irving, and Christopher Wright (Manchester: Manchester University Press, 2016), 1–19.
[14] For ritual and sensory resistance, see Greg Downey, "The Importance of Repetition: Ritual as a Support to Mind," in *Ritual, Performance and the Senses*, eds. Michael Bull and Jon Mitchell (New York: Bloomsbury, 2015), 45–62; Hwa Yol Jung,

However, evil the smells of the Middle Passage and slavery became, slaves consistently found within the European classification of the African race as pungently different a veil they could use to create spaces of resistance. The shroud of odor, originally a classification of the other that Europeans applied to justify narratives of African inferiority and the slave trade, was reserved as a hidden cultural transcript by African slaves who hoped to create spaces of resistance distanced from increasingly fearful owners during the Age of Revolutions. African medical and dietary traditions involved much olfactory worship that many Europeans and colonists found distasteful and feared enough to increasingly avoid and draft laws to attempt to control. Still, the strange smells from African fires on white plantations frequently kept white masters in white houses. Spaces of resistance smelled because Africans knew smell would keep masters at bay, at least enough for artfully created, though minor and ephemeral, times and spaces of freedom.[15]

THE ETHNOGENETIC OLFACTORY

Despite a general focus on the British Atlantic, *The Smell of Slavery* asserts that odor became structurally important for discourses of both oppression and resistance throughout the broader and transnational spaces of the Atlantic World.[16] The English and French planters and scholars depicted in Chapter 2 often interchanged knowledges within a vast transnational Republic of Letters that included colonial leadership, personal letter

"Phenomenology and Body Politics," *Body and Society* 2, 2 (1996): 1–22. See also David Howes, "Olfaction and Transition; An Essay on the Ritual Uses of Smell," *Canadian Review of Sociology and Anthropology* 24, 3 (1987): 398–416; Alfred Gell, "Magic, Perfume, Dream," in *Symbols and Sentiments*, eds. Alfred Gell and Gilbert Lewis (London: Academic, 1977), 25–38; James Aho, *The Orifice as Sacrificial Site: Culture, Organization, and the Body* (New York: Aldine de Gruyter, 2002).

[15] For more on sensory literacy and sensory skills, see Arjun Appadurai, *Modernity at Large: Cultural Dimensions of Globalization* (Minneapolis: University of Minnesota Press, 1996), 35–38; Andrew Newman, "Early Americanist Grammatology," in *Colonial Mediascapes: Sensory Worlds of the Early Americas*, eds. Matt Cohen and Jeffrey Glover (Lincoln: University of Nebraska Press, 2014), 76–98.

[16] For critiques of the importance of African retention in the anthropological study of Afro-Caribbean religion, see Stephan Palmié, *The Cooking of History: How Not to Study Afro-Cuban Religion* (Chicago: University of Chicago Press, 2013), 6–12; Stephan Palmié, "Ecué's Atlantic: An Essay in Methodology," *Journal of Religion in Africa* 37, 2 (2007): 275–315; Stephen Shennen, "Ethnic Ambiguity: A Cultural Evolutionary Perspective," in *Ethnic Ambiguity and the African Past: Materiality, History, and the Shaping of Cultural Identities*, eds. Francois Richard and Kevin MacDonald (Walnut Creek, CA: Left Coast), 272–285.

exchanges, and scientific discourse. Within these multinational networks, racialization was commonly part of a language that coded races for reasons of status and economic trust. For slave societies in the Atlantic World, there were similar structural aspects of resistance to these forms of racialization, born within a "common wind" of transnational interchange between plantations, islands, and nations.[17]

For many African slaves and free blacks, these patterns of retention involved deep connections to libidinal spaces for smelling within diverse spiritualist traditions either retained as survivals or developing through processes of creolization in the New World.[18] Numerous historians have noticed these trends that link African patterns of herbalism, odor, and spirituality throughout the Greater Caribbean. These scholars' consistent notes are important for understanding the penetrative importance of olfactory cultural analysis within many different aspects of slave studies, including anthropology, history, and literary criticism.[19] Pablo Gomez's analysis of the sensory knowledge of environments in *Experiential Caribbean* (2017) notes the importance of many of these herbal smells and scented divinations within the early-seventeenth-century inquisition records of the New Kingdom of Granada healer and African-born Francisco Mandinga.[20] Karol Weaver's *Medical Revolutionaries* (2006) described many forms of similar slave medical management through the

---

[17] For transnational slave knowledge, see Julius Scott, "A Common Wind: Currents of Afro-American Communication in the Age of the Haitian Revolution" (Ph.D. Dissertation, Duke University Press, 1986); Kevin Dawson, "The Cultural Geography of Enslaved Ship Pilots," in *The Black Urban Atlantic in the Age of the Slave Trade*, eds. Jorge Cañizares-Esguerra, Matt Childs, and James Sidbury (Philadelphia: University of Pennsylvania Press, 2013), 163–184; Linda Rupert, *Creolization and Contraband: Curaçao in the Early Modern Atlantic World* (Athens: University of Georgia Press, 2012).

[18] Pablo Gómez, *The Experiential Caribbean: Creating Knowledge and Healing in the Early Modern Atlantic* (Chapel Hill: University of North Carolina Press, 2017), 95–117; Pablo Gómez, "The Circulation of Bodily Knowledge in the Seventeenth-Century Black Spanish Caribbean," *Social History of Medicine* 26, 3 (2013), 383–402.

[19] For more examples of African religious resistance in the New World, see Lizabeth Paravisini-Gebert, "Women Possessed: Eroticism and Exoticism in the Representation of Women as Zombie," in *Sacred Possessions: Vodou, Santería, Obeah, and the Caribbean*, eds. Margarite Fernandez Olmos and Lizabeth Paravisini-Gebert (New Brunswick, NJ: Rutgers University Press, 1997), 37–58; George Brandon, *Santería from Africa to the New World: The Dead Sell Memories* (Bloomington: University of Indiana Press, 1993), 86–91; Colin Dayan, *Haiti, History, and the Gods* (Berkeley: University of California Press, 1995), 98–152; Niya Afolabi, "Axe: Invocation of Candomblé and Afro-Brazilian Gods in Brazilian Cultural Production," in *Fragments of Bone: Neo-African Religions in a New World*, ed. Patrick Bellegarde-Smith (Urbana: University of Illinois Press, 2005), 108–123.

[20] Gómez, *Experiential Caribbean*, 105–106.

use of such herbal medicines applied on Hispaniola. To cure numerous fevers, African healers would sometimes use a "decocotion" made from "pois-puans (literally, stinking peas; Cassia occidentalis)." It was assumed at the time that "the plant's name came from its foul stench ... [S]laves also roasted it and drank it as a type of coffee."[21] In 1786, the Consul Superieur of Le Cap put many of these herbal practitioners on trial in Saint-Domingue. As Kate Ramsey provided: "A number of these practices described in the indictments resemble ways that ... strong roots in Kongo culture, have long been served, including the use of pepper, other hot spices, and gunpowder in ritual preparations, performances, and therapies."[22]

Similar olfactory and herbal agency emerged from slaves and free blacks throughout colonial South America. Laura de Mello e Souza offered how late sixteenth-century Brazilian laundress Isabel Maria de Oliveira would place "scented roots inside the clothing of the men she wanted to win over ... [M]any people accused this unmarried woman of being a sorceress." Isabel was later interrogated by the Holy Office as a possible witch and "claimed that she used these roots so the clothes she ironed would smell fragrant and pleasing to her customers."[23] Rachel Harding, in her analysis of the importance of female practitioners to South American religious traditions, summarized the practices of a black freed-woman in Minas Gerais in 1742, Luzia Pinta, who often diagnosed patient's diseases through the smelling of their heads.[24] Harding also described medicinal bags in her work on colonial Brazil, portraying the often strong-smelling roots that were carried as simples to protect slaves

---

[21] Karol Weaver, *Medical Revolutionaries: The Enslaved Healers of Eighteenth-Century Saint Domingue* (Urbana: University of Illinois Press, 2006), quotes on 73. For the more on the denigration of African sciences and environmental expertise in contemporary discourse, see Clapperton Chakanetsa Mavhunga, "Introduction: What Do Science, Technology, and Innovation Mean from Africa?," in *What Do Science, Technology, and Innovation Mean from Africa?*, ed. Clapperton Chakanetsa Mavhunga (Cambridge, MA: MIT Press, 2017), 1–28.

[22] Kate Ramsey, *The Spirits and the Law: Vodou and Power in Haiti* (Chicago: University of Chicago Press, 2011), 28–39, quote on 39.

[23] Laura de Mello e Souza, *The Devil and the Land of the Holy Cross: Witchcraft, Slavery, and Popular Religion in Colonial Brazil* (Austin: University of Texas Press, 2003), quotes on 151.

[24] Rachel Harding, *A Refuge in Thunder: Candomblé and Alternative Spaces of Blackness* (Bloomington: University of Indiana Press, 2000), 34–36. For more on Candomblé and African retention, see Beatriz Góis Dantas, *Nagô Grandma and White Papa: Candomblé and the Creation of Afro-Brazilian Identity* (Chapel Hill: University of North Carolina Press, 2009), 134–149.

from their masters through the magic placed upon them by the *feticeiro*, José Francisco Pereira, who was prosecuted for his supposed witchcraft in 1731.[25] James Sweet's *Domingos Álvares* (2011) similarly described the odors of ethnic African agency through the "fetid smell" of the "sack of medicinal plants" that the healer Domingos would carry on his divining missions throughout eighteenth-century Brazil, in the employ of masters or as a freedman.[26] João Reis likewise defined the importance of folkways of scent to African cultures in later Brazil of the nineteenth century, who battled against emerging medical professionalism. Therein, slave and free black Catholic confraternities resisted state attempts to control their keeping of the dead through using lavender water to scent their unburied deceased brethren.[27]

Odors within material waters and cultural designs regarding the mysticism of water were common in many of these different African spiritualisms within the Atlantic World. The diasporic tradition of Mami Wata, the mermaid or water spirit of many African nations, similarly represents the retention of African survivals and olfactory rituals within South America.[28] Mami Wata, or Water Mama, ceremonies sometimes included dancers who would perform inside a mobile ring of their fellow slaves. In 1775 Suriname, such a dance involved the retention of ways of smelling as divining. The ceremony, according to the Dutch governor Jean Nepveu, involved the regularly Dahomey-born dancers moving within a circle of onlookers and smelling-out the metaphorical poison within certain spectators who were then forced out of the circle. Nepveu described that "they pretend that they can not stand the smell of poisoners who are among the crowd, and who drive them mad; when these are driven away, they start dancing again."[29]

[25] Harding, *Refuge in Thunder*, 24–25.
[26] James Sweet, *Domingos Álvares: African Healing, and the Intellectual History of the Atlantic World* (Chapel Hill: University of North Carolina Press, 2011), 99–101.
[27] João José Reis, *Death Is a Festival: Funeral Rites and Rebellion in Nineteenth-Century Brazil* (Chapel Hill: University of North Carolina Press, 2003), 92–94, 234–240.
[28] Henry John Drewal, *Sacred Waters: Arts for Mami Wata and Other Divinities in Africa and the Diaspora* (Bloomington: University of Indiana Press, 2008); Henry John Drewal, "Performing the Other: Mami Wata Worship in Africa," *The Drama Review* 32, 2 (1988): 160–185.
[29] Alex van Stipriaan, "The Ever-Changing Face of Watramama in Suriname: A Water Goddess in Creolization since the Seventeenth Century," in *Sacred Waters: Arts for Mami Wata and Other Divinities in Africa and the Diaspora*, ed. Henry John Drewal (Bloomington: University of Indiana Press, 2008), 525–548, quote on 528. See also Ian Harwood, "The Hot/Cold Theory of Disease: Implications for Treatment of Puerto Rican Patients," *Journal of the American Medical Association* 216, 7 (1971): 1153–1158.

The importance of water spirits within the African diaspora, often ritualized through these broadly applied smelling rites and symbolism reminiscent of ring shouts, possibly led to later labor strikes among slave and free black populations in Rio de Janeiro in 1816.[30] Scented baths were also common throughout the slave communities of the Atlantic World, especially in Brazil where Catholic traditions of scent combined with African customs to create a creolized appreciation for odor to be used within soakings. In Brazil, African roots led to broader creolized rituals whereby different herbs were delineated through their hot and cold natures to be used in baths to cure specific ailments. Modern Candomblé still applies many of these traditional herbal definitions based on temperature, specifically within house baths, or *abo de casa*.[31]

Atlantic Africans also often used odor upon religious altars. Recent ethnographical works on altar worship has tied the understanding of performative spiritualism to the transcendent spasm caused when the "flash of the spirit" occurs after the dead and living are linked through an ephemeral moment of embodied holiness. Among the late-twentieth-century San of Namibia and Botswana, healing dances often involved the importance of the sense of smell within therapeutic movements tied to these forms of altar worship that were common during the era of slavery in the Atlantic World. Robert Farris Thompson has summarized that during these healing ceremonies "[b]lood sometimes rushes from the nostrils of a healer ... The red of the blood matches the red of the flames. It dramatizes *n/um* heat, 'boiling' up the shaman's back, vaporizing consciousness, driving the dancer to a higher plane. San

---

[30] Robert Slenes, "The Great Porpoise-skull Strike: Central-African Water Spirits and Slave Identity in Early Nineteenth-Century Rio de Janeiro," in *Central Africans and Cultural Transformations in the American Diaspora*, ed. Linda Heywood (Cambridge: Cambridge University Press, 2002), 183–208.

[31] Scented baths were probably more common throughout the Atlantic World than the limited and specific references from creolized Catholic traditions in Brazil and the Caribbean. Numerous references to similar herbs used for scenting baths are also common in the FWP narratives referenced later in this chapter. The African diaspora spread bathing traditions into many different American slave cultures, despite the lack of sources that summarize specific bathing procedures. For more on smell and bathing traditions, see Sharla Fett, *Working Cures: Healing, Health, and Power on Southern Slave Plantations* (Chapel Hill: University of North Carolina Press, 2002), 78–80, 112–114; Robert Voeks, *Sacred Leaves of Candomblé: African Magic, Medicine, and Religion in Brazil* (Austin: University of Texas Press, 1997), 95–96, 124–128; Margarite Fernández Olmos and Lizabeth Paravisini-Gebert, *Creole Religions of the Caribbean: An Introduction from Vodou and Santería to Obeah and Espiritismo* (New York: New York University Press, 2011), 178–183.

associate this trance-hemorrhage with blood streaming from the noses of dying elands; it is the sign or seal of passage from this world to the next. Such blood is medicine. In the belief that its smell repels all sickness, San shamans rub its crimson substance on their patients."[32] Similar practices are evident within earlier artwork throughout regions of southern Africa. As Thompson describes, numerous references from the eighteenth and nineteenth centuries portray a central healer with his nose highlighted through artistic styling and colored paints, often surrounded by a ring of dancers.[33] These dances that included olfactory importance reminiscent of Mami Wata rituals, practices of smelling within diverse ritual structures, and performances at altars were significant for much of African spiritual practice in the New World.

Despite the difficulty of discovering African religious practices from the era of the slave trade, many scholars have applied diverse reading methods to discover different ethnic practices from an African past that were also often informed by diverse Catholic, Protestant, and Islamic influences during the earlier centuries of the slave trade.[34] These African religious practices often influenced diverse New World syncretic religious traditions.[35] Often, these spiritualisms employed various African understandings of herbalism and ethnobotany.[36] Combining traditions helped

---

[32] Robert Farris Thompson, *Face of the Gods: Art and Altars of Africa and the African Americas* (New York: Museum for African Art, 1993), quote on 38.

[33] Thompson, *Face of the Gods*, 38–45, and 122–123.

[34] Kwasi Konadu, *The Akan Diaspora in the Americas* (New York: Oxford University Press, 2010); John Thornton, "Religious and Ceremonial Life in the Congo and Mbundu Areas, 1500–1700," in *Central Africans and Cultural Transformations in the American Diaspora*, ed. Linda Heywood (Cambridge: Cambridge University Press, 2012), 71–90; James Sweet, *Recreating Africa: Culture, Kinship, and Religion in the African-Portuguese World, 1441–1770* (Chapel Hill: University of North Carolina Press, 2003); Luis Nicholau Pares, "The Hula 'Problem': Ethnicity on the Pre-Colonial Slave Coast," in *The Changing Worlds of Atlantic Africa: Essays in Honor of Robin Law*, eds. Robin Law, Toyin Falola, and Matt Childs (Durham, NC: Carolina Academic Press, 2009), 323–346; Luis Nicolau Parés, "Ethnic-religious Modes of Identification among the Gbe-speaking People in Eighteenth and Nineteenth Century Brazil," in *Africa, Brazil, and the Construction of Trans-Atlantic Black Identities*, eds. Barry Boubacar, Elisee Akpo Soumonni, and Livio Sansone (Trenton, NJ: Africa World, 2008), 179–208; Paul Lovejoy, "Identifying Enslaved Africans in the African Diaspora," in *Identity in the Shadow of Slavery*, ed. Paul Lovejoy (London: Continuum, 2000), 1–29.

[35] Fernández Olmos and Paravisini-Gebert, *Creole Religions*, 1–23.

[36] For a sensory reading of the transmission of some of these botanical and medical cures, see Miles Ogborn, "Talking Plants: Botany and Speech in Eighteenth-Century Jamaica," *History of Science* 51 (2013): 251–282. See also modern sensory ethnobotany within Theresa Miller, *Plant Kin: A Multispecies Ethnography in Indigenous Brazil* (Austin: University of Texas Press, 2018).

to create a broader ethnogenetic olfactory that linked smelling traditions across African ethnic lines to create vast and creolized understandings of the importance of smell for the retention of African pasts. Often involving numerous aspects of the broader African olfactory explored in Chapter 3, slaves and free blacks who had crossed the Middle Passage found within their ancestral sensory repertoire various traditions of smelling-out, scenting goods, performing at fragrant altars, and herbal healing using goods classified partly through odor.[37]

OLFACTORY WARFARE: DOGS, MASTERS, AND SENSORY SKILLS

Many African cultural survivals of what was often deemed witchcraft by uninitiated planters similarly arose during numerous instances of slave and free black agency within the Atlantic World. Herbal remedies that were acknowledged for their scents informed countless slave medical traditions across plantations. Jason Young has designated the importance of conjurers and root doctors within many of these herbal traditions, who "often enjoyed 'even more importance than a preacher' because many" were regarded "with the respect that awe and fear excites." Analyzing the testimony of ex-slave Charles Hunter of St. Simon's Island in Georgia, Young presented that root doctors often assumed a mystical olfactory character involving scented charms, whereby local healers were repetitively illustrated through portrayals within numerous slave descriptions of the smoky rooms where conjurers and root doctors practiced.[38]

Walter Rucker has similarly examined the importance of root doctors and slave conjurers as human bridges for North American slaves to connect with African cultural pasts. The conjurer William Webb of nineteenth-century Kentucky had many of his fellow slaves fill bags with numerous herbs, which were then placed in front of the master's house

---

[37] For examples, see Robert Voeks, "African Medicine and Magic in the Americas," *Geographical Review* 83, 1 (1993): 66–78; Mary Galvin, "Decoctions for Carolinians: The Creation of a Creole Medicine Chest in Colonial South Carolina," in *Creolization in the Americas*, eds. David Buisseret and Steven Reinhardt (College Station, TX: Texas A&M University Press, 2000), 63–98; Schiebinger; *Secret Cures*, 117–129; William Aho and Kimlian Minott, "Creole and Doctor Medicine: Folk Beliefs, Practices and Orientations to Modern Medicine in a Rural and Industrial Setting in Trinidad and Tobago," *Social Science and Medicine*, 11, 5 (1977), 349–355.

[38] Fett, *Working Cures*, 72–80; Young, *Rituals of Resistance*, quotes on 128–129.

to entice dreams of slave retribution in the master's mind and thus induce better treatment. Henry Bibb, who was repeatedly beaten by his owner for running away, enlisted a similar conjurer to protect him from his master's whip. This was performed by sprinkling Bibb with herbs, powders, and protective roots. When these failed, and he was beaten again, Bibb enlisted another conjurer who provided a drink made with pungent cow manure and red pepper which, when ingested, would supposedly protect the slave from his cruel master.[39]

Although many scholars debate questions of slave memory as part of these narratives describing the Antebellum South, most have agreed that there remains great value within slave descriptions from later in their lives for understanding slave cultures and individual African consciousness within the confines of New World slave systems.[40] Throughout the Federal Writers Project (FWP) narratives, traditions of olfactory prominence are evident for numerous slaves and free blacks who relayed their reminiscences to interviewers during the Great Depression. For example, Uncle Jake (Juka), a legendary African American healer from North Georgia of the early twentieth century, was described as often living in a "lusty" cabin that smelled of the red pepper and onions hung from the rafters of his musty storeroom. The "smelly drippings" that were common in Jake's cabin are also suggestive of slave healers of decades prior who used odors of the environment to possibly maintain some distance between the slave population and white masters.[41]

Slaves within Arkansas of the early nineteenth century similarly used their knowledge of smells to create distance between their masters and the cabins they adorned with the scents of creolized diets. As one Arkansas observer, Dicey Thomas, noted: "You couldn't cook nothing without somebody knowin' it. Couldn't cook and eat in the back while white folk sit in the front without them knowin' it. They used to steal from the old master and cook it and they would be burning rags or something to

---

[39] Walter Rucker, "Conjure, Magic, and Power: The Influence of Afro-Atlantic Religious Practices on Slave Resistance and Rebellion," *Journal of Black Studies* 32, 1 (2001): 84–103.

[40] For debates, see Paul Lovejoy, "Autobiography and Memory: Gustavus Vassa, Alias Olaudah Equiano, the African," *Slavery & Abolition* 27, 3 (2006): 317–347; Charles Davis and Henry Louis Gates, *The Slave's Narrative* (Oxford: Oxford University Press, 1985), 42–43; Jonathan Clifton and Dorien Van De Mieroop, *Master Narratives, Identities, and the Stories of Former Slaves* (Amsterdam: John Benjamins, 2016), 18–33.

[41] *Federal Writers' Project: Slave Narrative Project, Vol. 4, Georgia, Part 2, Garey-Jones* (Washington, DC: Library of Congress, 1936), quote on 310–311.

keep the white folks from smelling it."[42] A similar tale, of a stolen chicken that had to be covered in "bedclothes" to hide odors from white masters, was related by the ex-slave Millie Williams from Texas.[43] As well, Benjamin Johnson, a former slave in Georgia, provided that his compatriots in the condition of servitude would be careful to hide all evidence of the chickens they stole from their masters for sustenance, as "you had to be careful an' bury all de feathers in de groun' 'cause if you burned 'em de white folks would smell 'em."[44] Combined, these tales of aromas portray direct attention to smell in the American South as a way to provide slaves different alimentary goods that would normally not be allowed as part of the diet generally provided from regularly austere plantation owners.

Slaves in North America were attuned to using their knowledge of smelling to hide dietary goods because they understood odor within the environment as essential from an African cultural past that defined smells as productive of cultural content and of great spiritual importance. Many slaves in North America used this greater attention to environmental odors to find their way through the backbreaking slave systems to which they were chained. Mildred Heard, a former slave from Georgia, wrote much of her ability to use scents to define her environment. Specifically, she noted that her nose was adept at smelling types of snakes encountered throughout the South.[45] These environmental skills allowed for slaves to surreptitiously maneuver to gather goods and important information. Slave narratives display glimpses of these differently creolized African American sensory worlds that frequently portray an intensive appreciation for generational forms of olfactory knowledge.[46]

African American slaves and later freedmen gained access to the knowledge of their times, judging sensory worlds carried on the Middle Passage important to their elegant causes of resistance. The conjurer Dr. Jones, an Antebellum Era figure described by freedwoman Patsy Moses from Texas, often would take baths to scent himself so dogs could not detect him as he

---

[42] *Federal Writers' Project: Slave Narrative Project, Vol. 2, Arkansas, Part 6, Quinn-Tuttle* (Washington, DC: Library of Congress, 1936), 288–295, quote on 289.

[43] *Federal Writers' Project: Slave Narrative Project, Vol. 16, Texas, Part 4, Sanco-Young* (Washington, DC: Library of Congress, 1936), quote on 170–172.

[44] *FWP Vol. 4, Georgia, Part 2*, quote on 322–323.

[45] *FWP Vol. 4, Georgia, Part 2*, 165–167.

[46] For more on slaves, environmental skills, and medicine, see Christopher Iannini, *Fatal Revolutions: Natural History, West Indian Slavery, and the Routes of American Literature* (Chapel Hill: University of North Carolina Press, 2012), 177–218; Susan Scott Parrish, *American Curiosity: Cultures of Natural History in the Colonial British Atlantic World* (Chapel Hill: University of North Carolina Press, 2012), 259–306.

traveled to provide conjuring through "frog bones," "snake skin," and other objects that he would place as charms on doorsteps of malevolent masters.[47] An ex-slave interviewed in Florida, Cindy Kinsey, described how slaves would also often tie rabbits' feet around their necks with stinking "akkerfedity" bags, usually filled with forms of excrement or other pungent charms, as a way to protect themselves during the era of the Civil War. She noted if a Union soldier would catch "you wif dat rabbit foots an dat akkerfedity bag roun youh nek, he sush turn you loose right now."[48] These scented protective charms worked wonders for slaves searching for their freedom in wartime and from their owners.

Conjure was common against masters, and was also used as a way to intimidate freedmen and freedwomen after emancipation. While questioning a former slave, Addie, her FWP interviewer noticed the African American woman became agitated about a conjurer who would visit her land each morning and spread his charms. Addie proclaimed: "Does you smell that funny scent? Oh, Good Lawd! Jus' look at dem white powders on my doorstep! Let me get some hot water and wash 'em out quick! Now Missy, see how dese Niggers 'round here is allus up to deir meanness?" Her understanding of conjure and the scent of African medicines came from her youth on plantations in antebellum Georgia when slaves worked their olfactory knowledge to both shield themselves from their master's dominion and intimidate fellow slaves.[49] Frequently, these African root doctors in the Americas would use diverse forms of material culture, sometimes implicating scents and odors of death, to create spaces of resistance. The use of goofer dust, the dirt of graveyards, as a weapon placed as a sprinkling in front of master's houses, or thrown in front of master's carriages, exemplifies the importance of funerary retention as part of these patterns of resistance through African spirituality and the productive powers of death. Goofer dust thus acted, specifically for Kongo slaves in the American South, as a *minkisi*, or material object that had implicitly synesthetic olfactory powers to influence the living in the natural world.[50]

---

[47] *Federal Writers' Project: Slave Narrative Project, Vol. 16, Texas, Part 3, Lewis-Ryles* (Washington, DC: Library of Congress, 1936), quotes on 142–145.

[48] *Federal Writers' Project: Slave Narrative Project, Vol. 3, Florida, Anderson-Wilson* (Washington, DC: Library of Congress, 1936), quotes on 191–193.

[49] *Federal Writers' Project: Slave Narrative Project, Vol. 4, Georgia, Part 4, Telfair-Young* (Washington, DC: Library of Congress, 1936), quotes on 110–111.

[50] Young, *Rituals of Resistance*, 163–166; Patrick Bellegarde-Smith, "Introduction," in *Fragments of Bone: Neo-African Religions in a New World*, ed. Patrick Bellegarde-Smith (Urbana: University of Illinois Press, 2005), 1–12.

Many of these African, African American, and ethnic olfactory pasts were informed by different traditions that ranged from the *juju* of Igbo customs to the *minkisi* of the Kongo.[51] As another illustration of olfactory diversity, Maggie Woods, a daughter of slaves from Summerville, Arkansas, described her use of conjure and medicine when discussing chitterlings mixed with other materials to create a salve. Her attention to both local environments and previous African sensory worlds represents such a talented bricolage of subjective agency within slave societies. Woods described her medicinal emollient as smelling "like chitlings. In that sack is the inside of the chitlings (hog manure). I boil it down and strain it, then boil it down, put camphor gum and fresh lard in it, boil it down low and pour it up. It is a green salve. It is fine for piles, rub your back for lumbago, and swab out your throat for sore throat."[52] Salves from animal goods and vegetal material were common throughout the Atlantic World. In South Carolina and Georgia it was often routine for both slaves and white society to also use African recipes for the creation of soups and soaps from the *bene* seeds of the *sesamun* plant, which was probably brought from Africa by slaves during the early years of Carolina settlement during the seventeenth century. Cultivators of the plant frequently applied their noses to create potent mixtures of cold and hot-pressed oils from the seeds.[53]

The Ole Heg Tale, a nineteenth-century legend from many areas of the New World including Belize, provides even more olfactory importance for the use of such vegetal material and *bene* seeds from African traditions. The tale comprises the legend of Ole Heg, an older female witch who frequented the dilapidated buildings of lost communities. To protect children from her hauntings at night, practitioners would use *asafoetida*, a pungent resin that would repel Ole Heg and her attempts at sucking the blood of her enemies. Many would also spread the aromatic seeds of the sesame on their floors to protect their children from these ephemeral attacks.[54]

---

[51] For more on survivals, see Douglas Chambers, *Murder at Montpelier: Igbo Africans in Virginia* (Jackson, MS: University of Mississippi Press, 2009), 57–59; Jerry Gershenhorn, *Melville J. Herskovits and the Racial Politics of Knowledge* (Lincoln: University of Nebraska Press, 2004), 93–122.

[52] *Federal Writers' Project: Slave Narrative Project, Vol. 2, Arkansas, Part 7, Vaden-Young* (Washington, DC: Library of Congress, 1936), quotes on 232–234.

[53] Dorothea Bedigian, "African Origins of Sesame Cultivation in the Americas," in *African Ethnobotany in the Americas*, eds. Robert Voeks and John Rashford (New York: Springer, 2013), 67–122, 78–80.

[54] Bedigian, "African Origins," 99–100. See also Melissa Johnson, *Becoming Creole: Nature and Race in Belize* (New Brunswick, NJ: Rutgers University Press, 2018), 83–86.

The poet and anthropologist Sarah Handy's Reconstruction Era ethnography "Negro Superstitions" similarly included tales of such scented slave and post-emancipation African American knowledge of environments, medicines, and olfactory traditions. Yvonne Chireau's summary of the racialized ethnography noted Handy's representation of "one doctor's treatment," which "included the burning of 'various vile-smelling powders' in a patient's room, followed by his opening a window 'to let the devil out.'"[55] As Chireau summarized regarding such structural applications of African and African American ritual traditions: "Over time, certain ingredients emerged as staple components in the material rhetoric of Conjure practices ... Materials were selected both for their sympathetic associations and for aesthetic purposes." Among these were included "acrid herbs to displace evil essences .... the most powerful charms required exuviae from the body itself: hair, nails, skin, or waste matter such as urine or excrement. The inventory of conjuring materials has remained remarkably consistent for hundreds of years."[56]

Other slaves and freedmen used their knowledge of smells and the environment to aid escapes from violent owners. The captured freedman Solomon Northrup was adept at understanding the scent tracking of the dogs that his Louisiana captors used to hunt fugitives. After his escape, he wrote of his cleansing swim in the bayou that he used to overcome the "slight, mysterious scent" that the "quick-smelling" hounds searched to chase fugitive slaves.[57] In the narrative of another escape from well-trained hounds, a slave named Burrus covered his feet in stinking pig's grease so that dogs could not catch him during his attempt to flee from slavery in North Carolina, as described by the ex-slave Fanny Cannady.[58] Other FWP narratives also portray how numerous slaves would often rub their feet with a vernacular-termed herb called "Indian turnip" to cover

---

[55] Yvonne Chireau, *Black Magic: Religion and the African American Conjuring Tradition* (Berkeley: University of California Press, 2003), quotes on 106–107; Sara Handy, "Negro Superstitions," *Lippincott's Magazine* 48 (December, 1891): 735–739.

[56] Chireau, *Black Magic*, quote on 48.

[57] Solomon Northrup, *Twelve Years a Slave* (Auburn, NY: Derby and Miller, 1853), quotes on 138–139. For more on runaways and political change, see R. J. M. Blackett, *The Captive's Quest for Freedom: Fugitive Slaves, the 1850 Fugitive Slave Law, and the Politics of Slavery* (New York: Cambridge University Press, 2018), 42–87; John Hope Franklin and Loren Schweninger, *Runaway Slaves: Rebels on the Plantation* (New York: Oxford University Press, 1999), 17–48.

[58] *Federal Writers' Project: Slave Narrative Project, Vol. 11, North Carolina, Part 1, Adams-Hunter* (Washington, DC: Library of Congress, 1936), 3–5.

their scents as they escaped from hounds, as remembered by Gus Smith, a freedman from Missouri.[59]

In the imbrued game of dogs played against their masters, as the ex-slave America Morgan portrayed, slave blood was often used to train dogs to recognize the stereotypical scents that masters believed existed within their slaves' bodies.[60] Charles Ball summarized such master's tactics within his slave narrative of the 1850s. He summarized how masters would use blankets scented from slaves sleeping upon their fibers to train dogs to locate the scents of specific African and African American bodies. One of Ball's overseers in South Carolina performed this skillfulness in front of slaves as a means to foment new fears that runaways would face from canines if they attempted to flee the slave system.[61] As Ball would later show during his own escape from captivity, which involved the killing of a hound through the slicing of the dog's potent nose and driving skull, slaves found numerous environmental aids to counter the proficient sensory skills educated upon the canine to hunt human property.[62]

Within a nation that was deemed moral and Christian, masters trained dogs to smell the odors of African bodies as part of a grand recital of silent escape and thunderous pecuniary ravenousness.[63] For slaveholders, as within the ironically toned poem *The Virginia Philosopher, or, Few Lucky Slave-Catchers* (1843) written in the wake of the trial of escaped slave George Latimer, dogs became the central "allies" within a game of "blood-hound noses skilled to catch" that pitted the proboscis of the hound against the olfactory environmental understanding of slaves hoping to flee from bondage. As the abolitionist Daniel Mann described during the middle of the nineteenth century, these dogs were often trained so harshly to

---

[59] *Federal Writers' Project: Slave Narrative Project, Vol. 10, Missouri, Abbot-Younger* (Washington, DC: Library of Congress, 1936), quotes on 331–332.

[60] *Federal Writers' Project: Slave Narrative Project, Vol. 5, Indiana, Arnold-Woodson* (Washington, DC: Library of Congress, 1936), 141–144.

[61] Charles Ball, *Slavery in the United States: A Narrative of the Life and Adventures of Charles Ball, a Black Man, Who Lived Forty Years in Maryland, South Carolina and Georgia, As a Slave* (Pittsburgh: Shryock, 1854), 253–255.

[62] Ball, *Slavery in the United States*, 409–411.

[63] For recent work on the human/animal question related to dogcatchers during slavery and after, see Bénédicte Boisseron, *Afro-Dog: Blackness and the Animal Question* (New York: Columbia University Press, 2018), 37–80. Much of this historical analysis relies on theories of cross-species sociality within Donna Haraway, *The Companion Species Manifesto: Dogs, People, and Significant Otherness* (Chicago: Prickly Paradigm, 2015).

detect and devour African bodies that "when they attack a negro even by mistake, it is a maxim that they must be made to conquer him, to keep up their courage and ferocity." Bodies torn to pieces in the mouths of dogs also commodified speaks to a modernity of nationalism and capitalism that never had faith, fairness, or fact at its ideological core.[64]

Throughout the capitalized Atlantic World, training of ravenous dogs generally related to the common black odor that was believed to be separate and distinct from individual slaves' scents. Masters trained different breeds of canines to recognize the universal odors of black sweat and black blood through a similar subconscious construction of a false perception that had penetrated their own nasal discernments. The biopolitical animal education to smell race created a market for slave-hunting canines within the American South and in other ports of the Atlantic World. Frederick Douglass specifically wrote in 1846 of the "blood-hound trainers" to be found selling their wares to nearly every plantation owner, and Harriet Beecher Stowe portrayed similar canine markets and profitable businessmen in *Uncle Tom's Cabin* (1852).[65]

Further exemplifying the common use of dogs throughout the institution of slavery, during the Haitian Rebellion many dogs trained in Cuba attacked rebelling slaves and were provided the eponymous terminology of "Cuban bloodhounds." However, the use of canines was limited at later stages of the war for Haitian independence as some European military leaders believed that the hounds of battle would turn on black allies due to the commonly held and false

---

[64] Daniel Mann, *The Virginia Philosopher, or, Few Lucky Slave-Catchers: A Poem* (Boston: Published for the Author, 1843), quotes on 28–38. Courtesy of the Huntington Library, San Marino, CA. For earlier English understanding of the use of dogs for hunting in the Americas, see the reading of Native American dogs as a form of livestock in Virginia DeJohn Anderson, *Creatures of Empire: How Domestic Animals Transformed Early America* (Oxford: Oxford University Press, 2007), 34–37; the Native American use of dogs prior to contact within Marion Schwartz, *A History of Dogs in the Early Americas* (New Haven: Yale University Press, 1998); and the use of dogs in animal hunts within, Nicolas Proctor, *Bathed in Blood: Hunting and Mastery in the Old South* (Charlottesville: University of Virginia Press, 2002), 65–73.

[65] Boisseron, *Afro-Dog*, 52–75, quote on 73; Harriet Beecher Stowe, *Uncle Tom's Cabin, or, Negro Life in the Slave States of America: With Fifty Splendid Engravings* (London: Clarke & Co, 1852), 58–60. See also Charlton Yingling and Tyler Parry, "Slave Hounds and Abolition in the Americas," *Past & Present* 246 (Forthcoming, 2020).

understanding of the propensity of indistinguishable black odors. The use of these trained dogs was so common in the Atlantic World that slaves came to know their escapes were regularly to be tested against the noses of hounds.[66]

Throughout the public spheres of the Atlantic World, advertisements and narratives relaying this market for dogs used to scent slaves further tied inherent pungency as an important distinction marking slave bodies, as with the print of "Training Bloodhounds" within Marcus Rainsford's *An Historical Account of the Black Empire of Hayti* (1805) (see Figure 4.1). Against these dogs and masters, olfactory cloaking became a potent weapon, born of a deep African attention to odors that survived the Middle Passage. The endurance of scented understandings of the environment, rebirthed in the New World, taught Africans listening to the common winds of rumor and transnational knowledge that struggling against the racial chaos of slavery was no waste but rather an assertion of identity and agency that could make itself into a world of fresh aromatic hopes and cultural survival. In the act of disobedience that was absconding from labor, slaves marked their own identities.[67] Often, that act of decoding racialized motifs of the slave as child or animal involved the use of smell and greater understandings of racial olfactory dialectics, whereby knowledge of the master's consideration of racial odors was used against the falsely educated though still biologically potent noses of dogs.[68]

---

[66] Philippe Girard, "War Unleashed: The Use of War Dogs during the Haitian War of Independence," *Napoleonica. La Revue* 15 (2012/2013): 80–105. For more on dog-training and the use of dogs in the French Caribbean, see Louis Sala-Molins, *Dark Side of the Light: Slavery and the French Enlightenment* (Minneapolis: University of Minnesota Press, 2006), 117–122.

[67] For more on dogs and runaways, see Sara Johnson, "'You Should Give them Blacks to Eat': Cuban Bloodhounds and the Waging of an Inter-American War of Torture and Terror," *American Quarterly* 61, 1 (March, 2009): 65–92; Franklin and Schweninger, *Runaway Slaves*, 149–181.

[68] For more the human/animal divide and dogs in the discourses of sensibility and abolitionism, see Markham Ellis, "Suffering Things: Lapdogs, Slaves, and Counter-Sensibility," in *The Secret Life of Things: Animals, Objects, and It-Narratives in Eighteenth-Century England*, ed. Mark Blackwell (Lewisburg, PA: Bucknell University Press, 2014), 92–113; Lynn Festa, "Person, Animal, Thing: The 1796 Dog Tax and the Right to Superfluous Things," *Eighteenth-Century Life* 33, 2 (2009): 1–44. See also Lynn Festa, *Sentimental Figures of Empire in Eighteenth-Century Britain and France* (Baltimore, MD: Johns Hopkins University Press, 2006), 153–161.

The mode of training Blood Hounds in S.ᵗ Domingo, and of exercising them by Chasseurs.

FIGURE 4.1 Print of "Training Bloodhounds, Saint Domingue." Included within Marcus Rainsford, *An Historical Account of the Black Empire of Hayti* (London, 1805), facing, p. 423. Courtesy of the Library Company of Philadelphia

ODOR AND OBEAH

Significantly extensive literatures on slave resistance within the Caribbean often focus on labor, class, and race in the making of radical formations that often led to the critical mass necessary for large-scale revolts.[69] Many works on African retention also explore the importance of cultural survivals for forms of everyday resistance to slavery.[70] Recent work on Obeah in the historical context of Jamaican slave societies has renewed interest in the study of African spirituality, cultural retention, and sensory engagements that could lead to rebellion.[71] As part of these narratives of sensory retention and cultural resistance, Obeah practitioners in the Anglo-Atlantic represent the use of African notions of smelling that survived the Middle Passage. White masters in societies with Obeah practitioners frequently became anxious about the power that spiritual practices could garner within slave cultures, especially after the widespread influences of the Vodou poisoner François Mackandal in Saint-Domingue of 1758 and the 1760 revolt led by the slave Tacky in Jamaica, himself an Obeah practitioner believed by other slaves to be invincible due to his herbal charms.[72]

Early references to Obeah within the literatures of the West Indies often note the mysterious powers of practitioners and the fears of their influence within slave communities.[73] Throughout the eighteenth century, the British came to know Obeah as a menacing and powerful spiritual force.[74] The fear white masters had of these untamable African medical

---

[69] For example, see Michael Mullin, *Africa in America: Slave Acculturation and Resistance in the American South and the British Caribbean, 1736–1831* (Urbana: University of Illinois Press, 1992), 269–281; Michael Craton, *Testing the Chains: Resistance to Slavery in the British West Indies* (Ithaca: Cornell University Press, 1982).

[70] For more examples, see Diana Paton, "Witchcraft, Poison, Law, and Atlantic Slavery," *William and Mary Quarterly* 69, 2 (2012): 235–264; Susan Dwyer Amussen, *Caribbean Exchanges: Slavery and the Transformation of English Society, 1640–1700* (Chapel Hill: University of North Carolina Press, 2009), 145–176; Jenny Shaw, *Everyday Life in the Early English Caribbean: Irish, Africans, and the Construction of Difference* (Athens: University of Georgia Press, 2013), 101–155.

[71] Kenneth Bilby, "An (Un)natural Mystic in the Air: Images of Obeah in Caribbean Song," in *Obeah and Other Powers: The Politics of Caribbean Religion and Healing*, eds. Diana Paton and Maarit Forde (Durham, NC: Duke University Press, 2012), 45–79; Dianne Stewart, *Three Eyes for the Journey: African Dimensions of the Jamaican Religious Experience* (Oxford: Oxford University Press, 2005), 58–68.

[72] Richard Robert Madden, *A Twelvemonth's Residence in the West Indies* (Philadelphia: Carey, Lea, and Blanchard, 1835), 72–75; William Shepherd, "The Negro Incantation," in *The Poetical Register and Repository of Fugitive Poetry for 1803* (London: Rivington, 1804), 413–415. See also Carolyn Fick, *The Making of Haiti: The Saint Domingue Revolution from Below* (Knoxville: The University of Tennessee Press, 1990), 61–72.

[73] For early references, see Thomas Walduck, "T. Walduck's Letters from Barbados, 1710–1711," *Journal of the Barbados Museum and Historical Society* 15, 2 (May, 1948): 137–149.

[74] James Grainger, *The Sugar-Cane: a Poem, In Four Books* (London: R. and J. Dodsley, 1764), 142–146. For more on Obeah, Atlantic medicine, and Grainger, see

practices can be seen through analysis of the many laws the English used to control African spiritualism within Jamaica, with many arising with the term "Obeah" after 1760.[75] As well, the creation of Obeah novels within the Anglo-Atlantic of the nineteenth century demonstrates the concern white planters had over the upset that the contagion of Obeah and her scented and common winds could cause their slave societies.[76]

British surgeon and traveler Benjamin Moseley's *A Treatise on Sugar* (1799) summarized the importance of Obeah in the minds of many of these fearful Jamaican planters. Within a work synthesized from observations that Moseley performed while in Jamaica from his first time on the island in 1768 until publication, *Treatise on Sugar* described for colonial and metropolitan readers an intense fear of Obeah among both slave populations and white masters. Moseley began his explanation by linking Obeah, shortened to Obi in his account, to ancient wisdom of Egyptians and Old Testament Semitic peoples who could manipulate the environment in ways most Europeans had lost touch with. Moseley summarized the "grave dirt, hair, teeth of sharks, and other animals, blood, feathers, egg-shells, images in wax, the hearts of birds, liver of mice, and some potent roots, weeds, and bushes" that Obi practitioners used to create "illness" in their enemies. Rather than judge these practices as mere superstition, Moseley's work accessed a tone of jealousy that "Europeans" were "ignorant" of these practices and their successful applications among Obi doctors. The Jamaican traveler continued: "Certain mixtures of these ingredients are burnt; or buried very deep in the ground; or hung up a chimney; or on the side of an house; or in a garden; or laid under the threshold of the door of the party, to suffer; with incantation songs, or curses, or ceremonies necromantically

Kelly Wisecup, *Medical Encounters: Knowledge and Identity in Early American Literatures* (Amherst: University of Massachusetts Press, 2013), 127–160; Emily Senior, *The Caribbean and the Medical Imagination, 1764–1834: Slavery, Disease and Colonial Modernity* (Cambridge: Cambridge University Press, 2018), 77–84.

[75] *Volume Two of Acts of Assembly, Passed in the Island of Jamaica, from the Year 1681 to the Year 1769* (Kingston, Jamaica, 1787), 6; Jerome Handler and Kenneth Bilby. "On the Early Use and Origin of the Term 'Obeah' in Barbados and the Anglophone Caribbean," *Slavery & Abolition* 22, 2 (2001): 87–100. For more on masters' suppression of slave medicine see Katherine Paugh, "Yaws, Syphilis, Sexuality, and the Circulation of Medical Knowledge in the British Caribbean and the Atlantic World," *Bulletin of the History of Medicine* 88, 2 (2014): 225–252.

[76] J. Alexandra McGhee, "Fever Dreams: Obeah, Tropical Disease, and Cultural Contamination in Colonial Jamaica and the Metropole," *Atlantic Studies* 12, 2 (2015): 179–199. See also Randy Browne, *Surviving Slavery in the British Caribbean* (Philadelphia: University of Pennsylvania Press, 2017), 132–143.

performed in planetary hours, or at midnight, regarding the aspects of the moon." As Moseley implicitly portrayed, these mixtures of environmental material created synesthetic sensations that included the redolent memories of African spiritualisms for Obeah practitioners throughout the Caribbean.[77]

Moseley summarized the inherent resistance in the practice of Obi by both men, who were more adept at using poisons and *calabashes*, and women, who were deemed more skillful at controlling the soul, the wind, and the weather. He prophetically noted: "Laws constructed in the West Indies, can never suppress the effect of ideas, the origin of which is in the centre of Africa."[78] Moseley continued his summary to tell the story of the most famous Obi practitioner in Jamaica at the time, Three Fingered Jack, who was believed to make zombie slaves out of a mixture of: "grave dirt, ashes, the blood of a black cat, and human fat; all mixed into a kind of paste." The rebel applied these goods in tandem with "[a] cat's foot, a dried toad, a pig's tail, a slip of virginal parchment of kid's skin, with characters marked in blood on it."[79] Jack became such an important and remembered character that many poems, plays, and novels were written about his exploits in the decades after his death in 1781.[80] The implications of zombie slaves pushed planters to attack and kill Jack for his attempted subversion of the slave system through the use of numerous animistic and usually scented objects.[81]

As Jack's use of numerous environmental objects portrays, his Jamaican location was an essential space for resistance through these aromatic forms of African understanding. In Barbados, practitioners of African medicines also often applied scent and the environment to use the high petroleum content of the island to their advantage in confidence games against their masters. One slave woman, during the 1790s, attempted to portray her witchcraft to white onlookers by lighting

---

[77] Benjamin Moseley, *A Treatise on Sugar: With Miscellaneous Medical Observations* (London: J. Nichols for G. G. and J. Robinson, 1800 [1799]), quotes on 190–192.

[78] Moseley, *A Treatise on Sugar*, quote on 194.

[79] Moseley, *A Treatise on Sugar*, quotes on 197.

[80] For many of these texts, see Errol Hill, *The Jamaican Stage, 1655–1900: Profile of a Colonial Theatre* (Amherst: University of Massachusetts Press, 1992), 100–102; Frances Botkin, *Thieving Three-Fingered Jack: Transatlantic Tales of a Jamaican Outlaw, 1780–2015* (New Brunswick, NJ: Rutgers University Press, 2017).

[81] Moseley, *A Treatise on Sugar*, 198–205. See also Wade Davis, *Passage of Darkness: The Ethnobiology of the Haitian Zombie* (Chapel Hill: University of North Carolina Press, 1988), 169–173; Elizabeth McAlister, "Slaves, Cannibals, and Infected Hyper-Whites: The Race and Religion of Zombies," *Anthropological Quarterly* 85, 2 (2012): 457–486.

a pungent bubbling brook on fire.[82] Later slaves would similarly try to trick their masters in Barbados through using the island's gas underbelly to prove their environmental skills and frighten their masters into offering better treatment.[83]

Numerous scholars have shown how these forms of Obeah and other African spiritualisms became a significant form of resistance that could create needed space between masters and slaves.[84] The correspondingly noteworthy form of resistance within the scented *myal* herbal practice that was a subsidiary to the spiritualism of Obeah was also a common way for slaves to connect to their African past through understandings of a different form of sensory herbalism than found within Western medical customs. Representing a deep attention to odor, the medical field of *myal* was possibly named for the aromatic weed *Eryngium foetidum* or from the similarly Kumina olfactory term *mwela*, or breathing power concerning plant life.[85] Slaves were often forced by poor medical care provided by masters to turn to the African medicine of *myal*'s aromas to keep their bodies and minds in decent health and working order.[86]

Obeah became communal by necessity, networked and organized in order to heal sick slaves.[87] Obeah practitioners sometimes also employed scented waters to wash diseased slaves, as in the specific case of the ill slave Cornelia in nineteenth-century British Guiana. The Obeah-man Willem, in a similar olfactory practice on another Guiana plantation, used an herb-

[82] George Pinckard, *Notes on the West Indies* (London: Longman, Hurst, Rees, and Orme, 1806), 299–300.
[83] Henry Fitzherbert, "The Journal Henry Fitzherbert Kept While in Barbados in 1825," *Journal of Barbados Museum and Historical Society* 44 (November/December, 1998): 117–190.
[84] Simon Gikandi, *Slavery and the Culture of Taste* (Princeton, NJ: Princeton University Press, 2011), 226–281; James Epstein, *Scandal of Colonial Rule: Power and Subversion in the British Atlantic during the Age of Revolution* (Cambridge: Cambridge University Press, 2012), 13–45. For more on spatial resistance in slave studies, see James Delle, *An Archaeology of Social Space: Analyzing Coffee Plantations in Jamaica's Blue Mountains* (New York: Plenum, 1998), 4–19.
[85] Stewart, *Three Eyes for the Journey*, 44–51; Monica Schuler, *"Alas, Alas, Kongo": A Social History of Indentured African Immigration into Jamaica, 1841–1865* (Baltimore, MD: Johns Hopkins University Press, 1980), 32–44.
[86] Jerome Handler and Kenneth Bilby, *Enacting Power: The Criminalization of Obeah in the Anglophone Caribbean, 1760–2011* (Kingston: University of West Indies Press, 2012), 29–38.
[87] Jerome Handler, "Slave Medicine and Obeah in Barbados, Circa 1650 to 1834," *New West Indian Guide* 74, 1–2 (2000): 57–90; Richard Sheridan, *Doctors and Slaves: A Medical and Demographic History of Slavery in the British West Indies, 1680–1834* (Cambridge: Cambridge University Press, 1985), 42–97.

scented broom as a healing device, in a comparable manner to African herbal traditions among the Ga language group of present-day Ghana.[88] Rather than the witchcraft and malevolent herbal practice that planters portrayed within Obeah, African herbal traditions helped to cure slaves, or at least provide some scented psychosomatic support, in spaces where white medicine and Christian morality had obviously failed.[89]

Many Obeah practitioners became adept at using poisons, on occasion citing knowledge about toxins from African traditions, as in the case of Igbo poisoning customs used in Martinique of the early nineteenth century.[90] These poisoned wells and bodies of the Atlantic, sometimes exaggerated by white officials to assert new forms of power, would occasionally be discovered through the feared scent of a poisoned well or the process of other Obeah practitioners smelling-out the accused poisoner.[91] Olfactory discovery of poison was, of course, avoided by slaves who wished to harm their masters through subversive means. Nevertheless, poison was a frequently pungent commodity. Africans' skills at understanding how to create poisons that smelled of other goods, or did not scent at all, allowed for tangible and often fatal forms of resistance in the Atlantic World. In Jamaica of 1789, one slave poisoned a well that became so pungent that the white masters whom slaves had hoped to murder discovered the plot through their own sense of smell. Deep in the well the slave had placed a mutilated, stinking, and poisoned dead chicken. When interrogated, other slaves on the plantation pointed to a brother and sister as the culprits. Upon entering the home of the sister, they discovered her Obeah wares: a "Calabash with greenish liquid ... recently emptied."[92] In part, due to the fears of poison, the British became obsessed with rooting out and surveying the stinking elements of Obeah within the West Indies of the early nineteenth century.[93]

---

[88] Juanita De Barros, "'Setting Things Right': Medicine and Magic in British Guiana, 1803–38," *Slavery and Abolition* 25, 1 (2004): 28–50.

[89] Kenneth Bilby and Jerome Handler, "Obeah: Healing and Protection in West Indian Slave Life," *The Journal of Caribbean History* 38, 2 (2004): 153–183.

[90] John Savage, "'Black Magic' and White Terror: Slave Poisoning and Colonial Society in Early 19th Century Martinique," *Journal of Social History* 40, 3 (2007): 635–662.

[91] Sasha Turner Bryson, "The Art of Power: Poison and Obeah Accusations and the Struggle for Dominance and Survival in Jamaica's Slave Society," *Caribbean Studies* 41, 2 (2013): 61–90.

[92] Bryson, "Art of Power," quotes on 70–72.

[93] For materials and the law regarding Obeah, see Danielle Boaz, "'Instruments of Obeah': The Significance of Ritual Objects in the Jamaican Legal System, 1760 to the Present," in *Materialities of Ritual in the Black Atlantic*, eds. Akinwumi Ogundiran and Paula Saunders (Bloomington: University of Indiana Press, 2014), 143–158.

Even as commentator Robert Renny discussed Obeah implements in his *An History of Jamaica* (1807) as forms of quackery, the British understood that although defined as charlatanism the social and spiritual powers that emerged from within the practice of Obeah needed to be analyzed and controlled. For Renny, these concerns focused upon the belief that Obeah could cause illness through movements within ephemeral spaces that allowed practitioners to enter the bodies of their fellow slaves.[94] Reverend H. Beame's *Report on the State of the Parish of St. James* (1825) also represented many of these British infatuations with the practice and threats of African spiritualism through portraying Obeah as an evil to be overcome by the Christian faith. To Beame, the slave population was made up of liars, thieves, abortionists, and polygamists who committed crimes out of inherent evil. In this judgment, Beame prejudicially described the superstitions of how, at African funerals in Jamaica, the gathered would "kill either a fowl or hog" that would transfer to Africa through the spirit world. Once there, the pig or bird would feed the slave who had returned to their African homeland upon burial.[95] These surveys represent that the British began to pay attention to the actual practices of Obeah due to the threats of social manipulation in slave cultures, focusing often on scented objects or ephemeral and transitory spaces that African slaves and freed people believed existed due to an understanding of different sensory spiritualisms.

Fearful of Obeah, British masters regularly turned to law with attempts to stop the preponderance of African practices in their West Indian colonies. Often these legal maneuverings left the definitions for Obeah quite vague, as a means to paint suspected criminals with a wide brush.[96] Slaves and free blacks throughout the Atlantic World often understood these vagaries and knew places where they could maneuver beneath English,

---

[94] Robert Renny, *An History of Jamaica: With Observations of the Climate, Scenery, Trade, Productions, Negroes, Slave Trade* (London: Cawthorn, 1807), 168–174.

[95] "Extracts from the Reverend H. Beame's report of the state of the parish of St. James describing religious instruction provided and comparing the 'disposition' of 'Africans' and 'creoles', and rural and urban people. Touches on polygamy, abortion, Obeah and stresses that 'effectively to promote the improvement of the Slave, the first effort must be with the free'," folios 217–218, in *Correspondence from the Bishop of Jamaica, Christopher Lipscomb, to the Secretary of State relating to his appointment and work, his visits to Grand Cayman, Honduras and the Bahamas, and to other mainly ecclesiastical matters* (Colonial Office, 1825) CO 137/267.

[96] Diana Paton, *No Bond but the Law: Punishment, Race, and Gender in Jamaican State Formation, 1780–1870* (Durham, NC: Duke University Press, 2004), 140–142, 180–184; Diana Paton, *The Cultural Politics of Obeah: Religion, Colonialism and Modernity in the Caribbean World* (Cambridge: Cambridge University Press, 2015), 6–16.

colonial Caribbean, and American legalism.[97] The British asserted laws against the production of *calabashes*, which could contain "poisonous or noxious" drugs and herbs, "pounded glass," and other materials meant to allow what white Christians believed was an easier path to connivance with the devil and evil spirits.[98] The practices of Obeah, under the new slave laws of the late 1820s, were frequently punishable by death. The ambiguity of how to prove Obeah, when it was a supernatural and transgressive phenomenon, was of utmost concern to those drafting the new slave laws. Accordingly, the British slave laws for Jamaica of 1826 summarized: "If any slave ... shall assault or offer any violence by striking or otherwise, to or towards any white person or persons in free condition ... [he or she] shall upon conviction be punished with death, transportation, or confinement to hard labor for life, or a limited time, or such other punishment as the court at their discretion shall think proper to inflict."[99] The very idea that an assault could be perpetrated without touching exemplified the white belief in the social, if not spiritual, functions of Obeah and the desire to control that reifying belief system.

These transgressive olfactory concerns also sometimes included colonialist worries over the ability of Obeah practitioners to inform the slave community to a new propensity for revolt. British violence against Obeah increased throughout the colonies to suppress these revolutionary sentiments. In 1806, one West Indian slave who practiced Obeah allegedly poisoned his master. As a letter from Grenadian Governor Frederick Maitland described: "[H]e was tried as the law instructs ... found guilty, and sentenced to be hanged, his head, when dead, to be cut off and placed on a pole." His accomplices were flogged, and "pounded glass, little filings of copper, and powdered" vegetables that have "injurious qualities" were found in his cabin.[100] Such representation of the manipulated dead

---

[97] For examples, see Natalie Zemon Davis, "Judges, Masters, Diviners: Slaves' Experience of Criminal Justice in Colonial Suriname," *Law and History Review* 29, 4 (November, 2011): 925–984; Ariela Gross, "Beyond Black and White: Cultural Approaches to Race and Slavery," *Columbia Law Review* 101, 3 (2001): 640–690.

[98] *Slave Law of Jamaica: With Proceedings and Documents Relative Thereto* (London: Ridgway, 1828), quotes on 28–30.

[99] Society for the Mitigation and Gradual Abolition of Slavery throughout the British Dominions, *The New Slave Laws of Jamaica and St. Christopher's Examined with an Especial Reference to the Eulogies Recently Pronounced Upon Them in Parliament* (London: Society for the Mitigation and Gradual Abolition of Slavery, 1828), quotes on 13–14.

[100] Frederick Maitland to William Windhorn, "Letter of December 7, 1806," in *Refers to importation of articles, with reference to salt fish; refers to an enslaved person of African descent who was convicted ten days previous of an attempt to poison the manager on the*

involved a colonial assertion of power used to prevent slaves from revolt and suicide.[101]

Still, however vile the punishments for Obeah became, slaves persisted, being much more intellectually agile and spiritually brave than their violent owners suspected. This wisdom was not always considered materially tangible. Government reports included summaries of the abilities of Obeah-men to "enter animals" and control their actions. Guiding buffalo, elephants, and snakes, as noted in the report which must have leaned on descriptions of the African pre-texts to Obeah due to the animals listed, could allow Obeah-men to influence masters and fellow Africans without laying hands upon their bodies. Learning of many African traditions of the olfactory and ephemeral, the British began to elaborate upon earlier legal documents that alerted Obeah-men were usually "discovered by a process analogous to the 'smelling out' of witches among the Zulu." Through these formal documents, the British relayed notations of African practitioners in the Caribbean who asserted their subject status within regimes of slavery that attempted to make African workhands into laboring agricultural implements.[102]

The African agency to smell-out was applied by many Obeah-men in a constant battle of wits and suffering whereby each Obeah-man could usually only work against other Obeah and *myal* practitioners. In Berbice, during the British era of control in the 1820s, such a tale of counteractive Obeah-men included the Obeah doctor Hans who was hired to smell-out the malevolent Obeah applied by the slave Frederick, who would boil highly scented goods in a pot that included "blood, negro hair, shavings of nails, head of a snake, a ram's horn." Hans discovered the evil in the pot through smelling-out the malevolence trapped inside the boiled appendage. In the years to follow, Hans bragged to those who asked him of his powers: "If I go to any house where poison is hid I can discover it from the smell."[103] African retention of these smelling-out skills, even as part of

estate; person was tried by two magistrates and three white men as the jury, and then was hanged; states that the man was connected with 'obye' [obeah]. Frederick Maitland, Grenada, folios 177–178, CO 101/44.

[101] Vincent Brown, *The Reaper's Garden: Death and Power in the World of Atlantic Slavery* (Cambridge, MA: Harvard University Press, 2008).

[102] *Report of the Lords of the Committee of the Council Appointed for the Consideration of all Matters Relating to Trade and Foreign Plantation* (London: N. P., 1789), quotes on 20.

[103] Randy Browne, "The 'Bad Business' of Obeah: Power, Authority, and the Politics of Slave Culture in the British Caribbean," *William and Mary Quarterly* 68, 3 (2011): 451–480, quotes on 477–479; Also see different testimonies of this smelling-out event in

intra-community contests amongst slaves, represents, like Mami Wata rituals, a deep African and multitemporal appreciation for the idea that evil could be detected through smelling.[104]

British officials often debated the level of violence to extend upon the bodies of the criminal Obeah practitioners within their West Indian colonies. During the middle of the nineteenth century, British administrators came to understand that Obeah worked throughout African communities of the West Indies as not simply malevolence against British masters and later bureaucrats. Though certain Obeah crimes such as murder continued to be prosecuted harshly during the era of emancipation, the general herbal medicine of Obeah and *myal* practitioners became less of a threat to British goals in the West Indies. As with the case of the healer Polydore from the Jamaican parish of St. Dorothy, who was believed to have removed a trapped shadow from a tree in 1831, officials were prone to commuting earlier punishments of imprisonment or transportation in favor of more lenient local sentences. This concern for mercy grew as many judges came to again assert Obeah as a form of medical "quackery" and desired removing corporeal punishment against those using "charms," "incantations," "magical arts" to hypnotize female populations, and "certain foolish ceremonies" to cure illnesses through "pretended remedies."[105] Even with some officials' desires to limit punishing the less vile herbal practices of *myal*, British officials still attempted to root out much of what they deemed malevolent Obeah after emancipation in the 1830s,

---

Colonial Office: *Copies of the Record of the Proceedings of the Fiscals of Demerara and Berbice* (London: House of Commons, 1825), 28–30. Courtesy of the John Carter Brown Library.

[104] For more on charms and retention, see Paula Sanders, "Charms and Spiritual Practitioners: Negotiating Power Dynamics in an Enslaved Community in Jamaica," in *Materialities of Ritual in the Black Atlantic*, eds. Akinwumi Ogundiran and Paula Saunders (Bloomington: University of Indiana Press, 2014), 159–176.

[105] "An Act for the Punishment of such Slaves as shall be found Practising Obeah, 1806," *in Refers to the 'Act for the better prevention of the practice of Obeah' and states that since its enactment 'a question of law has arisen as to its efficiency as an Act, in consequence of there being no Court specified, before whom the Criminal should be tried as was provided by the former Act' [of 4 November 1806]. The attorney general has expressed his opinion that a court comprising two magistrates and three freeholders was not competent to try a particular case. Asks that the matter should be referred to the law officers*, No. 48, CO 28/87/32, 103–104; "Proceedings in trials of T House, Polydore, and Industry convicted for Obeah, Howe Peter Browne, Marquess of Sligo, Governor of Jamaica, Jamaica," 1831, No. 315, folios 355–375, CO 137/209/59, quotes on 358–360, 362–364.

with wide-ranging laws applied extensively after the Morant Bay uprising of 1865.[106]

To enforce these laws, the British found much use for Herbert Thomas, a policeman and researcher into Obeah who became known as the "Obeah Catcher" during the 1870s and 1880s. Thomas, who investigated Obeah in the Morant Bay area, the central location for Obeah practitioners, published his reports in a pamphlet entitled *Something about Obeah* (1891).[107] Thomas portrayed "obeahmen" as essentially demonic. Their world was one of snakes, deformed faces, and slow gaits due to malformed feet. One cabin that Thomas discovered was full of "[w]ooden images, doll heads, bits of looking glass, fowl-bones, the skins of snakes and frogs, the comb and beak of a cock, a pack of cards, a razor, tiny carved calabashes, brimstone enclosed in a small bag" and "powdered torchwood." For Thomas, these different items were used for diverse goals and frequently included scented methods. Many practitioners would usually use "a little dirt from a grave" in their rituals. For damaging crops, this dirt would often be mixed with animal excrement and "a couple of rotten eggs and some other filth" to be buried in the fields.[108] These attentions to odoriferous goods, funerary practices, and the use of herbalism and charms linked African healers, even into the late nineteenth century, through aromatic chains to African ethnic pasts, where rituals of smelling paired with herbal aromas to recreate West, Central, and southern African traditions of odor that survived the Middle Passage.

THREATENING AROMAS IN ANGLO-ATLANTIC LITERATURE

As surveyors such as Moseley, Long, and the "Obeah Catcher" worked their nasal and racist forensics within Jamaican homes, English writers found within their profound descriptions, and the observations of earlier officials and planters, a character to develop within romantic literature

---

[106] Gad Heuman, *"The Killing Time": The Morant Bay Rebellion in Jamaica* (Knoxville: University of Tennessee Press, 1994), 36–42.

[107] Herbert Thomas, "Memorial, August 30, 1894," folios 536–555, in "Sends a further memorial from Inspector Thomas. Includes a pamphlet called 'Something about Obeah'," No. 340, folios 536–560, CO 137/561/74; Diana Paton, "The Trials of Inspector Thomas: Policing and Ethnography in Jamaica," in *Obeah and Other Powers: The Politics of Caribbean Religion and Healing*, eds. Diana Paton and Maarit Forde (Durham, NC: Duke University Press, 2012), 172–197.

[108] Herbert Thomas, "Something about Obeah," folios 556–560, in *Sends a further memorial from Inspector Thomas. Includes a pamphlet called 'Something about Obeah'*, No. 340, folios 536–560 (Colonial Office, 1891), CO 137/561/74, quotes on 6–7.

thriving in contemporary European salons. In these novel fictions, a mutual brand of reinforcement continued to reify the tautological links between smell and race alongside the often-threatening literary relations between Obeah practitioners and subaltern resistance. In these various literatures, as with *Atar-Gull* that started this chapter, endless and rebellious reflections of the aromatic persisted in the minds and noses of slaveholders and the writers who relayed Caribbean concerns with insurgency.[109]

Romanticism was a literary domain that often provided critiques of aesthetics and class as categories and hierarchies of capitalism emerged to greater force during the late eighteenth and early nineteenth centuries.[110] The reifying power of the African other passed into these forms of Romanticism due to the constant analysis of aesthetics within colonial explorations of Obeah and other African spiritualisms throughout the Caribbean. As Kay Dian Kriz has noted, Atlantic aesthetic process involved producing a difficult form of opposing and oppressive artistic hegemony: "If the curiosities represented become too thoroughly pacified in the process of visual and verbal representation, then their capacity for arousing the wonder and desire of the reader is sharply diminished. Too little pacification threatens to expose Otherness that cannot be known, and, even more worryingly, cannot be physically contained." As part of these patterns of containment, much West Indian artwork regarding slavery was systematically constructed to place a veil over the most horrendous aspects of the slave system by showing the "metropolitan ornaments" of happy slaves, dancing slaves, and the curiosities of the Western Hemisphere to entice continued emigration from England.[111] Generally, slaves could rarely be represented as able to inflict damage upon the slave system, due, in part, to the fears of "monstrous hybridity" that came with the

---

[109] For sensory studies and Victorian literature, see Catherine Gallagher, *The Body Economic: Life, Death, and Sensation in Political Economy and the Victorian Novel* (Princeton, NJ: Princeton University Press, 2006); William Cohen, *Embodied: Victorian Literature and the Senses* (Minneapolis: University of Minnesota Press, 2009).

[110] Orrin Nan Chung Wang, *Romantic Sobriety: Sensation, Revolution, Commodification, History* (Baltimore, MD: Johns Hopkins University Press, 2011), 2–4; Andrew Eastham, *Aesthetic Afterlives: Irony, Literary Modernity and the Ends of Beauty* (London: Continuum International, 2011), 4–6.

[111] Kay Dian Kriz, *Slavery, Sugar, and the Culture of Refinement: Picturing the British West Indies, 1700–1840* (New Haven, CT: Yale University Press, 2008), 195–198, quote on 34; Jeffrey Auerbach, "The Picturesque and the Homogenisation of Empire," *The British Art Journal* 5, 1 (Spring/Summer 2004): 47–54.

unanticipated Haitian Revolution.[112] Caribbean planters accordingly often portrayed slavery as a common good, whereby artwork focused on slaves who were happy to perform labor and for the time off afforded to them and their families.[113]

Despite these misleadingly picturesque efforts to contain the agency of slave voices speaking of resistance and the horrors of their experiences, romantic literature began to involve African characters within Caribbean settings who were increasingly portrayed as subjects providing narrative changes and intellectual potency.[114] Over time, the diverse range of sensory behaviors regarding slave agency found pathways into these English literatures of both the periphery and the core. This inclusion of African spiritualism within European narratives was partially because sensory encounters of Obeah offered multiple agencies for slaves and free blacks throughout the Atlantic World and provided writers interesting and rebellious characters that practiced different sensory technologies.[115] As T. W. Jaudon has argued, "the practice of obeah gathered together a set of bodily responses to the world unlike the

---

[112] Marlene Daut, *Tropics of Haiti: Race and the Literary History of the Haitian Revolution in the Atlantic World, 1789–1865* (Liverpool: Liverpool University Press, 2015), 172–174.

[113] Jack Greene, "Changing Identity in the British Caribbean: Barbados as a Case Study," in *Colonial Identity in the Atlantic World, 1500–1800*, eds. Nicholas Canny and Anthony Pagden (Princeton, NJ: Princeton University Press, 1987), 213–266; David Bindman and Helen Weston, "Court and City: Fantasies of Domination," in Book III of Volume III of *The Image of the Black in Western Art*, eds. David Bindman, Henry Louis Gates, and Karen Dalton (Cambridge, MA: Belknap, 2010), 125–170; Charles Ford, Thomas Cummins, Rosalie Smith McCrea, and Helen Weston, "The Slave Colonies," in Book III of Volume III of *The Image of the Black in Western Art*, eds. David Bindman, Henry Louis Gates, and Karen Dalton (Cambridge, MA: Belknap, 2010), 241–308; David Dabydeen, "Eighteenth-Century English Literature on Commerce and Slavery," in *The Black Presence in English Literature*, ed. David Dabydeen (Manchester: Manchester University Press, 1985), 26–49.

[114] For more on British perceptions of Caribbean landscapes and the picturesque, see Jefferson Dillman, *Colonizing Paradise: Landscape and Empire in the British West Indies* (Tuscaloosa: University of Alabama Press, 2015), 137–173; Tim Barringer, "Picturesque Prospects and the Labour of the Enslaved," in *Art and Emancipation in Jamaica: Isaac Mendes Belisario and His Worlds*, eds. T. J. Barringer, Gllian Forrester, and Barbaro Martinez Ruiz (New Haven, CT: Yale University Press, 2007), 41–63; Elizabeth Bohls, "The Planter Picturesque: Matthew Lewis's Journal of a West India Proprietor," *European Romantic Review* 13, 1 (2002): 63–76; Elizabeth Bohls, *Slavery and the Politics of Place: Representing the Colonial Caribbean, 1770–1833* (Cambridge: Cambridge University Press, 2017).

[115] For links between English Romantic literature and abolitionism, see Deirdre Coleman, *Romantic Colonization and British Anti-Slavery* (Cambridge: Cambridge University Press, 2005); Tim Fulford, Peter Kitson, and Debbie Lee, *Literature, Science and*

reasonable, objective forms of sense perception that were gaining traction in the Enlightenment." Obeah allowed for practitioners, followers, and writers who tried to understand the African spiritual past a conduit to access sensory worlds outside of the nation-state. These novel sensory dogmas oriented the individual reader to other bodily experiences through providing sensory power to different material goods.[116]

Among the many Western authors who wrote of African spiritualisms, Irish novelist Maria Edgeworth penned the multivolume *Belinda* (1801) with summaries of the social effects of Obeah as part of her Caribbean literary settings. Edgeworth wrote much on Obeah, as within "The Grateful Negro," which displayed a tone of both respect and anxiety concerning the role of Obeah as a part of Jamaican slave life.[117] Edgeworth's particular tale of Obeah in *Belinda* borrowed much from the work of surveyor Bryan Edwards. The narrative described the life of Belinda Portman in the West Indies and included discussions of the odor of Obeah as a means to show the darkness of West Indian slavery and African spiritualism. In Edgeworth's narrative, a troublesome Obeah-woman on the Delacour Plantation on Jamaica placed a hex on Juba, an African servant who would later marry an Englishwoman. The room of Juba's convalescence included the "strong smell of phosphorous," which later investigators concluded was part of the scented confidence game of romantic entanglement played by the Obeah-woman.[118] As with the creation of African agencies to alter sensory worlds, much of romantic literature about such carnivalesque moments where slaves could have power also partially acted as a release of fear where the comedic exposure

---

Exploration in the Romantic Era: Bodies of Knowledge (Cambridge: Cambridge University Press, 2008), 249–261.

[116] T. W. Jaudon. "Obeah's Sensations: Rethinking Religion at the Transnational Turn," *American Literature* 84, 4 (2012): 715–741, quote on 716; Jacques Rancière, *The Politics of Aesthetics: The Distribution of the Sensible* (London: Continuum, 2004).

[117] Frances Botkin, "Questioning the 'Necessary Order of Things': Maria Edgeworth's 'The Grateful Negro', Plantation Slavery, and the Abolition of the Slave Trade," in *Discourses of Slavery and Abolition: Britain and Its Colonies, 1760–1838*, eds. Brycchan Carey, Markman Ellis, and Sara Salih (Basingstoke: Palgrave Macmillan, 2004), 194–208; Alison Harvey, "West Indian Obeah and English 'Obee': Race, Femininity, and Questions of Colonial Consolidation in Maria Edgeworth's *Belinda*," in *New Essays on Maria Edgeworth*, ed. Julie Nash (Aldershot: Ashgate, 2006), 1–30; Maria Edgeworth, "The Grateful Negro," in *Works of Maria Edgeworth*, eds. Maria Edgeworth, Richard Lovell Edgeworth, Samuel Hale Parker, Eliakim Littell, and Robert Norris Henry (Boston: Samuel H. Parker, 1824 [1811]), 353–354.

[118] Maria Edgeworth, *Belinda* (London: Baldwin & Cradock, 1833 [1801]), 312–328, quote on 315.

of confidence games removed the seriousness of slave revolt for readers in the London core who had no daily terror of uprising.[119]

In the later *Hamel, Obeah Man* (1827), written by British traveler Cynric Williams, Obeah was portrayed through the antipodal character of Hamel, a sorcerer who lived within a highly scented world that planters feared. Hamel's smoke-filled room included "a human skull on a table in the midst" of the white men entering the abode. Williams's Gothic romance was possibly also part of a growing canon that asserted literature as a retreat from the fears of actually threatening African spirituality, as missionaries increasingly pushed Christianity upon slaves and Africans during the nineteenth century. Next to the skull in Hamel's feared chamber was "a calabash, containing a filthy-looking mixture, placed beside a small iron pot which flamed with burning rum, whose blue and ghastly light, sufficient to illuminate the cellar, cast a glare of deeper hideousness on the faces and persons of these practitioners." The consistent use of the language of dirt, dirtiness, and odor within Williams's text portrayed a West Indian imaginary that involved consistent links between scent and alterations caused by new sensory identities.[120]

These rituals and smells of Obeah persisted in many a later European and American mind, signifying the fear of losing control of their black laborers well after slavery. The diary of Amelia Culpepper, a European traveler of the 1880s whose grandfather lived on Barbados during the early nineteenth century, described the memory of such olfactory complexity and resistance. Culpepper relayed a tale from her Parisian depot of 1887 about the desire of Africans to recover the "smell of old times in Africa" that led to the murder of a slave owner in Barbados of decades prior. When the slave, Peter, returned home from his violent excursion, his African father was quick to sense the smell of blood on Peter's body. Both the slave who desired an olfactory past that was lost in the backbreaking world of slave labor and his father who could smell the master's blood represent that odor was an important aspect of both resistance and

---

[119] Kelly Wisecup and T. W. Jaudon, "On Knowing and Not Knowing About Obeah," *Atlantic Studies* 12, 2 (2015): 129–143. For humor and the carnivalesque, see Terry Castle, *Masquerade and Civilization: The Carnivalesque in Eighteenth-Century English Culture and Fiction* (Stanford, CA: Stanford University Press, 1986), 110–129.

[120] Cynric Williams, *Hamel, the Obeah Man* (London: Hunt and Clarke, 1827), quotes on 116–117; Janina Nordius, "Racism and Radicalism in Jamaican Gothic: Cynric R. Williams's *Hamel, The Obeah Man*," *English Literary History* 73, 3 (2006): 673–693; Janelle Rodriques, "Obeah(Man) As Trickster in Cynric Williams *Hamel, the Obeah Man*," *Atlantic Studies: Global Currents* 12, 2 (2015): 219–234; Senior, *Caribbean and the Medical Imagination*, 180–188.

retention in diverse slave societies. Such opposition to the system, which came partially from remembered scents, could not be allowed among the African coterie that had murdered their owner, as they were all later executed.[121]

What emerged in writings about these fictional spiritualists, the use of odors, and remembering an olfactory Africa was a romantic ideal that, even when derogatory, exposed the African figure as a character, a subject, with his or her own cultural constructions.[122] For example, American literary critic and novelist Major Haldane MacFall's *The Wooings of Jezebel Pettyfer* (1898) likewise portrayed the historical memory of white fears of the stench of Obeah. Numerous mentions were made of the "sour smell of negroes" that perpetuated life in the West Indies, many times attributed to the machinations of an Obeah-man. This "sorcerer," Jehu Sennacherib Dyle, was portrayed as powerful through his adeptness at manipulating odor, once tricking a female dog by "mixing de smell" of her puppies in order to get the terrier mother to return to her progeny.[123] Dyle's Obeah household was rendered as having a "strange odour, the faint sour smell of the dead." The aromatic home was fashioned by this enchanter, who often controlled animal populations enough to also have crabs move at his will. When Deborah Bryan, one of the white protagonists of the novel, encountered the dead body of Dyle, "fear of a sudden increased her vision, so that she saw – and seeing, uttered a low cry: the black mangled thing, that lay staring up at her out of eyeless sockets . . . and it came to her that the ghastly, rent, and disemboweled mass of flesh that sent up the sickly smell of death into her senses must once have been the besotted old sorcerer; but that which had been a human being, save for the grinning sightless head, lay shapeless now as offal flung upon a dunghill." Deborah wandered the area where she encountered the redolent and otherworldly ephemeral evil of the conjurer's aura, which was to blame for the many deaths of vultures in the season to come.[124]

---

[121] Amelia Culpepper, "Excerpts from Amelia Culpeper's Diary c. 1887," *Journal of the Barbados Museum and Historical Society* 47 (November, 2001): 80–82, quote on 81.

[122] J. R. Oldfield, "The 'Ties Of soft Humanity': Slavery and Race in British Drama, 1760–1800," *Huntington Library Quarterly* 56, 1 (Winter, 1993): 1–14; Jill Casid, "'His Master's Obi': Machine Magic, Colonial Violence and Transculturation," in *The Visual Culture Reader*, ed. Nicholas Mirzoeff (London: Routledge, 2002), 533–545.

[123] Haldane Macfall, *The Wooings of Jezebel Pettyfer; Being the Personal History of Jehu Sennacherib Dyle, Commonly Called Masheen Dyle. Together with an Account of Certain Things That Chanced in the House of the Sorcerer* (London: Simpkin, Marshall, Hamilton, Kent, 1898), quotes on 22–23, 154, and 189.

[124] Macfall, *The Wooings of Jezebel Pettyfer*, quotes on 341–343.

As part of these romantic narratives that consistently included imagery of both aromatic beauty and excremental contagion, the memorialized West Indies became a pungent place of remembered African spiritualisms. For masters who cackled at abolitionists, the smells were attributed to the black body, as a mark of the inferior and commodified object to be made into a laboring dependent. For slaves and free blacks, understanding that racialized European nose allowed for African cultural survivals of smelling to be smuggled through the Middle Passage. Once in the New World, those cargoes of the olfactory were recombined into new and creolized understandings of the vast importance of odor within new environments and for the creation and retention of African identities. This new force, of a trafficked and reborn African olfactory identity, was not lost on later writers of British, French, and American public spheres, who found great power in the use of African odors not simply as a racialized pungency but also to contrarily mark the African as an identifiable subject with ingenious aromatic aesthetics.[125]

SCENTS OF STRUGGLE

These many novels that employ sensory language to highlight the subject status of healers and the history of Obeah as recorded by prejudicial British officials later informed the analysis of Obeah in Jesuit Father Joseph Williams's *Voodoos and Obeahs* (1932).[126] Educated also by Long's aforementioned *History of Jamaica* (1774), and Edwards' *History, Civil and Commercial, of the British West Indies* (1793), Williams described Obeah through a multisensory lens partly attributable to his twentieth-century Catholic and anthropological training. Through these many cradles, Williams summarized a sacrificial exercise in aromatic

---

[125] For more on Caribbean languages of resistance and the landscape, see Mimi Sheller, *Citizenship from Below: Erotic Agency and Caribbean Freedom* (Durham, NC: Duke University Press, 2012), 191–211; Robin D. G. Kelley, *Freedom Dreams: The Black Radical Imagination* (Boston: Beacon, 2002), 29–35. See also the connections between Latin American and African American racial languages within Juliet Hooker, *Theorizing Race in the Americas: Douglass, Sarmiento, Du Bois, and Vasconcelos* (New York: Oxford, 2017), 195–202.

[126] For debates upon anthropological analyses of Obeah, see Stewart, *Three Eyes for the Journey*, 6–24; Stephan Palmié, "Afterword, Other Powers: Tylor's Principle, Father Williams' Temptations and the Power of Banality," in *Obeah and Other Powers: The Politics of Caribbean Religion and Healing*, eds. Diana Paton and Maarit Forde (Durham, NC: Duke University Press, 2012), 316–340. For more examples, see religious concerns with references to serpent worship in Henry Hesketh Bell, *Obeah, Witchcraft in the West Indies* (London: Low, 1893), 6–12.

terms, which compared the practice of Vodou and Obeah as similarly outside of reason. He noted how a practitioner could make a girl and a goat switch bodies in order to heal the human illness harming the child. This "blood baptism" ceremony peaked when "the odor of blood was in the air," as the child "stood quiet, though still wide-eyed, while red silken ribbon were twined" in the goat's horns. Following this framing, the goat's "hoofs" were "anointed with wine and sweet-scented oils," before the sacrifice wherein blood from the goat's slaughter covered the sick child.[127] The descriptive telling of Obeah rituals and Vodou in the twentieth century often relayed these deep concerns with religious conversion and demonic healing, as well as the desire to remove practices that were deemed inherently bewitching. However, many of these traditions remain vital to the lifeblood of modern Caribbean communities and often integrate traditions of smelling from historical trajectories of both African ethnicities and creolized slave cultures.[128]

For many African descendants within the later British Caribbean, Obeah and other African-influenced spiritualisms continued to provide the sensory alternatives they had offered during the era of the Atlantic Slave Trade, often persisting as bridges to a redolent African past through modern concepts of mystical duppy and other forms of African and creole spiritual ephemera. In her discussion of Vodou as existing within a society without a strong sense of privacy, Maya Deren wrote during the 1950s of a similar scented Caribbean use of the "warm aroma which rises and pervades" offerings provided to the god Ogoun. These materials became "fragrant fumes" in worshippers' "cupped hands" during ritual offerings to different Yoruba divinities.[129]

[127] Joseph Williams, *Voodoos and Obeahs; Phases of West India Witchcraft* (New York: MacVeagh Dial, 1932), quotes on vii–viii; Edward Long, Volume II of *The History of Jamaica, or, General Survey of the Ancient and Modern State of That Island With Reflections on Its Situation, Settlements, Inhabitants, Climate, Products, Commerce, Laws, and Government* (London: Lowndes, 1774), 416–424; Bryan Edwards, *The History Civil and Commercial of the British Colonies in the West Indies To Which Is Added, an Historical Survey of the French Colony in the Island of St. Domingo* (London: B. Crosby, 1798 [1793]), 164–175.

[128] For more Caribbean debates on healing and African spiritualisms, see Paul Brodwin, *Medicine and Morality in Haiti: The Contest for Healing Power* (Cambridge: Cambridge University Press, 1996), 144–146; Brian Moore and Michele Johnson, *Neither Led nor Driven: Contesting British Cultural Imperialism in Jamaica, 1865–1920* (Kingston: University of West Indies Press, 2004), 37–41.

[129] Maya Deren, *Divine Horsemen: The Living Gods of Haiti* (New York: Thames and Hudson, 1953), quotes on 132–133.

As part of Alfred Métraux's history of Vodou, a similar account was told of mid-twentieth-century spiritual cults in Haiti that understood the history of slavery and their Dahomey past through the ephemeral power of scenting to tie perceptions of odor to the memory of those who were once sold into bondage.[130] Although there are considerable differences in the practices of Obeah, Vodou, Santería, and Candomblé, one important similarity is that all the African-informed religious practices of the New World commonly associated an importance to smell within diverse "body logics" that became very much absent within the dominant Western sensory traditions codifying whiteness in North America and the British West Indies.[131]

Through a reading of African retention and the hybrid cultural patterns of creolization, Richard Price understood many "deep-level, unconscious principles" were "a key to unraveling the African-American past."[132] To explore these forms of conscious and subconscious retention, this chapter analyzed the patterns of olfactory spiritualism that survived the Middle Passage from a deep sense of an African olfactory within diverse ethnic traditions. Shapes without color and shades without form, aromatic slave resistance boiled beneath the slaveholding elite with the fragrant miasmas of remembered and redolent ethnic practices. Throughout the Americas, African ethnic retention of natural knowledge for use in new American environments allowed for these patterns of resistance to emerge out of the landscapes where slaves toiled due to the ability of workhands to recombine cultures from commonly remembered sensory worlds of Africa.[133]

Africans in the Atlantic World built an inventory of the senses that was much different than that of their prejudicial Western masters. This portfolio included dissimilar appreciation for the sense of smell as a form of

---

[130] Alfred Métraux, *Voodoo in Haiti* (New York: Schocken, 1972 [1959]), 26–28, 286–287.

[131] Diana Paton, "Punishment, Crime, and the Bodies of Slaves in Eighteenth-Century Jamaica," *Journal of Social History* 34, 4 (2001): 923–954; Thomas Campbell and Samuel Rogers, *The Pleasures of Hope: With Other Poems* (Dublin: Porter, 1803), 121–122; Tim Watson, *Caribbean Culture and British Fiction in the Atlantic World, 1780–1870* (Cambridge: Cambridge University Press, 2008), 1–16; Paton, *Cultural Politics*, 191–200. For "body logics," see Aisha Beliso-De Jesús, "Santería Copresence and the Making of African Diaspora Bodies," *Cultural Anthropology* 29, 3 (2014): 503–526.

[132] Price, "The Miracle of Creolization," quote on 57.

[133] For more on landscape and resistance, see Ras Michael Brown, "'Walk in the Feenda': West-Central Africans and the Forest in the South Carolina-Georgia Low Country," in *Central Africans and Cultural Transformations in the American Diaspora*, ed. Linda Heywood (Cambridge: Cambridge University Press, 2002), 289–318.

sensory literacy and bodily skill that could be used to learn about New World environments while also allowing Africans to cultivate forms of spatial resistance and mark their own identities. The councils of men and women, slaves and free blacks, which created the insurrections of the Atlantic World often found within redolent aromas an ephemeral space to pattern and produce transgressive and rebellious behavior. Between the idea of insurrection and the reality of revolt, aromas offered ties to an African past, medicines in a diasporic present, and olfactory hopes for a future where African culture and its aromas would prosper. Between the motion of resistance, the planning and patterning, and the act of insurgency, minor or widespread, lay the shadows of the spectral aromatic, haunting slaveholders with the scents of Africa.[134]

---

[134] For more on ideas of conjuring as central to African American Christianity, see Theophus Smith, *Conjuring Culture: Biblical Formations of Black America* (New York: Oxford University Press, 2006).

Conclusion

Race, Nose, Truth

Anglo-Atlantic culture deodorized through shifting negative olfactory identities to their African slave subjects throughout the Atlantic littoral. It was not an inferior English culture that smelled of a barbarian past while the continent wafted of perfumed and deodorized elegance. Rather, stinking was for the beastly objects who toiled in the fields of Jamaica, in the cotton dens of the Carolinas, or for those that suffered the slave ships of the Royal African Company.

England deodorized from the Renaissance to the twentieth century. Englishpersons did so by displacing pungency onto those they deemed inferior, through a discursive process reinforced within a transnational Republic of Letters that informed other European nations to follow similar patterns of sensory anti-blackness. This process of olfactory othering burgeoned through explicitly rendered cultural acts, *verschiebungs* that displaced onto African bodies odors that colonial Europeans perceived as markers of racial inferiority. Regardless of the material realities of cleanly African bodies espoused by Olaudah Equiano, other former slaves in the Atlantic World, and many travelers to Africa, common Western sensory consciousness shifted to define African bodies as inherently pungent.

Racism against Africans, as it was originally constructed during the 1600s, was initially an ambiguous assemblage based on diverse narratives of class, climate, and culture. These perceptions of odor, pooling within cultural discussions of landscape, disease, and religion, shifted from cultural ideas about inferiority to later inform biological ideas about human difference. To more completely define the African as subhuman for labor control and pecuniary manipulation during the Atlantic Slave Trade, polygenesis emerged with an associated racist nose to smell-out the perceived animalistic and diseased odors within African bodies.

Furthering their colonial interests in Africa during the 1800s, Englishpersons applied these sensory tools to construct new ideals of Scientific Racism and philosophies concerning cultural evolution and African profligacy. Schools of thought like phrenology, eugenics, and Social Darwinism all emerged to justify the previous few centuries' vile experiments in racial economics that birthed the modern global economy and held sway over the horrific system of slave trading and forced breeding that defined the first few hundred years of the malodorous experiment of capitalism.

RACIAL DYSTOPIAS AND THE AMERICAN OLFACTORY IMAGINATION

The general belief in the odors of inferior races peaked during the late nineteenth century, but that does not affirm that racism was not ordered through the nose prior, nor is it to say racism was not as vile or pervasive in the early eras of slavery as during the later days of lynched bodies on Mississippi oaks. The early modern European ideal of African odors worked to keep Africans in the open fields hewing wood and drawing water, stolen from African to American shores, not meant to spread their potent pungency in the metropoles of deodorizing Europe. Marking Africans as foul and odoriferous was part of an initial conception of the cultural other, but the more it cultivated and semantically linked to new and diverse ideas about African inferiority and biological inheritance the more it became economically determined and socially necessary to uphold the slave system. This olfactory ideology provided Western Europeans with fresh and embodied assurances that slaves were predestined to live in the stinking cane fields of the colonies, not in the deodorizing bedrooms, living rooms, and courts of Europe. These English and European olfactory traditions became American as new nations developed during the Age of Revolutions.[1]

---

[1] For similar justifications of slavery through racial science in nineteenth-century America, see the physiological applications of the spirometer within Lundy Braun, *Breathing Race into the Machine: The Surprising Career of the Spirometer from Plantation to Genetics* (Minneapolis: University of Minnesota Press, 2014), 27–54, 109–137, and the psychological constructs regarding bondage and race in Wendy Gonaver, *The Peculiar Institution and the Making of Modern Psychiatry, 1840–1880* (Chapel Hill: University of North

Many later American ideas of Republicanism, civic duty, and patriotism entrenched within these partially racialized sensory cultures.[2] Much of this fresh sensory understanding of race and nation emerged out of an Anglo-Atlantic discourse of sensibility and fellow feeling that united a form of sensible and deferential whiteness against those deemed unable to access forms of citizenship reserved for white bodies and minds.[3] The smolders of sensible racial knowing, the unformed and all-encompassing warming silhouettes of embodied othering, later became the burning spirits of Scientific Racism, which hardened the various and falsely conscious phantoms of racism into firmer forms of emotional and sensory disgust during the nineteenth century.[4] Part of this debate on disgust and race in the American public sphere of the nineteenth century involved arguments over the proper space for African Americans when emancipation would finally arrive to the United States, as it had to Britain and its

Carolina Press, 2018); Sander Gilman, *Difference and Pathology: Stereotypes of Sexuality, Race, and Madness* (Ithaca: Cornell University Press, 1985).

[2] Richard Cullen Rath, *How Early America Sounded* (Ithaca: Cornell University Press, 2003), 173–184; Lauren Klein, "Dinner-Table Bargains: Thomas Jefferson, James Madison, and the Senses of Taste," *Early American Literature* 49, 2 (2014): 403–433; Jay Fliegelman, *Declaring Independence: Jefferson, Natural Language & the Culture of Performance* (Stanford, CA: Stanford University Press, 1993); Wendy Bellion, *Citizen Spectator: Art, Illusion, and Visual Perception in Early National America* (Chapel Hill: University of North Carolina Press, 2011); M. B. McWilliams, "Distant Tables: Food and the Novel in Early America," *Early American Literature* 38 (2003): 365–394; James McWilliams, *A Revolution in Eating: How the Quest for Food Shaped America* (New York: Columbia University Press, 2005); Donna Gabaccia, *We Are What We Eat: Ethnic Food and the Making of Americans* (Cambridge, MA: Harvard University Press, 1998); Sarah Knott, *Sensibility and the American Revolution* (Chapel Hill: University of North Carolina Press, 2009).

[3] For more on sensibility, sociability, and the senses in the study of early America, see the readings on the importance of emotionality to political discussions within Nicole Eustace, *Passion Is the Gale: Emotion, Power, and the Coming of the American Revolution* (Chapel Hill: University of North Carolina Press, 2008), 4–13; the emotionality of early American novels within Julia Stern, *The Plight of Feeling: Sympathy and Dissent in the Early American Novel* (Chicago: University of Chicago Press, 1997), 2–8; and the language of sentimentalism and sociability in the Anglo-Atlantic within Norman Fiering, "Irresistible Compassion: An Aspect of Eighteenth-Century Sympathy and Humanitarianism," *Journal of the History of Ideas* 37, 2 (1976): 195–218 and G. J. Barker-Benfield, *The Culture of Sensibility: Sex and Society in Eighteenth-Century Britain* (Chicago: University of Chicago Press, 1992).

[4] For introduction to the increasing Southern assertion of whiteness, see Walter Johnson, "The Slave Trader, the White Slave, and the Politics of Racial Determination in the 1850s," *Journal of American History* 87 (June, 2000): 13–38.

colonies during the 1830s.[5] Whether debating recolonization of Africans in Sierra Leone and Liberia or simply arguing that African Americans should be integrated into American society, debates on race and nation grew into a furor that became increasingly sexualized, vocalized, and violent. As part of these deliberations, Southerners and proslavery advocates wrote often about the perceived racial inferiority of African bodies to continue their ardent justifications for slaveholding.[6]

Many literary works seemed to poke fun at such sensory conceptions of race asserted by Southern racists and hypocritical Northern abolitionists. As outlined at the end of Chapter 2, the Antebellum South created a vast academic debate that elaborated on many centuries of literary, religious, and scientific literatures about the smell of the black body. Northerners occasionally noticed the absurdity of these deliberations and provided much dissent against the proslavery declarations of African olfactory inferiority. For example, Massachusetts defender of free labor and newspaper editor Asa Greene's parodic *A Yankee among the Nullifiers* (1833) summarized what was deemed a putrefying machine, created by a fictional industrialist, which emitted "purifying and sweetening" agents throughout factories to cure the "native smell" that emanated from the "sooty skins" of African slaves. This machine, called the "Anti-African-Odor-Gas-Generator," was meant to disinfect and sweeten rooms where industrial slaves labored. In a work written as a response to the nullification crisis, Greene created the idea of a machine that would prevent the noisome odors of black bodies from influencing delicate white nostrils as a way to satirize absurdist arguments concerning the inherent smell of black bodies and the rights to slavery that those smells justified in the minds of many Southern intellectuals.[7]

As a part of the emerging literary worlds of science fiction and dystopian literature to be made famous by Edward Bellamy and Samuel Butler

---

[5] For similarities between the racial conceptions of abolitionists and slaveholders, see the examples provided within Roxann Wheeler, "'Betrayed by Some of My Own Complexion': Cugoano, Abolition, and the Contemporary Language of Racialism," in *Genius in Bondage: Literature of the Early Black Atlantic*, eds. Vincent Carretta and Philip Gould (Lexington: University of Kentucky Press, 2001), 17–38; and the analysis of bio-politics, the impressable body, and sentimentalism within Kyla Schuller, *The Biopolitics of Feeling: Race, Sex, and Science in the Nineteenth Century* (Durham, NC: Duke University Press, 2018), 35–67, 76–80.

[6] Larry Tise, *Proslavery: A History of the Defense of Slavery in America, 1701–1840* (Athens: University of Georgia Press, 1987); Lacy Ford, *Deliver Us from Evil: The Slavery Question in the Old South* (New York: Oxford University Press, 2010).

[7] Asa Greene, *A Yankee among the Nullifiers* (New York: Pearson, 1833), quotes on 90–94.

during the later nineteenth century, racial politics of the nose also became a vital ingress for tortuous and illogical racial distortions. Implicitly denying that such a machine as Greene's would be humorous, Jerome Holgate's dystopian fiction *Sojourn in the City of Amalgamation* (1835) described how similar machines would be necessary if the United States fell prey to the perceived ravages of miscegenation. For Holgate's tale of societal declension within a future Northern city, amalgamation included the compulsory breeding of white women and African men, often portrayed as brutes and primates through different sensory categories and craniometric descriptions. The representation of "amalgamation" that Holgate highlighted through his authorial pseudonym Oliver Bolokitten provided intense olfactory racism applied within a science fiction novel meant to critique abolitionist ambitions as sexually motivated.[8]

The most effusive scene within the dystopian narrative involved a Northern preacher in the "City of Amalgamation" who stumbled through a sermon because he had to constantly reach for a flask of aromatic lavender near his pulpit. The church where the preacher lambasted frequently positioned large machines "composed of fans and little vials, ingeniously intermingled" to prevent the odor of African bodies from invading the nostrils of the male visitors who prized the visual beauty of their darker wives but still could not bear the smells of the "evaporations" and "offensive air" that emanated from their "odoriferous" spouses. During a central scene in the work, when the scent of a recently arriving African American woman entered the church, the pastor began to choke. For another parishioner, the odor of the unperfumed woman entering his nostrils forced vomit out of his throat, copiously covering the processional rows.[9]

---

[8] Oliver Bolokitten, *Sojourn in the City of Amalgamation: In the Year of Our Lord 19—* (New York: Oliver Bolokitten, 1835); Tavia Amolo Ochieng' Nyongó, *The Amalgamation Waltz: Race, Performance and the Ruses of Memory* (Minneapolis: University of Minnesota Press, 2009), 14–15. For the history of primates in the comparative science of race and gender in the later twentieth century, see Donna Haraway, *Primate Visions: Gender, Race, and Nature in the World of Modern Science* (London: Verso, 1992), 1–16. See also Martha Hodes, *White Women, Black Men: Illicit Sex in the Nineteenth-Century South* (New Haven, CT: Yale University Press, 1999), 147–175. James Kinney, *Amalgamation! Race, Sex, and Rhetoric in the Nineteenth-Century American Novel* (Westport, CT: Greenwood, 1985); Karen Sánchez-Eppler, *Touching Liberty: Abolition, Feminism and the Politics of the Body* (Berkeley: University of California Press, 1997); Katy Chiles, *Transformable Race: Surprising Metamorphoses in the Literature of Early America* (Oxford: Oxford University Press, 2014).

[9] Bolokitten, *Sojourn*, 17–24; Elise Virginia Lemire, *Miscegenation: Making Race in America* (Philadelphia: University of Pennsylvania Press, 2002), 68–88; Justine Murison,

Like the dizzied preacher, those who could not stand these pejoratively natural odors were taken to a "perfumery" where white bodies drank enthusiastic alcoholic spirits made from special "boilers" meant to desensitize noses to more effortlessly encounter African smells. Nearby machines also removed the nasal hairs from the practitioners of miscegenation as physical evidence and medical measurement of a forced social patterning of anosmia. For Holgate, the truth of racism was in the body. The "stomachal tide" gushing forth from the flock that smelled not-yet-perfumed African sexuality was an embodied form of racism that correctly told the American body to hate the other. As the rest of the novel portrays through a complex romantic plot involving blackface, fears of forced breeding, and a white paramour turned redeemer, overcoming natural forms of disgust through perfume machines that sprayed camphor and lavender scents would be against nature, akin to the unnatural integrations of American society that Holgate believed were espoused by abolitionists of the 1830s.[10]

Because of the racist force of works like *Sojourn in the City of Amalgamation*, the ironic abolitionist tones of writers such as Greene took many decades to come to fruition as an assertion of the absurdity of racial odors for the general American public. Even within several abolitionist texts of the later Antebellum Era, the idea of Africans as a pungent other was retained as a marker of race through the senses. The famed abolitionist, supporter of freedmen, and founder of Berea College John Gregg Fee offered in his *Anti-Slavery Manual* (1848) that "Africans of the present generation in our country, have far less of that smell that their forefathers had." Such a supposition offered that, even when the most progressive of abolitionists spoke of African and African American bodies, they often were informed by a tacit American knowledge of embodied racism that began in the nose and prospered through forms of both racial disgust and abolitionist paternalism.[11] US Army

---

The Politics of Anxiety in Nineteenth-Century American Literature (Cambridge: Cambridge University Press, 2011), 70–71. See also Katherine Paugh, *Politics of Reproduction: Race, Medicine, and Fertility in the Age of Abolition* (Oxford: Oxford University Press, 2017); Sophie White, *Voices of the Enslaved: Love, Labor, and Longing in French Louisiana* (Williamsburg, VA: Omohundro Institute of Early American History and Culture, 2019).

[10] Bolokitten, *Sojourn*, 24–34.

[11] John Gregg Fee, *An Anti-Slavery Manual* (Maysville, KY: Herald Office, 1848), quote on 199. For more on American abolitionism and racism, see John Wood Sweet, *Bodies Politic: Negotiating Race in the American North, 1730–1830* (Baltimore, MD: Johns Hopkins University Press, 2003), 271–311.

Chaplain Stephen Alexander Hodgman, even while critiquing the hypocrisy of other abolitionists as falsely magnanimous during the Civil War, similarly noted: "Some of the very elite of American Society ... have been able, not only to dwell with them in the same country, and to tolerate their dark color and their African odor, but they even had such a partiality and affection for them, that they could not do without their presence in the nursery, in the kitchen, in the parlor, and in every other department of domestic life."[12] Such a sentiment also appeared within Harriet Beecher Stowe's *Uncle Tom's Cabin* (1852), where the author questioned the paternalism of abolitionists who believed in African colonization through the figure of the reluctant slaveholder Augustine St. Clare, who indicted the colonizers who would simply send slaves back "to Africa, out of your sight and smell, and then send a missionary or two to do up all the self-denial of elevating them compendiously."[13]

Two decades after Bolokitten offered his dystopian worldview of a wayward American future, Cephas Broadluck, a pseudonym for the American author Allen Gazlay, published *Races of Humankind with Travels in Grubland* (1856) as an allegorical and consistently awkward attack on comparable forms of sensory and sexual amalgamation. Much less direct and certainly more obscure and metaphorical than the work of Holgate, Broadluck defended the right of the racist nose to be disgusted through a winding representation regarding the political force of those "holding the black statue" who desired that the Caucasians of his dystopian world plug their noses and remove their sense of smell. In this dystopian world, the "Grubmaster of all Grubland" decreed that all those not holding the "black statue" would no longer be allowed to use their sense of smell. Broadluck reviled such controls, which he implicitly tied to a metaphor of abolitionism, as the nose alerted peoples to the dangers of the world around them.[14] The obscure metaphors of Broadluck's text point to an era directly before the Civil War, when the belief in the odors of African bodies was so potent and debated that

[12] Stephen Alexander Hodgman, *The Nation's Sin and Punishment, or, The Hand of God Visible in the Overthrow of Slavery* (New York: American News, 1864), quotes on 215–216.

[13] Harriet Beecher Stowe, *Uncle Tom's Cabin, or, Negro Life in the Slave States of America: With Fifty Splendid Engravings* (London: Clarke & Co, 1852), quote on 151; Martha Cutter, *The Illustrated Slave: Empathy, Graphic Narrative, and the Visual Culture of the Transatlantic Abolition Movement, 1800–1852* (Athens: University of Georgia Press, 2017), 190–192.

[14] Cephas Broadluck, *Races of Mankind; With Travels in Grubland* (Cincinnati, OH: Longley, 1856), 138–146.

allegorical connotations to black smells within a future dystopia would have been understood by the common reader. For the metaphorical abolitionists "holding the black statue," smell was not a perceived racial problem. For the racists that Broadluck defended, smelling Africans was an important signifier that black bodies and minds were inferior, and eradicating the right to smell therefore removed protective social mechanisms that Gazlay and his racist cohort deemed essential to protection of the white body politic.[15]

The men and women who lived beneath the protective blanched umbrella of racial knowledge in the Herrenvolk Democracy subsisted constantly with a preservation of racial superiority through their sensory organs. For these specific dystopian authors, discovering race through the sense of smell was a moral imperative for a nation that was soon to face the ravages of perceived sexual amalgamation. These racists knew that race existed because they sensed and felt disgust. The white lives of the nineteenth century were simplified through existing at the top of this racial hierarchy and through asserting that position using greater and more encompassing languages to justify their place atop orders of both civilization and aroma.[16]

As described at the end of Chapter 2, such embodied and often subconscious scented racism grew out of English literary fancy and later medical debates of the Atlantic World into a political, social, and legal assertion throughout the American nineteenth century. For Southern physician Samuel Cartwright, creator of the ridiculous medical diagnosis of drapetomania, the smell of African bodies would justify more than simply the continuance of slavery and the disease of wanting to escape bondage. As Cartwright argued in the "Natural History of the Prognathous Species of Mankind," later to be applied as an informal brief for the court's decision in *Dred Scott v. Sandford* (1857): "The skin of a happy, healthy negro is not only blacker and more oily than an unhappy, unhealthy one, but emits the strongest odor when the body is warmed by exercise and the soul is filled with the most pleasurable emotions. In the dance called *patting juber,* the odor emitted from the men, intoxicated with pleasure, is often so powerful as to throw the negro women into paroxysms of

---

[15] Broadluck, *Races of Mankind*, 144–146.
[16] For introduction to whiteness studies, see Peter Kolchin, "Whiteness Studies: The New History of Race in America," *Journal of American History* 89, 1 (2002): 154–173.

unconsciousness, vulgar hysterics."[17] The *Dred Scott* case set a precedent that citizenship was not accessible for African American freedmen in the United States. The arguments of African sub-humanity and wildness that upheld the case were justified through aromatic devices that included a conceptual haze of false racial knowledge.[18]

The use of blackface within minstrel shows of the nineteenth century also increasingly introduced these ridiculous representations of black ineptitude to immigrant populations of the new Herrenvolk Democracy upheld by fresh ideas of whiteness and citizenship. Many Americans came to believe these racial identities were sensory facts, often associating the absurd physical traits and sexual tones of the minstrel shows to actual black cultures. Frequently, African Americans would participate in these shows to earn money. Some, like Master Juba, became famous for their portrayals of African culture, both as resistance to the blackface tradition but also participating within the minstrel tradition for economic achievement. On the eve of the Civil War, the propensity of these minstrel shows heightened as the nation faced increasingly binary and difficult questions of race and integration.[19]

These shows often included songs that would frequently offer sensory traits of African bodies as a stereotypical portrayal of false racial narratives. The minstrel song "Who Will Care for Niggers Now?" was distributed by frequent racist minstrel publisher H. De Marsan of New York City. The tune included the tale of a wayward freedman unable to care for himself after the loss of his master. Probably written directly after William

[17] Samuel Cartwright, "Natural History of the Prognathous Species of Mankind," Applied as an Appendix in "The Dred Scott Decision: Opinion of Chief Justice Taney," *New York Day-Book*, November 10, 1857; reprinted in *Cotton is King, and Pro-Slavery Arguments*, ed. E. N. Elliot (Augusta, GA: Pritchard, Abbot and Loomis, 1860), quote on 707.

[18] For more on the *Dred Scott* decision, American racism, and citizenship, see Martha Jones, *Birthright Citizens. A History of Race and Rights in Antebellum America* (Cambridge: Cambridge University Press, 2018), 128–145; Kenneth Stampp, *America in 1857: A Nation on the Brink* (New York: Oxford University Press, 1992); Austin Allen, *Origins of the Dred Scott Case: Jacksonian Jurisprudence and the Supreme Court, 1837–1857* (Athens: University of Georgia Press, 2006).

[19] For blackface minstrelsy, see Eric Lott, *Love and Theft: Blackface Minstrelsy and the American Working Class* (New York: Oxford University Press, 1993), 38–62; Dale Cockrell, *Demons of Disorder: Early Blackface Minstrels and their World* (Cambridge: Cambridge University Press, 1997); John Hanners, *"It Was Play or Starve": Acting in the Nineteenth Century American Popular Theatre* (Bowling Green, OH: Bowling Green University Press, 1993); Louis Onuorah Chude-Sokei, *The Sound of Culture: Diaspora and Black Technopoetics* (Middletown, CT: Wesleyan University Press, 2016), 21–49.

Tecumseh Sherman's march to free Southern cities from the continued yoke of the Confederacy, the song presented a black voice searching the soundscape for his master's caring hands: "List to me, plantation niggers,/ As I in dis mud-hole lie;/ Though I feel starvation's rigors,/ Let me say a word, and die./ Niggers, does dis look like Freedom!/ I can't see it any how;/ Blacks are fools, and white folks lead 'em:/ But who cares for niggers now?" Such a preposterously constructed figure, "relieved of his master's corn-crib and bacon stack," was considered to be wholly imbued "wid de African scent" and therefore unable to come to terms with the responsibilities of his newfound freedom.[20]

Discourses of cleanliness and the African body similarly emerged within another minstrel to question the proper roles for abolitionism and secession in American life and whether a Civil War was even necessary to cure what many racists deemed the already improved organization of their social hierarchy. This additional De Marsan publication provided, through the racially performed language of a man in bondage: "It's been de way wid some, Eber since dis world begun,/ To bother deir heads about de nigger;/ First Bobolition comes to view,/ And den Secession too:/ And did fight is all about de nigger." Drawing from centuries of religious and political discourse that constantly reiterated proverbs about African odors and skin, the constructed idea of the wayward freedman and unnecessary Civil War combined through drawing connections between the slave's own body and a deep racial mark that could not be removed: "You may talk and you may write,/ You may work and you may fight,/ But what good does eber arise?/ You may paint and you may rub,/ You may wash and you may scrub,/ But a nigger is a nigger till he dies!"[21] Minstrel shows often portrayed these stereotypes as satire, but most worked to invade the mainstream of public consciousness through reiterations of racial expressions that perpetuated ideas from religion, literature, and politics that one could not "wash the blackamoor white."

These embodied aromatic traditions that continued to impose racism were birthed throughout the Early Modern Era and later justified a slave system that created horrific pungent experiences for captives on the Middle Passage. These capitalized shapes continued into the era of

---

[20] Anonymous, "Who will care for niggers now? A parody on: Who will care for mother now?" (New York: H. De Marsan, 54 Chatham Street, ND). Courtesy of the Huntington Library, San Marino, CA.

[21] Anonymous, "Pompey Moore" (New York: H. De Marsan, Publisher, 54 Chatham Street, ND). Courtesy of the Huntington Library, San Marino, CA.

Scientific Racism, justifying new and complex determinations of odor and race that further subjugated dark bodies throughout Western Europe's growing colonial empires. As with the nasal passages of British surveyors that increasingly entered Africa during the nineteenth century described in Chapter 2, the racist noses of many in the United States and Confederacy around the time of the Civil War believed that odor was a signifier of intellectual inferiority and provided evidence that Africans and African Americans would not be able to reach modernity unless conscripted into civilization through continued colonial paternalism or the continually stated rights to own black bodies.

AMERICAN FALSE CONSCIOUSNESS

During the American nineteenth century, racism against Africans and African Americans increasingly did not need to be consistently justified among racist white populations of North America as the atrocious discursive fields of xenophobia and othering linked to specific sensory experiences educated upon the body rather than from an ideal that consistently needed to be reinforced through scientific or religious narratives. Especially after the end of slavery in North America during the Civil War, racism increased due to these embedded racial experiences of the body. This racial familiarity manifested during the era of intense violence during the Reconstruction Era and well into the twentieth century through diverse racial categorizations, instances of lynching, and scientific racisms that were used to uphold the legal structures of Jim Crow.[22]

Established social ideas of polygenetic racism came to be understood as increasingly factual during the era of Social Darwinism, mixing with historical memory of Atlantic slavery to continue fashioning the odor of the black body well after emancipation. The representative bloodhounds of Canadian author and early Social Darwinist Grant Allen's *In All Shades* (1886) explicitly noted the slave dog's aptitude at latching onto the smell of an African body as second nature due to the pungency of the runaway's

---

[22] Mark Smith, *How Race Is Made: Slavery, Segregation, and the Senses* (Chapel Hill: University of North Carolina Press, 2006), 93–145; Robert Entman. *The Black Image in the White Mind* (Chicago: University of Chicago Press, 2010 [1971]), 228–282; LaRose Parris, *Being Apart: Theoretical and Existential Resistance in Africana Literature* (Charlottesville: University of Virginia Press, 2015); Sharon Kennedy-Nolle, *Writing Reconstruction: Race, Gender, and Citizenship in the Postwar South* (Chapel Hill: University of North Carolina Press, 2015), 1–24.

sweat.[23] Scientific Racism and Social Darwinism of the late nineteenth century took these miasmas of racial knowledge and applied an ordered system to scented bodies in pursuit of renewed racial domination. This science, emerging from earlier Atlantic networks of the racialized Republic of Letters, provided narrative stereotypes about the smell of black bodies and increasingly linked with natural philosophy to uphold what originally began within the literary fancy charted on the English stage and page.[24]

The works of Samuel George Morton, Josiah Nott, and George Gliddon specifically submitted for Americans numerous phrenological and craniological justifications for continued beliefs regarding racial superiority. Often, these phrenological discussions relied on defining temperaments and personalities through an understanding that different areas of the brain and skull determined sensory acuities.[25] Through many other cases of scientific dissemination, craniologists traveled throughout technical lyceums of the Atlantic World and Europe to offer performances of their skull observations for adoring and racist crowds.[26] For smelling, these performances often continued previous links between sensing, the

---

[23] Grant Allen, *In All Shades* (Chicago: Rand McNally, 1889 [1886]), 40–42, 190.

[24] For more on Social Darwinism and literature in the later Anglo-Atlantic, see Joseph Carroll, *Literary Darwinism: Evolution, Human Nature, and Literature* (New York: Routledge, 2012); Edward Beasley, *The Victorian Reinvention of Race: New Racisms and the Problem of Grouping in the Human Sciences* (New York: Routledge, 2012), 97–111. See also Daniela Babilon, *The Power of Smell in American Literature: Odor, Affect, and Social Inequality* (New York: Peter Lang, 2017), 171–183.

[25] Henry Clarke, *Phrenology Founded on and Deducible from Christianity: In Three Lectures on the Application of the Doctrines and Precepts of the New Testament to the Animal, Moral, and Intellectual Nature of Man* (Edinburgh: W. Tait, and J. Anderson, 1836), 30–31, 42–43; Samuel George Morton, *Crania Americana: Or a Comparative View of the Skulls of Various Aboriginal Nations of North and South America: to Which Is Prefixed an Essay on the Varieties of Human Species* (Philadelphia: Dobson, 1839), 51–66; Alexander Kinmont, *Twelve Lectures on the Natural History of Man* (Cincinnati, OH: U. P. James, 1839), 172–176.

[26] Shawn Michelle Smith, *American Archives: Gender, Race, and Class in Visual Culture* (Princeton, NJ: Princeton University Press, 2014), 29–50. For more on such performances, and opposing African-American counter-performances, see Britt Rusert, "The Science of Freedom: Counterarchives of Racial Science on the Antebellum Stage," *African American Review* 45, 3 (Fall, 2012): 291–308. See also the large crowds at the public autopsy of former slave Joice Heth in Benjamin Reiss, *The Showman and the Slave: Race, Death, and Memory in Barnum's America* (Cambridge, MA: Harvard University Press, 2001), 198–207, and the later performances of athletics, theatre, and otherness within Harvey Young, *Embodying Black Experience: Stillness, Critical Memory, and the Black Body* (Ann Arbor: University of Michigan Press, 2010).

size of the nose, and consequential concerns with moral aptitudes of different races.[27]

Those who submitted themselves to the treatments of phrenology would often be analyzed within self-completed workbooks, like O. S. Fowler's commonly updated guidelines within *Synopsis of Phrenology*. Following the guidelines of these books to self-monitor supposedly helped to improve specific sensory skills and instances of depression through cultivating aspects of the brain that phrenologists argued would cure personal concerns with their patient's place in the social order.[28] For some phrenologists, as within the *Orthodox Phrenology* (1870) of sculptor Ambrose Vago, the specific shapes and aptitudes of the nose defined the ability of certain persons to mark their own individuality. Certain nose shapes, for some believers of the pseudoscience, meant that individuals were more prone to adeptly perceive the character of those around them, making certain proboscis shapes common among creative types and writers.[29] Many Americans and Europeans who entered into these phrenological circles often believed that these nose shapes and sensory abilities determined their aptitude for judging the civilization, character, and class of those around them, a trait they had learned from racial falsities of the previous centuries that they increasingly cultivated as a pre-Freudian form of psychoanalysis that worked to educate sensory skills, flatter white minds, and teach bodies how to smell both the socially acceptable and culturally excepted.[30]

---

[27] J. G. Spurzheim, *Phrenology, or, The Doctrine of the Mental Phenomena* (Boston: Marsh, Capen & Lyon, 1832), 309–311; George Combe, *Elements of Phrenology* (Edinburgh: John Anderson, 1824), 86–87; J. Stanley Grimes, John William Orr, John P. Hall, and J. Pinkney, *A New System of Phrenology* (Buffalo, NY: Oliver G. Steele, 1839), 69–76; G. S. Weaver and J. Burns. *Lectures on Mental Science According to the Philosophy of Phrenology: Delivered Before the Anthropological Society of the Western Liberal Institute of Marietta, Ohio, in the Autumn of 1851* (London: James Burns, 1876), 42–45; Frederick Bridges, *Phrenology Made Practical and Popularly Explained* (London: George Philip & Son, 1860), 40–61.

[28] For example, see O. S. Fowler, *Synopsis of Phrenology, and the Phrenological Developments: Together with the Character and Talents Of* (New York: Fowlers & Wells, 1849), 15–19.

[29] Ambrose Lewis Vago, *Orthodox Phrenology* (London: Simpkin and Marshall, 1870), 49–52.

[30] For phrenology in the Atlantic World, see Britt Rusert, *Fugitive Science: Empiricism and Freedom in Early African American Culture* (New York: New York University Press, 2017), 65–112; Ann Fabian, *The Skull Collectors: Race, Science, and America's Unburied Dead* (Chicago: University of Chicago Press, 2010); Tim Fulford, Peter Kitson, and Debbie Lee, *Literature, Science and Exploration in the Romantic Era: Bodies of Knowledge* (Cambridge: Cambridge University Press, 2008), 127–148.

Tangential to these racialized discourses, scatological sciences also emerged again during the late nineteenth century to define those perceived as inferior through often belabored analyses of shit-stained ritual cultures. United States Army Captain John Bourke's *Scatalogic Rites of All Nations* (1891) summarized the intense olfactory of non-Western peoples during this era of New Imperialism whereby cleanliness and the lack of odor persisted as markers of civility. Although much of his fieldwork was spent with the Zuni nations of the American West, Bourke homogenized othered populations through structural anthropology and tales of excremental desires. The former soldier turned ethnographer specifically summarized Africans through collecting numerous well-trodden tales of a naturally stinking people who defecated in the open, drank rhinoceros feces in their nightly concoctions, slept on beds made of cow dung, tanned their animal skins with shit, and split their milk with cattle urine.[31] Within these fresh narratives of civilization and odor that emerged during the late nineteenth century, tied often to the back of the beaten horse of Scientific Racism, smells were increasingly linked to primitive peoples, further tying all non-Europeans to an earlier space of cultural evolution, whereby attributing smell as important within a culture negatively defined that nation as fundamentally primeval.[32]

---

[31] John Gregory Bourke, *Scatalogic Rites of All Nations: A Monograph Upon the Employment of Excrementitious Remedial Agents in Religion, Therapeutics, Divination, Witchcraft, Love-Philters, Etc., in All Parts of the Globe* (Washington, DC: W. H. Lowdermilk & Co, 1891), 30, 39, 148, 180; Stephen Greenblatt, "Filthy Rites," *Daedalus* 111, 3 (1982): 1–16.

[32] For example, see the description of former slave Joice Heth's purportedly wondrous ability to smell within Reiss, *Showman and the Slave*, 86–88. See also Nicolas Joly, *Man Before Metals* (New York: D. Appleton and Company, 1891), 171–172; Gerald Massey, *The Natural Genesis, or, Second Part of A Book of the Beginnings, Containing an Attempt to Recover and Reconstitute the Lost Origines of the Myths and Mysteries, Types and Symbols, Religion and Language, with Egypt for the Mouthpiece and Africa As the Birthplace* (London: Williams and Norgate, 1883), 77–83; J. Mount Bleyer, "The 'Sense of Smell' – In Relation to Medico-Legal Questions," *Journal of the Respiratory Organs* 1, 9 (September, 1889): 181–183; Charles Darwin, *The Descent of Man, and Selection in Relation to Sex* (London: John Murray, 1899 [1871]), 23–24, 114–115; John Van Evrie, *Subgenation: The Theory of the Normal Relation of the Races: an Answer to "Miscegenation"* (New York: John Bradburn, 1864), 13–17; John Van Evrie, *Negroes and Negro Slavery: the First an Inferior Race: the Latter Its Normal Condition* (New York: Van Evrie, Horton, and Company, 1868), 18–20.

The metropolitan cores in England and the imperial United States of the early twentieth century enlisted a scientific and medical knowledge supported by this virulent racism that increasingly applied both a propensity to use the nose within a culture and the perception of pungent bodies to mark categories of race and inferiority.[33] The vast and continuing Western racialization project through odor involved different scatological, monogenetic, and polygenetic justifications. Where racist scatology could not place non-Western peoples as inferior, a tradition of the biological inheritance of odors proliferated for those Social Darwinists increasingly avowing evolutionary racial hierarchies for imperial control. For instance, American doctors George Milbry Gould and Walter Pyle's *Anomalies and Curiosities of Medicine* (1896) asserted that certain races, especially after coitus, retained identifiable and specific biological odors. Following work by French biologist Jean Louis Armand de Quatrefages de Bréau and a recurrent citation from the famed German traveling anatomist Franz Pruner-Bey regarding the purported bumps on African skin, they declared: "Negroes have a rank ammoniacal odor, unmitigated by cleanliness ... due to a volatile oil set free by the sebaceous follicles."[34] Scientific assurances of bumps on skin and the production of specific organs, reminiscent of the work of Rush, Jefferson, Mitchell, and Long, demarcated pseudoscientific truths that justified race as a hardened category to be used for the continuing growth of Western colonial dominance over Africa and the rest of the colonial world where dark bodies were increasingly linked as a common racial and scented other.[35]

---

[33] Tracy Teslow, *Constructing Race: The Science of Bodies and Cultures in American Anthropology* (New York: Cambridge University Press, 2014), 32–73; Pat Shipman, *The Evolution of Racism: Human Differences and the Use and Abuse of Science* (New York: Simon & Schuster, 1994); Sari Altschuler, *The Medical Imagination: Literature and Health in the Early United States* (Philadelphia: University of Pennsylvania Press, 2018), 133–159; Banu Subramaniam, *Ghost Stories for Darwin: The Science of Variation and the Politics of Diversity* (Urbana: University of Illinois Press, 2014).

[34] George Gould and Walter Pyle, *Anomalies and Curiosities of Medicine* (New York: Bell, 1896), 398–400, quote on 399; M. De Quatrefages, "Physical Characteristics of the Human Races," *Popular Science* (March, 1873): 545–548; James Hastings, John Selbie, and Louis Gray, *Encyclopedia of Religion and Ethics* (New York: Scribner's Sons, 1908), 396–397.

[35] For European dialogues that "effectively homogenized" the diverse others of the world through a "grammar of sameness," see Benjamin Schmidt, *Inventing Exoticism: Geography, Globalism, and Europe's Early Modern World* (Philadelphia: University of Pennsylvania Press, 2015), 13–18, 118–139, and the mixed origins of Othello analyzed within Jonathan Burton, "'A most wily bird': Leo Africanus, *Othello* and the Trafficking

These scientific assurances of race appeared often within later American social discourses and legalism that increasingly codified whiteness as a social code for different manifestations of the Herrenvolk Democracy.[36] The imperative case for defining the separate but equal clause of Jim Crow, *Plessy v. Ferguson* (1896), specifically involved the accusation of blackness through the sense of smell. As Mark Smith has shown, because the sight of Homer Plessy was often so confusingly white, Southern jurists contemplated with difficulty how to categorize the test case and passing activist. In parts of their deliberations, Southerners came to the aromatic sciences as a way to define Plessy as black.[37] In the broader United States after *Plessy*, the rise of Jim Crow increased the marking of black bodies as pungent and produced later social places for American culture of the twentieth century to perpetuate olfactory stereotypes of African Americans.[38] Of course, such racialized and transnational olfactory ideologies passed into later narratives, even as Western experiments, like those of Canadian psychologist Otto Klineberg during the 1930s, defined that no differences in smell could be traced across the races.[39]

Regardless of these definitive tests, the materiality of factual science did not matter in the twentieth century as it similarly had not mattered during the Early Modern Era or on the African frontiers of the nineteenth century. Western racism was often so virulent as to be able to construct deeply embodied sensations that frequently resisted the realities of material odors. The transnational disease of olfactory racism that infected Western sensory consciousness involved the application of medicine, science, and literature that expanded the Western body into a space of

---

in Difference," in *Post-Colonial Shakespeares*, eds. Ania Loomba and Martin Orkin (London: Routledge, 1998), 43–63.

[36] For general concerns with race construction and whiteness in the nineteenth century, see Matthew Frye Jacobson, *Whiteness of a Different Color: European Immigrants and the Alchemy of Race* (Cambridge, MA: Harvard University Press, 1998); David Roediger, *The Wages of Whiteness: Race and the Making of the American Working Class* (London: Verso, 1991).

[37] Smith, *How Race Is Made*, 66–110.

[38] Robert Park, "The Bases of Race Prejudice," *The Annals of the American Academy of Political and Social Science* 140 (November, 1928): 11–20.

[39] Otto Klineberg, *Race Differences* (New York: Harper and Brothers, 1935). See also Charles King, *Gods of the Upper Air: How a Circle of Renegade Anthropologists Reinvented Race, Sex, and Gender in the Twentieth Century* (New York: Doubleday, 2019); Charles Lawrence, *The Id, the Ego, and Equal Protection: Reckoning with Unconscious Racism* (San Francisco: Stanford University Press, 1987); Robert Guthrie, *Even the Rat Was White: A Historical View of Psychology* (Boston: Pearson, 2004).

purity while displacing bodies of racial others into what were defined as excremental and wasteful cultural spaces. These processes often occurred structurally within other colonialist schemes against many different indigenous peoples. As Greg Grandin summarized regarding nineteenth-century Latin America, epidemiology and knowledge of diseases included a vast significance for "representing and defining racial and national identities."[40] Other colonialist schemes linked diseases, odors, and sexuality to provide justification for the dominance of one race over another. The specific scents of miscegenation were frequently applied as a Dutch rationalization for continued imperial control in colonial Java of the twentieth century. Explicit rules set standards whereby Dutch children were prohibited from playing with Javanese girls and boys, partly because of the pestilential odors that their sweat was believed to emanate.[41]

Racial science and olfactory observation remained a common way for Westerners to mark the other as European empires flourished during the twentieth century.[42] For the remaining British Empire of the twentieth century, the conceit of inherent black odors persisted to justify continued imperial goals in Africa and other areas of the Global South.[43] Within the

[40] Greg Grandin, *The Blood of Guatemala: A History of Race and Nation* (Durham, NC: Duke University Press, 2000), 85–98, quote on 82–83. See also Julyan Peard, *Race, Place, and Medicine: The Idea of the Tropics in Nineteenth-Century Brazil* (Durham, NC: Duke University Press, 2000), 81–108: Mariola Espinosa, *Epidemic Invasions: Yellow Fever and the Limits of Cuban Independence, 1878–1930* (Chicago: University of Chicago Press, 2009), 1–10; Daniel Nemser, *Infrastructures of Race: Concentration and Biopolitics in Colonial Mexico* (Austin: University of Texas Press, 2017); Karin Alejandra Rosemblatt, *The Science and Politics of Race in Mexico and the United States, 1910–1950* (Chapel Hill: University of North Carolina Press, 2019); Paul Ramírez, *Enlightened Immunity: Mexico's Experiments with Disease Prevention in the Age of Reason* (Stanford, CA: Stanford University Press, 2018).

[41] Ann Laura Stoler, *Carnal Knowledge and Imperial Power: Race and the Intimate in Colonial Rule* (Berkeley: University of California Press, 2002), 6–7, 173; Ann Laura Stoler, *Race and the Education of Desire: Foucault's History of Sexuality and the Colonial Order of Things* (Durham: Duke University Press, 1995), 1–18, 186–188. For similar use of separating children, based on beliefs of moral cleanliness, see Robin Bernstein, *Racial Innocence: Performing American Childhood from Slavery to Civil Rights* (New York: New York University Press, 2011).

[42] For examples, see Stephen Kern, "Olfactory Ontology and Scented Harmonies: on the History of Smell," *Journal of Popular Culture* 7, 4 (1974): 816–824; Alexander Butchart, *The Anatomy of Power: European Constructions of the African Body* (London: Zed, 1998), 42, 66; Barbara Thompson, "The African Female Body in the Cultural Imagination," in *Black Womanhood: Images, Icons, and Ideologies of the African Body*, eds. Barbara Thompson and Ifi Amadiume (Hanover, NH: Hood Museum of Art 2008), 27–48.

[43] Radhika Mohanram, *Imperial White: Race, Diaspora, and the British Empire* (Minneapolis: University of Minnesota Press, 2007), 99–108; Joseph Childers, "Foreign

United States, these narratives of miasma, disease, and smell continue to uphold environmental racism that links narratives of race to the dirtiness of the areas where darker bodies are deemed able to live due to more resilient sensoriums.[44]

SCENT AND THE DIALECTICS OF MODERNITY

Money is shit, but it does not smell. Muck and money go together. Children mark their food by licking it, by taunting others that their mark of uncleanness has made something theirs. Animals piss and shit to mark their territory. So does man. He marks his terrain through cordoning off what is shit and what is not. He does so through rhetoric, through changing language, by semantically defining what cannot be made clean. Like the animals who mark their land in a discursive battle of textual urine, man marks his territory through the shit-stained words of his popular culture. The public sphere contains a battle over consciousness that includes and enhances this throwing of shit. Sometimes this is shit itself, but more often it is shit as words, a carnival of fecal texts tossed by those who thirst for power and from those who are oppressed.

Still today, quick searches on the internet will find numerous stories of both important public figures and the unimportant dredges on the bowels of the web remarking about the inherent smell of black bodies and the shitholes of their cultural ancestries. If you are keen to feel disgusted at the place of racism on the anonymous internet, take a look at the pages of Reddit that attack political correctness through racial means. There you will find all the links of racial consciousness and odor found within this monograph. You will be disgusted to find that there are remaining and growing associations between the perceived laziness of Africans and African Americans and a supposed lack of bathing habits. You will find links between the curliness of African hair and its retention of odor. You

Matter: Imperial Filth," in *Filth: Dirt, Disgust, and Modern Life*, eds. William Cohen and Ryan Johnson (Minneapolis: University of Minnesota Press, 2005), 201–224.

[44] Carl Zimring, *Clean and White: A History of Environmental Racism in the United States* (New York: New York University Press, 2015); Mel Chen, *Animacies: Biopolitics, Racial Mattering, and Queer Affect* (Durham, NC: Duke University Press, 2012); Julie Sze, *Noxious New York: The Racial Politics of Urban Health and Environmental Justice* (Cambridge, MA: MIT Press, 2006); Pavithra Vasudevan, "An Intimate Inventory of Race and Waste," *Antipode* (2019): 1–21. See also Deborah Jackson, "Scents of Place: the Dysplacement of a First Nations Community in Canada," *American Anthropologist* 113, 4 (2011): 606–618; Hsuan Hsu, "Naturalist Smellscapes and Environmental Justice," *American Literature* 88, 4 (2016): 787–814.

will read a few of the scholarly set who may peruse these racist web pages and post on the evolution of the African body as needing smellier skin to repel the carnivorous beasts of Africa. Race science has returned with great force to inform bodies to sense race due to the millions of white nationalist tentacles and fascist intentions upon the varied and broad spectrums of the internet.

Racism is one of the many aspects of culture and language that is felt through the sensory organs.[45] Even as most of the ivory tower understands race is not genetic, the academy remains at an intense and losing racial moment in the West, at a place where most scholars are not correctly understanding the place of the body in the marking of race. The racist mind cannot simply be told that race does not exist, because racist knowledge is not entirely conscious. Rather, racial familiarity is embodied to such an extent within racialist perceptions that the experience seems to be biological. To deconstruct racism through educating the mind alone consequently creates a resistant body and an impervious body politic of racists and their many intellectual and embodied siege mentalities. To deconstruct how the five senses work to perceive the other, more attention must be paid to the subconscious experiences of disgust that are educated within the racialized social habitus.[46]

This deliberation must learn from a historical subaltern community of slaves and Africans that called out the primitive shit-stained contours of slavery and capitalism that bonded laborers to land and ledger.

---

[45] For more on the body, language, and sensory experience, see Michael Polanyi, *The Tacit Dimension* (Chicago: University of Chicago Press, 1966); George Lakoff and Mark Johnson, *Metaphors We Live By* (Chicago: University of Chicago Press, 2008 [1980]), 57–58; Asifa Majid and Stephen Levinson, "The Senses in Language and Culture," *Senses & Society* 6 (2011): 5–18; Thomas Sebeok, *Signs: An Introduction to Semiotics* (Toronto: University of Toronto Press, 2001), 11–23, 124–126; Peter Stallybrass and Ann Rosalind Jones, "Fetishizing the Glove in Renaissance Europe," *Critical Inquiry* 28, 1 (2001): 114–132; David Murray, "Object Lessons: Fetishism and the Hierarchies of Race and Religion," in *Conversion: Old Worlds and New*, eds. Kenneth Mills and Anthony Grafton (Rochester, NY: University of Rochester Press, 2003), 199–217; Mark Johnson, *The Body in the Mind: The Bodily Basis of Meaning, Imagination, and Reason* (Chicago: University of Chicago Press, 1987).

[46] For more on race, taste, and habitus, see Richard Lewontin, Steven Rose, and Leon Kamin, *Not in Our Genes: Biology, Ideology, and Human Nature* (New York: Pantheon, 1984); Pierre Bourdieu, *Distinction: A Social Critique of the Judgement of Taste* (Cambridge, MA: Harvard University Press, 1984), 190–192; William Ian Miller, *The Anatomy of Disgust* (Cambridge, MA: Harvard University Press, 1997); Alan Hyde, "Offensive Bodies," in *The Smell Culture Reader*, ed. Jim Drobnick (Oxford: Berg, 2006), 53–58; Richard Schechner, "Rasaesthetics," in *The Senses in Performance*, eds. Sally Banes and André Lepecki (New York: Routledge, 2007), 10–28.

Transgressive languages of odor can specifically be used to resist the continuing motifs of capital and associated racism that define categories of waste and purity to mark newly spiraling categories of the fetish within the repetitious corralling of the human form that late capitalism continues to materially and digitally encode upon the libidinal apparatuses.[47]

Reified in syntax through stereotyping on the stage, the pungent markers of the black race were sent for violent assertion on the flagellated fringes of Europe's colonial empires. The colonies usually accepted such suppositions and asserted olfactory colonialism upon their laborers. Anglo-Atlantic sensory consciousness, in this oversimplified but essential binary, desired a process of deodorization, cleanliness, and religious purity that was created by rhetorically shifting what was deemed foul and what was deemed fragrant. The Anglo-Atlantic body has been marking and making race for centuries. The scientific racists, and Enlightenment scholars before them, coded what the body had learned from popular culture through the centuries prior. When analyzing race, and when racism first sprung from the depths of human anxiety, it is improper to look only at the texts of ordered racial hierarchies as the initial cause, because ordering and finalizing are the ultimate steps in the scientific method. The earlier steps on the path that created European racism were the nascently polygenetic racial hypotheses, altered from the cultural summaries of the periphery, that were set forth by playwrights, politicians, and pastors of the London core. Smells portray how deeply engrained these racial ideals endured within the early modern English body, the place where racism was initially experienced. African medical practitioners did not desire such anesthetized anosmia within their religious devotions and medical practices. African retention of the idea of smelling-out witches, poison, and disease survived the Middle Passage.

---

[47] For late capitalism and the senses, see Fredric Jameson, *Postmodernism, or, The Cultural Logic of Late Capitalism* (Durham, NC: Duke University Press, 1991), 6–45; Dorothea Olkowski, *Universal (In the Realm of the Sensible): Beyond Continental Philosophy* (Edinburgh: Edinburgh University Press, 2007), 184–186, 202–255; Gilles Deleuze, *Difference and Repetition* (London: Bloomsbury, 2014); Felix Guattari, Paul Bains, and Julian Pefanis, *Chaosmosis: An Ethico-Aesthetic Paradigm* (Sydney: Power, 2006); David Howes, "Hyperesthesia, or, The Sensual Logic of Late Capitalism," in *Empire of the Senses: The Sensual Culture Reader*, ed. David Howes (London: Bloomsbury, 2005), 281–303. See also the alternative sensory epistemologies within Boaventura de Sousa Santos, *The End of the Cognitive Empire: The Coming of Age of Epistemologies of the South* (Durham, NC: Duke University Press, 2018), 166–180; Sami Khatib, "'Sensuous Supra-Sensuous': The Aesthetics of Real Absraction," in *Aesthetic Marx* eds. Samir Gandesha and Johan Hartle (London: Bloomsbury, 2018), 49–72.

African slaves used these smells to mark their own territory against their masters. This setting of rival geographies through smell constituted a structural marker of revolutionary agency through individual acts of everyday resistance.

Race, in modern academic parlance, is a social construct, but materialist drives incentivize many to still consider the importance of finding race within the body and the more scientifically misleading use of the genetic code, as a space to be divined by computers that have partially replaced the five senses and the accompanying embodied perceptions of the racial other.[48] Racialization began in the body, was written as science, and now is read by computers through a genomic code and quantitative spectrum that retains traits of disgust that allows historical correlation to mean racial causation in continuingly absurdist terminologies.[49] Such technology, as with earlier forms of Scientific Racism, is not neutral. Rather, it is white and patriarchal, born of a history of racial oppression that began in an Enlightenment obsessed with cataloging information as a means of racial control and labor appropriation. That desire for racial cataloguing continues today in the corporate algorithms of search engines that represent a white and neoliberal order circulating racial knowledge to reap the repetitious advertising profits of late capitalism.[50]

---

[48] Ashley Montagu, *Man's Most Dangerous Myth: The Fallacy of Race* (Cleveland, OH: World Pub. Co., 1997 [1942]); Stephan Palmié, "Genomics, Divination, 'Racecraft'," *American Ethnologist* 34 (2007): 205–222; Mark Smith, "Finding Deficiency: On Eugenics, Economics, and Certainty," *American Journal of Economics and Sociology* 64, 3 (2005): 887–900; Mikuláš Teich, "Mapping the Human Genome in the Light of History," in *Nature and Society in Historical Context*, eds. Mikuláš Teich, Roy Porter, and Bo Gustafsson (New York: Cambridge, 1997), 308–331.

[49] Gregory Cochran, Jason Hardy, and Henry Harpending, "Natural History of Ashkenazi Intelligence," *Journal of Biosocial Science* 38, 5 (2006): 659–693; Richard Herrnstein and Charles Murray, *The Bell Curve: Intelligence and Class Structure in American Life* (New York: Free Press, 1994); Michael Specter, *Denialism: How Irrational Thinking Hinders Scientific Progress, Harms the Planet, and Threatens Our Lives* (New York: Penguin, 2009); Nicholas Wade, *A Troublesome Inheritance: Genes, Race, and Human History* (New York: Penguin, 2014); William Tucker, *The Funding of Scientific Racism: Wickliffe Draper and the Pioneer Fund* (Urbana: University of Illinois Press, 2007); Michael Staub, *The Mismeasure of Minds: Debating Race and Intelligence between Brown and the Bell Curve* (Chapel Hill: University of North Carolina Press, 2018); Richard Lewontin, *Biology As Ideology: The Doctrine of DNA* (New York: Harper Perennial, 1991); Michael Levin, *Why Race Matters: Race Differences and What They Mean* (Westport, CT: Praeger, 1997).

[50] See the power of algorithms to consistently reproduce racial stereotypes within the digitized public sphere within Safiya Umoja Noble, *Algorithms of Oppression: How Search Engines Reinforce Racism* (New York: New York University Press, 2018), 1–14. See also Lisa Nakamura, *Digitizing Race: Visual Cultures of the Internet* (Minneapolis:

This genetic and computable coding of race currently pairs with the continued use of racism within political and public spheres. Consistent current political attention to immigration in both Britain and the United States often relies on using languages of smelling, disease, and cleanliness to describe the immigrant other.[51] Western culture digs into the body, into the very genes at the root of the human form, to discover race and causality. Skin color was never enough; smell was deeply embodied but still not sufficient. Now race is found encoded in the digital matrix of DNA as part of our increasingly technological lives.[52]

For American slaves who earned their freedom after the Civil War, smell often indicated freedom. Like the Africans who used smell as a pathway to resistance throughout the Atlantic World, freedmen in the American South after the Civil War were similarly appreciative of odor's numerous meanings. For many former African American slaves, emancipation celebrations that first began in 1863 involved a deep olfactory

University of Minnesota Press, 2008), 171–201; R. Alexander Bentley, Michael J. O'Brien, and John Maeda, *The Acceleration of Cultural Change: From Ancestors to Algorithms* (Cambridge, MA: MIT Press, 2017), 1–14.

[51] Desmond Manderson, "Senses and Symbols: The Construction of Drugs in Historic and Aesthetic Perspective," in *Law and the Senses: Sensational Jurisprudence*, eds. Lionel Bently and Leo Flynn (London: Pluto, 1996), 199–216; Alexis Shotwell, *Knowing Otherwise: Race, Gender, and Implicit Understanding* (University Park, PA: Pennsylvania State University Press, 2011). For more research on body odor and cultural relativism, see Terence Hannigan, "Body Odor: The International Student and Cross-Cultural Communication," *Culture & Psychology* 1, 4 (1995): 497–503.

[52] For more background, see Angela Saini, *Superior: The Return of Race Science* (London: Fouth Estate, 2019); Camisha Russell, *The Assisted Reproduction of Race* (Bloomington: University of Indiana Press, 2018); Sten Pultz Moslund, *Literature's Sensuous Geographies: Postcolonial Matters of Place* (New York: Palgrave Macmillan, 2015); Paul Rabinow and Nikolas Rose, "Biopower Today," in *Biopower: Foucault and Beyond*, eds. Vernon Cisney and Nicolae Morar (Chicago: University of Chicago Press, 2016), 297–325; Nikolas Rose, *The Politics of Life Itself: Biomedicine, Power, and Subjectivity in the Twenty-First Century* (Princeton, NJ: Princeton University Press, 2009), 155–167; Naomi Zack, *Philosophy of Science and Race* (London: Routledge, 2002), 58–118; Stephen Jay Gould, *The Mismeasure of Man* (New York: Norton, 2008); Tracy Teslow, *Constructing Race: The Science of Bodies and Cultures in American Anthropology* (New York: Cambridge University Press, 2014), 337–362; Sarah Chinn, *Technology and the Logic of American Racism: A Cultural History of the Body As Evidence* (London: Continuum, 2000), 141–167; Kieth Wailoo, "Inventing the Heterozygote: Molecular Biology, Racial Identity, and the Narratives of Sickle-Cell Disease, Tay-Sachs, and Cystic Fibrosis," in *Race, Nature, and the Politics of Difference*, eds. Donald Moore, Jake Kosek, and Anand Pandian (Durham, NC: Duke University Press, 2003), 235–253; Debra Thompson, *Schematic State: Race, Transnationalism, and the Politics of the Census* (Cambridge: Cambridge University Press, 2018), 222–264.

connection to the smell of pork as a signifier of liberty and new American opportunities. In modern North America, the pit-barbeque of smoking pigs during emancipation anniversaries continues to offer such a redolent remembrance of both the horrors of slavery and the promises of freedom.[53]

Throughout a work that portrays the invasions of civilization, Western education, and liberalism on African culture, *The African Witch* (1936) of Joyce Cary describes a central tale of African nationalism and educational disillusionment through a rebellious character in Africa of the twentieth century who similarly employs smell to throw aromatic symbolism and rhetoric back into the face of his oppressors. The novel involves the deeply rebellious and youthful character Musa, who furnishes upon the white soldiers blocking his path a taunt: "Hail, great lords of the muck-heap – a thousand salutations with dung! God damn you for ever and ever." It is within the language of smell and waste that Cary created Musa's comedic rebelliousness.[54] It is also within the spiritual and material spaces of the olfactory that African resistance in the diaspora and against the colonial European entrance to the Dark Continent was often asserted.

Sensory history can portray these important spaces for resistance to the false racial consciousness of the modern Western racist.[55] The uprisings against racial inequality during the Civil Rights Movement often involved even greater sensory expressions of music, dress, and hairstyles that marked African American and African identity as increasingly subjective.[56] Within representations of odors exists a specific specter of

---

[53] William Wiggins, *O Freedom! Afro-American Emancipation Celebrations* (Knoxville: University of Tennessee Press, 1987), 80–83. See also the persistence of racial motifs of oppression and resistance within Afrofuturism in Chude-Sokei, *Sound of Culture*, 179–224; Erik Steinskog, *Afrofuturism and Black Sound Studies: Culture, Technology, and Things to Come* (Cham: Palgrave Macmillan, 2018), 37–74.

[54] Joyce Cary, *The African Witch* (New York: Harper, 1962 [1936]), quotes on 77–81.

[55] See also "bodily antiracist" within Ibram Kendi, *How to be an Antiracist* (New York: One World, 2019), 69–80.

[56] For more on forms of sensory resistance, see Anita Sridhar Chari, *A Political Economy of the Senses: Neoliberalism, Reification, Critique* (New York: Columbia University Press, 2016); Francine Masiello, *The Senses of Democracy: Perception, Politics, and Culture in Latin America* (Austin: University of Texas Press, 2018), 22–32; David Howes, "Introduction: Empire of the Senses," in *Empire of the Senses: The Sensual Culture Reader*, ed. David Howes (Oxford: Berg, 2005), 1–20; Terry Eagleton, *The Ideology of the Aesthetic* (Malden, MA: Blackwell, 1990), 7–28; Mark Smith, *Sensing the Past: Seeing, Hearing, Smelling, Tasting, and Touching in History* (Berkeley: University of California Press, 2007), 15–28; Bryan Nelson, "Politics of the Senses: Karl Marx and

resistance that can be articulated within the body and smelled outward upon the languages and institutions of oppression. For Black Nationalist playwright Amiri Baraka, in the *Slave Ship* (1967) odor was include as part of an essential cultural memory for African Americans to understand both the tragedy of slavery and the triumph of survival. The entire play splashes in odors of pestilence. From a dark stage emerge odors from stage directions that are meant to elicit perceptions of "Pee, Shit, Death." The play, like the Atlantic World in her most vile and tragic moments, explores slave traders who made Africans sleep in filth and shit and how those victims used dialectical languages of excrement as a means to cry resistance through calling traders "White shit-eaters" and "Devils, Devils, cold walking shit." Baraka's play exposes memories of a slave trade that involved sensory warfare. As masters tried to control the senses of their property, that chattel asserted the rights of the subject with their own sensory narratives of culture, identity, and world-forming.[57]

Early modern European science took the original thoughts of the fearful masses and used the power of the printed word to shift stench upon the other. At times, the other was able to throw that shit back, through printed words and the material of scents that eluded the hegemonic confines of the superstructure. In the culmination of this olfactory discourse, African peoples were increasingly perceived as stinking. Racism became emboldened within the Western body, felt and sensed without concern for material realities. Different African nations were progressively placed between man and animal, deemed inferior because of a pungent liminality and considered susceptible to a cultural ethos that negatively prized scents and smells, odors that many Europeans were not willing to reward as culturally vital after the rise of hygiene and the Reformation against sensuous religiosity. Africans resisted these narratives of odor through

Empirical Subjectivity," *Subjectivity* 4, 4 (2011): 395–412; David Howes, *Sensual Relations: Engaging the Senses in Culture and Social Theory* (Ann Arbor: University of Michigan Press, 2010) 204–234; Judith Farquhar and Margaret Lock, "Introduction," in *Beyond the Body Proper: Reading the Anthropology of Material Life*, eds. Judith Farquhar and Margaret Lock (Durham, NC: Duke University Press, 2007), 1–15; Richard Shusterman, *Body Consciousness A Philosophy of Mindfulness and Somaesthetics* (Cambridge: Cambridge University Press, 2011). See also the use of carnal hermeneutics to resist the ocularcentric egotism of modern sensory oppression within Hwa Yol Jung, "Phenomenology and Body Politics," *Body and Society* 2, 2 (1996): 1–22.

[57] Imamu Amiri Baraka, *Slave Ship*, in *Crosswinds: An Anthology of Black Dramatists in the Diaspora*, ed. William Branch (Indianapolis: University of Indiana Press, 1993), 250–259, quotes on 251–253. For more on Baraka, see Fred Moten, *In the Break: The Aesthetics of the Black Radical Tradition* (Minneapolis: University of Minnesota Press, 2003).

asserting that Western distastes for odor were absurd and did not allow for the increased knowledge that could come with cross-cultural familiarity concerning herbs, rituals, and medicine. Smelling thus became a discursive arena for discussions of religion, race, and capital throughout the Early Modern Era.[58]

Even when cleansed, racialized bodies did not change their odors, because the perception of smells was not solely materially oriented. Rather, scenting was and remains embodied and constructed through the false sensory consciousness of economically determined phenomenological experience. Mixing the sight of a black body with a vast cultural motif buried deep within the sensory membranes, groups of racially incentivized Englishpersons, Western Europeans, and Americans smelled Africans as pungent regardless of the material of bodily odors. These perceptions frequently continue today, personified within the racist mind and felt in the racialist body as a biological experience of tacit knowledge, disgust, and phenomenological truth that must be understood if the academy is to make any inroads against the substantial return of racist and fascist modernity within the contemporary West.[59]

---

[58] For more on race, the body, and the senses in modernity, see the embodied defenses of racists within Robin DiAngelo, *White Fragility: Why It's so Hard for White People to Talk About Racism* (Boston: Beacon, 2018); the sensory analysis of race, masochism, and the color line within Amber Jamilla Musser, *Sensational Flesh: Race, Power, and Masochism* (New York: New York University Press, 2014), 88–117; the role of music and difference in Jennifer Lynn Stoever, *The Sonic Color Line: Race and the Cultural Politics of Listening* (New York: New York University Press, 2016), 229–276; the importance of the body to religious resistance in Anthony Pinn, *Embodiment and the New Shape of Black Theological Thought* (New York: New York University Press, 2010), 101–142; and the racial constellations explored within Alexander Weheliye, *Habeas Viscus: Racializing Assemblages, Biopolitics, and Black Feminist Theories of the Human* (Durham, NC: Duke University Press, 2014). See also Utz McKnight, *The Everyday Practice of Race in America* (London: Routledge, 2010), 44–61.

[59] For persistence of racism, especially in American contexts, see Robert Sussman, *The Myth of Race: The Troubling Persistence of an Unscientific Idea* (Cambridge, MA: Harvard University Press, 2014), 43–106; George Yancy, *Black Bodies, White Gazes: The Continuing Significance of Race* (Lanham, MD: Rowman & Littlefield, 2008); C. Wright Mills, *The Racial Contract* (Ithaca: Cornell University Press, 1999); Kimberly Brown, *The Repeating Body: Slavery's Visual Resonance in the Contemporary* (Durham, NC: Duke University Press, 2015); Michelle Alexander, *The New Jim Crow: Mass Incarceration in the Age of Colorblindness* (New York: New Press, 2012). See also perceptual remnants within Deepika Bahri, *Postcolonial Biology: Psyche and Flesh After Empire* (Minneapolis: University of Minnesota Press, 2018); B. Keith Payne, Heidi Vuletich, and Jazmin Brown-Iannuzzi, "Historical Roots of Implicit Bias in Slavery," *Proceedings of the National Academy of Sciences* 116, 24 (2018): 11,693–11,698; Jack Glaser, *Suspect Race: Causes and Consequences of Racial Profiling* (Oxford: Oxford University Press, 2015).

Index

Abercromby, Ralph, 148
Abolitionism xiii–xvii, 28, 33, 97, 103–105,
    111–112, 125–128, 133, 149, 172,
    198–204, *See* Slave Ship
Achebe, Chinua, 142–143
    Arrow of God (1964), 143
    Things Fall Apart (1958), 142
Adams, John, 104
Aesop, 42, 70, *See* Washing the Ethiopian
Africanus, Leo, 24, 43, 53–57, 120
    Geographical Historie of Africa (1600),
        56–57
    Taqiyya, 57, *See* Islam
Age of Revolutions, 156, 160, 196, *See*
    American Revolution
Ahoho, 141, *See* Ants
Albanese, Denise, 20
Allen, Grant, 205
    In All Shades (1886), 205, *See* Dogs
Altar Rituals, 130, 138, 164–166, *See*
    Funeral Rites
Alvares, Domingos, 163
Alvares, Manuel, 55, 136
    *Ethiopia Minor and a Geographical
    Account of the Province of Sierra
    Leone*, 55
American Philosophical Society, 108–110,
    See Rush, Benjamin
American Revolution, 96, 147, 153, *See*
    Republicanism
American West, 208
Ananse, 140, *See* Spiders

Anderson, Warwick, 124
Angola, 90, 98
Animal Sacrifice, 191–192,
    See Vodou
Anosmia, 73, 159, 200, 214, *See* Nose
Antebellum Era, xvii–xix, 118, 167–168,
    198–200, *See* Civil War
Anti–Semitism, 50–53, 72–73, *See* Browne,
    Thomas
Ants, 141, *See* Ahoho
Apprenticeship, xvi, 114, *See* Emancipation
Archive, 21, 33–35, 127–128, 138–139,
    145–146, 156, *See* Static Africa
Arkansas, 167–170
Asante, 135–137

Babilon, Daniela, 33–34
Backscheider, Paula, 35
Bacon, Francis, 60
    New Atlantis (1627), 60
Badiou, Alain, xii
Ball, Charles, 33, 153, 172, *See* Slave
    Narratives
Bandello, Matteo, 62
Baptist, 136, *See* Protestant
Baraka, Amira, 218
    Slave Ship (1967), 218
Barbados, xvi, 87–89, 97–100, 148,
    178–179, 189, *See* Sugar
    Revolution
Barr, J.S., 105
Barth, Henry, 132

Bassa, 136, *See* Gold Coast
Bathing, 3, 38–41, 85–88, 99, 120,
    125–132, 136, 164, 179, 212–214,
    218, *See* Soap
Beame, Reverend H., 181, *See* Obeah
Belize, 170
Bellamy, Edward, 198
Bene Seeds, 170, *See* Sesame
Beng, 145
Benin, 129, 141
Berbice, 183
Bernier, Francois, 47
Best, George, 86
Bibb, Henry, 167, *See* Slave Narratives
Bight of Biafra, 83
Birds, 88, 177, 181, 190
Black Magi, 52
Blackface, 60, 203, *See* Mistrel Shows
Blood Nobility, 89, 102, *See* Monogenesis
Blumenbach, Johann, 47, 91, 105, *See*
    Monogenesis
Boccalini, Trajano, 66
    New-Found Politicke (1626), 66
Body Politic, 5, 23, 42, 106, 117, 202, 213,
    See Hobbes, Thomas
Bohun, Ralph, 78
    *Discourse Concerning the Origine and
    Properties of Wind* (1671), 78, *See*
    Torrid Zone
Book of Jeremiah, 42, 51, 69, *See* Old
    Testament
Bosman, Willem, 88, 99
Botswana, 164
Bourdieu, Pierre, 93
    Habitus, 93, 213, *See* Taste
Bourke, John, 208
    Scatalogic Rites of All Nations (1891),
    208, *See* Scatology
Boyle, Robert, 1–2, 78
    *Suspicions about the Hidden Realities of
    the Air* (1674), *See* Miasma Theory
Brace, Jeffrey, 147, *See* Slave Narratives
Brazil, 101–102, 162–164
Bréau, Jean Louis Armand de Quatrefages
    de, 209
Breton, Nicholas, 10
    Smale Handfull of Fragrant Flowers
    (1575), 10
Brisson, Pierre Raymond de, 105
    Voyages to the Coast of Africa (1792),
    105

British Empire, 79, 95, 135, 211, *See*
    Colonialism
British Guiana, 179
British Virgin Islands, xiv
Brome, Richard, 67
    The English Moor (1659), 67
Brown, Kathleen, 27–28
Browne, Patrick, 95
    Civil and Natural History of Jamaica
    (1756), 95
Browne, Thomas, 72
    Psuedodoxia Epidemica (1646), 72, *See*
    Anti-Semitism
Buffalo, 183
Buffon, Georges-Louis Leclerc, Comte de,
    47, 101, 105, *See* Monogenesis
    Histoire Naturelle, 105
Burgess, Anthony, 72
    Spiritual Refining (1664), 72
Burton, Henry, 70
    Truth's Triumph over Trent (1629), 70,
    See Reformation
Burton, Richard, 116, 141–142
    Mission to the King of Dahome (1864),
    116
Butler, Samuel, 198
Byrd, Jodi, 65

Cadamosto, Alvise, 54, *See* Henry the
    Navigator
Calabash, 178–185, 189, *See* Medicine Man
Camp, Stephanie, 158
    Rival Geographies, 128, 215
Candomblé, 164, 193, *See* Brazil
Cannady, Fanny, 171, *See* Slave Narratives
Cannibalism, xix, 117, *See* Diet
Cape Verde Islands, 77
Capitalism, xii–xx, xxv–xxvii, 14, 22–24,
    28, 35–38, 43–47, 76, 81, 87,
    112–121, 129, 154, 173, 186, 196,
    213–215, *See* Commodification
Caribbean, xiv–xx, 20, 28–32, 77–80,
    87–89, 100–101, 113–116, 148,
    152–157, 161, 175–193, *See*
    Colonialism
Carnivalesque, 124, 188
Carolinas, 96, 195
Cartwright, Samuel, 202
Cary, Alfred Joyce, 217
    The African Witch (1936), 217
Catesby, Mark, 96

Catholic, 9, 48, 55–57, 76, 102, 163–165, 191, *See* Protestant
Cats, xii, 134, 178
Cattle, 90, 142–143, 156, 167, 208
Central America, 116–117, *See* Pim, Bedford
Ceremonial Songs, 144–145, 177, *See* Ring Shout
Chanvalon, Thibault de, 91
Charles, Earl Grey, 115
Chicken, 168, 180, 185, *See* Diet
Chireau, Yvonne, 171
Chitlings, 170, *See* Pigs
Citizenship, 25, 92, 103, 197, 203, *See* Civilizing Process
Civil Rights Movement, 217
Civil War, 118, 169, 201–205, 216, *See* Antebellum Era
Civilizing Process, 7, 13, 36–39, 131, 218, *See* Cleanliness
Clapperton, Hugh, 131, 135
Clarkson, Thomas, 149, *See* Abolitionism
Cleanliness, xi, 2–3, 27–28, 36–38, 42, 72, 85–87, 99, 125, 129–132, 145, 153, 204, 208–211, 216, *See* Bathing
Climatology, 25, 56, 80, 84, 104, 110, 195
Moral Climatology, 110, 115
Clothing, xviii, 69, 90, 115, 125, 139, 162, *See* Skin
Coffle, 147, 154, *See* Middle Passage
Cogan, Thomas, 11
The Haven of Health (1636), 11
Coleridge, Samuel Taylor, 63, *See* Shakespeare, William
Coles, William, 11
Adam in Eden (1657), 11
Collier, George, 113, 151
Report on Captured Negroes in Tortola (1825), 114
Collyer, Joseph, 96
New System of Geography (1765), 96
Colombia, 102
Colonialism, xii–xx, 18, 27, 38, 43–45, 65, 79, 85–106, 110–117, 121–133, 139–143, 157–162, 177, 182–186, 195–196, 205, 209–217, *See* Caribbean
Commodification, xii–xvi, xx, 6, 18–22, 28, 35–38, 65, 77–83, 92, 103, 118, 124–125, 129, 133, 147, 152–154, 173, 191, *See* Capitalism

Common Wind, 30, 161, 174
Confederacy, 204–205, *See* Civil War
Congo, 54, 90, 98, 131, 144, 149, *See* Kongo
Congo Jack, 149
Conjuring, 65, 155, 166–171, 190, *See* Obeah
Connecticut, 147
Cooper River, 148, *See* South Carolina
Corry, Joseph, 82
Observations upon the Windward Coast of Africa (1807), 82
Craniology, 199, 206, *See* Phrenology
Creole Jack, 149
Creolization, 31, 127, 158–161, 166–170, 191–193, *See* Survivals
Crocker, William, 136
Cuba, 173
Culpepper, Amelia, 189
Curse of Ham, xix, 25, 52–53, 58, 73, 94, *See* Monogenesis

Dahomey, 116, 141, 163, 193
Darwin, Erasmus, 16
Botanic Garden (1791), 17
Davis, Natalie, 57
Dawdy, Shannon, 90
Dekkar, Thomas, 68
Lust's Dominion (1657), 68
Demons, xii, 125, 182–185, 192, 218, *See* Witchcraft
Denham, Dixon, 131, 135
Deren, Maya, 192
Diet, xix, xxvi, 54–55, 79, 99, 125, 140, 144, 160, 167–168, 212, *See* Taste
Digital Racism, 212–216, *See* Genetic Code
Dillon, Elizabeth, 59
Divining, 33, 139, 146, 163, *See* Smelling–Out
Dodoens, Rembert, 11
New Herbal (1578), 11
Dogs, 34, 158, 168–174, 190, 205, *See* Slave Narratives
Douglas, Niel, 149, *See* Abolitionism
Douglass, Frederick, 173, *See* Slave Narratives
Dr. Jones, 168, *See* Slave Narratives
Drayton, Michael, 70
Dred Scott v. Sandford (1857), 202–203, *See* Citizenship

Du Pratz, Monsieur Antoine-Simon Le Page, 90–91
Dupuis, Joseph, 135
 Journal of a Residence in Ashante (1824), 135
Dutch, 54, 90, 163, 211
Dystopia, 198–202

Ebed-Melech, 51
Edgeworth, Maria, 188
 "The Grateful Negro," 188
 Belinda (1801), 188
Edwards, Bryan, 188–191
 History, Civil and Commercial, of the British West Indies (1793), 191
Egba, 138
Eggs, 177, 185
Elephants, 73, 140, 183
Elizabeth I, 58
Emancipation, xvi, 114, 171, 184, 197, 205, 216, *See* Runaway Slaves
English Civil War, 69–71, 87
Episteme, 8, 85
Equiano, Olaudah, 33, 125, 133–134, 147–149, 195
 Interesting Narrative (1789), 125, *See* Slave Narratives
Ethiopia, 42, 51, 55, 89, 123
Ethnobotany, 145, 165, *See* Herbal Medicine
Ethnogenesis, 34, 127, 134, 139, 158, 166, *See* Creolization
Eugenics, 196, *See* Social Darwinism
Evans, William McKee, 52
Excrement, xiii–xiv, 23, 33, 38, 90, 143–148, 152–154, 167–171, 185, 190, 208, 212–213, 217–218

Falconbridge, Alexander, xii, 148
 Account of the Slave Trade on the Coast of Africa (1788), xii, *See* Middle Passage
Fanon, Frantz, xii, 112, *See* Colonialism
Federal Writers Project, 33, 167–171, *See* Slave Narratives
Fee, John Gregg, 200
 Anti-Slavery Manual (1848), 200
Feerick, Jean, 58
Fennell, Christopher, 157
Fenning, Daniel, 96
 New System of Geography (1765), 96

Fernando Po, 114
Fish, 40, 54, 65, 99, 147
Florida, 96, 169
Flowers, x, xvii, 55, 101, *See* Gardens
Floyer, John, 3
Flux, xiii, 152, *See* Excrement
Folklore, 34, 40–41, 75, 102, 139–141
Fowler, O.S., 207
 Synopsis of Phrenology, 207
France, 156
French, xviii, 27, 40–41, 89–91, 98–101, 105, 119–120, 130, 144, 150, 155–156, 160, 191, 209
Freud, Sigmund, 42, 207
 Verschiebung, 42, 195
Friedman, Emily, 34
Frobisher, Martin, 86
Frogs, 169, 185
Funeral Rites, 130, 142, 153, 169, 181, 185, *See* Altar Rituals

Goofer Dust, 169, *See* Conjure
Galen, 10, 56, 110
 Humoral Medicine, 1, 110
Gambia River, 129
Gamble, Samuel, 107, *See* Sandown
Garden of Eden, 87
Garden, Alexander, 146
Gardens, 16, 75, 177, *See* Weeds
Gazlay, Allen, 201–202
 Broadluck, Cephus, 201–202
 Races of Humankind with Travels in Grubland (1856), 201, *See* Dystopia
Genetic Code, 215–216, *See* Digital Racism
Georgia, 119, 152, 166–170
Gerard, John, 11
 General History of Plants (1633), 11
German, 132, 209
Geurts, Kathryn, 143
Ghana, 130, 180
Ghosts, 40, 123, 134–144, 182, 190, *See* Smelling-Out
Gikandi, Simon, 25–26
Giraffes, 73
Gliddon, George, 206, *See* Phrenology
Global South, xviii, 22, 122–124, 211, *See* Colonialism
Goats, 56, 62, 99, 192
Gold Coast, 89, 113, 130–132, 136, 150
Goldsmith, Oliver, 16, 100, *See* Industrial Revolution

Gomez, Michael, 158
Gomez, Pablo, 161
Gould, George Milbry, 209
  Anomalies and Curiosities of Medicine
    (1896), 209
Grainger, James, 79
  The Sugar Cane (1764), 79
Grandin, Greg, 211
Grease, 90, 96, 171, *See* Skin
Great Chain of Being, 106
Great Depression, 167, *See* Federal Writers
  Project
Greene, Asa, 198–200
  A Yankee among the Nullifiers (1833),
    198, *See* Nullification Crisis
Greenhill, William, 67
  Sound-Hearted Christian (1670), 67
Guinea, 55, 100, 105–107, 130, 136
Gunpowder, 142, 152, 162
Gutenberg, Johannes, 9
  Printing Press, 8, 13

Hair, ix, 31, 52, 89, 95–96, 102–104, 171,
    183, 212, 217
Haiti, 40–41, 75, 173, 187, 193, *See* San
  Domingue
Haitian Revolution, 187
Hall, Gewndolyn, 158
Handy, Sarah, 171
  "Negro Superstitions," 171
Harding, Rachel, 162
Hartman, Saidiya, 38
Heard, Wildred, 168, *See* Slave Narratives
Heath, Robert, 67
  Clarastella (1650), 67
Heng, Geraldine, 73
Henry the Navigator, 54
Herbal Medicine, 10, 33, 137, 141–145,
    158–166, 176–180, 184–185, 219,
    See Myal
Herbert, George, 70
  Remains (1652), 70
Herbert, Thomas, 77–78
Herrenvolk Democracy, 118, 202–203,
    210, *See* Whiteness
Heywood, Thomas, 60
  The Four Prentices (1615), 60
Hillary, William, 79
Hispaniola, 40, 162, *See* Haiti
Hobbes, Thomas, 106, *See* Body Politic
Hodge, Arthur, xiv

Hodgman, Stephen Alexander, 201
Hoffer, Peter Charles, 32
Holgate, Jerome, 199–200
  Bolokitten, Oliver, 199–201
  Sojourn in the City of Amalgamation
    (1835), 199–200, *See* Dystopia
Holy Office, 161–162, *See* Catholic
Home, Henry, 104
  Sketches of the History of Man (1774),
    104
Hunter, Charles, 166, *See* Slave Narratives
Hutchinson, Thomas, 83
Huxley, Elspeth, 142
  The Flame Trees of Thika (1959), 142
Hyenas, 137

Ibn Botlan, 53, *See* Islam
Igbo, 133, 142–143, 170, 180, *See* Survivals
Industrial Revolution, 17
Insoko, 130, 134
Islam, 43, 52–57, 130, 165
Ivory Coast, 145

Jackson, John Andrew, 125, *See* Runaway
  Slaves
Jacobson–Widding, Anita, 144
Jamaica, xiii, 95–99, 116–117, 128,
    155–156, 176–188, 195, *See* Obeah
Jaudon, T.W., 187
Java, 211
Jefferson, Thomas, xi, 108, 209
  Notes on the State of Virginia (1784), xi
Jim Crow, 35, 45, 93, 205, 210, *See*
  Reconstruction
Jobson, Richard, 129
  Golden Trade (1623), 129
Johnson, Benjamin, 168, *See* Slave
  Narratives

Kemble, Fanny, 119
  *Journal of a Residence on a Georgian
    Plantation in 1838–1839* (1863),
    119
Kentucky, 121, 166
Kenya, 142
Kidd, Colin, 57
Kiechle, Melanie, 28
King George II, 3
King, Henry, 60
  "The Defense," 60
King, Thomas, 138

Kinsey, Cindy, 169, *See* Slave Narratives
Klineberg, Otto, 210
Kongo, 144, 162, 169, *See* Congo
Kriz, Kay Dian, 186
Kumina, 179

Latimer, George, 172
Laundry, 129, 162, 168, *See* Soap
Leopards, 137
Leprosy, 94, 109–110, *See* Monogenesis
Leviticus, 94, *See* Old Testament
Liberia, 132, 198, *See* Emancipation
Ligon, Richard, 87–89
    *A True and Exact History of the Island of
       Barbadoes* (1657), 88, *See* Bathing
Linnaeus, Carolus, 47
Lions, 73, 137, 141
Locke, John, 106
Long, Edward, 97–100, 128, 185, 191, 209
    History of Jamaica (1774), 97, 191
Lopes, Duarte, 24, 43, 54–55, 120
    Report of the Kingdome of Congo (1597),
       54
Lord Mayor's Pageants, 73–74
Lord Peter, 92
Louisiana, 90–91, 171
Lowe, Donald, 13
Lynching, 196, *See* Reconstruction

MacFall, Major Haldane, 190
    The Wooings of Jezebel Pettyfer (1898),
       190
MacGaffey, Wyatt, 145
Machin, Lewis, 66
    The Dumbe Knight (1608), 66
MacQueen, James, 115
Maggots, 147
Maitland, Frederick, 182
Makandals, 182, *See* Calabash
Malaria, 83, 104
Mali, 54, 135
Mami Wata, 163–165, 184
Mandeville, John, 49–55
Mandinga, Francisco, 161
Mann, Daniel, 172
Marabout, 130, *See* Islam
Marees, Pieter de, 54
    Description *and Historical Account of the
       Gold Kingdom of Guinea* (1602), 54
Mark of Cain, 25, 73, 94, *See* Monogenesis
Markham, Gervase, 66

The Dumbe Knight (1608), 66
Marsan, H. De, 203–204, *See* Minstrel
    Shows
Martens, Stephanie, 106
Martinique, 91, 180
Massachusetts, 136, 198
Massey, Gerald, 137–139
    The Natural Genesis (1883), 137
Master Juba, 203, *See* Minstrel Shows
McClintock, Anne, 133
McKenzie, P.R., 138
Mead, Richard, 3, *See* Miama Theory
Measles, 94
Medicine Man, 143, 155–156, 164–169, *See*
    Obeah
Mello e Souza, Laura de, 162
Memmi, Albert, 126, *See* Colonialism
Mercantilism, xxvii, 18, 118, *See* Capitalism
Métraux, Alfred, 193, *See* Vodou
Miasma Theory, xiii, 1–5, 27–28, 78–80,
    95, 113–115, 153, 212, *See* Royal
    Society
Middle Passage, xii, 25, 33, 89, 126–128,
    146–160, 166–168, 174–176, 185,
    191–193, 204, 214, *See* Slave Ship
Miller, Joseph, 158
Minas Gerais, 162, *See* Brazil
Minkisi, 169, *See* Kongo
Minstrel Shows, 101, 203–204, *See*
    Blackface
Mirror of Misery (1814), xiv, *See*
    Abolitionism
Mississippi, 196
Missouri, 172
Mitchell, John, 94–97, 109, 209, *See* Royal
    Society
Monogenesis, 24–25, 86, 119, 209, *See*
    Curse of Ham
Montgomery, James, xvi
    The Negro's Vigil (1834), xvi, *See*
    Abolitionism
Moody, Thomas, 114
Morant Bay, 117, 185, *See* Jamaica
Morgan, America, 172, *See* Slave Narratives
Morgan, W.B., 121
Morocco, 56
Morton, Samuel George, 206, *See*
    Phrenology
Moseley, Benjamin, 177–178, 185
    A Treatise on Sugar (1800), 177
Moses, Patsy, 168, *See* Slave Narratives

Moss, Henry, 109
Mozambique, 100, 105
Myal, 179, 183–184, *See* Herbal Medicine

Namibia, 164, *See* San
Nash, Richard, 92
Native Americans, 20, 90, 96, 208
Ndembu, 144, *See* Zambia
Necromancy, 139, 153, 177, *See* Funeral
    Rites
Nepveu, Jean, 163, *See* Suriname
Nevis, 149
New France, 91, *See* Louisiana
New Imperialism, 115, 208, *See*
    Colonialism
New Kingdom of Granada, 161
New York City, 157, 203
Newton, John, xiii, 148
    Thoughts upon the African Slave Trade
    (1788), xiii, *See* Abolitionism
Nigeria, 132–134, 142–143
North Carolina, 171
Northrup, Solomon, 171, *See* Slave
    Narratives
Nose, xviii, 1–3, 7–10, 16, 30, 43–47,
    75–76, 84–87, 104–106, 110,
    118–119, 126–129, 136–137, 144,
    165–168, 172–173, 185, 191,
    196–201, 205–209, *See* Cleanliness
Nott, Josiah, 206, *See* Phrenology
Nullification Crisis, 198, *See* Antebellum
    Era

Obeah, 33–35, 176–192, *See* Creolization
Ogilby, John, 89, 130, 134–135
    Africa (1670), 134
Ogoun, 192, *See* Yoruba
Oji, 141, *See* Ghana
Old Testament, 42, 51–52, 70, 177, *See*
    Curse of Ham
Ole Heg Tale, 170, *See* Witchcraft
Oliveira, Isabela Maria de, 162
Onions, 167
Orientalism, 141, *See* Xenophobia
Origins Debate, 24, 45, *See* Slavery and
    Capitalism
Orisha, 138, *See* Yoruba

Palm Oil, 54, 130–131, 152, *See* Perfume
Panama Canal, 116, *See* Pim, Bedford
Paramaribo, 139, *See* Suriname

Paternalism, 200–201, 205, *See* Antebellum
    Era
Pepper, 162, 167, *See* Spices
Pereira, Jose Francisco, 163
Perfume, 3, 12–13, 44, 54, 74, 99–101,
    129–135, 139, 152–155, 163, 200,
    See Bathing
Peyrère, Isaac de La, 86
    Prae-Adamitae (1655), 86, *See* Polygenesis
Phrenology, xviii, 105, 136, 196, 206–207,
    See Craniology
Pigs, 151, 178–181, 217, *See* Diet
Pim, Bedford, 116–117, 141–142
    The Negro and Jamaica (1866), 116
    Dottings on the Roadside (1869), 117
Pinckard, George, 100, 148
Pinta, Luiza, 162
Plant Roots, 137, 162, 177, *See* Weeds
Plessy v. Ferguson (1896), 210, *See* Jim
    Crow
Plessy, Homer, 210
Poison, 156–158, 163, 178–183,
    See Obeah
Polydore, 184
Polygenesis, 24–25, 44, 84–89, 95–99,
    103–104, 111, 119–120, 196, 209,
    See Scientific Racism
Pope Leo X, 57
Portuguese, 43, 54–55, 131, 150, *See* Brazil
Pory, John, 57
Pouchet, Georges, 119–120
    The Plurality of the Human Race (1864),
    119, *See* Scientific Racism
Prester John, 49, 53
Price, Richard, 193, *See* Creolization
Priest, Josiah, xix
    Slavery (1849), xix, *See* Antebellum Era
Primates, 199
Primitive Accumulation, xii, 46–47, 87, *See*
    Capitalism
Protestant, 20, 49–50, 64, 84–85, 115, 165,
    See Catholic
Pruner-Bey, Franz, 209
Pseudoscience, xviii, 93, 109–110, 125,
    207–209, *See* Scientific Racism
Public Sphere, xvi–xviii, 13, 23, 45, 69, 73,
    92, 115, 124, 191, 197, 212–216, *See*
    Republic of Letters
Purchas, Samuel, 120
    Purchas' Pilgrims (1626), 54
Pyle, Walter, 209

Queen of Sheba, 49
Quran, 53, *See* Islam

Race Coding, 5, 44, 87, 120, 174, *See* Public
    Sphere
Rainsford, Marcus, 174
Ram's Horn, 183
Ramsey, Kate, 162
Rancière, Jacques, 59
Rape, xiv, 61, 101, 156
Rasmussen, Susan, 143
Rath, Richard Cullen, 32
Rattray, Robert, 137
Rawlins, Henry, 149
Reconstruction, 171, 205, *See* Jim Crow
Reddit, 212, *See* Digital Racism
Reformation, 8, 12, 24, 70, 76, 218, *See*
    Protestant
Reis, Joao, 163
Renaissance, 16, 49–50, 59, 69, 195
Renny, Robert, 112, 181
    An History of Jamaica (1807), 112, 181
Republic of Letters, 85, 100, 120, 160, 195,
    206, *See* Public Sphere
Republicanism, 197, *See* Citizenship
Rhinoceros, 208
Ring Shout, 31, 165, *See* Ceremonial Songs
Rio de Janeiro, 164, *See* Brazil
River Bonny, 151, *See* Nigeria
Romanticism, 186–190
Rotter, Andrew, 18
Royal African Company, 195, *See* Middle
    Passage
Royal Society, 1–3, 93–97, 109, *See* Miasma
    Theory
Rucker, Walter, 166
Runaway Slaves, xiii, 125, 171–172, 205,
    See Federal Writers Project
Rush, Benjamin, 108–113, 209, *See*
    American Philosophical Society

San, 164–165, *See* Namibia
San Domingue, 157, 162, *See* Haiti
Sandoval, Alonso de, 55
Sandown, 107, *See* Gamble, Samuel
Sante Will, 136
Santeria, 193, *See* Cuba
Scatology, 208–209, *See* Excrement
Schiebinger, Londa, 158
Schotte, J.P., 104
    Synochus Atrabiliosa (1778), 104

Scientific Racism, xviii, 25, 47, 103–106,
    136, 196–197, 205–215, *See*
    Polygenesis
Scotland, 134, 148
Scott, James, 30, 123
    Hidden Transcripts, 30, 123–124, 160
    Weapons of the Weak, 30, 123, 159
Scramble for Africa, xx, 93, 104, 111–112,
    121, *See* Colonialism
Senegal, 98
Senior, Emily, 79
Sensorium, 13, 74, 85, 139, 143–146, 212
Serres, Michel, 37
    The Parasite (1982), 37
Sesame, 170, *See* Bene Seeds
Seth, Suman, 79
Settler Colonialism, 22, 43, *See* Colonialism
Shakespeare, William, ix–x, 15, 35, 42,
    60–65, 74–76, 214
    Othello (1603), 61–63
    Sonnets, ix
    The Tempest (1610), 64–65
    Titus Andronicus (1594), 42, 61–62
Sharp, Granville, 149, *See* Abolitionism
Sheep, 90
Sherman, William Tecumseh, 204, *See* Civil
    War
Sierra Leone, xvii, 55, 82, 113–115, 132,
    198 See *Emancipation*
    Free Town, 114
Skin, x–xiv, xviii, 23–25, 40–42, 48–56, 61,
    69–71, 75, 84–86, 90–97, 101, 109,
    115, 169–171, 178, 202–204, 209,
    213, *See* Leprosy
Slave Narratives, 33, 171–172, *See* Federal
    Writers Project
Slave Ship, xiii, 30, 123, 146–154, 195, *See*
    Middle Passage
    Anna Maria, 151
    Brookes, 149–150, *See* Abolitionism
    Rodeur, 150
    San Antonio, 150
Slavery and Capitalism, 46, *See* Origins
    Debate
Sloane, Hans, 79
Smallpox, 94
Smellie, William, 105
Smelling-Out, 33, 136–139, 143–146, 158,
    163–166, 180–183, 214, *See*
    Divining
Smith, Bruce, 35

Smith, Gus, 172, *See* Slave Narratives
Smith, Mark, 28, 45, 118, 210
Smith, Samuel Stanhope, 102, *See* Hair
Smith, William, 131
Smoking Moor, 74
Snakes, 156, 168, 183–185
Soap, 119, 129–133, 152, 170, *See* Bathing
Social Darwinism, xviii, 137–139, 196, 205, 209, *See* Scientific Racism
Social Death, 154, *See* Middle Passage
Sofala, 105, *See* Mozambique
Soubise, Julius, 101, *See* Minstrel Shows
Soudan, 131, 135
South Carolina, 125, 146–148, 170–172
Spanish, 55, 150–151
Spices, 162, *See* Pepper
Spiders, 140, *See* Ananse
Stafford, John, x
    The Academy of Pleasure (1665), x, *See* Whiteness
Static Africa, 127, 146, *See* Archive
Stepan, Nancy, 103
Stinking Peas, 162
Stono Rebellion, 32, 157, *See* South Carolina
Stowe, Harriet Beecher, 173, 201
    Uncle Tom's Cabin (1852), 173, 201
Sue, Eugene, 155
    Atar Gull
        Or, The Slave's Revenge (1846), 155
Sugar, xv, 87–91, 98, *See* Capitalism
Sugar Revolution, 87, *See* Barbados
Suicide, 62, 151–153, 183
Sullivan's Island, 148, *See* South Carolina
Sultan of Sego, 135
Suriname, 139, 163
Survivals, 128, 139, 158–166, 170, 176, 191, *See* Creolization
Süskind, Patrick, 8
Swediaur, Franz, 109
Sweet, James, 53, 163
Swetnam, Joseph, 70
    Araignment of Lewd, Idle, and Unconstant Women (1615), 70

Tachard, Guy, 90–91
    Relation of the Voyage to Siam (1688), 90
Tacit Knowledge, 15–18, 24–26, 47, 83–85, 97, 196, 219, *See* Public Sphere
Tacky, 176, *See* Jamaica

Taste, xxii, 11–12, 151, 160, 213, 219, *See* Diet
Taylor, Charles, 19
Teeth, 53–54, 177, *See* Diet
Texas, 168
Thistlewood, Thomas, xiii, *See* Rape
Thomas, Dicey, 167, *See* Slave Narratives
Thomas, Herbert, 185
    Something about Obeah (1891), 185
Thompson, George, 132
Thompson, Robert Farris, 144, 164–165
Thornton, John, 158
Three Fingered Jack, 178, *See* Jamaica
Tomkis, Thomas, 4
    Lingua (1622), 4
Torrid Zone, 111–113, 118, *See* Caribbean
Tortoises, 140
Tryon, Thomas, 2–3
    Letters upon Several Occasions (1700), 2, *See* Cleanliness
Tuareg, 143, *See* Nigeria
Tucker, Sarah, xvii
    Abbeokuta, or Sunrise within the Tropics (1853), *See* Emancipation
Turner, Victor, 144

Uncle Jake, 167, *See* Slave Narratives
Uruguay, 102

Vago, Ambrose, 207
    Orthodox Phrenology (1870), 207
Van Allen, Charles, 118
    "Suggestions upon Animal Odor," 119
Van Beek, W.E.A., 143
Vaughn, Virginia, 62
Villault, Sieur
    Relation of the Coasts of Africk Called Guinee (1670), 130
Virey, Julien, xviii, xix
    Natural History of the Negro Race (1837), xviii, *See* Polygenesis
Virginia, xi, 94, 172
Vodou, 40, 162, 192–193, *See* Haiti
Vomit, 199–200, *See* Excrement

Warner–Lewis, Maureen, 158
Washing the Ethiopian, 24, 41, 59, 69–72, 88, 99, 141, 204, *See* Aesop
Weaver, Karol, 161
Webb, William, 166, *See* Slave Narratives
Weeds, 54, 107, 177, *See* Flowers

Weemes, John, 72–73, *See* Anti-Semitism
Welsh, James, 129, *See* Benin
White, Graham, 31
White, Shane, 31
Whiteness, x–xi, 18, 33, 41, 47–48, 52, 67, 71, 91, 98–101, 118, 193, 197, 202, 210, *See* Herrenvolk Democracy
Whitney, Geffrey, 69
  A Choice of Emblemes (1586), 69, *See* Washing the Ethiopian
Wilberforce, William, 149, *See* Abolitionism
Wild Man, 92, 106, *See* Civilizing Process
Wilkinson, William, 130–131
  Systema Africanum (1690), 130
Williams, Cynric, 189
  Hamel, Obeah Man (1827), 189
Williams, Father Joseph, 191
  Voodoos and Obeahs (1932), 191
Wilson, John Leighton, 132

Western Africa (1856), 132
Witchcraft, xii, 64, 103, 117, 136–142, 162–166, 170, 178–183, 214–217, *See* Demons
Woods, Maggie, 170, *See* Slave Narratives
Wroth, Mary, 60
  Urania (1621), 60

Xenophobia, 137, 205, *See* Whiteness

Yellow Fever, 82, 118
Yeo, James, 150
Yoruba, xvii, 138, 192, *See* Nigeria
Young, Jason, 158, 166

Zambia, 144, *See* Ndembu
Zimbabwe, 134
Zombies, 178, *See* Obeah
Zulu, 183
Zuni, 208, *See* Native Americans